Studies in the
Legal History of the South

EDITED BY PAUL FINKELMAN AND KERMIT L. HALL

This series explores the ways in which law has affected

the development of the southern United States and

in turn the ways the history of the South has affected

the development of American law. Volumes in the series focus

on a specific aspect of the law, such as slave law or civil rights

legislation, or on a broader topic of historical significance to the

development of the legal system in the region, such as issues of

constitutional history and of law and society, comparative analyses

with other legal systems, and biographical studies

of influential southern jurists

and lawyers.

FREE
TO WORK

James D. Schmidt

FREE TO WORK

Labor Law, Emancipation,

and Reconstruction,

1815–1880

THE UNIVERSITY OF GEORGIA PRESS

ATHENS AND LONDON

© 1998 by the University of Georgia Press
Athens, Georgia 30602
All rights reserved
Designed by Betty Palmer McDaniel
Set in 10.5 on 14 Berthold Bodoni Antiqua
by G & S Typesetters, Inc.
Printed and bound by Maple-Vail
The paper in this book meets the guidelines for
permanence and durability of the Committee on
Production Guidelines for Book Longevity of the
Council on Library Resources.

Printed in the United States of America
02 01 00 99 98 c 5 4 3 2 1

Library of Congress Cataloging in Publication Data

Schmidt, James D.
Free to work : labor law, emancipation, and
reconstruction, 1815–1880 / James D. Schmidt.
p. cm. – (Studies in the legal history of the South)
Includes bibliographical references and index.
ISBN 0-8203-2034-x (alk. paper)
1. Labor contract–Southern States–History. 2. Free
choice of employment–Southern States–History.
3. Labor market–Southern States–History.
4. Afro-Americans–Employment–Southern
States–History. 5. Reconstruction. I. Title.
II. Series.
KF3457.S36 1998
344.7501–dc21 98-22487

British Library Cataloging in Publication Data
available

To my parents

Contents

Acknowledgments

A member of Harold Hyman's seminar in American legal and constitutional history at Rice University once described this project as "the velcro topic" because an ever increasing list of avenues for investigation seemed to adhere to it. Indeed, the work's expanding scope has owed much to the assistance of fellow researchers as well as librarians and archivists. My efforts have been aided immeasurably by the library staffs at Rice University, University of Houston, University of Houston Law Library, University of Georgia, Emory University, Mercer University, University of North Carolina–Chapel Hill, University of Michigan, Northwestern University, the National Archives, and Northern Illinois University. Comments by fellow bound laborers in Professor Hyman's seminar helped me focus my inquiries, and I would like to thank especially Ken Deville, who encouraged me to explore the connections between labor contracts and vagrancy laws. Either through course work, examination committees, conference comments, correspondence, or informal conversations, I have also benefited from the comments of Thomas Haskell, Martin Wiener, Ira Gruber, John Boles, Gale Stokes, Chandler Davidson, John Inscoe, Wayne Durrill, David Montgomery, Peter Way, Wythe Holt, Robert Steinfeld, Sally Hadden, Lea VanderVelde, Christopher Tomlins, and numerous others. Mike Vorenberg and Ginger Frost read the entire manuscript and offered many insightful and helpful comments. The series editor for the University of Georgia Press, Paul Finkelman, also offered helpful comments. The other reader, Paul Cimbala, sharpened my analysis of the Freedmen's Bureau considerably, in addition to providing useful comments on other sections. Colleagues at Northern Illinois University, especially Mary Furner, Simon Newman, John Jentz, and Allan Kulikoff, offered helpful suggestions. Special thanks go to my adviser, Professor Hyman, for encouraging me to broaden my inquiries and for supporting my work even when I argued with him. In the book's final stages, I have been assisted by Malcolm Call, David DesJardines, Kristine Blakeslee, and other staff at the University of Georgia Press. My copy editor, Grace Buonocore, saved me from numerous miscues. Beth Green from Northern Illinois University also read the manuscript in its final stages and detected many infelicities of expression. The mistakes that remain are, of course, my own.

Finally, I wish to thank those closest to me. My parents, Dean and Vera Schmidt, have been a consistent source of encouragement throughout my academic career. My stepsons, Mike and Drew Banghart, have helped me keep my sanity during the final stages of this project by talking about fishing, golf, computer games, and Marxism. Finally, Andrea Smalley, even after listening to endless hours of redundant ruminations, has been the most ardent supporter of this project and its author.

FREE
TO WORK

Introduction

In October 1865 Freedmen's Bureau commissioner Oliver Otis Howard ordered that "vagrant laws made for free people" would be extended to freed
slaves. At first blush it might seem that Howard was being ironic. If emancipated African Americans were subject to statutes restricting both their mobility and their labor, how could they be free? Historians of Reconstruction
and emancipation have asked this rhetorical question and concluded that
laws regulating work contradicted the antebellum North's commitment to
free labor. Even a quick look at the history of northern law, however, reveals
that Howard was quite serious. Howard's proclamation, then, raises important questions about the role of law in understanding emancipation and Reconstruction. This study attempts to answer those questions. I began simply
by asking: Why did the northerners who sought to establish "free labor" in
the South during Reconstruction use a legal system of contracts, enticement,
and vagrancy and apprenticeship laws that seemed to contradict free labor?
Trying to answer this question, I soon discovered, opened up a much broader
inquiry: What was the role of law in the creation of free labor? Seeking to
answer these questions, I found that they were integrally related. In fact, I
came to conclude, understanding the outcomes of Reconstruction in both
the North and the South requires looking at the ways in which Americans of
the middle nineteenth century used the state to create a capitalist market in
labor and how they sought to explain and legitimate their actions.[1]

My extended answer to these questions does not try to erect a general
theory for the role of the state in capitalist development, but some basic
definitions are critical to understanding my argument. First, we must have a
sense of what "free labor" is. Historically speaking, "free labor" meant many
things to the men and women of the nineteenth century. To evangelical Pro-

testants, it meant simple self-ownership, but to radical urban artisans and republican ideologues, it meant possession of productive property. Applied to daily life, these abstractions implied social, occupational, and geographic mobility. Through wage labor, free labor's advocates believed, propertyless workers could accumulate capital and eventually buy land or a small business, thereby escaping poverty and relieving the United States of a permanent proletariat. Even if laborers could not elude proletarianization, they could avoid unfair treatment by unrestricted movement in the labor market, simply quitting one job for another. In either case, harmony would prevail between labor and capital. Free labor also meant the new milieu of social relations that resulted from the breakdown of the master-journeyman-apprentice system in the skilled crafts. As master craftsmen responded to widening markets after 1815 by expanding output, ancient methods of production eroded rapidly. Journeymen moved out of their masters' homes and into working-class communities. Old rituals of work and time faded as new industrial class relations emerged. In many ways, the "free-labor ethic" was a response to this transformation. Ideally, free labor removed both the legal restraints of indentured servitude and the customary paternalism of the master-servant relation.[2]

Most accounts of the emergence of free labor embed it within historical context, as they rightly should. Moreover, many of them are informed by an explicit or implicit Marxist framework. It may be helpful, as a result, to turn to Marx himself for a definition of free labor and its market. Marx understood that the emergence of a capitalist system depended on commodified labor power. In *Wage Labour and Capital*, Marx wrote that labor power is "a commodity, which its possessor, the wage-worker[,] sells to capital." For Marx, this transaction took place in an open market, where the laborer purchased the "means of subsistence." He did so for a simple reason: "in order to live." Moreover, for Marx, this sale of labor power took place "piecemeal," on a daily basis without legal restraint. "The worker leaves the capitalist to whom he hires himself whenever he likes, and the capitalist discharges him whenever he thinks fit, as soon as he no longer gets any profit out of him, or the anticipated profit," Marx wrote. The only restraint on the labor market so conceived was that the worker could not leave "the whole class of purchasers." It was always the worker's "business to dispose of himself, that is, to find a purchaser within the capitalist class."[3]

As we shall see, Marx's definition of the capitalist labor market provides a neat summary of the point American labor eventually reached. For him, workers worked to avoid want. Most historians who try to define free labor have followed this line. With the capitalist revolution, work became governed by a competitive market, by human necessity, and by an internalized sense of industrial time. While this definition provides a valid description of a point in capitalist development, it necessarily ignores one part of how that unfettered market came into being. Because Marxist historians who follow this line locate the emergence of the capitalist labor market completely in the social relations of production, they miss the role of the state. Marxist historians spend a good deal of time talking about the state's role in the creation or destruction of productive property, but they spend less effort on the role the state played in the creation of a labor market. Usually, the state appears as the enforcer of the general sanctity of labor contracts or the deterrent to collective action. Yet Marx recognized that the state was central to the growth and progression of capitalism, even if he did not often investigate the process. In the famous words of Marx and Engels in *The Communist Manifesto:* "The executive of the modern State is but a committee for managing the common affairs of the whole bourgeoisie." Understanding the creation of the labor market requires attention to how precisely the bourgeoisie managed their affairs through the state.[4]

Exploring "the state" is a tricky business, for the United States did not possess in the nineteenth century the centralized, modernizing bureaucracies that Marx envisioned. As Stephen Skowronek has pointed out, Americans then and now maintain that the country was "stateless." Still, recent theoretical writing on "the state" suggests that a state did exist in nineteenth-century America. Theda Skocpol, drawing on Max Weber and others, provides a usable definition of the state. "A state," she writes, "is any set of relatively differentiated organizations that claims sovereignty and control over a territory and its population, defending and perhaps extending that claim in competition with other states." The organizations that constitute a state exercise administrative, judicial, and policing powers to collect funds, maintain domestic order, and protect the state's own interests. For our purposes here, Skocpol's most important function of the state is to "enforce the constitutive rules of the state and society." While Skocpol is concerned primarily with the period after the Civil War, Skowronek helps locate the antebellum state in political parties and, more important for our purposes, the courts.[5]

To turn attention to the antebellum courts might suggest that the recent historiography on labor law answers the question nicely. Indeed, scholars such as Christopher Tomlins, Robert Steinfeld, and Amy Dru Stanley have significantly deepened our knowledge of the nature and meaning of labor law in the nineteenth century. Although the contributions of these scholars are significant, I believe this literature suffers from three deficiencies if it is to be used to understand the questions posed above. First, it does not consider antebellum, wartime, and postbellum developments as a whole but rather focuses on one or the other. Second, it does not investigate closely enough what "free labor" or a capitalist labor market actually is. Finally, I would suggest, these works as well as the theoretical literature on the state ignore or downplay the importance of class. To return to Marx, the state in a capitalist society is a bourgeois state.[6]

Attention to the bourgeoisie as a class, then, is central to my analysis. My definition of class involves five interrelated propositions: (1) Although the social origin of class can be seen as the relation to the means of production or to productive property, it can also be delineated as the relationship to labor power, that is, some people sell labor power, and others buy it. (2) Certain people serve the interests of the buyers of labor power, even if they do not purchase it themselves. Together, I would dub the buyers of labor power and their servants the bourgeoisie. (3) Members of the bourgeoisie use the state both to facilitate the buying and selling of labor power and to mediate the social problems caused by the capitalist social relations the transaction produces. (4) The bourgeoisie uses a wide variety of means to legitimate and explain its use of the state to create a capitalist market. (5) In historical context, this process through which the bourgeoisie used the state has been erratic and contested. The nineteenth century witnessed the emergence of more than one bourgeois vision for a labor market, and it saw considerable resistance from the recipients of bourgeois law.[7]

The last two points of my definition suggest the need to define one further set of terms I use consistently below. In trying to understand the state by exploring law, I have envisioned law not so much as a set of legal rules but as a discourse or a language. As with the other terms above, I do not wish to engage in theoretical debates, especially the extended ones that spin around structuralism, poststructuralism, postmodernism, and deconstruction. However, some working definition is in order, and I find the one supplied by Kathleen Brown in her book on colonial gender relations to be particularly valuable. A discourse for Brown is "the use of language delineating a community and its interests." For her, a discourse arises in a particular historical time and place, but it "subsequently acquires a myriad of other meanings and uses as material or political circumstances change, or as it is appropriated by different groups of people." Employing a similar conception, I have referred frequently below to the various discourses surrounding the creation of a capitalist market in labor. These languages originated with reform writers and in the social contests of antebellum statehouses and courtrooms, yet they came to have broader meanings. The analysis below traces how legal and reform discourses penetrated popular consciousness in ways that shaped the creation of a state apparatus in the Reconstruction South and the postwar North.[8]

With these definitions in mind, what follows is a relatively straightforward investigation of the questions I posed at the outset. The book takes up these questions in two sections. The first section (chapters 1 and 2) considers the antebellum period and centers mainly on legal developments regarding labor contracts and vagrancy laws. I have focused on these elements of law because they were the most common embodiments of state power employed by the northerners who undertook the social Reconstruction of the South. By 1860, I argue, northern courts had erected two competing models of labor law in a capitalist society. One posited a right to security for both employers and workers lodged in unbreakable, definite contracts. This vision, still the dominant one by the eve of the war, harkened back to much older, precapitalist conceptions of labor, for it controlled the workers' ability to sell their labor power freely in the market. The other conception, contained within an emerging right to quit, suggested that workers could leave their employers at any time and employers could discharge them at any time so long as workers received cash wages. Although not dominant by 1860, this legal construction looked forward to a fully developed capitalist labor market in which labor power was utterly commodified and free to circulate to the highest bidder. At the same time, the state began to erect modern vagrancy laws that would police the outer edges of the labor market. As Marx foretold, workers could leave individual employers, but they could not leave the market altogether. All of this did not occur in a consistent way, however. After about 1815, northern judges created significant differences in the workings of the law based on class, and white southerners moved toward a system of labor law that diverged considerably from its northern counterpart. Moreover, this legal discourse did not exist in a social vacuum. Reform writers and others helped create popular notions of law that influenced both lawmaking during their own time and subsequent actions during emancipation and Reconstruction. In doing so, they drew on discourses of class, gender, and republicanism.

The book's second part (chapters 3–6) looks at how the interconnected discourses of law and labor created during the antebellum period influenced Reconstruction. Here I argue that the mostly middle-class northerners who made Reconstruction drew on the conflicted heritage of antebellum labor law. Both during the war and after, northerners clung to one of three general positions, all of which had roots in the inchoate state northern labor law had reached by 1860. For convenience's sake, I have labeled these "conservative," "moderate," and "liberal." Conservatives looked backward to the right to security and direct state enforcement of work, while liberals looked forward to the right to quit with or without state policing of the perimeters of the labor market. Embodying more directly the conflicted state of labor law, moderates advocated an unstable mixture of all the elements present in antebellum discourse. I have chosen to explore this general conceptualization by looking at three examples: wartime Reconstruction in Louisiana, the adoption of the Thirteenth Amendment, and the operations of the Freedmen's Bureau in a handful of states. The evidence here shows, I believe, how northern legal discourse penetrated popular consciousness by the time of the war and, more important, how it influenced state policymaking at the ground level. The Freedmen's Bureau is particularly important, for it represents the first broad effort in American history to build the apparatus of a modern, administrative state. I suggest that the effort failed because of the underdeveloped state of northern law that bureau agents tried to implement via their own popular conceptions. The bureau also failed because of the reception that law received from southerners, both black and white. When northerners tried to graft capitalist law onto a precapitalist society, the task proved too great. At home, however, bourgeois jurists, legislators, and reformers were completing the legal transition to a capitalist market in labor like the one Marx described. Courts removed or weakened the remaining restraints on individual labor contracts, while state legislatures passed tramp acts that enhanced the law's power over the meanings of work, gender, and class.

The Right to Quit

"The principles in this case have so long been settled that it seems a waste of time to argue upon them," a weary Sidney Breese began an Illinois Supreme Court opinion in 1862. The impossibility of a worker recovering wages after voluntarily leaving an employer, Breese believed, had been firmly established at law. However, the principles of labor law that Breese found so settled in the second year of the Civil War were far from fixed as northerners began to confront the questions about labor and law raised by the destruction of slavery in the South. In fact, the northerners who would use the power of the federal government to construct wage labor in the Reconstruction South grew up in a time when legal debate had created conflicting roles for the state in a capitalist labor market. While most legal and social commentators concurred that certain vestiges of servitude were illegitimate in a free-labor economy, they could not agree on the legal principles guiding wage-labor contracts. Many northern jurists believed in the unquestioned sanctity of contracts and in a right to security for workers and employers. Consequently, they envisioned an active role for the state in a capitalist labor market. However, a growing and vocal minority believed in a right to quit and a labor market less controlled by law. Although jurists constructed these theoretical debates about law and labor without regard to social conditions, in practice, the contractual rights of wage labor became defined by workers' class positions. Consequently, legal discourse left the Reconstructors with competing models on which to draw, models that had not resolved questions concerning the role of law in regulating capitalist labor contracts. Moreover, these competing principles would encounter a southern legal culture that had diluted the sanctity of contract and the right to security without establishing the right to quit.[1]

In recent years, the use of labor contract law in Jacksonian America's emerging capitalist order has become a topic of considerable debate among historians. According to some legal scholars and labor historians, strict enforcement of labor contracts resulted from the common position of jurists and capitalists in the exploiting class. Others have seen contract law as a response to the decline of indentured servitude, as a new discourse of power couched in older language, and as a vestige of "feudalism." Still another view denies the power of contract law to configure the employment relation and the conditions of free labor. Clearly, law and the state played a role in the formation of a capitalist labor market. Yet, for antebellum northerners, that role was by no means clear by the coming of the Civil War. For the Reconstructors, free labor would have more than one legal meaning.[2]

BADGES OF SERVITUDE

For the most part, northern courts agreed that certain practices were *not* free labor. By the second decade of the nineteenth century, northern legal thinkers had begun to abandon traditional definitions of "servants," undermining the property rights that masters had previously held. As property rights in labor declined, jurists and others believed that free laborers could not be subjected to physical punishment. Moreover, they discontinued the doctrine of specific performance and thereby established the principle that a worker could not be compelled to labor for a particular individual.[3]

By 1860, most northerners could agree that free labor involved limits on the power of masters, but this consensus took some time to build. Whether applied to slaves, indentured servants, or apprentices, a clear demarcation of power had constituted the heart of the premodern master-servant relation. Traditionally, legal powers of masters had been vast, and they remained so in the early nineteenth century. As late as 1810, Massachusetts masters could still have runaway apprentices and servants arrested and committed to the house of correction. In the same year, Pennsylvania laws authorized justices of the peace to issue arrest warrants for any apprentice who was "a stubborn and disorderly person" or one who "hath absconded from his [master's] service, contrary to the law, and to the great detriment of [his master]." In New York, masters could bring actions in trespass if their servants had been beaten by others, and they could sue for enticement if other masters employed their laborers.[4]

Notwithstanding these vestiges of paternal authority, master-servant discourse embraced considerable tensions by the early nineteenth century. Such ambiguities surfaced most transparently when treatise writers attempted to state precisely the actual definitions of a master and a servant. Anchored in the eighteenth century, Tapping Reeve voiced the traditional bonds of servitude in his 1816 treatise on family law: "A master is one who, by law, has a personal authority over another, and such person, over whom such authority may be rightfully exercised, is a servant." Reeve still envisioned servants within a traditional household, in which a patriarchal master governed all inhabitants and servants occupied a distinct position in hierarchies inherited from colonial America. For more forward-looking writers such as Nathan Dane, the matter was not so clear. In his 1823 *General Abridgement and Digest of American Law*, Dane echoed Reeve's construction of servitude, noting that "a *servant* is one over whom authority may be rightfully exercised by another." But he also acknowledged that "servant" was coming simply to mean "persons employed by others" and might include wives, attorneys, and other agents. By recognizing this caveat to customary definitions, Dane described the emerging world of free labor more accurately than Reeve, but he still emphasized power distribution.[5]

New York treatise writer John Dunlap most clearly represented the mixture of traditional and contractual language that had begun to constitute the dominant antebellum vision of free labor. Writing in 1815, he averred that masters' rights arose from "the property that every man has in the service of his domestics, acquired by the contract of hiring, and purchased by giving them wages." Like slave masters, then, employers acquired property rights in their employees, yet they did so through the "modern" avenue of contract. Further confusing the matter, he saw this relationship as equitable. Service contracts rested on "the principles of natural equity, that the servant shall serve, and the master maintain him, throughout all the revolutions of the respective seasons, as well as when there is work to be done, as well as when there is not."[6]

Dunlap's analysis neatly summarized an emerging view of the wage bargain, one that would remain in place into Reconstruction. In this view, workers sold more than commodified parts of their labor power; rather, they sold the whole of their labor power, thereby vesting their employers with a right to that "property." Thus, a capitalist transaction secured a noncapitalist, reciprocal relationship under which the servant worked diligently during the busy spring and summer in return for a home and a meal during the cold, sparse winter months. In essence, Dunlap described a free-labor world in which workers voluntarily obligated themselves to a defined period of service. But service was not servitude, for the contract limited the property rights the master had acquired in the transition. In this formulation, servants had not sold their persons into service; rather, they had bargained away the whole of their disembodied labor power. This minimal limitation on employers' powers represented a tenet of free labor on which most northerners eventually came to agree.

As legal writers grew unsure about servitude, laborers themselves also began to challenge the institution in the courts, and by doing so, they helped clarify the nature of the modern employment relation. By 1840 northern courts had firmly established another crucial difference between servitude and free labor by taking away the prerogative to administer corporal punishment to nonapprenticed servants. Dane had noted that masters were to chastise servants "with great moderation, without passion, and with the proper instrument," and workers pressed for even greater limits on this element of power by charging employers who beat them with assault and battery. In *Commonwealth v. Baird*, the Pennsylvania court declared in 1831 that although corporal punishment might preserve order in factories that employed minors, the law would not support it. In 1838 the Connecticut court considered a similar case against a Litchfield clock maker and reached similar conclusions. While apprentices might be punished, the power could not "be lawfully exercised, by a master over his hired servant, whether that servant [was] employed in husbandry, in manufacturing business, or in any other manner, except in the case of sailors."[7]

Courts resolved the matter of corporal punishment for servants in a relatively compressed period in the 1830s, but constructing the contractual relations of free labor started much earlier and took much longer. If free labor meant anything, it meant the ability of workers to circulate freely in a labor market. Yet existing master-servant law contained the power to hinder workers' movements. Given the right legal instruments, masters might detain workers against their will and compel them to perform their contracts. This power, what legal writers call specific performance, obstructed the development of commodified capitalist labor. Although some historians contend that specific performance was never established by colonial courts, litigations in the early Republic reveal that similar legal remnants of bound labor remained by the end of the revolutionary period. Still, as Robert Steinfeld has noted, these legal encumbrances on free labor faded by the 1820s. The death of specific performance freed workers to sell their labor power, although the terms and conditions of that sale were still an open question by the end of the antebellum period. At the least, though, most northerners by 1860 could agree that employers could not themselves compel performance of a contract to labor without any hope of relief.[8]

Doctrinal debate on specific performance commenced in the late eighteenth century when servants began to bring litigations against masters who attempted to detain them against their will. The Pennsylvania Supreme Court faced some implications of this question in 1793 when it considered the case of *Respublica against Catharine Keppele*. On December 22, 1789, the Philadelphia mistress had secured a five-year indenture for Benjamin Hannis, an eleven-year-old orphan boy. When Hannis's patrons obtained a writ of habeas corpus to force Keppele to surrender him before his time expired, she appealed, and the court was forced to decide the status of indentured apprentices. Mr. Sergeant, Keppele's attorney, argued strenuously for the enforcement of long-held traditions. "Servitude by indenture is founded upon the immemorial usage of Pennsylvania," he declared. Indigent families needed indentures to avoid their children "being brought up meanly, and in habits of idleness and vice." If the court allowed such children to escape before their time expired, no one would receive them in the future. The boy's attorney, on the other hand, "urged that servants were considered in Pennsylvania, in a very degraded state." They could be whipped, and their service could be extended if they ran away, conducted business, or married. A parent might have the right to assign a child to such a position, but a guardian never could, he maintained. In carefully worded opinions, each justice considered the custom of indentured servitude and decided the boy could not be assigned to it. While some members of the court sustained indentures for the poor or upheld parental powers to bind out children, Justice Bradford decried the indentures altogether. No parent, he argued, could rightfully place a child in an institution that sanctioned prison terms or additional servitude for desertion. "Such a contract which would subject the infant to the severe penalties of our laws, and to be sold to anyone who will buy his service, cannot be for [the child's] benefit."[9]

Eight years later the Pennsylvania court extended protection against servitude when it entertained a former slave's claim for wages. The slave, a man named Peter, had been captured behind British lines during the Revolutionary War by William Steel, an American officer. After the war, Steel brought

Peter to Lancaster County, Pennsylvania. Perhaps with the assistance of the state's antislavery Quakers, Peter obtained his freedom six months later through a habeas writ. After several years passed, he sought remuneration for the time he had labored for Steel. Barred in his initial attempt by a ruling that the suit was insufficient, Peter brought his case before Pennsylvania's high court. Again, the judges eroded the foundations of servitude and allowed Peter the wages he asked. "When one does work for another by compulsion, whom he is under no legal or moral obligation to serve," Justice Jasper Yeates wrote, "the law will . . . imply and raise a promise on the part of the person benefited thereby, to make a reasonable compensation." [10]

The opinions in these Pennsylvania litigations revealed the emerging northern consensus on specific performance. Bradford's opinion expanded the assault on servitude, the selling of one's person into service, and on its institution of enforcement, criminal penalties for desertion. Increasingly, free labor meant that masters did not retain power over the bodies of their servants. Yeates's opinion went further, for he began to separate labor power from the laborer. Even though Peter had been forced to work, indeed because he had been forced to work, the labor must be remunerated. This view contradicted flatly the idea of servitude, the purchase of a laborer's body. Moreover, it upheld the coming world of wages, of compensation for disembodied labor power.

By the turn of the nineteenth century, then, the function of law in supporting slavery and servitude had become ambiguous in the northern states. By the time the Indiana Supreme Court heard the case of Mary Clark in 1821, northerners had begun to draw distinct lines between servitude and free labor. In its particulars, the litigation resembled those of Hannis and Peter in that Clark sought release from an indenture through habeas corpus. But in 1821 she could use the force of Indiana's antislavery constitution, which declared indentures for African Americans void whether made in Indiana or elsewhere. A former slave, Clark had bound herself as a housemaid to G. W. Johnson for twenty years. Having become dissatisfied with the arrangement, she applied for release and appealed to the state supreme court after a circuit court validated the indenture. [11]

Upholding her release, Justice Jesse L. Holman discussed fully the relationship between servitude and free labor. A Baptist clergyman and later a Jacksonian Democrat, Holman dispensed with arguments about race by resorting to the rhetoric of equality of laws. Clark was a citizen, and under the state constitution, all citizens possessed "equal right and ability to contract."

The constitution also forbade involuntary servitude, but Clark's indenture was made freely. Consequently, Holman believed, it must be tested by the principles of obligations incurred by writing—that is, contracts. By starting from this standpoint, Holman introduced the implicit conflict between the traditional master-servant relation (which relied on customary and legal support for the master's authority) and the "modern" employer-employee relation (which posited legal equality through contract). When courts intervened to settle differences between contracting parties, he pointed out, the litigants' feelings became "irritated against each other, and the losing party feels mortified and degraded in being compelled to perform for the other what he had previously refused." Conflict became even more severe if the outcome placed the losing party under the control of his or her adversary. Degradation manifested itself most plainly "in the case of the common servant, where the master would have a continual right of command, and where the servant would be compelled to continual obedience." Accordingly, the court would not abide such a situation, for it would "leave a party to exercise the law of the strong." Unlike a minor who might be considered to have no legal will, Clark was an adult and could "regulate her own conduct." She possessed "the right to exercise volition" and to declare "her will in respect to the present service."[12]

Based on these arguments, Holman rescinded Clark's indenture, declaring that neither the common law nor Indiana statutes authorized compulsion of specific performance. By this simple principle, he distinguished the central difference between forced and free labor. Slavery and involuntary servitude used the law directly to control the laborer's body and to coerce labor, contrary to the will of the worker. In striking down these ancient principles, Holman perceived that in a polity committed to formal equality, power relationships could not be so transparent. Obliging a servant to return to a master whom she or he wanted to depart was equivalent to "absolute slavery; and if enforced under a government like ours, which acknowledges a personal equality, it would be productive of a state of feeling more discordant and irritating than slavery itself." Holman could have limited his analysis to slavery or indentures alone, but he extended it to cover all contracts. If the law sanctioned labor compulsion, it would either end contracts altogether or would "produce in their performance a state of domination in the one party, and abject humiliation in the other."[13]

Though not fully developed, Holman's argument voiced a new theme that many northerners were coming to realize by 1821—that the destruction of overt forms of labor control did not signify the end of legal labor discipline itself. In essence, Holman had stumbled across the idea of commodified labor, the concept that employers did not have to control laborers' bodies in order to extract work. As he implied, contracts could secure reliable labor without resorting to force, and a few years later Holman recognized this idea explicitly when he penned an opinion that enforced the contract of an Indiana farm laborer. Yet for contracts to work in a capitalist economy and liberal polity, they had to contain at least a nominal right to quit. Workers must be free to circulate, or the use of contracts would be moot.[14]

CONFLICTING VISIONS OF FREE-LABOR LAW

Between 1815 and 1860, jurists, attorneys, and litigants created two competing definitions of contracts for labor. Each implied a differing place for the state in a capitalist labor system. The dominant path regarded state interference as normal and offered (at least in theory) security for both individual employers and employees. The other, although limited in numerous ways, envisioned a labor market substantially free of state control for individual workers.

By the antebellum period, labor law had come to encompass many types of actions, yet the law of contracts became increasingly important. As legal and labor historians have long noted, criminal conspiracy cases became a focal point for the labor movement. In addition, the ability of workers to recover damages after industrial accidents became an issue of heated contention as early capitalist manufacturing chewed up more and more laborers. When considering the question of the state's role in creating and sustaining a capitalist labor market, however, the nature of labor contracts occupied the central place. Certainly, contracts did not receive the attention by labor leaders or social critics that criminal conspiracy or industrial accident cases did. Nor have they until recently been much explored by historians. Yet grasping the nature of a contract for labor is essential to understanding both the employment relation in antebellum America and the assumptions Reconstruction-era northerners took into the emancipated South.

Above all, a labor contract defined the labor market. To be sure, most workers in antebellum America did not sign formal contracts as such. Rather, they worked under oral agreements or semiformal workplace rules. In a capitalist society, though, any employment relationship becomes a contract, a promise to perform some action in exchange for a payment, in cash or in kind. Obviously, envisioning labor in such a way was essential for its commodification. In fact, jurists and treatise writers who struggled to define labor contracts sometimes likened them to other commodity exchanges. Thus, delivering a certain amount of work might be analogous, in fact equivalent, to transferring a certain amount of grain. As Justice Yeates had argued, this delivery of a commodity was what raised the promise to pay. It created the conditions needed for a cash exchange, and, in a wage labor world, it bound recipients to complete their part of the bargain by paying for the commodity of labor. A labor contract, then, meant, for the worker, a promise to deliver labor power and, for the employer, a promise to pay for that labor power. These elemental concepts ran aground, however, when one party to the contract failed to fulfill the promise.

How the judicial system, and hence the state, dealt with these failures created the core of Jacksonian-era labor law. These failures to perform the promises inherent in a capitalist contract for labor received their fullest discussions in cases involving what were called "entire" or "special" contracts. Such agreements obligated a worker to labor for a definite period of time for a set amount of cash, payable either at the end or in installments along the way. Again, most workers, especially industrial workers, did not toil under agreements of this kind, yet judicial reasoning about these sorts of contracts should not be seen as a narrow discussion of obscure legal doctrines. Rather, entire contracts isolated and clarified the cash nexus at the heart of capitalist labor, for they made workers' promises to perform and employers' promises to pay definite and open to examination. Although often indirectly stated, the legal nature of the capitalist wage bargain and labor market received more attention in entire contract cases than anywhere else in antebellum America.

By 1860, participants in northern legal culture had developed consistent sets of arguments about entire contracts, yet they had reached no synthesis. In most states in the antebellum North, laborers who voluntarily abandoned entire contracts could not collect money due under the agreement, nor could they treat it as rescinded and recoup the actual value of their work. In landmark cases such as *Stark v. Parker* (Massachusetts, 1824), eastern courts established the "entirety" rule, requiring full performance before wages could be paid. However, by the 1830s entirety faced a growing challenge from a different construction of free labor based on the concept of *quantum meruit.* *Britton v. Turner*, an 1834 New Hampshire case, introduced this rule to a wide audience and provided ammunition for workers' attorneys. An equitable remedy envisioning payment for time actually served, *quantum meruit,* or "apportionment," assumed that all work bestowed some benefit to its recipient and that acceptance of that benefit implied a promise to recompense the laborer. For advocates of *quantum meruit*, a contract could thus be "apportioned" so that workers could be paid for however much time they had worked, whether they had completed the whole time stipulated in the contract or not. Nonetheless, those favoring strict enforcement of contracts found this remedy redundant, claiming that entirety protected workers as well as employers. If a servant was discharged without a sufficient cause, they pointed out, he or she could collect wages as if the contract had been completed.[15]

Judicial decisions about entire contracts in specific and labor contracts in general shaped the nature of the wage bargain and, more important, the emerging capitalist labor market itself. In the first instance, entirety lent the force of the state to the exchange of labor for cash. To be sure, workers deprived of the means of production toiled for cash in order to feed themselves and their families, and employers paid wages because they wanted the labor commodity that workers delivered. Still, state action both legitimated this social pattern and created means to enforce it. By undergirding both the promise to deliver and the promise to pay, law helped ensconce the wage bargain as *the* central economic relationship. In the second place, contract rules influenced the actual workings of the labor market. Entire contracts restricted the ability of workers to move about to sell their labor power, and they limited the powers of employers to dispose of laborers at will. The dissolution of servitude left employers with the threat of forfeiture or nonpayment of wages as the only real means to control workers' movements in the labor market. For workers, entire contracts offered a wisp of certainty in an increasingly uncertain economic world.

Judicial reasoning about entire contracts diverged along two lines. On the one hand, the majority of judges and other legal commentators upheld the notion of entirety and supported what might be called a right to security. For them, a promise to deliver a set amount of labor had to be performed in full before the state could obligate the recipient to accept the exchange and pay. Practically speaking, this reasoning meant that workers could not quit before their contracts expired, unless they wanted to forgo all payment. At the same time, these jurists believed that an employer who discharged a worker before the end of a contract could be penalized by being forced to pay for the whole term, as if the labor had been performed. On the other hand, a minority of judges believed that accepting labor on an ongoing basis raised a promise to pay for it. This conception implied a right to quit, and concomitantly a right to fire, for it reduced the exchange to a daily act that could be terminated at any time.

STATE CONTROL AND THE RIGHT TO SECURITY

Although English precedents had existed for centuries, U.S. courts created the foundations for entire contracts during the antebellum period. The New York Supreme Court established the first American precedents for entirety between 1815 and 1822, but the leading American support for entirety was *Stark v. Parker.* Decided by the Massachusetts Supreme Court in 1824, the case involved a farm servant. A hired man on Thomas Parker's farm, John Stark left before the term expired and tried to recover for the time he had served. In *Stark,* Justice Levi Lincoln sternly proclaimed that courts possessed a duty to enforce contracts and "withhold aid and countenance from those who seek, through their instrumentality, impunity or excuse for the violation of them." He was satisfied that "the law will not admit of the monstrous absurdity that a man may voluntarily and without cause violate his agreement, and make the very breach of that agreement the foundation of an action he could not maintain under it." Charges that employers drove workers away were "wholly groundless," and the law offered remedies for cause if this unlikely event did happen. These remedies, the ability of workers to recover their full pay, took somewhat longer to establish. Though applied much less often in the antebellum North, this principle received a full hearing in *Costigan v. the Mohawk and Hudson Rail Road Company,* an 1846 case in the New York Supreme Court. The railroad had hired Costigan to superintend its Albany-to-Schenectady road from May 1, 1843, to May 1, 1844, at a salary of fifteen hundred dollars. On July 1, 1843, it discharged him for no apparent reason. When a referee awarded Costigan the remainder of his pay, the railroad appealed, arguing that Costigan was bound to find other employment instead of suing the railroad for what it owed. Justice Samuel Beardsley declared that "nothing is better settled than that . . . the plaintiff is entitled to recover pay for the entire year" when discharged without cause.[16]

For the most part, then, supporters of entire contracts envisioned an active role for the state in a capitalist labor market, especially when it came to controlling the movements of workers. They saw the apportionment of contracts offered by the *Britton* doctrine as contrary to law and productive of

social ill. While apportionment's supporters pleaded for equity, the central
concern of jurists, attorneys, and employers who opposed *quantum meruit*
was that it would encourage the breaking of contracts. As Justice William B.
Peck of Ohio noted, *quantum meruit* "lessens the sanctity of these agreements and tends to encourage their violation." A Maine attorney phrased
it more bluntly: *Britton* was simply "an evasion of law." The Maine court
agreed, noting that *Britton* was "more equitable" but warning that "if it were
permitted to the laborer to determine the contract at his pleasure, no well
founded reliance could be placed, at any time, upon due observance of it."
Similarly, New York jurist Samuel Wells claimed it was "preposterous" to say
that a worker could leave his employer's service without cause or on "mere
fancy." Arguing a case before the Illinois Supreme Court in 1847, prominent
Belleville attorney and state assemblyman William H. Underwood pressed
vigorously for strict enforcement. "To tolerate a recovery in a case like this,
would be to impair and destroy the obligation of contracts," he insisted. "It
would encourage men to disregard their contracts, and occasion damages,
which no one but the party injured could fully appreciate or ascertain." To
these men, promises implied a duty that they be kept. Laborers must be
taught this lesson, even if it agitated the communities in which they lived and
worked. As Massachusetts justice Marcus Morton noted in 1837, "Laborers,
and especially that most improvident part of them, sailors, may excite sympathy; but in a government of equal laws they must be subject to the same
rules and principles as the rest of the community." [17]

Like their counterparts would be during Reconstruction, these men were
true conservatives in that they expected the state, rather than the market,
to take the greater role in ordering society. Indeed, they were backward-
looking traditionalists who saw the equitable arguments for apportionment
as an undesirable change. To them, the "equitable principle" in *Britton* was
of "recent innovation" and applied only to slight deviations from a contract.
Entire contracts were "reasonable, convenient, [were] founded in practical
wisdom, and ha[d] long received sanction of law." *Britton*, the Ohio Supreme
Court proclaimed in 1860, was "an innovation upon the long established
principles governing *entire* contracts." The court did not dispute the equity
of the New Hampshire rule, Justice Peck admitted, but it was not prepared
to adopt it because "so radical a change . . . should originate with the legislature, and not with the judiciary." [18]

To the most stringent adherents of the sanctity of contract, no exceptions
existed. For example, these lawyers and judges did not accept the common

principle that exempted minors from the entirety rule because they were incapable of ascertaining their best interests. Asking the court to adopt *Stark* for minors in 1824, a Massachusetts lawyer maintained that a child's contract should be construed as entire because of "the habits of industry and virtue which would probably be acquired from a faithful performance of it." For Vermont jurist Isaac P. Redfield, even acts of Providence did not absolve contractual obligations. "It is vain to say that the plaintiff was hindered from performing the service by the act of God," he wrote in a blistering dissent to a decision releasing a laborer who had been ill. "That is never an excuse for the non-fulfillment of a condition precedent." [19]

These proponents of entirety saw contracts as a form of legal labor discipline. Whether for adults or minors, contracts would inculcate "habits of industry and virtue" and effect order in the labor market and in the workplace. Even though equity might be an ideal concern, the common law and the courts' general duty to bolster promise keeping came first. Yet it would be unfair to see all opponents of apportionment as uncomplicated oppressors. Redfield was a particularly complex jurist. A biographer credited him with infusing equitable principles into the common law and with seeing law as "a broad and noble science, not a mass of arbitrary rules." In an 1836 case Redfield ruled that any work that could not be rejected necessitated payment. Such a principle was imperative "to prevent one party gaining an unconscionable advantage over the other." Sounding like a Jacksonian labor radical, Redfield asserted that "the laborer is entitled to his own labor, or its product, where it is in such a shape that he cannot carry it away." [20]

More than a technical dispute over contracts, what separated conservatives from their opponents was a deeper conflict about the social value of work. Supporters of entirety envisioned merit only in benefit added. By implication they valued skilled labor but not unskilled, and they regarded wages as arising from the products of labor, not from work itself. These jurists and lawyers usually were very careful to distinguish cases involving skilled artisans, especially house builders, from those involving unskilled "service." Litigations involving builders, they pointed out, involved mutual recision of the contract or slight deviations from its form. More important, they argued that the employer must possess the ability to accept or reject the product. However, unlike Redfield, they saw the inability to reject labor as a bar to recovery, instead of the very fact that justified remuneration. When recovery was allowed, they contended, the employers had benefited by acquiring the finished commodity though voluntary acceptance. Manual labor could not be returned, as a Maine lawyer maintained in an 1852 case involving a lumberjack. "We cannot deliver the labor back, [as] we could an unfinished article of property, a carriage, a house, a bridge," he insisted. Such contentions assumed that skilled labor was intrinsically more valuable and socially important than was simple service. Breese made this clear in *Lee v. Quirk*, an 1858 litigation for recovery under a year-long farm contract. "Merely working for the defendant," he wrote, "does not give the plaintiff a right to recover, if a special contract existed under which the work was done, and that contract violated by the plaintiff himself."[21]

Such statements suggest a precapitalist, or at most protocapitalist, view of law and the labor market, a view considerably different from the one that eventually triumphed after the Civil War. The judges, attorneys, and litigants who supported entire contracts saw them as cementing stable, almost hierarchical, relationships. As such, they represented one step beyond indentured servitude. Moreover, these men had not yet come to understand fully the commodification of labor taking place in the North's developing economy. They were much more comfortable thinking in terms of artisanal labor, in which independent craftsmen sold a tangible product, not their labor power.

Indeed, leaders of the working men's parties and the trade unions confined valuable labor to "producers." In the eyes of George Henry Evans, an English-born New York printer, laborers were "those who do the work and fight the battles; who produce the necessaries and comforts of life; who till the earth and dig for its treasures; who build the houses and the ships; who make the clothes, the books, the machinery, the clocks and watches, the musical instruments, and the thousands of things which are necessary to enable men to live and be happy." Radical Frances Wright directed an 1829 address to "the intelligent working classes, . . . the producing laborer and useful artisan." For New England carpenter Seth Luther, the producing classes' interests concerned everyone. "We believe," he told a group of New England workers in 1832, "[that] the interests of all classes are involved in the *intelligence* and *welfare* of those who labour—those who produce *all* the wealth and enjoy so *small* a portion of it themselves." Producing a tangible commodity in the artisan tradition indicated social worth; mere service did not suffice because it implied loss of skill and degradation to the status of manual labor, which was what the Jacksonian labor movement was trying to prevent.[22]

This version of labor related not only to work itself. It also carried fundamental political assumptions. "The industrious classes have been called the
bone and marrow of the nation; but they are in fact the nation itself," Wright
proclaimed. "The fruits of their industry are the nation's wealth; their moral
integrity and physical health the nation's strength; their ease and independence is the nation's prosperity; their intellectual intelligence is the nation's
hope." Artisans, historian Sean Wilentz has argued, saw themselves as "co-
operative yet independent craftsmen." By earning their competence they believed they became the natural citizens of a virtuous republic. John Commerford, a New York chair maker who rose to the presidency of New York
City's General Trades Union in 1835, put the case clearly. In a republic, he
believed, the value of a man's labor would indicate his worth, and productive
citizens would not become "the willing tools of other men." [23]

In essence, jurists, attorneys, and litigants who supported entirety looked
to a different conception of the capitalist labor market. Much more anchored
in the older economic conceptions voiced by artisans in the early part of the
century, they believed that contracts formed reciprocal obligations binding
on both parties. Under this conception, a contract was not truly a capitalist
device; rather, it was an indenture modified to fit the discourse of an emerging liberal-capitalist polity. This vision encompassed a role for labor law in
which employers could turn directly to the state to control workers, but one
also in which workers could turn to the state to protect themselves against
avaricious bosses. Viewed this way, jurists' use of master-servant discourse
represents their continued adherence to the hierarchical, but relatively more
stable, relationships of a precapitalist world. In that world, both masters and
servants could expect less opportunity but more security.

APPORTIONMENT, A LIBERAL-CAPITALIST MARKET, AND THE RIGHT TO QUIT

If entirety and its accompanying right to security represented a precapitalist
model, apportionment of contracts and the emerging right to quit pointed
toward a liberal-capitalist market in labor. In essence, jurists and others who
supported this emergent "right to quit" were true nineteenth-century liberals, who believed that the state's role in the economy should be limited. As a
result, they imagined labor and the labor market quite differently than conservatives did. Without possessing all the words, they had arrived at a full

capitalist conception of work. Whether they recognized it or not, they had come to see labor power as a commodity in itself, now wholly disembodied from worker or product. In their view, labor power could be put in very small parcels and sold on a daily basis. Consequently, proponents of apportionment argued for the right of workers to leave at any time, and they saw this right as equitable and just for workers. Ironically, then, labor's ostensible allies pointed the way to a more fully developed capitalist labor market in which workers could become more thoroughly alienated.

Arguments about the right to quit came to the fore as soon as courts began to establish entirety as the rule for labor contracts. In the Massachusetts Supreme Court, H. H. Fuller, the worker's attorney in *Stark*, employed three of the standard arguments in favor of *quantum meruit*. First, he contended, it was an "equitable principle. . . . And this principle ought particularly to be applied to the case of hiring to labor, in which the personal comfort and convenience of the laborer are so much concerned." Next, he argued that by accepting Stark's daily labors as they progressed, Parker took on a responsibility for compensation. Finally, he suggested that *quantum meruit* would promote labor stability. Deduction for damages would induce the laborer to stay, and the ability to recover would prevent employers from making "the laborer's situation uncomfortable towards the end of the term of service, in order that the laborer may leave him and forfeit his wages." Like Holman, Fuller realized that apportionment need not dilute labor discipline. Following assumptions similar to those that northerners would later employ in the post–Civil War South, he posited that contented laborers might work even harder than those subject to compulsion.[24]

In *Stark*, the Massachusetts court had tried to solve the abandonment problem definitively, but its harsh condemnation added to smoldering resentment against the entirety rule. By denying any wages to a worker who had completed ten and a half months of a year-long contract in *Lantry v. Parks* (1827), the New York court fostered more agitation for relaxing full performance. The harsh ruling in *Lantry* provided a stimulus for change, and *Hayward v. Leonard* (Massachusetts, 1828) supplied a means. *Hayward* was the most important in a series of decisions in which courts allowed builders to recover for work after the person who hired them rejected the structure. Azra Leonard had engaged Nathan Hayward to build a house. Leonard watched the structure going up and directed Hayward to make some changes along the way. The builder completed the home, but he broke the contract by not following its instructions to the letter. In 1828 Chief Justice Isaac

Parker for the Massachusetts Supreme Court upheld a lower-court judgment in favor of Hayward. Because Leonard derived obvious benefit from the house and because he had rescinded the contract by approving changes while observing the work, Hayward could recover *quantum meruit*. The chief justice made it clear, however, that this case differed from *Stark v. Parker*. Stark deserved no compensation because "he had stipulated to labor for a year, and before the expiration of the time, voluntarily and without fault of Parker, left his service." In approving *quantum meruit* for Hayward, the opinion explained, the justices meant "to confine [themselves] to cases in which there [was] an honest intention to go by the contract, and a substantive execution of it, but some comparatively slight deviations as to some particulars." [25]

Parker's careful distinctions did not last long. In 1834 *Hayward* was used to perpetrate what the Massachusetts court had tried to prevent—a ruling in support of *quantum meruit* after an abandonment without cause. In *Britton v. Turner*, the New Hampshire Supreme Court affirmed the right of workers to recover wages for the time they served, and by doing so, it inaugurated a debate over the nature of labor contracts that lasted into Reconstruction. *Britton* resembled *Stark* closely in its particulars. Britton contracted to work for Turner from March 1831 to March 1832 for $120, but he left two days after Christmas, 1831. This time it was the employer's lawyer on the defensive. "Although courts in modern times may have succeeded in getting around the old law," the attorney conceded, precedents like *Stark* and *Lantry* still supported entirety. "To hold out inducements to men to violate their contracts, when fairly entered into, is of immoral tendency." The New Hampshire Supreme Court listened to his advice and then issued a carefully crafted opinion in support of apportionment. After a series of qualifications, the court held that workers could be awarded any excess wages after damages for the breach of contract had been deducted. Citing *Lantry*, Justice Joel Parker called entirety "very unequal, not to say unjust. . . . By the operation of this rule . . . the party who attempts performance may be placed in a much worse situation than he who wholly disregards his contract." Comparing building cases to service contracts, he concluded that the discrepancy did not justify a different rule. Employers accepted labor on a day-to-day basis just like Leonard had done with his house, Parker submitted. The employer received a benefit for which the worker deserved compensation. By balancing the employer's responsibility for services rendered with the laborer's liability for the breach, the rule would prevent employers from driving away laborers before the end of their terms and would induce workers to stay. In closing, Parker lauded apportionment as a panacea for labor disputes: "It will in most instances settle the whole controversy in one action, and prevent a multiplicity of suits and cross actions." Extending Holman's concerns about coerced performance, Parker believed that labor discipline could function just as effectively if workers were paid whether they completed the contract or not. In other words, the cash nexus, not legal control, provided the ultimate and most effective control over workers.[26]

Concerns by conservatives about the possible results of apportionment pushed the New Hampshire court to modify *Britton* further in 1838. Workers wishing to recover must wait until their contract expired; in other words, they must act as if they had worked until the end. This restriction, the court hoped, would alleviate the dangers inherent in *Britton*. "It is desirable not to give the temptation of a payment in ready money, instead of delayed payment, to those who already have, perhaps, too much encouragement, at least all they deserve, to faithlessness of their contracts," Justice Nathaniel G. Upham wrote. Upham's concerns reveal the conundrum of using binding contracts to discipline workers at the inception of a capitalist labor market while simultaneously trying to legitimate the cash nexus. Although jurists continued to wonder about such uncertainties, *Britton* had established the right to quit firmly in the minds of workers and their attorneys, as the numerous antebellum litigations for contract apportionment attest.[27]

Even with restrictions, the proponents of apportionable contracts saw this conception of labor law as both equitable and progressive. By the immediate prewar period, liberal jurists had opened a deepening fissure in legal discourse as arguments about apportionment began to present a serious challenge to entirety and wage forfeiture. As the Vermont court remarked, "the ancient, rigorous doctrine" in relation to entire contracts had been much relaxed by 1850. By the mid-1850s, equitable arguments for *quantum meruit* also found their way into treatises. When the eighth American edition of *Chitty on Contracts* appeared in 1851, the editor noted that the *Britton* court had come to "manifestly just and sensible conclusions." Theophilus Parsons in his 1853 treatise on contracts gave even more credence to *Britton*. If the New Hampshire court's qualifications were kept in mind, he argued, "it might seem that the principles of this case are better adapted to do adequate justice to both parties, and wrong to neither, than those of the numerous cases which rest upon the somewhat technical rule of entirety of the contract."[28]

As much as conservatives wanted to cling to tradition, entirety faced increasing criticism between 1830 and 1860. Joel Parker had called entirety "very unequal," and lawyers and judges who came after him made the same charge. A Connecticut court found entirety to be "rigid and unreasonable," and a Vermont lawyer asserted that apportionment would be both just and equitable. Milo L. Bennett, a Vermont Supreme Court justice, made the case for apportionment forcefully in *Fenton v. Clark* (1839). Perhaps the most pro-worker of any prewar justice, Bennett stated straightforwardly that "it is not the object of the law to punish the party for a violation of his contract." To Bennett, entirety often produced "manifest injustice" for hired laborers. Primarily concerned with an equitable outcome, he believed that upholding entirety on technical grounds was "leaving the substance, and adhering to the shadow." Since the case in question involved a worker's sickness, Bennett may have seen it as anomalous, but his comments were most severe when he considered how entirety compelled workers to stay with cruel employers. A worker who was maltreated had to "submit to it, or leave his employer, not only subject to answer for such damages as he [the employer] may have sustained, but even at the peril of forfeiting all his former earnings." [29]

Certainly, opinions such as Bennett's helped workers survive in the day-to-day world of an economy undergoing the transformation to industrial capitalism. Yet apportionment also helped clear the way for the eventual triumph of a liberal-capitalist market, for it reduced the employment relation almost exclusively to the cash nexus. Proponents of apportionment focused on Joel Parker's point about daily acceptance. To them, the fact that labor could not be returned meant that its recipient incurred at least a moral, if not a legal, obligation to pay for it. When the Indiana court allowed a man who had cleared land for another to collect wages, its opinion adopted Parker's analysis in full. Unlike a house, the land cleared could never be rejected or returned to its original condition. In view of this fact, the employer had plainly derived benefit, and his daily acquiescence in letting the work continue meant that he received it. For such jurists, work possessed inherent value. Bennett clarified this point when he noted that he found it difficult to imagine "any very sound ground of distinction" between cases in which a builder raised a structure that deviated from the design and those in which a servant working under a special contract abandoned it. "In both, the defendant has had some benefit from the plaintiff's labor, and in neither can the parties be placed *in statu quo* by rescinding the contract." [30]

These views conformed neatly with the emerging bourgeois consensus

on the nature and value of work. Although middle-class employers and reformers sometimes shared with artisans a view that valued work for its products, not for its physical exertion, they more often emphasized the merits of
work itself. A nice illustration of the middle-class view appeared in Edward
Everett's "Lecture on the Workingman's Party," which he delivered to the
Charlestown, Massachusetts, lyceum in October 1831. Everett, a noted Massachusetts educator and politician and later the Constitutional Union Party's
vice presidential candidate, believed that work was the natural pursuit of all
people. "Nature is so ordered as both to require and encourage man to
work," he contended. "He is created with wants, which cannot be satisfied
without labor; at the same time, that ample provision is made by Providence,
to satisfy them, with labor." Work with "the muscles of the hand" was what
counted for Everett. Work must also be steady and difficult. Throughout the
ages, men such as Demosthenes, Julius Caesar, Lord Bacon, Washington, and
Napoleon had been judged by how hard they worked. At points, Everett's
address resonated with artisanal language, as when he noted the value of
"the man, whose honest industry just gives him a competence." Instead of
applying this standard only to productive labor, though, Everett related it to
all work. Enumerating how many workers it took to produce a telescope, he
included trades such as the glass and brass makers but also noted the day
laborers who scooped the sand that made the glass. All labor was dignified
because there was "no operation of manual labor so simple, so mechanical,
which [did] not require the exercise of perception, reflection, memory, and
judgment; the same intellectual powers, by which the highest truths of science have been discovered." For the conservative Everett, a workers' party
would embrace practically everyone, and his broad definition differed significantly from that of artisans, who emphasized skilled trades alone. As
Bruce Laurie has pointed out, such middle-class definitions could be used as
a defense against de-skilling. In the hands of Jacksonian poor-law reformers
or Civil War–era policymakers, they also could be employed to enforce a
general duty to work.[31]

CLASS AND WORKERS' RIGHTS

Of special importance to the minds of the Reconstructors, participants in
northern legal culture also envisioned workers' rights differently based on
class. For middle-class professionals, courts secured the right to wages after
being fired, while they gave artisanal capitalists considerable power to re-

solve disputes within the standards of their craft. For industrial workers, courts somewhat hesitantly legitimated factory regulations intended to limit the right to quit and to discipline the shop floor and more eagerly supported contractual rules intended to control collective action. Finally and most important for Reconstruction, courts gave farmers considerable power to control agricultural workers' right to quit. By 1860, then, courts had ensconced in free-labor law the axiom that class mattered.

While the proletarianization of the workforce in textile and other industries was the most significant alteration in the antebellum North's class structure, economic growth generated other new occupations. Besides operatives, it produced an expanding class of accountants, clerks, and managers. In relations with their employers, such "servants" often entered into long-term contracts to protect their salaries from downturns in the market. Seeking to maintain their middle-class position, they often sued for their entire wages if they were discharged. By doing so, they enhanced the right to security, but only for their own class.[32]

A combination of the class of the worker and the nature of the work influenced the outcomes of these suits. Sympathetic with middle-class professionals, jurists generally affirmed their right to recover entire wages. In 1842 the Pennsylvania Supreme Court denied recovery to a bookkeeper for a textile mill because he made mistakes in the accounts. Nevertheless, the court noted that if the dismissal was unjust, nothing prevented the servant from being paid for time worked plus "the wages he would have earned had the contract continued in full force." Daniel P. Ingraham, a conservative New York judge, observed in an 1850 case involving a clerk that a servant might obtain his whole compensation after being discharged if "it appear[ed] that he was idle and could not obtain other employment." As noted earlier, the New York Supreme Court issued the landmark opinion on this issue in the 1846 *Costigan* decision, a case that rested on the nature of employment for professionals. Costigan's attorney, N. Hill Jr., declared that though the demand for common labor was "constant and uniform," his client's profession of superintending railroads was "peculiar, and the call for it limited." M. T. Reynolds, the company's attorney, rejoined that the nature of Costigan's calling was no excuse. Many branches were open, and even if Costigan could not find employment, he was "not entitled to a life of ease and enjoyment with leisure for mental improvement, which he should have earned in a laborious occupation." For Reynolds, middle-class respectability had to be earned and retained by constant exertion. Justice Beardsley refused to accept this line of analysis. If the company could claim that Costigan had to find other employment, it had to be in the same area and in the same occupation. They could "not insist that he should, in order to relieve their pockets, take up the business of a farmer or a merchant." The courts, Beardsley implied, would neither enforce nor sanction downward social mobility for the middle class.[33]

If the nature of professional occupations often helped employees, it sometimes worked against them, as an 1858 Wisconsin case demonstrates. Much like Costigan, William Brewster had been discharged, and his employer's attorneys argued that Brewster was bound to seek employment. "He could not unnecessarily remain idle for any portion of the time," they asserted. "He must do everything in his power to render the damages as light as possible to his employer." Brewster had left a lucrative Chicago business in 1856 and concluded a five-year written contract with Peter Gordon to superintend his Wisconsin logging concern. Because Gordon resided out of the state, he entrusted his two large sawmills at Oconto, northwest of Green Bay, to agents. Brewster managed these mills and their pineries during the winter and acted as a general agent during the summer for a yearly salary of $2,000. On May 10, 1857, Gordon discharged Brewster, refusing to pay him the $300 owed for the current year. Brewster sued not only for his back pay but for the whole $8,000 remaining under the contract. The lower-court jury gave Brewster $4,480, the amount he could have earned less what he had received from another job he had procured. The high court found this amount excessive and decided that Brewster could recover only what he earned up to the discharge. In so ruling, the court relied on its own assessment of the labor market: "In any business the price of labor fluctuates greatly within four years, particularly is this true of the lumbering business in this country."[34]

Although professionals did not consistently recover wages, their class position and the conditions of their employment placed them in a privileged place. So too did the social station of builders and other artisans involved in labor contract cases. Most of these litigants were not "workers" at all. Workers proper in the transforming artisan world of Jacksonian America were journeymen in the traditional artisanal system. Increasingly unable to become shop-owning masters, journeymen experienced a decline in their skill levels as they approached the status of factory operatives.[35]

While this vast social transformation engendered class conflict that artisans expressed through working-class organizations, most journeymen did not carry their conflicts into the courts. However, a few state supreme court cases before the Civil War did involve workers identifiable as journeymen. In these cases, courts ruled in favor of employers, but more hesitantly than in litigations involving agricultural laborers or others involved in preindustrial work patterns. A joiner working a year-long contract at $1 per day for a New York cotton mill in 1816 recovered a quarter's wages, but a joiner working under a $180 yearly contract for a Grand Isle, Vermont, boat builder lost his wages when he left after six months. In 1845 Thales B. Winn, a journeyman tailor who pressed clothes and oversaw the work of young women employed in Porter Southgate's shop in Vermont, lost a suit for back wages against his merchant-tailor employer. Ten years later, gilder John Nounenbocker won his claim for extra wages against Thomas Hooper, who ran a gold and silver gilding establishment at 14 Dutch Street in New York City. In 1856 Michigan's supreme court allowed a gunsmith laboring by the day to recover wages, even though he did not complete the piece on which he was engaged.[36]

A more detailed illustration of journeyman-master conflicts comes from a Maine litigation. On January 5, 1835, shoemaker Leonard Cobb promised to work in Josephus Stevens's shop for ten months at $10 per month, but he reserved the right to leave and to have a third party determine the value of his work. Stevens protected his interests by inserting a clause stating that if Cobb worked for any other area shoemaker, he would forfeit his wages. On June 11 Cobb left after an altercation that had prompted Stevens to exclaim that "if he hated every body as bad as he did Cobb, he should not want to live long." The Maine court decided that Cobb's contract was void for vagueness and that Stevens's "violent hatred" constituted a reasonable cause for leaving. Cobb recovered $32.86 in wages.[37]

Though journeymen were not absent from antebellum courtrooms, most artisan cases involved carpenters, joiners, masons, painters, and builders who were either independent workers or master craftsmen. Many were large contractors who had long since left the artisan system behind. Their contracts diverged significantly from the service arrangements signed by farmworkers, mill hands, professionals, and even their own journeymen. Time contracts were not unknown, but most artisans' contracts established a price for the whole job. In addition, they often described the work in very specific terms, as in the agreement Amasa G. Smith made in 1829. Smith was to build a meetinghouse in Lowell, Massachusetts, for $8,000 following plans provided by the church's committee. Among the provisions in the covenant were stipulations that the roof was to be "well strengthened, and covered with slate," and that all materials used were to be "good and well seasoned."[38]

Given the intricate nature of master artisans' contracts, courts were often asked to decide cases of skill, and when doing so they incorporated both judgments from other artisans and the customs of the artisan world. In 1839 the Maine Supreme Court approved the use of fellow artisans in evaluating work. "In particular branches of trade or manufacture," the court believed, "the opinions of persons skilled in these respective matters should be received, as well as to the value, as the fidelity and excellence of the work." Reviewing the erection of an ironworks, the Pennsylvania court concluded that the construction of blast furnaces was "an art." In such vast and highly capitalized enterprises, success depended on skill, and if the company called in a man avowing expertise in construction, "the rules of law applicable to other artisans, attach[ed] to him." If he failed to meet accepted standards, he could not recover. However, not all jurists were willing to allow custom to overcome law. Indiana justice Thomas L. Smith would not allow juries to consider "customary prices charged by other workmen." Such a practice would give the builder an "unfair advantage, for he could stop when he pleased and compel the owner to pay him a full price for what work he had done."[39]

When jurists assessed the remedies available to master artisans, they usually relied on the standards pronounced in the 1828 *Hayward* case. Even before the Massachusetts court had acted, New York judge Jacob Sutherland had argued that if work was not done exactly according to the contract, a builder could still recover for the actual value. A New York court twenty years later saw this concept as valuable to employer and employee alike. An artisan should not be able to force an employer to accept work because the employer's circumstances may change. If one person hired another to build a house and subsequent events rendered it impossible for him to pay, it would be "commendable for him to stop the work, and pay for what has been done and the damages sustained by the contractor," the court maintained. As time passed, the Massachusetts court also elaborated on the reasoning behind the *Hayward* rule. Samuel S. Wilde argued in 1847 that if a defendant had derived any benefit, "it would be unjust to allow him to retain that without paying anything." However, he applied the rule cautiously to cases in which "the labor ha[d] been performed in good faith, and not to those where the party ha[d] intentionally . . . failed to comply with the stipulations of his contract." In an 1851 builder's case, Dewey noted that the rule was introduced to modify entirety so plaintiffs could recover even if they "had not literally complied with all the minute stipulations of the contract." The defendants' attorneys had asserted that in cases under the *Hayward* rule the contract had been substantially performed, but Dewey would not accept this line of reasoning. If it were adopted, he predicted, the builder would be "entirely remediless, and wholly at the mercy of his employer." The employer could simply elect at any time to reject the work and thus evade paying for it.[40]

Not all jurists were willing to allow master artisans to recover. In *Pullman v. Corning*, New York judge Henry Welles deemed the *Hayward* rule more fitted for "a court of conciliation, than of law." He could "see no just ground for making a distinction between a building contract and any other." This outcome might cause some hardship, but courts had no right to make contracts or dispense with rules of law. Welles pointed out that the mason in the case had not supplied materials. "All that he contributed was his labor," and that had been "unskillfully and negligently performed." In essence, he was closer to a worker than to an independent artisan.[41]

Welles's comments echoed Sidney Breese's disdain for those who simply labored, and taken together, their views pointed to the central difference between workers and the master artisans involved in building cases. An odd case in Connecticut in the late 1850s articulated even more explicitly the differences between master builders and members of the working class. In the spring of 1857 Lewis Corbin contracted with the town of Vernon to repair a road, for which he was to receive a cash payment plus any stone he removed. The enterprising Corbin then made a contract with the American Mills to construct a mill dam with this stone. Blasting stone to build the road, one of Corbin's workmen accidentally blew a two-ton boulder onto and through the roof of a nearby paper mill, smashing a machine. The owners of the paper mill sued Corbin for damages, and he tried to claim that American Mills was liable. Reviewing the complicated litigation, Justice William Wolcott Ellsworth admitted that it was not always easy to tell the difference between the relation of "master and servant" and that of "independence in the employee." For Ellsworth, the issue rested on whether the servant was acting solely within "his master's will and not his own." Corbin obviously did not fit this description. He had "sole control and oversight of the work—hired his own men, as many as he pleased, set them to work as he pleased, and dismissed them if they did not serve him with fidelity." Corbin resembled any other "mechanic or master builder," and "such a contractor [was] in no proper sense a hired servant or agent."[42]

Even though Corbin's predicament did not fully involve the employment relations of industrial capitalism, many litigations coming before antebellum courts did. In a series of litigations starting shortly after 1815, courts consid-

ered the applicability of entire contracts to true industrial workers. At a time
of rapid and disruptive economic change, owners and workers alike tried to
use entire contracts to bolster their economic fortunes. In some places, operatives asked for year-long arrangements to protect themselves from the
vagaries of the market. In others, owners experimented with unbreakable
long-term agreements to regulate the labor supply. The New York Supreme
Court appraised the latter usage in *McMillan v. Vanderlip* (1815). Vanderlip
had contracted with McMillan to spin yarn at three cents per run for one
year. He quit the job after about thirteen weeks and sued McMillan for the
work already completed. Some ambiguity about the terms of the contract
clouded the case, but the court held that "the contract was entire, and [had
to] be performed as a condition precedent before any action could be maintained for the price of labor." Vanderlip's long-term agreement evoked the
premodern employment relation of the agricultural contracts on which entirety lay based, and the court had little trouble sustaining it.[43]

Entire contracts might be used by entrepreneurs such as McMillan to discipline the workforce, but they carried an implicit danger. If markets for
cotton or woolen goods soured and mill owners wanted to slow down production, they could be saddled with workers for the entire year. The hazards
of entire contracts to textile mill owners became clear in two cases decided
in the 1830s. In both instances, operatives who were not supplied with work
tried to use entirety in their favor. In an 1835 Connecticut case, a wool spinner had contracted to labor for a dollar per day for an entire year. When his
employer failed to provide work, he sued, claiming he had made an entire
contract. After the operative won a judgment from a Litchfield jury, his employers sought an arrest of the judgment from the state's high court. Not
wishing to reverse the case at so late a stage, the court reviewed it "with some
anxiety to sustain it if possible" but overturned the award because no work
had been performed. A similar case faced the Massachusetts Supreme Court
two years later. In April 1836 spinner Solomon Thayer had agreed to work
until April 1, 1837, in David Wadsworth's factory at a set rate per yard. The
owners were unable to keep his loom occupied, so he left in late August.
Following a local custom, the owners settled for the first quarter of Thayer's
work but refused to go beyond that, setting up his breach of contract as a
defense. In arguing the case, both attorneys relied on *Stark v. Parker*, Thayer
to prove Wadsworth's liability, and Wadsworth to prove Thayer's breach of
entirety. The lower-court judge ruled that an entire contract existed as a bar
to recovery, and the jury returned a verdict for the mill owner. However, in

the high court, Justice Charles S. Dewey reversed the judgment. More important, he implied that entirety might not apply to industrial contracts at all. "The legal principles of [*Stark*] are undoubtedly correct," he maintained, "but care should be taken to apply them to cases depending on similar facts, or those substantially analogous to them."[44]

Dewey's implication that agreements for labor in textile manufacturing were materially different from the farm contract in *Stark* was correct. Most hirings in New England textile firms were not contracts at all. Rather, operatives submitted to work (and in Lowell, live) under a list of regulations. Although operatives nominally bound themselves to year-long contracts, the key provision was the requirement for notification before quitting. In daily practice, firms in Lowell, Massachusetts, the hub of the New England textile industry, did not enforce yearly terms or notice requirements with any consistency. As textile concerns expanded, and especially as labor unrest became more pronounced, owners and courts began to recognize the value of notification rules in disciplining the workplace. Yet this realization came slowly, and courts proceeded cautiously and uncertainly in affirming it. When initially requested to graft agrarian concepts of entirety onto industrial work relations, they resisted, and the function of contracts in disciplining textile workers was not firmly established until the 1850s.[45]

Initially, notices before quitting may have been intended to rationalize the labor market more effectively than entire contracts. An example from Massachusetts in the late 1820s demonstrates textile firms' use of regulations for this purpose. A weaver named Reeves, who had recently arrived in America, walked into the weaving room at a Mr. Stevens's Andover textile mill on July 3, 1828, and asked the overseer "if he had a loom idle." The overseer answered, "Yes," and set Reeves to work. Two weeks later, Reeves disappeared for a couple of days and then went to work at another mill on July 21. Before he left, Reeves received ten dollars under the company's piece rate for the weaving he had completed. Finding him at the other mill, Stevens sued Reeves for breach of contract, presumably to recover the ten dollars and to teach other wayward workers a lesson. The industrialist's attorneys claimed it was common knowledge among weavers in the area that quitting required a fortnight's notice. Asked to construe this custom as a bar to payment of wages, the Massachusetts court balked. Justice Isaac Parker found that the contract was not one for a specific time, notice was not a general custom, and Reeves had not been informed of it as part of the factory regimen.[46]

Although notification requirements in Stevens's factory were aimed at wandering weavers, the practice eventually became another means of work-place control. Two key cases that elaborated on the purpose of notification occurred in Massachusetts in the 1840s. The first, *Hunt v. Otis* (1842), directly raised the question of whether failure to give notice fell under the entirety rule. Elvira Hunt, a textile operative, left her job without giving the four weeks' notice required by the company's oral agreement with her. Hunt then sued Otis when the company refused to pay wages she had not yet received. After being instructed that Hunt's failure would not necessitate forfeiture but that the company could deduct for breach of contract, the jury awarded the $59.64 she requested. Hearing the company's appeal, the high court decided such regulations did not constitute a special contract. Justice Samuel Hubbard acknowledged the company's claim that this regulation was "important to them in due management of their business, not merely in regard to this case, but as to others." Still, he did not consider a notification requirement to be "a special contract for specific labor for a definite period." Even if the regulation were viewed in "the most favorable light" for the company, Hunt would not have to forfeit more than four weeks' wages. If the regulation had been in writing and signed as part of the contract, Hubbard suggested, the court might have held otherwise. But as the agreement stood, Hunt "did not *expressly* agree to labor for any specific time." Entirety, which governed "special contracts," could not apply.[47]

Massachusetts's industrialists apparently acted on Hubbard's suggestion. When the court again considered notification six years later, the requirement was embedded in a long list of written instructions adopted by the Dwight Manufacturing Company, a textile mill organized after the Lowell model. Again the plaintiff, Mary Rice, had quit her job without four weeks' notice. The jury in the lower court ruled in her favor after instruction that the obscurity of the regulations voided the contract. Reacting to this antilegalist action, the higher court decided in favor of the mill owners. However, the justices recognized that "the services might have been, to some extent, meritorious and valuable to the defendants, and it might be equitable that a reasonable compensation should be made for them." Although the court upheld entirety, then, its reasoning supported the inviolability of the cash nexus and the potential severability of contracts. While applying the law as it stood, Massachusetts's jurists understood that mill owners needed impersonal market relations, not vestiges of bound labor from an agrarian world that was rapidly fading. The decision in Rice's case exemplifies the emerging liberal notion of a free-labor market even more clearly when compared with the court's decision in the cases following *Stark*. The same court that invariably denied recovery for farmworkers proposed that apportionment might be possible for a mill girl.[48]

While the Massachusetts cases did not directly address the intention of regulation papers or notification, a Maine litigation in 1853 considered the matter fully. Frank L. Harmon and his wife, Almeda, sought the wages she had earned as a weaver at the Salmon Falls Manufacturing Company before their marriage. Almeda had commenced work on September 27, 1847, under a regulation paper that required two weeks' notice before leaving and that designated the agreement as an express contract. The Harmons' attorney, Mr. Luques, claimed that regulations such as these did not constitute a contract at all. They contained no certainty nor any statement about duration. Furthermore, they evaded the essence of contract doctrine "because there was no *mutuality*. The company were at full liberty to dismiss the laborer at any moment." Unexplained when handed to her, the paper was "a mere intimation of the company's wishes, as to the hours of work and mode of behavior." Luques's argument subscribed the terms of industrial discipline, accepting regulation of work time and work rhythms, but he would not allow these to be engrafted to older concepts. As he pointed out to the court, "It is not even pretended that the company suffered any damage by want of notice of quitting." Industrial contracts could not fall within agricultural categories. If a worker left without notice, one loom might lay idle for a time, but a whole year's crop would not be lost.[49]

J. N. Goodwin, the mill's attorney, also set up regulation papers as a means of workplace control, frankly outlining the firm's motives. Though the amount sought was small, he noted, the case presented "principles of deep importance, especially to those who [were] conducting the business of . . . large manufacturing establishments." Goodwin dismissed Luques's arguments about definiteness and certainty, basing this point on the central difference between industrial and agricultural work time. "The company," he alleged, "from the nature of its business, cannot beforehand fix more exactly the time of each operative's services." The stimulus to contracts for textile mills was not rationalization of the market but management of the shop floor and limitation of workers' control. Goodwin then got to the heart of the matter. Mill regulations were "indispensably necessary for protection against 'strikes' and such losses as must almost certainly ensue from a sudden cessation of the operatives to carry on the machinery."[50]

If Goodwin spoke for other companies, by the 1850s regulations had become a precursor to the post–Civil War "yellow dog" contract, intending to prevent strikes and govern workers while at their machines. Although it could be said that these contracts restricted the labor market in a larger sense, they did not do so in the same way as agricultural compacts. In actual effect, industrial regulations aimed to rein in large bodies of workers who demanded higher wages or better working conditions and who did not intend to leave the company permanently.

Reviewing the Harmons' case, Chief Justice Ether Shepley wasted no time in discarding their claim and affirming the company's contract. Shepley expressed deepest sympathy for the mill owners. Manufacturers, he asserted, concluded agreements for the delivery of vast quantities of goods. If workers could idle machines until replacements could be procured, no one could trust the industrialist, nor could he obtain "indemnity for losses occasioned by the fault of others." Shepley accepted Goodwin's suggested cure for this problem completely. Contracts requiring forfeiture of wages for leaving machines were "the only valuable protection" against strikes. Though the courts should not be instrumental in making such agreements, they should not "shirk from the duty" of enforcing them. Workers who violated them could not "expect to obtain relief by the rules of moral right and wrong, or by those of equity jurisprudence or the common law." Having gone this far, Shepley even dispensed with the concept of mutuality. "The position is quite novel," he professed, "that a contract will not be valid unless each party assumes precisely the same obligations." In other words, while individual wage negotiations might have to be just, the conditions of work that ensued after the bargain did not.[51]

Shepley's opinion was one of the baldest manifestos for employers' powers issued from any antebellum court. Yet it demonstrates that the role of law in industrial work discipline rested not on the formal doctrine of contracts but on the nature of work and workplace control. This latter goal underlay another industrial case decided in the Massachusetts Supreme Court at about the same time. This litigation examined what might happen when an operative in the Lowell mills followed the rules, laboring faithfully for a year and giving a fortnight's notice before leaving. Under such circumstances, the operative was supposed to be given a "line" or "honorable discharge," without which he or she could not obtain employment elsewhere in Lowell.[52]

In 1852, Catherine Cassidy sued the Suffolk Manufacturing Company of Lowell because it had denied her a line. Trying to clarify the custom, the trial court heard many explanations of the custom's purpose and operation.

According to Alexander P. Wright, the company's agent, reasons for refusing a line included "bad temper, producing disturbance in the room . . . [and] any such conduct as would render the hand unserviceable elsewhere, such as insulting the overseer, trying to get the other hands discontented." The implication was that Cassidy had committed one of the enumerated offenses. On July 19, 1849, she was dismissed by her overseer, John Clark, for "improper conduct" after working since May 29, 1848. Cassidy and her friend Bridget Gaiten then sought work at Boott Mills, but Cassidy was turned down for want of a line. In early August 1849 William Markland, overseer at the Lowell Company, hired her for a week, but again she had to leave because of her missing reference. With a crippled mother to care for, Cassidy attempted in October to secure her honorable discharge by convincing her neighbor, John Montague, to accompany her on a visit to her former overseer. The pair called on Clark at the mill, and Montague told the overseer he "thought it a rather hard discharge" and "how hard it was for her and her mother." The trio then proceeded to see the agent, Wright, who first assured Cassidy that she might come back to work for the company because "she was a very good girl, there was nothing against her." Not receiving Wright's condescension with due deference, Montague told him they might sue, to which Wright responded that "he would spend $5,000 rather than change the line he had given her." In December, Cassidy finally acquired a line from a previous employer and worked for Markland at the Lowell Company for thirteen months. By the time her suit reached the supreme court, she had married Bernard Thornton and presumably retired from the mills.[53]

The case went to the supreme court, where Chief Justice Lemuel Shaw was asked to determine its legitimacy. Shaw declared the plaintiff's suit insufficient and affirmed unhesitantly employers' right to exercise workplace control. Cassidy had claimed that her twelve months' service by itself gave her a right to the line. Shaw answered that if an unsatisfactory operative secured an honorable discharge simply by staying an allotted time, "it would be the certificate of a falsehood, tending to mislead and not to inform other employers." Indeed, employers had the right to adjudge operatives' conduct "in all respects, including not only skill and industry in such employment, but conduct in point of morals, temper, language, and deportment, and the like." Because of their relation to each other, Lowell companies had a "common interest . . . in maintaining their discipline."[54]

Contract cases involving professionals, artisans, and workers demonstrate how much class mattered in determining the contractual rights of free labor.

Middle-class professionals sought and won (temporarily) a right to security, while artisans used law to help shore up their declining control over their craft. Industrial workers, however, gained much less legal power. Although they obtained a somewhat restricted right to quit, they also lost the ability to seek economic security. More important, they faced increasing contractual restrictions against their actions on the shop floor and in collective wage bargaining.

As important as industrial cases were for the development of contract law, agricultural litigations created the most critical relation between law and class that would influence emancipation and Reconstruction. Because bound labor had always been prevalent in northern farming and southern plant-ing, a tradition of restricting farmworkers already existed. Indeed, the most stringent advocates of entirety hinted that the rule might be restricted to farm cases. Consequently, as labor contract law developed in the antebellum North, jurists most firmly established the principle that entire contracts could be used to limit the right to quit for farmworkers, thereby governing their behavior in a capitalist labor market.

Entire contracts between farmers and their hired hands emerged from a combination of volatile labor markets, seasonality in crop production, and the class position of farmworkers. Labor requirements for cultivation of small grains and hay varied throughout the growing year. In fall and winter, farmers might take care of their places with members of the family, but the harvest season from July through September required additional hands at a moment's notice. If workers could not be procured, heavy ripened wheat could be downed by a brief shower and would rot in the field. Farm labor markets formed around these exigencies. In the Midwest, hands followed the harvest northward from the Ohio Valley into Canada. Often young, un-married men trying to move up to farm tenancy and then ownership, they worked on farms in the summer and then drifted into logging, meatpacking, or casual labor in cities during the winter. Fully aware of their prized status at harvest time, workers could command daily wages far above what they would earn under monthly-wage arrangements.[55]

Many farmers solved the problem of high-priced harvest labor through long-term contracts. Workers could be hired in the spring at a lower monthly wage and be kept through the harvest season. Under such agreements, land-owners both lowered labor costs and secured workers to gather crops. For example, Allen O. Brown decided to work for Frederick W. Kimball in Or-leans County, Vermont, for six and a half months starting on April 4, 1838, for $12 per month. Brown would receive his pay at the completion of the contract, $50 in cash and $28 in sheep. Chester W. Olmstead made a similar contract with farmer Jonathan Beale in Norfolk, Massachusetts. Barnabas Eldridge hired Nelson Rowe to work for eight months on his farm in Kendall County, Illinois, at $90 for the entire time. Near Stephenson, Illinois, William Hanna contracted with John B. Angle on May 15, 1857, to labor until October 1 at $18 per month. Hirings of this sort were usually informal wage bargains struck between employer and laborer after brief negotiations such as those carried on between Lot Davis and Ann Maxwell. Davis contacted Maxwell on an April day in 1844 and asked her for work on her farm near Waltham, Massachusetts. He told her he would rather work for her at $12 per month than for a dollar a month more on a nearby milk farm. The two struck a deal for seven months' labor, and Davis began work that afternoon.[56]

Farmers wanted to control wages, but more important, they aimed to restrict laborers' movements in the market by using contracts for fixed periods of time, thereby invoking the law of entirety. Most contracts began in March and lasted through October, but some ran the whole year. *Stark v. Parker* had involved just this sort of arrangement. John Stark had agreed to labor for Thomas Parker for a whole year at $120. A similar contract made in Connecticut in August 1854 stipulated work for the entire year with a payment of $160 at the end. In Bureau County, Illinois, James Swanzey hired John Moore to work for one year starting March 5, 1856, with pay of $200 at the end. Annual arrangements offered the farmworker economic security and relatively little work in the winter months in return for the strenuous exertion of spring and summer.[57]

While valuable for farmers in controlling the labor market and for laborers in assuring themselves a job, such long-term binding contracts presented potential problems for both parties. From the farmer's perspective, she or he might be bound to a hand who disobeyed commands or shirked labor. From the laborer's point of view, he or she might be forced to withstand mistreatment to be paid. Two customs arose to solve these problems: trial hiring and at-will clauses. Usually, trial hirings involved a test period of one month and then a longer term for the season. A Cayuga County, New York, farmer hired a hand for a month in April 1856 with the proviso that if he liked him he would keep him on for six more months. A Grafton, New Hampshire, worker started on November 11, 1833, for one month and then agreed to a contract for a year at $120. In Ohio, David P. Larkin and John Buck agreed to a somewhat different kind of trial hiring, one that recognized explicitly both the geographic mobility and the variable wages of farmworkers. Buck decided to work for Larkin starting on October 17, 1860, for six months at $11 per month, and then for another six months at $13 per month if he did not leave for Pennsylvania.[58]

Trial hirings worked to the advantage of employers by testing out workers' reliability, and some at-will clauses were inserted for the same purpose. In Wisconsin, an employer who concluded an at-will arrangement noted that "he would not hire a man to work for him if they could not agree, or either was dissatisfied; that when that was the case he would pay them off and let them go." While the aim might have been workplace control, such contracts also benefited laborers by ensuring their ability to respond to the market, and these arrangements were common, even early in the nineteenth century. On May 15, 1835, for instance, John Tyrell agreed to work for brothers William and Harry Sutton for six months. Under the contract, they could discharge him at pleasure, and he could leave without any forfeiture of wages. Isaac P. Whitcomb concluded a year-long contract with Daniel C. Gilman in 1859 with an identical proviso. At least some workers recognized the value of such clauses and insisted on them. In rural western New York in 1859, a worker informed his prospective employer that he "would not hire for any certain time, or any longer than they could agree." Consequently, his eight-month contract provided that he was "not bound to remain" if conflict arose. When at-will contracts came before the courts, some refused to uphold them, but others saw them as giving either party the right to end the contract as long as bona fide disagreement existed.[59]

In such cases, avoiding conflicts with workers through at-will clauses undermined the original purpose, regulation of the market. This dilemma arose because response to the labor market and conflicts in the field were the two most common reasons why farmworkers left their employers. Farm laborers in the antebellum North were highly mobile, relocating often in pursuit of higher wages or better conditions. Through day-to-day interactions with servants from other farms, they obtained valuable information about local wage rates and working conditions. They often broke contracts, even at the risk of forfeiting wages. When Nelson Rowe deserted Barnabas Eldridge in June 1843, he did so to "go to the South" with another agricultural worker. Eli Heald migrated to Pennsylvania after three months of a six-month contract on Abraham Badgley's St. Clair County, Illinois, farm. Already displaying an awareness of local wage rates when he contracted with Ann Maxwell, Lot Davis continued to eye the market as he stayed at her Waltham establishment. In mid-July, Davis resolved that he was "going to look for work," and he informed his mistress of his decision. Maxwell replied that "there was work enough for him to do" and that "she should not pay him any wages, if he left." Undeterred, he departed and sued her for his pay.[60]

Some workers left simply to look for better wages, but others breached their contracts because of open conflicts with their employers. Sometimes these disagreements were about payments due. In *Lantry v. Parks*, Lantry left because he resolved that "he would work no more . . . till he ascertained if he could collect his wages." Swan Erickson, a Swedish immigrant, departed Daniel J. Hansell under similar circumstances. Though Erickson had trouble understanding English, he objected when his employer refused to pay by the month as he thought the contract stated.[61]

More often, conflicts concerned work pace and worker's control. Not un-like their southern counterparts, northern farmers wanted faithful and doc-ile servants, but hired hands tried to preserve control over their time and conditions of labor. Two examples from Illinois illustrate the nature of these disputes. Already upset because John Angle had made him cart bricks for a new house, William Hanna became even angrier on an August day in 1857. When Angle tried to speed up the pace at which Hanna was driving a team of horses pulling a flax-cutting machine, the hired man refused. Angle then put Hanna on the reaper to pitch off the crop. After once more round the field under the summer sun, Hanna jumped off the machine, stuck his fork in the ground, declared the work was too hard, and said he would not do it. In response to Hanna's complaint, Angle threatened to hire someone else, after which Hanna quit. Farmworker John Moore clashed with the son of his employer, James Swanzey, on the family's Bureau County, Illinois, place. When the younger Swanzey complained on August 25, 1856, that Moore and another hand had hauled no more than two loads of hay that day, Moore walked off.[62]

Some farmers were probably glad to see such workers go, but others tried to retain hired hands even after quarreling with them. Wishing to keep hands on the farm, they overcame their temper and their desire for discipline in the field. When Frederick Kimball wanted Allen O. Brown to help haul a load of boards in July 1838, both became angry, but after talking it over, Kimball asked Brown to stay. Caught between the two brothers who had hired him, John Tyrell encountered a similar attempt to get him to remain. In July 1835 he argued with Harry Sutton at Harry's St. George, Vermont, farm. Harry fired him, but when Tyrell went to pick up his belongings at the other brother's farm, William Sutton tried unsuccessfully to persuade him to postpone his departure. A New York farmer grew angry when his hired man refused to water and feed cattle on Sunday. However, his ire did not overcome his preference for keeping his help. He simply informed the hand that he could "go to hell, but to mind and first work his time out."[63]

When farmworkers who had left their employers attempted to recover their wages, they found a sympathetic ear and a reward for time served from local justices of the peace and juries. High courts were not so understanding. Although state supreme courts upheld awards in some cases, they more often overturned them. Some of these cases confronted issues of power distribution and workplace control on the farm directly. When the Illinois court heard William Hanna's case for wages, for instance, it reversed the ninety-dollar judgment he received from the circuit court jury and disregarded his complaints about the work rhythms of flax harvesting. Since he had been dismissed, Hanna should have benefited from the reciprocity of entirety, but Justice Pinkney H. Walker could not countenance farmhands determining working conditions. Hanna "was employed on the farm in the performance of labor incident to that occupation," Walker intoned, "and he had no right to insist upon the right to perform only the lighter portions of it, and an exemption from the more onerous portions."[64]

While opinions such as Walker's bolstered control of farmhands in the fields, other jurists assisted farmers in regulating hands' behavior in the market. Moreover, the arguments they heard and the opinions they issued often recognized explicitly the seasonality of farm labor and the traditional use of contracts in governing it. "We think well established principles are not thus to be shaken," Levi Lincoln concluded his *Stark v. Parker* opinion, "and that in this commonwealth more especially, where the important business of husbandry leads to multiplied engagements of precisely this description, it should least of all be questioned, that the laborer is worthy of his hire, only on the performance of his contract, and as the reward of fidelity." Himself an active farmer and agricultural reformer, Lincoln knew the value of farm labor and farm contracts from experience. In *Larkin v. Buck*, the Ohio Supreme Court noted that in farm labor, "the value of the service, and the amount of the compensation, vary with the season and the character of the work required."[65]

Jesse Holman, who had penned the perceptive statement of the principles of free labor in Clark's case, explained the function of labor contracts with equal lucidity a few years later. "But it is well known that the labor of a man on a farm is far more valuable in the spring and summer than in the winter months," Holman wrote. "And it would be contrary to every principle of justice, to permit a man under a contract to labor through the winter months and recover of his employer for that time as for monthly wages, when in all probability the employer would not have hired him during those months, but in consideration of his services for the balance of the term." Holman realized completely the bargain implied in long-term contracts. The farmer hired a hand at lower wages during the winter to make sure he was available for seasonal work during the summer.[66]

The prime reason for requiring entire performance in these contracts before wages could be collected was made clear by both Redfield and Breese. According to a farm servant's attorney, the leading British case on entirety suggested an "implied understanding" that servants were entitled to their pay even if they did not serve out the term. Redfield responded that no such understanding existed in the United States for domestic servants. Nor did it prevail "in the case of men hired for the farming season, where the loss of a single month's labor might cost the loss of the products of an entire season." Addressing the case of Swan Erickson, the Swedish immigrant who had left because he was not paid, Breese rapidly disposed of the "pretext" of a possible language barrier as "too flimsy to deserve notice." The worker had made his pledge to stay for the season, and he had to abide by it. Breese's indignant opinion went beyond this simple lecture about the sanctity of contracts. Rather, he focused on the problem of laborers absconding at a particular point in the agricultural cycle. Erickson "left his employer in the midst of the harvest, probably under the promise, from some meddlesome person, to give him higher wages," Breese reported. "This is contrary to justice and good morals, and cannot be tolerated."[67]

Erickson had done exactly what he should have done in a capitalist society; he responded to the job market as well as any classical economist or free-labor Republican could have desired. Farmhands like him put liberal jurists such as Breese in a peculiar position. Breese was not antiworker. In another context, he eased the operation of the fellow-servant rule, which limited workers' claims in industrial accident cases. Farm labor was another matter altogether. Especially in the grain belt and especially during harvest, many farmers believed success required restrictions on farmworkers' mobility. Reliance on day labor was common, but farmers who sought more rationality turned to long-term contracts. Such agreements were not an outright invention of a new capitalist economy so much as an incomplete mutation of traditional customs as indentured servitude slowly transformed into the wage relation. Breese, Redfield, and Lincoln knew farmers' needs in the changing economy almost instinctively.[68]

This mixture of master-servant discourse with the language of wage relations also appeared in a case involving a housekeeper on a Pennsylvania farm. Mary Albright had begun serving John Ranck and his one child on his Lancaster County farm for three dollars per month under an express contract. When she started in 1854, Ranck's farm had been worked by sharecroppers, but in 1856 he resumed personal management, employing additional farmhands and several artisans to improve the place. Albright saw this as a change in the nature of her work, demanded a raise, and left on July 13, 1858, when Ranck refused to grant it. Considering the case in 1860, the Pennsylvania Supreme Court admitted that the change in circumstances had indeed increased her duties. Nevertheless, "by her original contract of hiring, she had sold to him the right to all her time and labour, if they were needed for housekeeping." By not objecting immediately, the opinion argued, she accepted the new terms. "Her silence was an assent," Justice William Strong concluded.[69]

Strong's rhetoric resonated with both traditional and modern constructs, and it reveals the fluid state that labor contract law had reached by 1860. The justice recognized the cash nexus: Albright "sold" complete control over her "time and labour" to Ranck. But the wage bargain and the employment relation were not equivalent. As a servant and as a woman, Albright's failure to resist became a positive act, conferring her acquiescence to new employment but not to new wages. Her status as a servant subtracted from her importance as an actor in the market. In Albright's case, both class and gender girded power structures. For the farmhands she served, class was ultimately the overriding consideration. Schooled in an agrarian world, jurists viewed both farm servants and domestic help in traditional terms and felt safe in supporting the entire contracts such servants accepted. In other words, the class of the workers counted more than the class of their employers. Drawing on a long agrarian tradition, farm contracts in antebellum America possessed clear purposes, purposes that war-era northerners would carry into emancipation and beyond.

CAPITALIST CONTRACTS IN THE SLAVE SOUTH

The bourgeois northerners who had come to believe in a society organized by contracts and in rights defined by class encountered during Reconstruction a society similar in appearance but divergent in structure. Southern courts decided labor cases starting from the same English and American precedents as did those in the North, yet the social realities of a slave society produced a different strain of law with different social meanings. While southern courts also limited the right to quit, the demands of planters led judges to augment the planters' power to discharge workers by weakening the right to security. This power to dispose of workers at will left planters well prepared to view labor as a commodity but ill equipped to consent to rights for workers.

As in the North, class figured prominently in broad patterns of litigation. For all the charges raised by slavery's apologists against northern free labor, the South possessed its share of workers outside the normal bounds of slavery. Slaves who hired their own time, free black workers, and urban artisans and mechanics created anomalies in the hegemony of the legal system of slavery. Some southern states adopted the entirety rule in use in the North for white manual laborers, but most southern prewar labor contract law was dominated by one particular type of litigation, that between planters and overseers.[70]

To be sure, southern courts sometimes enforced labor contracts in ways identical with northern law. Even though the contracts of overseers came to constitute a distinct and powerful area of litigation, some cases mirrored farm laborer agreements in the North. If overseers abandoned their arrangements without cause, southern jurists enforced the entirety rule with a zeal worthy of their northern brethren. The Louisiana court considered contract abandonment in *Hays v. Marsh* and pointed out directly the threat to the plantation. "The agricultural interests of the country are mainly under the control of this description of men [overseers]," the opinion declared, "and if they could abandon their employers in the time of greatest need . . . it is plain that great and remediless mischief would ensue." The Louisiana court realized that sugar cultivation required constant attention, and abandonment near harvest time could not be tolerated. As such its decision echoed the arguments of northern jurists who enforced entirety of contract harshly against agricultural workers who absconded during harvest. Agricultural production necessitated intensive labor and intensive labor management at certain seasons, and courts in both the North and South were not prepared to allow agricultural workers to influence work arrangements to any great extent.[71]

Most litigations, however, involved planters who fired their overseers, not overseers who left their employers. In considering these frequent conflicts, southern courts constructed a legal order in which reserving the employer's power rested on the ability to discharge rather than bind workers. Consequently, contract apportionment, at least for overseers, became much more common in the South. Nevertheless, like northern doctrines, these rules resulted from the needs of the producers. Owners depended on overseers to make the crop and care for their property in slaves. Owners required the flexibility to dispose of overseers who threatened the stability of the plantation and endangered agricultural success. Therefore, southern courts created an agricultural contract system that in many ways was the opposite of the northern model, a system in which planters expected agricultural stability to rest on the ability to violate labor agreements. In the broadest sense, the South's version of free-labor law aimed to resolve the class conflicts of a biracial slave society, not a truly capitalist one in which the inviolability of contracts had become sacrosanct.

The very nature of overseers' contracts suggested the mixture of openness and control that planters desired. Indeed, the wage bargain itself revealed the planters' preference for flexibility. Some employers agreed to give their overseers from one-twentieth to one-fourth of the proceeds of the farm in lieu of wages. Others paid a cash wage plus provisions for the employee, his family, and his stock. Most offered wages of $150 to $500, payable at the end of the year. This restriction of pay, similar to northern farm contracts, both invoked the entirety rule and created the potential for conflict. Another source of potential conflict arose in the production bonuses some planters offered. In Mississippi, for example, Robert Sale contracted with Harden Hariston for $650 plus a $25 bonus if he could make two hundred bales of cotton weighing five hundred pounds per bale. Improving the management and productivity of the plantation prompted some overseers to push slaves further than their masters wanted. Plantation regulations created another source of friction, for once employed, many overseers lived under lengthy sets of rules governing their behavior and that of slaves. Such rules covered everything from how, when, and what to plant to the specific dictates for the discipline of slaves.[72]

Most important, some planters reserved the right to discharge their overseers at will. For example, a South Carolina planter stipulated that he could discharge his overseer for good cause and be liable for only the time served rather than for the whole salary. In the Red River cotton district of Arkansas, it was "invariably understood" that planters could discharge an overseer and pay him for his services and that "the overseers always reserved to themselves the right to quit at any time upon becoming dissatisfied, and to settle and receive their wages in proportion to the time they had served." A contract between Jesse Whatley, overseer, and George Jones, planter, provided for payment of four hundred dollars for the year or "thirty three dollars and thirty three cents a month if the said George Jones [wished] to terminate this agreement before the end of the aforesaid year." When John Ball of South Carolina fired John E. Morton after a month, he considered the overseer's poverty and "allowed him ¼ yrs. wages which was more than he deserved." At inception, then, some overseers' contracts accepted easy dissolution and apportionment of wages.[73]

Contracts without at-will clauses, which appear to be the majority, created a serious dilemma for planters. Both the common-law entirety rule and the Civil Code in Louisiana required payment of the entire year's wages if an employer dismissed an employee without cause. These rules, envisioned as supplying equity in contract arrangements, left planters in a predicament. If they fired an incompetent overseer in, say, March, they might be liable to pay for the remainder of the year. On the other hand, if they avoided this unpalatable outcome by keeping him on, they risked mismanagement of their farms and slaves.

Trying to resolve this dilemma, southern courts upheld and even encouraged the violability of contracts between planters and overseers. The leading case and impetus for change in other states was *Byrd v. Boyd,* a decision handed down by the South Carolina court in 1825. In an opinion upholding recovery of wages by an overseer who had been dismissed, Justice David Johnson noted, "The relation of employer and overseer is one which the state of the country renders almost indispensably necessary to every planter and collisions do and must necessarily arise, and it is fit that there should be some settled rule on the subject." Johnson was sure that overseers could not recover when they abandoned without cause and that masters could not prevent recovery when they discharged without cause. There was, however, "a third class of cases": "The employer reaps the full benefit of the services which have been rendered, but some circumstance occurs which renders his discharging the overseer necessary and justified." In these cases, Johnson held, overseers could recover for the time they had served.[74]

By 1860 most other southern states had adopted *Byrd* specifically or had devised a similar rule. Adopting the South Carolina court's reasoning, Mississippi justice J. S. B. Thacher noted, "The strict rule of law, governing contracts, has been much relaxed in this country in relation to those made between employer and overseer." The Tennessee Supreme Court also recognized *Byrd* in an 1853 case. William T. Jones had been fired after eight months' service. The court was quick to hold that "abuse and cruelty toward the servants, and . . . neglect and mismanagement of the farm and stock" constituted sufficient cause for firing him. And although the high court would not allow the lower-court jury's $275 award for Jones's whole year's wages, it did sanction recovery for the time actually served. "This liberal rule has been adopted in South Carolina, and we think it just and reasonable," the court declared. Courts in Alabama, Arkansas, North Carolina, Texas, and Louisiana took similar courses. Knowledge of these rules apparently became widespread among overseers. In 1858 Robert P. Ford left Catherine P. Danks's Louisiana plantation, but he was subsequently "advised by others that it would be better to return and be discharged." If overseers possessed information about their legal remedies, the key for planters in avoiding payment of full wages was inducing the court to recognize a sufficient cause for the dismissal. As a result, civil actions for overseers' wages became investigations of the employment relation and its conflicts.[75]

While most of the events leading to discharging an overseer came from the conflicts inherent in a slave society, a few cases resulted more directly from the exigencies of the market. In considering such actions, some justices recognized a limited capitalist role for the apportionment of contracts. In 1849 an Arkansas judge held that instead of recovering their whole wages, overseers could recoup only the actual loss or injury they had sustained. Without such a rule, he believed, "extreme injustice" would befall planters who found themselves unable to retain an employee because of "events that could not have been foreseen and were beyond their control." A Texas jurist also justified recovery for time served by the vagaries of the market. "The planter might, in the course of the year, remove elsewhere, or his plantation might be sold for debts," he noted. "Would there be any justice in an overseers' exacting compensation for the whole year?"[76]

Most cases did not involve market decisions as such. Rather, planters fired overseers for reasons deeply connected with slavery. In the first place, many overseers found themselves out of work because of the way they handled slaves. Sometimes such charges were brought in conjunction with allegations of sexual impropriety, but more often owners simply alleged injury to their chattel. Courts did not construe threats of violence to slaves as grounds for discharge, but actual harm usually justified an end to the contract. In 1838 Dabney Garth, the overseer on Bird Posey's Missouri farm, beat a slave to death with a handspike. The Missouri Supreme Court held that Posey was justified in disposing of Garth. "He not only had a right to discharge him," Justice William Scott declared, "but it was his duty to do it."[77]

In addition to cruelty, planters also fired overseers for what they saw as general mismanagement, and the courts upheld their actions. One common form of mismanagement was simply being absent from the plantation. In North Carolina, for instance, Gray Armstrong found that his overseer, John Fly, was "very often seen at grog shops, and at a bowling alley at the depot, in the working hours of the day and on sundays, during the three months while he had charge on the farms . . . and was at one time observed playing at cards at about 10 o'clock in the morning, of a week day. Frequently during this time, he was proven to be excited with spirits, but not drunk." Fly claimed his activities did not cause "any special injury" to Armstrong, but the North Carolina court disagreed. Armstrong, the court ruled, "was not bound to wait until his crops were ruined before he removed the cause of the impending evil."[78]

More common than disregard for the plantation were complaints that overseers seized too much control to themselves. Many overseers, as William Scarborough has pointed out, saw themselves as semiprofessionals. As such, they wanted more influence in plantation decision making than planters were willing to concede. Texas overseer Thomas P. Rutledge quit his employers in 1847 because they would not allow him to whip slaves, and Mississippi cotton planter Theophilus Prichard quarreled with Richard Martin in 1851 over which tasks should be assigned to which slaves. A Georgia overseer refused to commence work under his contract unless the planter "would give up to him the plantation, negroes, and stock to his entire and exclusive control and management." Generally, courts refused to countenance such assertions of worker control. "An overseer contracts to do everything according to the means furnished by his employer, which a prudent and economical man would do in attending to his own business," a Mississippi judge intoned in 1854. North Carolina was even more direct. "It cannot for a moment be admitted," Justice William H. Battle wrote in 1859, "that an overseer has a right to control of the slaves under his charge, against the known wishes, much less the positive commands, of the owner." The Louisiana court considered refusal by the overseer to follow the planter's explicit orders on the method of whipping slaves to be "sufficient cause" for discharging him.[79]

Mistreatment of slaves and mismanagement of the plantation were the most common reasons for firing an overseer, but numerous dismissals stemmed from a more general class conflict between southern planters and their hired managers. Many planters agreed with the Alabaman who wrote that "the great mass of overseers [were] totally unqualified" to manage slaves. Overseers fought back against these charges. One complained bitterly that he and his fellows were expected to manage plantations and slaves "for wages scarcely if at all in advance of that given to an Irish ditcher." Another suggested sarcastically, "The wise and good show some charity, and instruct and pull us up out of the mire and dirt, rather than getting on our shoulders, and bidding us GOD speed."[80]

With these tensions in the background, disagreements over management of the plantation often became contests about personal honor that ended in violence between employer and employee. This incipient class conflict came before the courts when owners or overseers tried to use personal disputes to excuse breaches of contract. In *Byrd v. Boyd*, the conflict involved southern constructions of class, gender, and honor. The overseer had "managed the crop well, but in July he made use of abusive language to the [planter's] daughter for which he was turned away." In another South Carolina litigation, Henry Suber claimed he left H. D. Vanlew because a slave woman had complained that he "was too familiar with her" to Vanlew's wife, who had believed the allegation. Suber told the court that "he felt he was above any such thing." A Louisiana overseer added a suit for slander to his claim for wages when his employer accused him of stealing, and a Texas manager claimed five hundred dollars' damages for "injury to his reputation as an overseer."[81]

Such disputes grew out of a mixture of class tension, the honor ethic, and racial ideology, a combination that made overseers unwilling to be treated as servants. For example, Richard Martin explained (and the Mississippi court accepted) that while he would be glad to do his duty, he "would not worship" his employer. In Darlington, South Carolina, Caleb Boone had a similar but more violent reaction to his employer's aristocratic pretensions. Boone believed that John Lyde "wanted him to knuckle to him too much," and when Lyde tried to fire him, the overseer "got into a great rage and got a rail to strike Lyde." Boone's confrontation with Lyde did not produce actual violence, but other conflicts did. Near Macon, Georgia, Benjamin Stiles ambushed his employer, Simeon Henderson, and "brutally beat him with the barrel of his gun." Justice Eugenius A. Nisbet deemed this act a breach of contract and "incompatible with the peaceful exercise of all the rights of dominion over his property on the part of the employed." Nevertheless, the

Georgia court as well as others allowed apportionment of contracts in such situations.[82]

These conflicts centered on a fundamental disagreement about the distribution of power in the employment relation. Planters and agricultural writers believed contracts established the undisputed dominance of owners. "Subordination to the master is the first of an overseer's duties," the editors of the *Southern Planter* asserted bluntly. An overseer must be unfailingly loyal. "Of his own free will he has sold them [*sic*] to [his employer] for one year, and as an honest man he must stand by his bargain." While the journal's editors framed the terms of power within a mixture of the lexicons of slavery and capitalist contracts, another contributor placed them in gender discourse. To advance the interests of his employer, the writer noted, an overseer "has one of the requisites of a good wife, 'a keeper of the home.'" Some overseers, at least, recognized such assertions of power and refused to accept them. In regard planters' unwillingness to contract early for the next year, one overseer noted, "I cannot see what Mr. Farmer wants, unless it is to put the overseer off until the last hour of the day, and then he will have him in his power, and say you may take this, or that, and let it alone."[83]

By the time of the Civil War, labor contract law had diverged along sectional paths. In the South as in the North, differing methods of agriculture and industry underlay different forms of contract law. As such, contractual relations in labor resulted not from undifferentiated capitalism itself but from the specific needs of its many forms of production. Insofar as it pertained to overseers, southern labor contract law was an expression of capitalism only peripherally. Instead of upholding the sanctity of contracts like their northern counterparts, many southern courts encouraged violability by expanding grounds for discharge and allowing overseers to collect for the time served. Such practices grew out of the class relationship between planter and overseer, the needs of staple agriculture, and, most of all, the peculiarities of slavery. The high level of conflict between owners and managers meant that disputes occurred almost inevitably. Jurists acknowledged the "collisions" between these two classes and relaxed the entirety rule for discharge to fit the prevailing practice of open contracts. Plantation agriculture fostered this course. The planter required an overseer who would produce crops and maintain stability and good health among the owner's valued slave property. If the overseer failed, he had to be dismissed immediately, or crops and slaves—all the owner's property—might be lost.[84]

At one level, northern and southern law diverged, creating regional mean-

ings for free labor and free-labor law. At another plane, however, the bourgeois northerners who would make Reconstruction could agree with their
cousins in the southern planter and merchant classes. Certainly, middle-class
northerners had come to see the sanctity of contract as essential to labor
discipline, especially in agriculture. Yet they also had begun to define the
legal rights of workers by class. Bourgeois professionals, master artisans and
journeymen, industrial workers, and farmhands all owned a particular position in the North's legal structure because of the nature of their labor and
their class. With the contractual rights of laborers increasingly defined by
class, it was only a short step to measures that made work not only a moral
duty but also a legal requirement.

The Duty to Work

"Idleness is sometimes sluggish and solitary, earns nothing, but constantly consumes and corrupts the man who lives by himself, and makes him a vagabond, and worse than useless," declared Harvard law professor Nathan Dane in his *General Abridgement and Digest of American Law*. Dane's sentiment, articulated in the 1820s, would have received a warm response from the bourgeois northerners who brought free labor to the emancipated South. Indeed, the mostly middle-class northerners who would do the work of Reconstruction came from a society in which poor-law reformers, lawmakers, and jurists had created a central place for vagrancy law in discourse about work and its relation to society and culture. When combined with the growing contractual vision of free labor, this language led middle-class northerners to assume that the state could enforce a general societal duty to work, but it left them less sure that the state could compel labor directly for an individual employer. In turn, many northerners also came to believe that the state's regulation of vagrancy must be paternal and reformatory, aimed primarily at establishing bourgeois culture. Here, too, northern Reconstructors would confront a southern legal world with subtle though significant differences. While southern lawmakers in the antebellum period had also formed vagrancy laws as instruments of class hegemony, they had retained both corporal punishment and a stronger emphasis on forced labor, elements antithetical to northern conceptions. Northerners carried to the South, then, a way of understanding poverty that was divergent enough from southern conceptions to cause conflict but similar enough to prevent its resolution.[1]

THE LANGUAGE OF POVERTY

In ways largely lost to the twentieth century, nineteenth-century northerners, especially reform writers, moved vagrancy to a central place in social discourse. This lingual transformation did not occur, however, in a social vacuum. In essence, reform writers fashioned a language of class in which the beggar stood as the antithesis of the emerging bourgeois culture of the industrializing North. Vagabonds and beggars, bourgeois commentators believed, contradicted central social values about class, gender, and political participation. This class-based language of poverty provided northerners who would go south during Reconstruction with their primary point of reference for imagining the millions of unemployed workers generated by emancipation.[2]

In part, increased bourgeois attention to vagrants and beggars resulted from rising humanitarian sentiment. This transformation reflected the influence of Enlightenment thinking and evangelical religion as well as changes in the face-to-face community necessary for shaming punishment. However, as Thomas Haskell has suggested, the rise of humanitarian sensibilities also involved the late-eighteenth-century evolution in capitalism. In short, as market relations connected individuals outside their local communities, they gained a heightened awareness of personal power over previously intractable problems such as slavery.[3]

With regard to more distant issues such as slavery, the connection between humanitarianism and capitalism may have rested on broader forces engendered by market relations. But examining the relationship between the capitalist transformation and humanitarian reform of the poor and vagrancy laws requires attention to another facet of market society—class formation. The existence of a group of elite and middle-class reformers who shared a common culture was central to the ways in which vagrancy was imagined in Jacksonian America. An assorted group of master artisans, entrepreneurs, and professionals became increasingly aware of the gap between themselves and the incipient Jacksonian working class. Although the separation between master artisans and their workers may have still been unclear, the chasm between the middle and elite classes and the smaller vagrant underclass was unmistakable. This split generated contradictory impulses for reformers. On the one hand, separation engendered a humanitarian inclination to assist those in the underclass with a view toward closing social fissures. On the other, it motivated attempts to cement class alienation through legal institutions. The latter tendency was especially strong because of the nature of the vagrant underclass. When seen in the terms of Jacksonian social theory, vagrants and beggars seemed strangely perverse. Their behavior defied expectations about relationships between people, and between people and the state. In addition, in their clothing or lack of cleanliness, beggars emphasized the gap between themselves and the respectable classes.

Focusing on class does not mean that reformers' humanitarian sentiments were insincere. The very authenticity of these feelings was what made the question of vagrants and beggars so acute. Elite and middle-class spokespeople, many of whom denounced vagrancy in the harshest terms, also expressed the most sincere altruism toward the poor. Matthew Carey, a wealthy Philadelphia businessman, philanthropist, and political economist, denounced Malthusian critics of the poor laws and urged greater charity. Many "benevolent and liberal" individuals, he believed, were "by these pernicious and cold-blooded doctrines prevented from indulging the feelings of their hearts." A committee investigating the charitable and public institutions of New York in 1856 deplored conditions in the poorhouses, workhouses, jails, and penitentiaries. The committee stressed that these institutions were overcrowded, dingy, and inhumane; they mixed the sexes promiscuously and exposed the young to untold corruptions. "Common domestic animals are usually more humanely provided for than the paupers in some of these institutions," they concluded. From New York, John Van Ness Yates, one of the country's first social investigators, wrote that legal removal of paupers to their place of residence was inconsistent with "the spirit of a system professing to be founded on principles of pure benevolence and humanity." Removal also contradicted "the genius of a free government" and entailed "an invasion upon natural and inalienable rights." Yates found contracting out and auctioning paupers to be morally objectionable because the poor were "frequently treated with barbarity and neglect by their keepers." In addition, when he described the poorhouses he hoped the state would construct, Yates envisioned them as happy, cheerful abodes connected to a farm where the deserving poor could pursue "some healthful labor, chiefly agricultural," and their children would be "carefully instructed, and at suitable ages, to be put out to some useful trade or business."[4]

From the outset, however, such feelings were ambivalent. Unitarian clergyman Joseph Tuckerman exemplified the complexities of Jacksonian reformers' humanitarianism. Tuckerman argued forcefully for personal action to reach the alienated poor. However, in an 1833 report he wrote for a Massachusetts committee studying the state's poor laws, he advanced a differing view. Citing English political economist Thomas Chalmers, Tuckerman argued that public provision for the idle poor quelled the impulse to charity among respectable members of the community. The vagrant poor themselves incurred the blame for the inability of elites to give. "Every individual of the reckless and vicious poor," he averred, "contributes his or her share, to the hardening of the heart against the best sympathies of common nature." This diminution of charity could be overcome if the system of legal provision was abolished and "a more humane and Christian" system of local and private charity substituted in its place. The commissioners believed it was "the sure and benignant [sic] effect of this [kind of] charity, unlike that of the law, which alienates, to bind more closely together those who impart, and those who receive." [5]

Tuckerman's direct discussions of class, however, were anomalous. For the most part, bourgeois reformers remained unable to describe the structures that underlay the fissure. As a result, they turned to metaphors to describe the nature of a beggar. Most commonly, these images dehumanized the objects of humanitarian concern, rendering them into animals or diseases that must be controlled. The resort to metaphor can be seen in reformers' descriptions of beggars as "vicious." In the context of the violence of Jacksonian culture and by modern gauges, asking for a few cents in the street hardly seems dangerous. Nevertheless, Yates worried that the street beggar, "that profligate and disgusting character" who plagued Europe, was becoming prevalent in New York. The beggar's concentration in the state's growing urban areas justified "a rigid police, for compelling the sturdy vagrant to abandon his vicious pursuits." Yates's solution was the workhouse, where vagrants and beggars would be subjected to "a rigid diet, hard labor, employment at the stepping mill, or some treatment equally efficacious in restraining their vicious appetites and pursuits." [6]

A concern over vagrancy and the "corruptions of mendacity" pervaded Carey's account. His most powerful image related to legalized French begging. France, he claimed, contained "an aggregate of nearly a million of souls in a state of beggary, prowling abroad, and preying on the public to an enormous amount." Like Tuckerman in Massachusetts, Carey was humanely concerned for the poverty-stricken, yet simultaneously he could not overcome his alienation from them. This tension helped prompt the extremes of his rhetoric. Beggars again became something less than human, "prowling" and "preying" on respectable society.[7]

While Yates and Carey used animal metaphors, an 1827 Pennsylvania committee found disease a more appealing image. Its revulsion appeared most strongly in a description of New York City's social welfare institutions. There, part of the pesthouse was set aside for "the reception of vagrants, whose filthy condition unfit[ted] them for the Alms House." In this building, "by no means the least useful," vagrants were "cleansed of their vermin, their clothes [were] burnt, and [they were] otherwise purified." Such vivid sensory images translated the reformers' vague disgust into concrete, eradicable behavior; vagrancy became associated with pestilence and open to harsh treatment. The Pennsylvanians' imagery also highlights the role of material culture in defining vagrancy. The offense came in vagrants' "filthy condition," especially in their clothing. They must be "purified" by removing them from society to a metaphorical pesthouse.[8]

Revulsion toward the underclass based on bourgeois standards of material culture such as cleanliness formed part of a larger middle-class consciousness, but these sentiments existed in an uneasy tension with humanitarian impulses. This contradiction, which became more obvious as the Jacksonian period progressed, appeared most transparently in the program of the New York Association for Improving the Condition of the Poor. The AICP aimed to overcome ambivalence about begging by treating it as a face-to-face encounter. The organization was founded after the Panic of 1837 by Robert Milham Hartley, the Presbyterian owner of a New York mercantile firm who left it in the 1830s to become a full-time temperance advocate. The panic put thousands out of work in New York City and vastly increased the number of vagrants and beggars. Hartley garnered support from other members of the Protestant middle and lower-middle classes and established the AICP as an umbrella organization for New York City charities in 1843. The group worked for housing reform, immigration laws, and juvenile delinquency reform. However, its chief goal was "to discountenance indiscriminate almsgiving, and to put an end to street begging and vagrancy."[9]

To achieve the latter purpose, the group developed a system for separating "worthy" recipients of charity from the "unworthy." Instead of dispensing food, clothing, or money, the group encouraged almsgivers to hand out paper tickets that the AICP provided. Beggars then had to present the tickets to an AICP member who would investigate their claims. With these tickets and an examination form listing character traits such as virtuous/vicious and industrious/idle, the AICP hoped to categorize the poor and stabilize the power relationship between the classes. This would not be accomplished by using an impersonal and formalistic legal system but by individual contact across class lines. Correcting the problem, the AICP emphasized, would "require nothing less than a *volunteer individual guardianship over the poor,* with faithful efforts for their moral and physical elevation."[10]

In 1847 the organization printed two letters alleging to show the system at work. Perhaps concocted for promotional purposes, they depict how the system was intended to work, and they betray some of the motivations beneath it. The first letter concerned an encounter between a female AICP visitor and a poor African American woman. The poor woman presented the visitor with tickets, and the latter discovered that the woman's husband "drove a cart, owned some property, and was unusually well off for a person of his class." His wife, the visitor reported, pursued begging "on the ground that there could be little harm in a poor woman like herself begging a little from the rich." The visitor quickly disabused her of this belief. "I tried to impress on her mind," the visitor recounted, "the wickedness of such a life of deceit and imposture, with the warning that I would watch her, and if she was again seen begging it would be my duty to report her as a vagrant, and the police would probably send her to the penitentiary. She became alarmed, and promised to do better in the future, and, I have no doubt, is entirely cured of her begging and vagrant propensities." In this case, the visitor experienced a sense of power over an elusive situation. She resolved the problem of the unworthy and temporarily overcame her estrangement from them. Moreover, both her actions and her report of them allowed her to assert the power of her class to set cultural norms.[11]

The report of "a gentleman living up town" displayed the potency of the ticket system even more clearly. The gentleman was beset by a common household nuisance. "My door was so frequented by vagrants and beggars, chiefly foreigners, as to prove a serious annoyance to me," he related. This situation discomfited him. "So importunate were they, and so pitiful often were their tales of distress, that we knew not how to send them away." He noticed, upon observation, that his neighbor was not bothered by beggars, and he inquired why. "'Oh, ho,' said [the neighbor], 'we give them nothing but tickets, and they never come back.' 'Tickets!' [the gentleman] rejoined; 'what do you mean?'" The neighbor then explained the AICP system, the uptown gentleman adopted it, and he "pretty much cured" his problem in about a week. "Of all the cures for vagrancy," he concluded, "this is the most complete." The gentleman had found a way out of the dilemma. He could give yet not give. He could assuage humanitarian sentiments by handing out paper, but he could be sure that a respectable organization of his peers would see that his gift did not complicate the problem.[12]

Members of the AICP confronted the dilemmas of vagrancy and humanitarianism more directly than most other antebellum reformers. On a macrosocial level, they and fellow reformers faced the task of devising a new method for sifting out the growing number of seemingly unworthy poor produced by an industrializing society and dealing with them in an ideological context that increasingly disfavored corporal punishment. In addition, the dilemmas created by vagrants for humanitarians reached a personal level. Begging momentarily bared class divisions in the face-to-face act of the outstretched hand, connecting the impersonal with the personal and rendering power structures uncertain.

If beggars and vagrants disturbed bourgeois notions of class, they also disrupted gender conventions and standards of middle-class domestic life. As Christine Stansell, Mary Ryan, and others have noted, the fight to construct bourgeois definitions of manhood, womanhood, and childhood became central to class formation itself. As a result, the home became a contested sphere of class conflict. These larger social changes appeared clearly in reform discourse. Like late-twentieth-century reformers, antebellum writers believed vagrancy and public support undermined the basic rhythms of life. Reformers from Philadelphia asserted in 1827 that because of public support, "the incentives to industry ha[d] been weakened, the ties which connect society ha[d] been relaxed, and the desire to honest independence lessened." The basic problem involved the sense of security that public pensioners developed. "The certainty of a comfortable and easy life in the winter," the report continued, "is a perpetual and very effectual encouragement, to a thoughtless, dissipated, and self-indulgent course during the summer."[13]

Concern about relaxation of "the ties which connect society" centered attention on gender roles and the Victorian home. The constant use of masculine pronouns by reform writers and in vagrancy statutes was more than nineteenth-century literary practice. Apart from female prostitutes, vagrants were male in the consciousness of most reformers and legislators. Purveyors of middle-class culture defined vagrancy in part as the abandonment of supposed male responsibilities in the home. Addressing a workingman's political party in 1831, Edward Everett maintained that a man who refused to work was more alarming than a mere idler. "In almost every case," Everett observed, "he must be something worse,—such as a spendthrift, a gamester, or an intemperate person; a bad son, a bad husband, a bad father." This person was blameworthy because he had abandoned his familial, male responsibilities. "[He who] leaves to want those whom he ought to support, even if he does not pass his idle hours in any criminal pursuit, has no right to call himself a working man." Everett anchored the source of vagrancy in the degeneration of domestic relations and gender roles. His emphasis was as much on the individual's loss of masculinity as on his working-class status. By contrast, Tuckerman reversed the relationship, blaming vagrants for the breakdown. A lack of discipline often left children open to early contact with vagrants who would corrupt them. Without proper constraints, children might gravitate to taverns, where "the restraints of domestic discipline, and the pleasures of domestic affection and virtue are lost." [14]

Concentrating on gender and domestic roles illuminates an important facet of the meaning of vagrancy as a criminal offense. "Independence" was central to masculinity in Jacksonian America. In Republican thought, personal autonomy meant economic independence through ownership of productive property or through the "simple competency" of artisanship. In political thought, it meant that men's votes could not be controlled by economic dependence on other men, and it was used as a primary basis for denying suffrage to women and others. But members of the antebellum northern middle class expected that political and economic independence would be checked by Tuckerman's "restraints of domestic discipline." Viewed this way, vagrants denied both halves of male gender roles. They made themselves economically dependent on others through the state, and they became independent from the constraints of the home, abandoning their patriarchal duties. Such behavior left reform writers such as Yates willing to abolish all poor relief to any "male person, with the use of his faculties" between the ages of eighteen and fifty. Reformers implied that vagrants and beggars maintained an alienated relationship both with the middle-class home and with society and culture in general. [15]

Constructing class alienation in terms of masculine independence returned the issue to politics. In fact, Tuckerman had grasped the alienated position of the Jacksonian underclass and desired at least some effort to bridge the gap, yet the strains that vagrancy placed on Jacksonian social theory pushed him toward entertaining means of discipline. As historians of the early Republic have noted, the dependent poor presented a particular problem for republican ideology. Republicanism visualized a society of independent landholders, and poor people dependent on others or the state violated this vision. While dependence alone may have been reformers' primary concern with regard to the "worthy" poor, vagrants and beggars presented a far more complicated problem.[16]

The Tuckerman committee's description of the wandering poor focused on the critical interrelationships of dependence and independence involved in being a vagrant. The report identified the wandering poor as "outcasts; possessed of nothing, except the miserable clothing which barely cover[ed] them; accustomed to beggary, and wholly dependent upon it; with no local attachments . . . ; with no friendships, and neither feeling nor awakening sympathy." It continued: "Is it surprising that they are debased, and shameless; alternately insolent, and servile; importunate for the means of subsistence, and self-gratification, and averse from every means, but that of begging to obtain them?" This passage captured a central problem of vagrancy. Homeless people were not simply dependent on the public. Bound by no or few social ties, they were also independent in a certain way, and Tuckerman's characterization captured this tension. Vagrants were "alternately insolent, and servile," impudently independent and fawningly dependent at the same time. The committee's solution was to compel this section of the poor to work. If a man able to labor refused to do so, the commissioners contended, he incurred "a debt to the community for all that he receive[d] from it"; they stated further, "If he refuses to pay this debt, the Government may of a right compel him to pay it." In other words, a dependent position involved reciprocal obligations that had to be fulfilled.[17]

LABOR MARKET INTERVENTION AND
PATERNALIST CORRECTION

To realize the bourgeois vision, reformers furnished the means for turning social discourse into legal power by erecting a paternal state. Doing so required retaining elements of existing poor laws such as the apprenticeship of pauper children. It also required jettisoning, for the most part, community control and corporal punishment, while retaining the power to intervene in ✓ the labor market inherent in older vagrancy laws. Most important, it required redefining the "crime" of vagrancy as the contradiction of bourgeois culture and instituting paternalist correction as a way to inculcate the values of an industrial society. Although reformers failed to achieve the methods they would have liked in some cases, they did establish firmly that in a bourgeois culture the state had the power to enforce a duty to work.

Paternalist correction and labor market intervention, while most important in vagrancy laws themselves, appeared also in bound apprenticeship. The binding out of pauper children persisted as an anomalous form of state-sanctioned unfree labor long after the disappearance of indentured servitude in the North. Most states in the antebellum period authorized binding out by statute. Iowa and Indiana, as with other states, allowed binding out of poor children until age twenty-one. Many states tied bound apprenticeship directly to adult vagrancy. In 1834, New Hampshire allowed local overseers of the poor to bind out children whose parents could not support them or would not apprentice the children themselves. Maine, in 1857, authorized local officials to apprentice children without the consent of their parents. Bluntly interventionist, many of these laws also sounded a note of paternalist kindness. Maine lawmakers called on local officials "to protect and defend" bound apprentices, and New Hampshire legislators commanded them to "make their Contract equitably, and for the benefit of the person bound out," and to "enquire into the usage of apprentices" and "endeavor to redress any wrongs and injuries, they may sustain." Although striving to maintain "equity" in contracts, both the Maine and New Hampshire laws recognized gendered differences in the nature of those contracts. Maine required apprenticeships to teach boys to read, write, and cipher but girls only to read and write. New Hampshire required masters to teach boys to read and write but girls only to read and to "do such work and business, as [was] suitable to their Circumstance and condition."[18]

Poor children certainly occupied the imaginations of reformers and lawmakers, but bourgeois spokespeople were even more concerned with what they saw as a rising tide of adult vagrancy. The transformation that such people effected in vagrancy laws during the Jacksonian period becomes clear only by comparison with English and colonial concepts of the offense. The "crime" of vagrancy originated as a response to the disorder of late medieval England. The decline of feudalism, the rise of enclosure, the onset of the plague, and the reduction in poor relief from monasteries all destabilized labor and forced workers to tramp the roads in search of employment. Consequently, Parliament passed the Statute of Labourers in 1349 and 1350, restricting migration and setting wage rates, and it enacted increasingly severe enforcement statutes in following years. By the mid-sixteenth century, labor regulation gave way to a new conception of vagrancy laws, one that envisioned their purpose as social discipline. Parliament associated vagrancy with theft and other crimes and punished it with whipping, branding, slavery, and death for repeat offenders. By the turn of the seventeenth century, England started to develop new laws and institutions to deal with the poor. The Poor Relief Act of 1601 (commonly called 43 Elizabeth or the Old Poor Law) initiated state aid for the poor. Simultaneously Parliament started to separate vagrancy into categories based on specific acts.[19]

In British North America many colonial assemblies directly copied the English poor laws. The basic elements of the Old Poor Law, local responsibility for the poor and cash or in-kind relief outside institutions, transferred across the Atlantic. Local officials determined eligibility based on the law of legal settlement, an increasingly arcane set of rules that determined a person's place of residence. People deemed ineligible by local overseers of the poor were either "warned out" (told to move on under pain of criminal prosecution) or "removed" (taken back to their home communities, often against their will).[20]

Colonial vagrancy codes relied on the law of removal coupled with corporal punishment. These acts subsumed a variety of behaviors, but they commonly defined the offense as returning to a town after being removed or warned out. Town magistrates undertook few prosecutions, but through the pillory and the public whipping post, the community punished wayward members. Harsh criminal laws and sentences survived up to the time of the American Revolution, but by the turn of the nineteenth century, reliance on community control eroded across the northeastern United States. Lawmakers began to abandon corporal punishment in favor of paternalist correction or forced labor.[21]

Although reformers accomplished a good deal of their agenda in most states, they succeeded less fully in some states. Pennsylvania, for example, was atypical in its devotion to a lenient interpretation of the Old Poor Law. Poor-law reformers in the state were as strident in their rhetoric as elsewhere, employing some of the more extravagant descriptions of the evils of vagabonds. However, when the state revised its poor laws in 1836, legislators did not proceed as drastically as critics might have liked. More a restatement than a revision, the statute retained most of the provisions of the old poor-law system. The law of settlement remained, as did removal and the eighteenth-century definitions of vagrancy. (In fact, the state did not possess a separate vagrancy statute until after the Civil War.) As in the past, overseers of the poor were allowed to bind out poor children as apprentices until age eighteen for females and twenty-one for males. The statute required local officials to provide work for poor persons according to their abilities and allowed localities to employ the poor in repairing public roads. The law viewed these requirements as the bound duty of those in charge, for it imposed stiff penalties for neglect of office. The one major change that reformers won was imposition of the workhouse test. Touted by English utilitarian Jeremy Bentham as the key to poor-law reform in England, the clause in the Pennsylvania law stipulated, "If any poor person shall refuse to be kept and employed in such a [work]house, he shall not be entitled to receive relief from the overseers during such a refusal."[22]

Because of its workhouse test, the 1836 revision could be seen as a restrictive policy, as indeed poor-law revisions in England and in some other states were. Nevertheless, outdoor relief persisted in nineteenth-century Pennsylvania. In Philadelphia, where a local law of 1828 had authorized a new workhouse and tried to cut off outdoor relief, aid was suspended for only five years, from 1835 to 1840. Even then, some assistance in kind, such as fuel, was granted. Moreover, local workhouse enabling acts outside Philadelphia largely ignored reform principles. Scores of these local acts cleared the Pennsylvania legislature between 1790 and 1900, and although diversity and attention to local demands prevailed, common elements appeared. These acts abolished the old office of overseer of the poor, replacing it with a board of poorhouse administrators. All called for the erection or purchase of houses of employment, the transferral of the poor to these institutions, and the provision of indoor work. Eligibility was based on residency, and officials could refuse aid to persons who declined to take an oath and give information about their legal settlement.

However, outdoor relief continued within the limits of what might be called a budgetary workhouse test. Local directors retained the right to administer outdoor relief to the poor provided that "the expense of their maintenance [did] not in any case exceed that for which [they] could [have been] maintained at the poor houses." Directors had the power to bind out apprentices, though this, too, was often tempered by stipulations that indentures for work not be made more than thirty miles away from home. These provisions eased the operation of the workhouse system and retained the spirit, if not the exact form, of local control embodied in the Old Poor Law. If the specific provisions did not uphold local control, one last section in most of these laws did. Almost all the acts until at least mid-century were subject to approval in local referenda. Apparently, local voters often failed to endorse workhouses, because similar laws for the same counties appeared in the statutes over a period of several years.[23]

On the whole, however, reformers in the antebellum North thought that the state could and should compel unemployed people to work, and legislators in many states agreed. Although some states (such as New Hampshire) eventually abandoned the practice, most state governments in the antebellum North authorized hiring out, binding out, or auctioning off adults charged with vagrancy. Most common in midwestern states, statutes that provided for hiring out allowed local poor-law officials to act as administrators of a labor bureau. Iowa, Illinois, Indiana, and Michigan all sanctioned hiring out, usually under year-long contracts. In Iowa, for example, courts could place vagrants in annual contracts with half the proceeds going to the county and the other half to the worker. The use of year-long contracts in an agricultural state suggests that legislators intended to help farmers in the same way the civil courts were doing. Such practices were not confined to the developing West, however. The New England states also allowed hiring out at one time or another, and some scattered evidence suggests that local officials used their statutory authority. A reform writer charged in 1834 that the town of Framingham, Massachusetts, had been selling its poor to the highest bidder, who then parceled them out to individual homes, and a Connecticut newspaper reported in 1837 that Chatham (presumably, Massachusetts) would sell its poor.[24]

Hiring out looked to move labor directly toward employers, but these statutes also contained paternalist language. The Massachusetts law of 1834 that reaffirmed the state's eighteenth-century practice of hiring out directed poorhouse masters "to have the general inspection of the conduct of persons so let out to hire, and the treatment they receive[d]." Under this sort of construction, hirings out represented something other than a regular labor contract. In fact, an earlier law in New Hampshire had addressed just this issue. In 1791, lawmakers there had stipulated that contracts for binding out were "as good and effectual as if such person had him or herself for the same term of time." Yet later language about binding out retreated from equality of law. Most tellingly, several states brought bindings out of adults under the laws that governed regular apprenticeships for children. Iowa's law code of 1851 represented the most clear example of this legal shift and contained an ambivalent mixture of the languages of free and bound labor. The statute authorized district courts to "contract for the services" of adults as "laborers or servants" for up to a year, but such contracts were to be treated as if the person had been a minor apprenticed with his and his parents' consent.[25]

Hiring out tied vagrancy laws directly to labor control, albeit for reducing public expenditures. As in southern criminal codes before and after the Civil War, the state intervened in the labor market directly by funneling unemployed workers to private employers. This practice differed considerably from the more common practice of employment at hard labor for the state or for the local community. In the latter case, labor was either a form of punishment or, at most, an attempt to force inculcation of a capitalist work ethic. Although this form of incarceration constricted the labor market, it did not place workers in jobs. Yet even in states that employed hiring out, vagrancy laws functioned in a second, and ultimately more important, way — as paternalist correction meted out at the behest of the middle class.

Central to most state vagrancy laws was reformation of behavior. In Iowa's 1839 act, the state requested sureties for good behavior, and the courts could place detainees in year-long contracts if they could not post bond. In 1831, Illinois initiated good behavior bonds by which a vagrant would "betake himself to some honest employment for support" so that he or his family would not become public charges because of "his idleness, immorality, or profligacy." Connecticut law allowed keepers of workhouses to punish inmates who were "refractory and stubborn, and refuse[d] to work, or to perform their work in a proper manner." When inmates displayed "great obstinacy, and perverseness," the master might reduce miscreants to bread and water until they were "brought to submission and obedience." When Zephaniah Swift compiled Connecticut's laws in 1822, he noted that vagrancy statutes aimed "to promote industry, and restrain vagabonds and beggars," to support such offenders, and to punish them for their "misconduct."[26]

With reformation as the goal, state lawmakers outlined a relatively consistent list of offensive behaviors. Although phrases in Jacksonian vagrancy laws harkened back to the Tudor period, this language took on new salience in a society increasingly sundered by class. Statutory definitions of the "crime" of vagrancy usually included idleness, begging, and "wandering" or "roaming." These central tenets all led back to the tensions between dependence and independence, between manly agency and domestic discipline, that reform writers had captured but not established. These definitions focused the offense on the seeming rootlessness of Jacksonian northerners, especially young men. Oftentimes, statutes also included proscriptions of gaming or drunkenness, offenses also associated in reformers' minds with the emergent working class. Lawmakers often included desertion of families as well. Here, too, vagrancy laws looked to the mobility in Jacksonian society, especially among young working-class men. These laws banned any pattern of behavior considered morally unacceptable or liable to transform citizens into public charges.[27]

The basic structure of Jacksonian vagrancy laws, then, aimed at class-based, paternalist reformation, and sometimes lawmakers made these intentions explicit. Commonly, vagrancy was not a crime whose administration was confined to local constables. Rather, states allowed citizen involvement. Connecticut authorized justices of the peace to issue warrants on the word of "any substantial householder," and Illinois authorized arrests upon the oath of a "resident citizen." In defining vagrancy, Indiana lawmakers singled out people who did not have "visible property to maintain themselves" or who did "not follow some calling." Similar language in the Illinois law went further, punishing those unable to support themselves "in a respectable way." With regard to the operation of correction, some states clearly asserted paternalist purposes. Many states allowed time off for good behavior. Connecticut lawmakers in 1853 allowed stewards to release any prisoner who had "so conducted himself while confined" that he should not have been imprisoned any longer. With regard to time spent in the workhouse, New Hampshire lawmakers issued the most direct statement of paternalist intentions. Punishments in the workhouse, they advised, should not exceed "such reasonable correction as a parent may inflict upon a refractory child."[28]

New Hampshire lawmakers' direct equation of adults with children was the most direct statement of the paternalist intentions behind Jacksonian vagrancy statutes, but the tenor of other statutes certainly led in that direction. Reformers had created a discursive system in which centuries-old phrases took on new meaning as signifiers of class. Law, then, became a text for the expression and realization of class power. Without the power of the law, idleness, begging, or wandering would have been social behaviors open to scorn, but they would not have been "crimes" on which the full force of the state could potentially be brought to bear. With the power of the law, bourgeois reformers could attempt to use the state to alter the behavior of the less respectable classes. Such efforts were paternalist in that they necessarily created hierarchical relationships in which adults, once rendered as "vagrants," became legal children, stripped of their full rights as members of the Jacksonian polity. Statutory correction was also paternalist in that it created a group with power who defined and attempted to realize the best interests of a legally weaker group. That reformers accomplished these ends testifies to the power of language to shape law and vice versa. That they did not get all they wanted, however, evinces the limits of law to shape social relations. In the case of vagrancy, both the accomplishments and the limits appeared most clearly in the case of New York.

Reform of vagrancy and poor-law legislation in New York started earlier and produced perhaps the most thorough changes of any state. The Revolutionary War aggravated the state's vagrancy problem, but the rhetoric of the Republic also brought sentiments that undermined the permanence of colonial solutions. The first hint of the new ideals' impact on vagrants appeared in 1785 when the state legislature allowed officials to substitute six months' confinement at hard labor for corporal punishment. Although it conceivably applied to all criminals, the act singled out "all idle and disorderly vagrants, not having a visible means of livelihood and all common prostitutes." Earlier that year, state legislators passed "an Act for apprehending and punishing disorderly persons." More inclusive than earlier colonial legislation, this law outlawed the activities of idlers, wanderers, beggars, prostitutes, and men who abandoned their families and place of legal settlement. Such offenders could be kept at hard labor in the bridewell (a prison) for up to sixty days awaiting trial before a justice of the peace. If the justice of the peace adjudged an offender to be a "disorderly person" within the scope of the law, he could sentence him or her to six months in the bridewell. During the confinement the convict could be "corrected by whipping in such a manner and at such times and places, as according to the nature of such person's offence, as [the keepers] in their discretion" thought fit. If disorderly persons' place of legal settlement could not be determined, they could be kept "until they [could] provide for themselves" or until the justices could "place them in some lawful calling as servants, apprentices, mariners, or otherwise." Finally, the offender's money could be confiscated and clothing sold to pay for the cost of conveyance to his or her place of settlement upon release. By the late eighteenth century, state officials started to think about abandoning the specific definitions of the state's colonial laws and its more severe forms of corporal punishment. These attempted changes reflected uncertainties about vagrancy and the poor that New Yorkers were to confront for the next several decades.[29]

In the early nineteenth century, New York City experimented with ingenious methods of dealing with its seemingly intractable vagrancy problem.

In 1816, the city erected Bellevue Penitentiary specifically for vagrants, petty offenders, and troublemaking paupers from the almshouse. Under pressure from the New York Society for the Prevention of Pauperism, the city also installed a tread wheel. Invented by building contractor Samuel Cubitt for the punishment of British vagrants, this contraption consisted of a revolving drum fitted with steps. Vagrants lined up on the wheel and began ascending it in unison, coming down to rest after they reached the top. The wheel was connected to a grinding stone for the production of meal. Bellevue installed two of these machines in 1823, and on them inmates ground about forty pounds of meal per day, saving the city about nineteen hundred dollars a year. Reaction against the device grew quickly. In 1826 the Common Council suspended the wheel's use for females and ordered the Police Committee to investigate. Shortly thereafter, the wheels were removed.[30]

Calls for social welfare reform also became louder after the turn of the century. Laws of 1784, 1788, and following years had retained the colonial system of settlement and removal. Influenced by the debate over the Old Poor Law in Britain and the ideas of political economists, middle-class reformers in New York began to think about changing their system. In 1819 the New York legislature appointed a committee to look into the matter. Its report claimed that the poor law encouraged begging and that these "idle, vicious and intemperate" souls should be excluded from the public dole. Nothing became of this report, but in 1823 the legislature appointed J. V. N. Yates to examine the problem again. Yates's report and proposal to the legislature, perhaps the most comprehensive study of poverty during the antebellum period, produced a new poor law for New York.[31]

Yates suggested far-reaching measures. He wanted to simplify the law of settlement and to end removal altogether. In addition, he intended to exclude all healthy men from public relief and to make begging a specific crime. Most important, Yates hoped for the creation of a separate system of workhouses where vagrants and beggars could be punished. The legislature passed a revision based on his suggestions in November 1824. However, it dropped all Yates's severe provisions, constructing a scattered system of poorhouses that mixed all types of impoverished people, exactly what Yates did not want. The confused poor law of 1824 allowed counties (except the thirty-eight it excluded) to levy property taxes to build poorhouses and employ supervisors. These supervisors could devise rules of discipline including hard labor and solitary confinement on bread and water for intractables. Counties were also allowed to continue contracting the poor to local employers. Once the houses were constructed, overseers of the poor were to conduct all paupers applying for relief to the poorhouse. Further, if the county supervisors approved, justices of the peace could apprehend "disorderly persons" under the 1788 act and convey them to the poorhouse to be confined at hard labor up to six months. Beggars under the age of fifteen could also be so incarcerated. Finally, the law ended removal, prescribing relief of the sick, infirm, and poor in the county where they requested it. Healthy vagrants and beggars were to be treated as disorderly persons, which meant that they were funneled back to the poorhouse.[32]

The state incorporated these provisions into its 1827–28 revised statutes, and they served as the basic vagrancy law in New York until after the Civil War. The section concerning vagrants and beggars in the revision combined the 1788 disorderly persons act, the 1824 poor law provisions, and an 1821 rider on child begging. It streamlined the definitions but left punishment open. The law denominated three classes of people as vagrants. First, it included idle persons without visible means or visible employment, the heart of American vagrancy statutes. Second, it proscribed persons "wandering abroad and lodging in taverns, groceries, beer-houses, out-houses, market-places, sheds or barns, or in the open air, and not giving a good account of themselves." Third, it discouraged three kinds of beggars: those wandering about, those going door to door, and those standing in public places. A separate section sent child beggars to the county poorhouse until released or bound out as apprentices. A special law passed for New York City in 1833 added prostitutes, destitute habitual drunkards, and men who abandoned their families.[33]

Punishment was left to justices of the peace and other public officials. They were to make critical distinctions, sending vagrants one of two ways. First, if the accused was "not a notorious offender, and [was] a proper subject for relief," the person would be sent to the county poorhouse for up to six months of hard labor. Second, if the offender was "an improper person to be sent to the poor-house," the convict would be committed to the bridewell or house of correction if the county had one, if not to the common jail. These offenders could be incarcerated for sixty days, with up to half their time on bread and water. Since most counties could not raise the funds for separate facilities, these provisions meant that creating a separate system of alms-houses and workhouses had been given up in most areas of the state.[34]

The changes New York legislators wrought in the state's vagrancy laws did not go as far as some reformers wanted, but they did change the nature of the offense. The statutes in place by the early 1830s more clearly focused the "crime" as a transgression against the emergent bourgeoisie. The "crime" no longer represented an infraction against specific communities and their administration of local poor laws. Rather, it came to center on the ways working-class people, especially the very poor, lived their daily lives.

Moreover, these laws did not become dead letters. Throughout the Jacksonian period, police in New York City arrested men and women, black and white, for vagrancy and begging. During July 4 holiday celebrations in 1824, for example, city police sent 106 people to the penitentiary as "vagrants, thieves, &c." In May 1840, the city incarcerated 108 people specifically for begging. In Philadelphia, too, police frequently sent unemployed workers to the workhouse under vagrancy codes. Sometimes, arrests may have represented manipulation of the law, rather than direct enforcement. A local justice of the peace in Cumberland County, Pennsylvania, committed 195 people as vagrants during the winter and spring of 1859, but his case for reimbursement from the county revealed that he made the arrests to give shelter to homeless people, rather than to punish them. Such instances notwithstanding, most vagrancy arrests represented less than humanitarian ends. In 1844, a New York newspaper reported an incident involving "an Italian mendicant" who happened to walk into a city counting room while the mayor was there. He presented the mayor with papers dubbing him a proper applicant for charity. The mayor then "politely invited his customer to a walk, which terminated at the city prison." "Begging is prohibited by law," the paper intoned, "and as the Mayor lays himself out to enforce the laws, the mendicant was committed." Whether this event actually occurred or not, the newspaper's narrative suggests that vagrancy arrests happened as a matter of course and that they could become moments at which class and state power were acted out in an open, even derisory, way.[35]

Even if local police did not enforce vagrancy codes consistently, the laws remained important as texts for the expression of reformers' class-based aims. Bourgeois reformers plainly wanted to rid the streets of beggars, whether they succeeded or not. They clearly desired to stop "idleness," "wandering," and "roaming." And they certainly hoped to shore up domestic discipline by punishing people who deserted their families, with good reason or without. Moreover, reformers and the legislators who carried out their wishes intended for law to establish both class divisions and hierarchical relationships for paternal intervention across class lines. To do so, of course, was not to create a series of legal statuses. Rather, law served to make the discourse of social relationships real by giving it the force of the state. Thus, legal texts legitimated the language that reformers had elucidated elsewhere, giving it much more power to penetrate the culture.

JUDICIAL VISIONS

The reform language embedded in statutes also surfaced in judicial discussions of vagrancy. Detainees did not often challenge vagrancy laws during the antebellum period, but when they did, courts had the opportunity to discuss the "crime" more fully than lawmakers did. These opinions illuminate the ways in which popular discourse entered the law and the manner in which law empowered reform language. In part, judges used popular conceptions of vagrants to uphold the state's power of summary conviction and thereby invalidate poor people's claims to basic civil rights. In doing so, these jurists helped to establish the administrative power of the modern state as superordinate to the legal rights created by constitutional provisions or by liberal discourse. In turn, they supported bourgeois reformers' desire to use the state for paternal intervention. Judicial favor for intervention itself also invoked reformers' emergent social language of poverty, with its emphasis on the duties of home and work. Taken as a whole, then, the decisions in these few litigations reveal once again the inchoate popular legal culture on which middle-class northerners would rely during Reconstruction.

Vagrants' independence from home, work, and community, and their dependence on the state, reformers believed, justified intervention to reconstitute social relations. Such concerns returned the matter to the legal system and focused attention on what civil and political rights vagrants might possess. As Dane noted, Massachusetts's vagrancy laws had operated "with great tenderness generally, in some cases perhaps too great." Reformers such as Tuckerman converted supposed lenient enforcement into an outright deficiency in the legal system. He complained, "[Under current law] a vagrant, however dependent and miserable, and unfit for self-direction, must now be left free, while he chooses to be at large, till he has committed some *crime*." The culpability of the dependent and undeserving poor related to their lack of self-reliance, and Tuckerman carried this principle to its political conclusion. "To me," he continued, "it seems most absurd, to talk of the personal rights, and of the constitutionally guaranted [sic] freedom of those who not only have nothing, and who, though able, will do nothing, for self-support, but whose example is every day extending corruption to those around them."

For Tuckerman and many of his fellow northerners, rights and freedom were based not so much in property ownership, as republicanism envisioned, as in work and self-reliance. Without the latter, talk of rights would become senseless. Rights by implication rested on yet another foundation, discipline, which provided the basis for reforming lost men. Change would come about through "the Christian discipline of the [work]house, [whereby] some at least of these poor vagrants, all of whom would otherwise die as miserably as they have lived, would be made to live virtuously, and to die happily." In Tuckerman's scheme, discipline and work underlay virtue and thus political participation and civil rights.[36]

As Tuckerman indicated, the legal system sometimes denied reformers their wish to deprive vagrants of all rights. This relationship between vagrancy and civil rights received little discussion in the prewar period, but in a group of opinions on summary conviction judges did explore the issue. The most cohesive discussion appeared in a trio of New York litigations. The first of these cases, *People v. Phillips*, was decided in August 1847 by Judge John Worth Edmonds. Eliza Phillips probably could not have found a more sympathetic ear on any other high court in the nation. Edmonds had grown up in New York and had studied law under Martin Van Buren. In the 1830s he was an influential Democrat in the New York legislature, opposing the Second National Bank and supporting abolition of imprisonment for debt. From 1843 to 1845 he had been inspector of the state prison at Sing Sing, and he helped organize the Prison Discipline Society, the Prison Society, and the Women's Prison Association of the City of New York. Edmonds was influential in the movement to abolish corporal punishment in New York, although at times he expressed a desire to exclude African Americans and immigrants from prison reform.[37]

Phillips had been charged and detained at Blackwell's Island under the 1833 vagrancy law for New York City as a common prostitute. The case was carried to Edmonds on a writ of certiorari. Apparently this was a common procedure, for Edmonds noted that he had "been frequently called upon to discharge from the penitentiary prisoners committed on summary convictions for vagrancy on the ground of some alleged defect or irregularity of the sitting magistrate." The judge released Phillips and took the opportunity to indict the process of convicting vagrants. The problem, Edmonds began, was that summary conviction was in derogation of the common law. He then examined the history of summary conviction in the context of trial by jury and due process and laid out carefully how the proceedings should take place. The central theme of his opinion was the need for a clear record of the case. Without it, the magistrate would be liable in trespass and would have no defense. More important, without a record the defendant would "be deprived of all means of inquiring whether he had been justly condemned and also deprived of an effectual remedy against a wanton excess of jurisdiction." The vagrant could try a suit in trespass, but that "would not come until after he had suffered the wrong." This turn of events, Edmonds implied, would be unjust. While the vagrant's "conviction would be exceedingly prompt and summary, his remedy for the wrong done him would be very slow and burdensome." [38]

Edmonds's more general section that closed the opinion suggests that he was not merely tampering with fine points to protect magistrates from litigation. A proper record must go beyond appearances, he insisted. It should "not be merely to record the fact of judgment, but to show that the proceedings required by justice had been regularly observed and the sentence legally supported by the evidence." Reviewing the decisions of other state courts on summary conviction, Edmonds concluded that its "manifold dangers" had led these tribunals to "assert and maintain the principles on which personal liberty is dependent." In the end, he avowed that New York's laws did and must do the same: "These principles are deeply imbedded in the system of laws in our state also, and as thousands of our citizens are yearly subjected to the operation of this summary and dangerous jurisdiction, it is of the highest importance that the rules which have been adopted for the purpose of restraining it, within due bounds, should be strictly and carefully preserved." In other words, Tuckerman's views of legal rights could not be sanctioned; vagrancy did not unfit people for full citizenship. [39]

Edmonds was a radical; a few years after he rendered this opinion he became an avowed Spiritualist. Yet his opinion should not be dismissed. It proves that vagrancy laws and other laws against petty crime were being enforced regularly in the antebellum North, at least in New York. In a broader sense, Edmonds provided an alternative vision. He used the common law as a way to solve the moral problem of vagrancy. Through reasoned and equal application of stated principles, he would mediate the effects of vagrancy laws for both his class and for the "offenders." [40]

Another New York opinion, issued by Judge Josiah Sutherland in 1860, also produced freedom for the offender, but Sutherland arrived at this conclusion by a different route. In the years since Edmonds wrote, the legislature had created a commitment form for New York City vagrancy arrests based on the judge's suggestions. They had also sanctioned the use of habeas corpus and certiorari as means of appeal. In the case before Sutherland, Catharine Forbes had been convicted as a prostitute and had appealed to Sutherland on the habeas writ.[41]

Sutherland began from the assumption that vagrancy had not been a common-law crime. Consequently, the words of the statutes must be strictly construed. At issue was whether the 1827 revised statutes and the 1833 law for New York City prohibited something more than mere idleness. Sutherland thought they did. In Forbes's case, the law implied "a want of any lawful business, occupation or means whereby to sustain herself." Sutherland then proposed a new justification for vagrancy laws. The intent of the law was "not to punish common prostitutes as a sin or moral evil, or to reform the individual." Instead, the object was "to protect the public against the crimes, poverty, distress or public burdens, which experience has shown common prostitution causes or leads to." Vagrancy laws were police regulations for the public good, and if a person fit the description, "he [could] be convicted and imprisoned whether such a condition [was] his misfortune or his fault." He continued, "His individual liberty must yield to public necessity or the public good." Though Sutherland seemed strained by the words, he concluded that vagrancy laws were "constitutional, but should be construed strictly and executed carefully in favor of the liberty of the citizen." Sutherland's position foreshadowed the way later lawmakers would try to resolve the vagrancy problem. He wanted to turn vagrancy purely into a positive act of commission, to enumerate a list of specific restrained behaviors and remove them for the elusive "public good." Again, the legal system offered an alternative to reformers' ideas.[42]

A short opinion issued a month later by Judge Daniel Phoenix Ingraham concluded New York's antebellum litigation on summary conviction. William Gray had brought his case before Ingraham on habeas corpus, a practice that Ingraham believed was "not to be commended." The police justices had tinkered with the forms to combine the habitual drunkard section of the 1833 law with the idleness section of the state's revised statutes. This irregularity notwithstanding, Ingraham would not dismiss the charge. "The offence is being a vagrant," he declared unequivocally. "It is not necessary that the commitment should state all the particulars necessary to make out the offense." He attempted to align himself with Sutherland by asserting that he was talking about the *commitment*, not the *charge*. But he was making an artificial distinction; he clearly saw vagrancy as a status offense. "The words defining the particular causes of vagrancy, may therefore be regarded as surplusage, and the charge of being a vagrant and being committed thereof is sufficient," he concluded.[43]

Ingraham's opinion regarded vagrancy as a pattern of behavior, and it reflected the legal and cultural standards prevalent in 1860 better than those of his colleagues. Edmonds's opinion was too extreme to be adopted widely; Sutherland's idea was only catching on. Moreover, Ingraham's opinion was more in line with judges' thinking elsewhere. Judge William Strong of Pennsylvania reviewed the state's vagrancy laws in 1862 and reasoned that since summary conviction had a long history in English colonial law, the framers of the state constitution must have found it acceptable. Summary conviction, then, did not abrogate due process or the right to trial by jury. Five years earlier, Pennsylvania chief justice Ellis Lewis had also authorized summary conviction, noting that vagrants were "nuisances to the body politic which ought to be suppressed at every hazard." In an 1862 opinion on two separate cases, the Massachusetts Supreme Court affirmed that state's vagrancy laws, taking a line similar to that argued by Ingraham in New York. The vagrants, Judge Hoar proclaimed, were "under necessity to work" for their dependents, had opportunities for employment, but yet "neglected all lawful business." Moreover, one of them had "habitually misspent his time by frequenting houses of ill-fame, gaming houses, and tippling shops." In his opinion, Hoar invoked common elements of reform language, focusing on the daily lives of the detainees. The essence of vagrancy, Hoar asserted, was a pattern of behavior displayed over time.[44]

These higher-court justices were not alone in envisioning vagrancy as a crime against middle-class culture. An 1849 opinion by a local judge in Cincinnati went even further and directly employed reformers' assertions about the duty to work and the need for paternalist intervention. In the case, George Williams had been committed by the mayor for vagrancy. Mr. Forrest, Williams's attorney, argued that the man's conviction abrogated the right to trial by jury and raised "the delicate question, whether a man being poor was considered evil in itself." Judge Warden delivered the opinion for a divided court. Warden said he "never entertained a doubt that idleness, the essence of vagrancy, was in itself evil." Indeed, he averred that every system of philosophy had punished vagrancy. "All systems of civilized society, established on principles of equality, in recognizing certain rights also demanded the performance of certain duties, and it was peculiarly the spirit of our own institutions that men were not allowed to enjoy rights without performance of certain duties; and this he held to be the beauty of democracy." The city charter, Warden concluded, gave citizens the "power to protect themselves as a family and in its nature the power was of a paternal character," though for protection, not for reform, which should be left to "higher tribunals." Consequently, not every "case of correction" required trial by jury.[45]

Warden's opinion reveals how the language created by bourgeois reformers found its way into legal culture. Two other antebellum vagrancy appeals, one from Maine and the other from Philadelphia, illustrate even more clearly the broader interplay between reform language and legal constructions of the "crime" of vagrancy. The first of these cases involved an 1834 constitutional challenge to the Maine vagrancy law. Adeline G. Nott of Portland had been committed to the workhouse by the overseers of the poor. The statute allowed such actions against "all persons of able body to work and not having estate or other means to maintain themselves, who refuse[d] or neglect[ed] so to do; live[d] a dissolute life, and exercise[d] no ordinary calling or lawful business, sufficient to gain an honest livelihood." Nott's attorney, R. A. L. Codman, urged the Maine Supreme Court to find that the action derogated the natural rights of all people by "authorising the commitment to a dungeon or work-house, of a citizen without trial or hearing, and that too, by persons invested with no judicial power." The law violated "the spirit and genius" of the state constitution on the same grounds and breached due process by denying the right to counsel and the right to present witnesses and face those of the prosecution.[46]

Writing for the court, Justice Nathan Weston ignored Codman's arguments, resting denial of the appeal on social utility. Weston's opinion advanced three arguments in favor of vagrancy laws and workhouses: relief, reform, and sanitation. First, vagrants were obligated to pay for their support. "The indigent have no claim to be supported in idleness," Weston declared. "Their poverty generally grows out of an unwillingness to labor, or is occasioned by reckless or improvident habits." Consequently, poor people "have no just right to complain, if they are sent to, employed and governed in a work house, provided for the purpose of making their support less burthensome." Nott's health and strength, Weston reasoned, "constitut[ed] a fund, of which [the overseers] ha[d] a right reasonably to avail themselves, to contribute to her maintenance." Nott had a social duty to work, to supply her own relief.[47]

Weston carefully avoided the tension between dependence and independence embedded in Maine's vagrancy laws and refused to confront directly the issues of gender hidden not far beneath the surface of the case. For the purpose of convicting her, Nott was independent and wholly responsible for her own well-being, a condition she would not have been accorded in Jacksonian culture, economy, or political system had she not been before the court. Yet while Weston held that she was an independent agent before the law, he balanced this assumption precariously with her behavior. She had voluntarily chosen to become dependent and had therefore forfeited her "right to complain" (and apparently to appeal, as well). Her sacrifice of independence allowed the state to claim its guardianship over her, further complicating the matter by placing her in an even more dependent position.

Second, the justice professed that the law was intended for Nott's own benefit. It would show her how to "draw an honest livelihood. That she may be removed from temptation, and compelled to cultivate habits of industry, to be again restored to society, as a useful member, as soon as may be." Despite the conditions, Nott would eventually come to realize the law's benevolence, Weston assured. "When enlightened conscience shall do its office, and sober reason has its proper influence, she will regard the interposition as parental; as calculated to save instead of punishing." Paternalist correction would lift the fallen woman. So gender (and dependence) ultimately got the upper hand in Weston's mind. Because Nott was a woman, it was far easier for Weston to imagine her as child, in need of the "enlightened conscience" of her fatherly correctors.[48]

As a final, "collateral" reason, Weston suggested that removing Nott from society was a sanitary measure. Overseers' actions could be "viewed as a police regulation, to preserve the community from contamination." Likening the woman to a "victim of contagious disease," Weston dismissed the due process claim. "There may be cases of so pressing a character," he contended, "that they cannot await the forms of law, ordinarily provided for the protection of right, and the suspension of wrong." By 1834, then, common elements of the Jacksonian language of poverty had begun to seep into the courts. By likening vagrants to victims of disease (and in this case, to contagion itself), reformers could place vagrants safely outside the realm of normal life, and jurists such as Weston could place them outside the constitutional protection of the law. Paradoxically, to be restored to society vagrants first had to be placed beyond its boundaries.[49]

The second litigation, *Commonwealth ex relatione Joseph v. McKeagy, Superintendent of the House of Refuge* (Philadelphia, 1831) was exceptional in several ways. It dealt with the problem of juvenile vagrancy, and it involved a boy of apparently solid middle-class parentage. These circumstances were probably the only reasons for it being brought to the Philadelphia County Court of Common Pleas in the first place. Yet these unusual conditions prompted a full discussion of the law and popular notion of vagrancy.

The case involved fourteen-year-old Lewis Joseph, the only child of Abraham Joseph. Lewis grew up in a home with "every comfort of life" and with a mother who was "both a respectable and intelligent woman, much devoted to him." Lewis received an education in Philadelphia's "best private schools." However, the boy developed a habit of wandering the streets of the city, once for ten days, until he was returned in "a perishing condition" by Constable William McGinley. His father feared Lewis was stealing from him for support, and in March 1830, he took Lewis to the Philadelphia House of Refuge to have him committed. The superintendent refused, but a Mr. Goodman, a manager of the house present at the time, convicted Lewis of being a vagrant and "adjudged him to be 'a proper subject for the House of Refuge.'" Soon, Abraham Joseph reconsidered, admitting that "his excited feeling on the occasion betrayed him into error," and sought to have Lewis released under habeas corpus because of the summary nature of the commitment. The attorney for the house, poor-law reformer William Meredith, argued that Lewis was a vagrant and, failing that, that he had been placed in the institution with the full knowledge of his father to "submit his son to the discipline and regulation of the house."[50]

Judge King began his lengthy opinion by discussing the authority of institutions like the House of Refuge. He noted that its summary powers were warranted in periods of public emergency and that juvenile delinquency in Philadelphia indicated that such an emergency did exist. Moreover, summary conviction did not conflict with constitutional rights. Since the adoption of the state constitution of 1790, King noted, "this power ha[d] been exercised without question in cases of infant and adult vagrancy indifferently; and no one ever supposed, that the right of trial by jury . . . was infringed by the exercise of this beneficial and useful jurisdiction." The only change had been from "a temporary, but degrading punishment" in the eighteenth century to one of "public care and solicitude" for the minor vagrant by which "the public assume[d] the guardianship of this person during his minority with a view to his future usefulness." King captured the legal changes of the early nineteenth century in this statement, but he did not consider the implications.[51]

Most of King's opinion dealt with Meredith's first argument and tried to outline the meaning of vagrancy and its social consequences. To begin with, King in effect called upon his own character witness for Lewis. His colleague, Justice Freytag, had described the boy as "of a lively temperament, passionately fond of military music, and apparently incapable of resisting its charms." Although Freytag had once thought of sending Lewis to the house, he "consider[ed] him in no respect a vagrant." Such an opinion was important, King averred, because a vagrancy charge was "in its character degrading, if not infamous." Pennsylvania courts had even ruled that "calling a person 'a vagrant' [was] actionable in itself."[52]

King then examined the case under Pennsylvania's 1767 vagrancy act. Lewis was not an emigrating pauper, a person living idly, or a wandering beggar. He might be a loiterer, but this section could not fairly be applied to children, for to allow a magistrate to pass such a "degrading conviction" on a child would be a power that "would not be endured in any community." Although Lewis's father had referred to him as a vagrant when trying to have him committed, King argued that the question of vagrancy was "not referable to the opinion of a witness; it [was] an offense composed of an aggregation of circumstances" that resided in the details of each case.[53]

The key to vagrancy was a constant pattern of behavior. King compared Lewis with an example raised by Meredith. In a previous case, King had upheld the conviction of a young woman for vagrancy. However, the woman "had given herself up to a course of most shameless abandonment" though she was old enough to marry or work. Like Adeline Nott, this unnamed woman had been accorded an unusually high status in order to convict her of a crime. Lewis, on the other hand, had proved himself to be "good tempered, docile, and intelligent" and receptive to "that gentle but firm discipline . . . that was necessary to root out from his mind the luxuriant weeds produced by weak indulgence, bestowed by an erring parent on a sportive and volatile disposition." Overall, King concluded, Lewis had shown "none of that malicious capacity for wickedness, and that wanton and continued indulgence in it; nothing of that wandering and abandoned course of life, which alone would justify . . . pronouncing him a vagrant." King concluded that Lewis should have the stain of vagrancy expunged from his character and be restored to society.[54]

The imagery in King's opinion revealed nicely the popular as well as legal conception of vagrancy. The prevailing theme was disorder, from the "luxuriant weeds" in Lewis's head to the "wanton" indulgence in wicked actions. What made such behavior as this into vagrancy was its incorrigible nature, the inability to respond to "gentle but firm discipline." Unlike the merely misbehaving Lewis, a confirmed vagrant lived his or her life wandering about with no fixed spot in the community. These images again pointed to the dominant cultural conception of vagrancy as the antithesis of the nineteenth-century social system of gender and class.

As these two appeals indicate, key concepts of social discourse on poverty in the antebellum North penetrated the legal world as well. Although alternatives existed, reform writers and jurists constructed the "crime" of vagrancy in similar terms. Vagrancy meant independence from the informal social discipline of work and the home and dependence on the state; it equaled the abandonment of gender roles. Vagrancy also meant membership in a group alienated from the middle class by these activities and by dirty hands and torn clothing. Finally, vagrancy meant that with the social reality of self-reliance gone, the rights based on it became meaningless. These concepts would figure prominently when Republicans in Congress and Union army officials were given a free hand to construct free labor after emancipation. Before the war, however, these ideas were only in a formative stage, slowly working their way into the consciousness of upper- and middle-class northerners. At the same time, a considerably different ideological and legal world had developed in the South.

HONOR AND FORCED LABOR IN THE SLAVE SOUTH

The people of Virginia, the Reverend Hugh Jones wrote in 1724, were "never tormented with vagrant, and vagabond beggars." Although early in the South's history, Jones's comment presaged southern attitudes toward poverty and vagrancy that would prevail through the onset of the Civil War. Elite southerners generally believed their states had few poor people, and by the 1850s proslavery writers who exploited this tradition advocated an anticapitalist conception of society and charity. This mythology could not hide the fact that slavery automatically impoverished a third of the South's population and pushed many of the region's nonslaveholding whites into destitution as well. Neither could the prevailing fictions mask completely the existence of laws concerning poor and vagrant southerners. Supposedly free of pauperism, many southern states nevertheless constructed a system of poorhouses at about the same time as the North. While undertaking reform occasionally, southern lawmakers also retained much of the older definition of vagrancy that had been disposed of in the northern states. Planter-dominated legislatures and courts focused vagrancy on honor and continued corporal punishment and forced labor. Many southern states passed vagrancy acts that prescribed periods of forced labor longer than those in the North. However, these laws functioned not to train a disciplined workforce or even to secure an additional source of labor. Their specific purpose was usually to compel people to work for support or to make work a punishment for disreputable behavior. Apart from these precise goals, they also helped legitimate forced labor in general. Southern lawmakers followed their northern brethren in making vagrancy a symbol of class, but that symbol had a different face.[55]

Southern poor laws in the nineteenth century grew from the region's adherence to chattel slavery, not from a system of laws that diverged from the start. During the colonial period, assemblies in the South had adopted poor laws similar to those in the North and in England. In 1727, for example, Virginia lawmakers punished vagrants and deserting husbands with bound labor and the whip. Later the colony adopted the English practice of whipping vagrants from constable to constable until they reached home and ended the use of corporal punishment in favor of bound labor. Most of the seaboard colonies also experimented with workhouses in the colonial period. In Charleston, the town's vestry won support from the assembly for a workhouse in the 1730s, and by the 1750s the structure had become crowded, prompting an enlargement. Although towns in the South created such institutions, town governments and vestrymen continued to dispense relief to paupers outside the workhouse. All in all, southern poor laws remained in the English tradition. As part of this tradition, the vagrancy laws intended to put "masterless men" back into a dependent relationship of home or labor. Vagrants had committed an act against the social order, and they threatened to disrupt the system of poor relief by not paying the rates or by abandoning their dependents to the parish. They were a social problem that had to be controlled in a society with the assumptions of an organic world, in which all people were in some type of dependent relationship to each other.[56]

During the antebellum period, the meanings of vagrancy and poverty in the South, as in the North, derived from a social language about poverty embedded in the region's basic modes of production. In part, this frame of reference was articulated by the region's proslavery ideologues, who discussed southern poverty in relation to northern free labor. One of slavery's most zealous champions, Virginian Edmund Ruffin, asserted that free labor must eventually degrade into the "pauper slavery" of the poorhouse, where "the pauper, whether laborer or otherwise, receiving support from the parish, [was] neither more nor less than a slave to the administrators of the law and dispensers of the public charity." Such a person, he contended, ceased "to be a free agent in any respect." Addressing Cincinnati's Young Men's Mercantile Library Association in 1849, Elwood Fisher echoed Ruffin, claiming that poverty was virtually unknown in Virginia and Kentucky. Fisher then reversed the realities of poverty North and South: "The pauper in an alms house is a slave," Fisher declared. "He works under a master, and receives nothing but a subsistence." Vindicating the South against the "reproaches of the North," Iveson Brookes charged that the North's industrial cities witnessed "a condition of squalidness, hunger, and sickness without medical aid" not to be found among the slaves of the South, "because the humanity and pecuniary interests of the owner combine[d] to prevent such wretchedness."[57]

George Fitzhugh carried the argument even further, constructing a theory to explain poverty and its relief. Fitzhugh eschewed liberty and equality as "absurd and impracticable," preferring instead to see morality as originating in a divine series of dependent relationships. Free-labor societies such as England and the northern states had broken these relationships, released the poor from their natural bonds, and unleashed a competition of all against all. As a result, England (and by implication, the North) had enacted laws to force the poor to work. Legal coercion, however, did not solve the problem, for the wealthy were left without safe recipients for benevolence. Where free labor ruled, "public and private charity [was] a fund created by the labor of the industrious poor, and too often bestowed on the idle and improvident," Fitzhugh pointed out. "It is apt to aggravate the evils which it intends to cure." Because southerners had not abandoned hierarchy, however, the elite could dispense charity with the control needed to make it safe. Because the South had not abandoned dependence and subordination, it had no conflict between rich and poor; it was "wholly exempt from the torrent of pauperism, crime, agrarianism, and infidelity which Europe [was] pouring from her jails and alms houses on the already crowded North." The South had its poor, he admitted, but none who were "over-worked and under-fed." The relationships of southern society meant that poor relatives and friends were nourished in the homes of their betters.[58]

By focusing on the degrading lives of the northern poor, proslavery writers attempted to defend slavery by diverting attention both from the extreme and obvious destitution of slaves and from the less noticeable privation of the region's poorer whites. In part, their representations did reflect prevailing modes of relief as well as a broader popular consciousness about poverty. The local dependent poor were often seen as a part of the community and did not receive the scorn they sometimes did in the North. Although Robert Greenhow, president of the Richmond overseers of the poor in the 1810s, noted that Richmond discouraged begging, he focused on the operation of assistance. He assumed it was beyond question that "the poor of every community, [were] as integral and component parts thereof, as the members of individual families" were. It followed from this premise that "every civilized society [was] bound from the nature of its compact to *offer aid and assistance to all* of this description, within their bounds." Such views led some dispensers of southern poor relief to act as advocates for their charges. In Savannah, Poor Board member James Watts assured Mary Evans that he would help her get paid for her second stay in the workhouse and informed her of the proper procedures to use. Watts appears to have kept a close eye on the records, for he told her that he had "frequently wondered why [she] did not come forward with [her] account." However, a less contemptuous view toward the poor need not always have implied a more humane one. As attorney and diarist William Valentine observed, North Carolina had its paupers, many of whom were "decrepid [sic] and miserably afflicted, calling forth the sympathy of every humane, and . . . human bosom." Yet he confessed that many of his acquaintances were "too callous to this destitute portion" of the state's people.[59]

Perhaps because of this insensitivity, many southerners failed to find comfort in the words of slavery's defenders. Southerners of all classes feared poverty and viewed the poorhouse as a place to avoid at all cost. Valentine believed the local poor regarded the poorhouse as a penitentiary and "loathe[d] it as a disgrace and infamous notoriety." "The consequence is but few comparatively go there." While some consigned themselves to public dependence, he concluded, "The paupers are too proud to go to the Poor House. Many of them rather suffer than go there." Quite early in the nineteenth century, public assistance was seen as an option of last resort for the South's poor. When Catherine McGolnick of Savannah, Georgia, applied to have her sister relieved in the city's poorhouse in 1811, she assured authorities that she had "hitherto done what lay in [her] power for her but [was], last necessitated to apply to the public for assistance." McGolnick's sister was quite ill, was not receiving proper nourishment, and was finally ready to enter the house. To McGolnick, her sister's illness was yet another crisis in a life mired in poverty. Living in a house across from Savannah's cemetery, with two small children of her own and another young sister to support, Mc-Golnick struggled to keep the family from outright deprivation. "[I] have no other support but what I get by my industry," she wrote, "and what I am able to do is barely sufficient to keep my family from want." Such feelings, of course, were part of the more widespread cultural fear of impoverishment in America's fluid social structure, and these sentiments appeared in the southern middle class as well. When North Carolina attorney David Schenck contemplated his engagement and approaching marriage, the prevailing male middle-class fear of poverty haunted him. His law career had not yet become successful, and he worried that he could not "obtain all the luxuries and blessings" his betrothed might expect: "My pride will not submit to poverty — it would almost kill me to be unable to gratify the wishes of my wife."[60]

It might seem that such fears, based in gender, class, and racial identities, would have produced widespread public discussion about poverty in the South. But as numerous historians have pointed out, the region did not experience the ideological conflict that characterized poor relief in the Jacksonian North. Elite southerners were slow to abandon the traditions of the Old Poor Law. This regional distinctiveness has been ascribed to many causes, most notably the agricultural and anti-institutional nature of southern society. Since southern states for the most part did not adopt the precise measures of discipline embraced by northern poor and vagrancy laws, some historians have been tempted to see southern poor laws as somehow more humane. This assertion essentially adopts the line taken by proslavery advocates, albeit with an ironic twist. And to the extent that the well-disciplined almshouse was not prevalent in the South, it is accurate.[61]

Yet taken as a whole, the southern poor laws remained harsher in letter and spirit than those in the North, and more important, southern poor laws, lenient or not, served to construct and maintain the southern elite. In fact, southern communities lacked poorhouses often more because of neglect than because of humanity. Moreover, southern vagrancy laws retained punitive measures that had been abandoned, or at least eased, in the North. All the same, southerners did not exhibit the same harshness of *rhetoric* as did poor-law reformers in the North. The southern legal system endowed the providers of charity with the control and certainty that Fitzhugh argued must underlie all philanthropy — that their acts would have no real economic impact on the lives of recipients. The most significant function of these laws, then, was not their effect on poverty or "crime" (although these were undoubtedly both intended goals and actual outcomes) but rather in the way they helped designate who was, and who was not, a member of the ruling white elite. As Barbara Bellows has argued, elite benevolence bolstered racial control by making it obvious that poor whites were the proper objects of charity. While this is certainly accurate, poor relief also strengthened class lines. In their role as public stewards, elites asserted their power as a class vis-à-vis poor whites and clarified the lines of division that Fitzhugh asserted were critical to almsgiving.[62]

To say class legitimation was the broader effect of the poor laws does not mean southerners failed to relieve distress. Lacking an equally sophisticated institutional structure, southerners did not pursue the systematized charity of the North; instead, they relied on traditional means of social welfare. Some areas relieved the poor by placing them in private homes or auctioning them to the highest bidder. In many locales of North Carolina, the poor were sold in public. Before the construction of his Hertford County's poorhouse, attorney and diarist William Valentine recalled, "The miserable poor were put at auction and knocked down to the lowest undertaker!" The state did not explicitly forbid the practice until 1876. Many southern legislatures did authorize the construction of poorhouses, but outdoor relief remained prevalent. A South Carolina law of 1824, for example, allowed overseers to continue to board paupers with relatives and friends. The Virginia poor laws, the governor wrote in 1824, relied almost entirely on "pecuniary aid." As late as the 1850s Virginia's poor were not institutionalized. Figures from the Richmond almshouse show a low number of recipients for indoor relief. Out of a total population of 27,463 in Henrico County, an investigator in 1854 found 135 in the almshouse, or about 0.49 percent of the population. The operation of the Beckford Parish Poorhouse in Virginia illustrates the mixed functions of southern social welfare institutions, especially those in rural areas. Located in upstate Virginia, the house served as a hospital, lunatic asylum, and nursing home. The most common residents were elderly Virginians, who entered in their fifties or sixties, often described as insane. Apart from being a kind of nursing home, the Beckford Poorhouse also functioned as a foundling hospital, recording the births of one to four children per year in the 1820s and 1830s. Some of these children left the house with their mothers, while others were bound out by the overseers.[63]

Elite dispensations of relief, safely controlled, indirectly upheld paternalist patterns of social interaction. The vagrancy and poor laws passed by planter-dominated legislatures shored up the control of elite southerners more directly by mandating forced labor. Apprenticeships for poor orphans, bastards, and other poor children represented one form of bound labor. A carryover from the colonial South, this practice remained common in the nineteenth century. Apprenticeships might be undertaken by local overseers of the poor or by the families of poor children themselves. When Lot Dooling moved his family out of South Carolina in 1827, for example, he left behind a daughter bound out to a Mr. Bramblett, near Laurens. Local authorities also used and the courts upheld bound apprenticeship for free black children. In 1844, for instance, the overseers of the poor in Henry County, Virginia, labeled as bastards the children of Retha Harris, a free black woman and the wife of a slave, and indentured them to John S. Brewer. Brewer agreed to pay their mother a dollar each per year while they were between the ages of fourteen and seventeen and also to give each child twelve dollars for the last year of her service. The indenture for Milly also specified that Brewer teach her "all the art, trade and mystery of washing and spinning." When Harris sought the release of Sally, Joannah, and Milly in 1848, the Virginia Supreme Court overturned a lower-court decision in her favor.[64]

Pauper apprenticeship involved direct contact and control between the elite and the poor of both races. For such control to function as class legitimation, however, those who received the labor extracted in the indentures had to uphold their end of the bargain. Masters were legally obligated to perform their half of the bargain, but they did not always comply, and in some cases, apprentices sued. Often the apprentices in these cases lost, but a South Carolina court in 1840 took the side of the apprentice and made clear the desired role for elite patrons. The recipient of the indenture had discharged the apprentice for the "immoral behaviour" of being "disobedient and vicious." "It is the duty of every master," Judge John S. Richardson wrote, "to persevere, and strive to correct and improve his apprentice *throughout* the whole term of service. When the Doctor yielded to her perverseness, and dismissed his froward pupil, he himself failed in his primary undertaking." In such rulings, the court affirmed that if one undertook to act as part of the elite, that role must be maintained.[65]

While apprenticeships controlled the labor of poor children, southern vagrancy laws prescribed forced labor for adults. As in the northern states, southern legislatures defined vagrancy broadly. Most statutes included references to "idlers" and "ramblers," in others words, people who refused to work for wages or those who moved about from place to place in search of work. Many of these laws also defined as vagrants husbands who deserted their wives. Gambling constituted a third common area of offense, especially "steamboat gambling." Punishments for vagrants under these statutes usually combined forced labor with physical pain. Offenders could be hired out or auctioned to the highest bidder with the proceeds going either to a local poor fund or to the vagrant's family. Missouri's and Arkansas's statutes represent a typical vagrancy law of this stripe. Both states' definitions included loitering or "rambling" idlers, beggars, steamboat gamblers and gambling-house keepers, and husbands who abandoned their families. Minors convicted under these laws were bound out as apprentices. Offenders over twenty-one were offered at auction for six-month terms, with the proceeds used to pay court costs and to support the vagrant or his family.[66]

African Americans living outside slavery constituted a specific target of labor control. Most states had comprehensive special codes for "free persons of color," and these often included vagrancy sections intended to constrain free blacks in labor contracts. In addition, southern legislatures passed vagrancy acts specifically aimed at free blacks. In 1820 the Virginia legislature empowered overseers of the poor to investigate free blacks and commit them to the workhouse if they had no employment. In 1859 Georgia passed a law that anticipated aspects of the postwar Black Codes. Free blacks living without employment could be arrested for vagrancy. A first offense meant a two-year reassignment to bondage; a second arrest meant a permanent return to slavery. In essence, these laws enacted the suggestions of proslavery writers about how to avoid pauperism. Laws against free black "vagrancy" constructed an additional prop for the slave codes.[67]

Coerced labor was one motive of southern vagrancy laws, and on one level it enforced the hegemony of planter dominion over larger structural work patterns. Still, labor discipline was not the main purpose of vagrancy laws in the antebellum South. After all, the question of labor discipline had been supposedly solved by slavery; only the margins needed policing. Vagrancy laws served a broader function of social control by delineating the cultural membership in the elite and asserting its claims to power. Poor whites may not have constituted a large underclass in the Old South, but they did present a general threat to the vision of a well-ordered society. Moreover, they sometimes colluded with slaves in runaway attempts and in the market for goods stolen from plantations. By patrolling this slice of the southern social structure, elites helped affirm their ability to exercise hegemony over levels of society to which they were not intimately connected. Like their northern counterparts, they enacted laws that operated as means of regulating behavior that the respectable classes found unacceptable and of establishing the perimeters of propriety. Unlike northerners, who intended to accomplish these means primarily through institutions, most southern states retained corporal punishment or other harsh sentences, at least in their statutes.[68]

Southern legislators substantiated this general purpose of social control by using definitional sections to outline improper behaviors and by prescribing severe penalties for their commission. North Carolina used jail, labor, and the whip for incorrigibles. Aimed at idlers and gamblers, the law approved a ten-day sentence for the first arrest. If a second arrest occurred within twenty days, the offender was subject to a month's imprisonment, for which he had to pay all costs. If he refused or could not pay, he was bound over for trial. When convicted by "a jury of good and lawful men," the vagrant could be hired out by the court for up to six months. But persons "of ill fame" who could not be hired received thirty-nine lashes and their freedom. A similar end was met by vagrancy laws that dealt with prostitution. For example, Texas's 1857 Penal Code mentioned vagrancy only in the chapter on disorderly houses. The code defined a disorderly house as "one kept for the purpose of public prostitution, or as a common resort for prostitutes, vagabonds, and free negroes." Vagabonds, wandering and homeless men or women, were lumped in this statute with other social undesirables.[69]

Although comprehensive statutes were common, many southern vagrancy acts policed gaming specifically. When North Carolina passed a supplementary vagrancy act in 1841, it singled out people "endeavouring to maintain themselves by gaming or other means." Gambling as vagrancy received its most thorough examination in South Carolina. In December 1836 South Carolina passed a new vagrancy act specifically aimed to control gambling and prostitution in the vicinity of South Carolina College in Columbia. Upholding the constitutionality of the new statute a year later, Judge Baylis J. Earle of the South Carolina Court of Errors argued that vagrancy in itself did not constitute "a distinct offense." Rather, vagrancy laws were "intended to afford some adequate security to the public, against the danger apprehended from the several classes of persons enumerated, all of whom, from their want of honest employment, or from their vicious pursuits," could have been considered "a danger to society." With this object in mind, vagrancy proceedings were "merely inquisitorial," aiming to examine the life and livelihood of a suspect character, ascertain the likelihood of crime, and require security bonds if the person seemed to be a threat. In some ways, Earle's analysis pointed to the twentieth-century justification for vagrancy as a supposed benign form of crime prevention. But his opinion also drew a line between members of the public who needed "adequate security" and those who could be incarcerated because they were "vicious" and "a danger to society." Constructing the "crime" in this manner met two purposes. In the narrow sense, it allowed Earle and his colleagues to envision themselves as men who would not participate in professional gambling or other disreputable acts. On a broader level, it helped legitimate their position as purveyors of standards of respectable behavior to the remainder of South Carolina society.[70]

While often more specific than their northern cousins, these statutes still proscribed a way of life or a certain status more than they did specific acts. In the broad sense, vagrancy was not so much a crime as it was a description or an epithet, and southerners sometimes used slander and libel actions to rebuild their reputations after being labeled as vagabonds. In South Carolina, a Mr. Brown acted as informer to get a Mr. Colson tried under the 1787 vagrancy act. After being acquitted, Colson sued Brown under a clause of the 1787 law stating that if a conviction ensued from an accusation made "through malevolence, or resentment, without reasonable cause" the informer was bound to pay the five-pound fine and face a suit for civil damages. Brown claimed that no malice had been intended, but the lower court rejected his arguments. In April 1809, however, the South Carolina Supreme Court reversed the decision on the grounds that no conviction had occurred. In 1822 the state of South Carolina indicted Michael P. Walsh on libel charges because he told an unnamed victim: "[You are] the meanest man and the greatest rascal that I ever came across, or heard of; you are worse than the lowest of vagabonds, &c."[71]

Given such meanings, vagrancy arrests became informal rituals of affirmation for middle-class and elite members of southern communities, even quite late in the antebellum period. The language that separated the respectable classes from social outcasts appeared clearly in the young David Schenck's description of an arrest that occurred in January 1853. "The Sheriff (Lowe) was taking a young (18 yrs) vagabond to jail and he broke and run," Schenck recorded. "Every boy and young man followed, and kept near him till he got near Mr. Alx'rs woods, there got horses and dogs and caught him. There was much excitement and lots of fun. It was certainly a 'rich' race." The object of the chase, Martin Harriss, "excited sympathy of everyone when taken," Schenck reported. "He was an object of pity." Harris was actually being pursued on a bastardy indictment, not one for vagrancy, so Schenck's account is particularly interesting. A "vagabond" was seen as someone wholly other, a person whose misfortunes were at once to be pitied and enjoyed as a diversion. For a boy who was also eighteen at the time, the event helped secure Schenck's sense of social place. The event also played a role in ensconcing Harriss's location in the suspect classes. Harriss himself seemed to perceive that he had slipped across some sort of boundary, for when faced with the indictment, "his soul seemed to sink within him, and his hopes of happiness [were] forever blighted."[72]

This event and Schenck's perceptions of it capture the broader significance of southern vagrancy laws. By illustrating the behaviors southern lawmakers and planter society found unacceptable, laws became a text through which elites could assert their hold on the class and power structure, all within the objective cloak of law. Prohibitions against "rambling" or "loitering" proscribed mobility at the lowest levels of society. Hard labor, whipping, or incarceration for "idlers" punished them for not supporting themselves or their families by what lawmakers considered "honest means." Such proscriptions defined people who did "ramble" or "loiter" as outsiders to accepted society, as practitioners of dishonesty. Gambling and prostitution sections played a similar role, enforcing the code of honor that determined the gentlemanly avenues of vice. These constructions allowed southerners to adopt the more benevolent position toward relief that the proslavery writers touted. Southern dispensers of charity did not face the central problem of indiscriminate almsgiving that so troubled northerners because power structures remained relatively demarcated. Their want of northern sensibilities, however, did not mean that they lacked feeling for the poor. The main difference was that southern aristocrats or middle-class parvenus used slavery and, more important, the legal system to buttress the dependent relationships of their society and to temper the dilemmas that beset northerners. Whatever the actual force planters and wealthy merchants wielded in the whole of southern society, they knew they controlled their slaves, and they believed that the remainder of society was in a dependent relationship to them. With the question of dependence resolved, southern elites felt free to be charitable, at least in word if not in deed.

Just as southern and northern labor contract law diverged, so too did the two regions' poor and vagrant laws, but more subtly. Ideologically, southerners did not exhibit the extreme contempt for paupers and vagrants common in the North. With slavery to institutionalize the dependence of the very poor, southern elites believed they could be more lenient toward destitute whites. Nevertheless, they used vagrancy laws to help demarcate cultural membership in the respectable classes and to control behavior they found unacceptable. In pursuing such a goal, southern elites were not as far from their northern counterparts as they might have appeared. Northern vagrancy laws had also evolved into one means for the respectable classes to assert their legitimacy. Congressmen, missionaries, Union army officers, and others who would be active in the postemancipation South had imbibed these ideas and the legal rules that embodied them. For them, erecting free-labor society on the ruins of slavery meant establishing the northern system of labor contract and vagrant laws. In doing so, they would unwittingly aid southern elites in their attempts to reestablish labor control and would elicit charges of reviving slavery.

Northern Principles Go South

Above all, emancipation was a legal event. The process that slaves and their allies carried out in the Civil War South destroyed a legal apparatus that had instituted and perpetuated the region's central mode of production. What freedpeople and their associates could not create single-handedly, however, was a system of law to replace the one that had been vanquished. That power came to rest in the emergent national state of the Civil War era. As emancipation proceeded, Union army officers and members of Congress became the people who would define what free labor meant in a legal and constitutional sense. When these northern policymakers tried to establish a legal system for a free-labor South during emancipation, they imported popular notions of northern legal principles. The crisis of law caused by the destruction of slavery led them to discuss openly and combine in novel ways legal concepts that had remained only vaguely connected during the antebellum period. Yet northerners failed to resolve their debate about the role of the state in the labor market, leaving Union policy without a unitary or clearly defined guiding principle.

By the end of the Civil War, many northerners had come to believe that the destruction of slavery necessitated sweeping change in the emancipated South. When Carl Schurz grappled with how the Union might respond to the changes wrought by the Civil War and emancipation, he had a broad vision. "The whole organism of southern society," the German-born Radical Republican wrote in late 1865, "must be reconstructed, or rather constructed anew to bring it in harmony with the rest of American society." By envisioning social reconstruction, Schurz captured what Union officials, politicians in Washington, white southerners, and freed slaves had been pursuing for more than three years. For the former two groups, remaking the South had already proved to be a daunting task, as they uncovered competing models for what distinguished "the rest of American society." As northerners tried to implement their divergent ideas of freedom, they clashed with each other nearly as often as they did with southerners. When Major General Nathaniel P. Banks set up labor regulations in Louisiana in 1863, for instance, the *New York Principia* labeled them the "Governmental Establishment of Slavery in New Orleans."[1]

Banks's labor rules provoked such condemnation because the relationship between work and the law was central to the meaning of emancipation. As important as abstract elements of free-labor ideology were in determining the outcome of emancipation, more important were legal precepts received from the prewar North. Antebellum labor law offered officials in the South and in Washington both general assumptions regarding unemployed, unskilled laborers and specific legal rules with which to discipline their lives and labor. The very existence of these rules predisposed many northerners to desire a *system* of labor (a set of principles enforced by courts) instead of letting the market regulate conditions. Moreover, emancipation forced northerners to connect explicitly elements of criminal and civil law that had previously remained detached. In itself, this linkage caused a great deal of criticism. It revealed relationships between law and labor that had not been apparent before, relationships that had penetrated the thinking of many northerners but which they did not care to discuss openly. The systems of labor that Banks and others promulgated were also problematic because antebellum law was not cohesive. By 1860 northern (and southern) courts and legislatures had developed many options. Radical abolitionists often voiced these alternative views, but even they sometimes reverted to dominant themes of legal and social discourse. Whether radical or not, the actions of Union policymakers, both in Washington and in the field, demonstrate that the bourgeois vision outlined by reformers and lawmakers in the decades before the war was beginning to enjoy wide use as a point of reference for talking about labor and the state. These popularized notions of labor law, and their accompanying inconsistencies, became both guiding principles and points of conflict during wartime Reconstruction.[2]

FREE LABOR IN WARTIME LOUISIANA

Legal definitions for free labor began to emerge most clearly during emancipation in wartime Louisiana. There, Union army officers sought to use the power of military law to create a free-labor system. In doing so, as Eric Foner and others have noted, they prefigured much of what would happen later in emerging Union policy. However, they did not act solely or even centrally out of racial reasons, as earlier historians argued. Nor did they simply concoct labor policy on the spot based loosely on northern ideology, as Foner suggests. Rather, army officials based these early actions on the competing strains of free-labor law and their accompanying social discourses that had emerged in the prewar North.[3]

Banks was not the first Union representative to regulate labor in Louisiana. After occupation of New Orleans and surrounding areas by forces under General Benjamin Butler, army officers searched for ways to organize labor and poor relief. Butler inaugurated a mass program of public works for New Orleans, but his subalterns also influenced the outcome of labor for African Americans in the process of emancipation. Slaves fleeing plantations formed "contraband colonies" such as Camp Parapet north of the city. There, Lieutenant George H. Hanks, who would later become the first superintendent of the Bureau of Negro Labor, required work in return for support. Hanks's actions recalled the work requirements of the northern poor-law system. Another officer, General Thomas W. Sherman, forbade occupants of the colonies to "stroll away," borrowing directly the language of vagrancy laws. In October 1862 Butler appointed a northern civilian to oversee the sugar harvest on abandoned estates and then met with planters from St. Bernard and Plaquemine Parishes to organize plantation work. Butler promised these Unionists that if they paid wages and ended corporal punishment, the army would assist them in enforcing labor. November brought more clarification as Butler set up a three-member Sequestration Commission to convey the previous agreement to other parishes. Butler and his subordinates had sketched a new labor law for the state, but it remained only in the formative stages when the general's controversial actions in other areas of administration prompted his removal in December 1862. For the most part, any official in Butler's labor and welfare system had been no more than overseer of the poor and local constable rolled into one. Still, Butler's tenure initiated the army's role in securing work discipline, a part taken up with alacrity by Butler's replacement.[4]

Nathaniel Prentiss Banks was a nearly perfect embodiment of northern legal and social theory. Having started life as an industrial operative in Waltham, Massachusetts, he benefited from an unlikely rags-to-riches story. Dubbing himself the "Bobbin Boy," Banks used his rise from the working class to political advantage, serving as Speaker of the U.S. House and as Republican governor of Massachusetts before the Civil War. Although he opposed slavery, Banks was a moderate Republican, alienating Massachusetts radicals, who labeled him a political "trimmer." A friend of Lincoln's as well as Secretary of State William Seward's, Banks commanded an army against "Stonewall" Jackson in the Shenandoah Valley campaign and carried out a policy of conciliation there. On December 17, 1862, Banks relieved Butler, again believing he had come to make peace with Union loyalists.[5]

After the harsh rule of Butler, Louisianans expected Banks to be less severe. "It is supposed that Gen. Banks intends to pursue a liberal course here," the *New Orleans Picayune* assured its readers shortly after he arrived. In his initial actions, the general did not disappoint the local citizens. "The war is not being waged by the Government for the overthrow of slavery," Banks declared in his first official proclamation. Yet he believed that as a work of Providence, the war was ending slavery in a way that even abolitionists could not have foreseen. Banks remained unclear about the status of slaves in Louisiana, part of which was under Union control and part of which was not. It seemed at the time that parts of the state would be exempt when the Emancipation Proclamation became official on January 1, 1863. Consequently, Banks advised slaves "to remain upon their plantations until their privileges [had] been definitely established." Slaves could "rest assured that whatever benefit the Government intend[ed] [would] be secured them," but he warned them not to take the law into their own hands. At the same time, he promised anxious planters that "no encouragement" would be given to laborers "to desert their employers," yet he went on to say that "no authority exist[ed] to compel them to return." For the time being, he urged planters to devise a system whereby some "equitable portion" of the proceeds from coming year's crops could be "set apart and reserved for the support and compensation for labor." In essence, Banks had pronounced the minimum requirements of free labor as envisioned by most northerners: the absence of specific performance, the sanctity of entire contracts, and the necessity of the cash nexus.[6]

While the status of African American laborers remained unclear into January 1863, officials in Banks's army, with or without his permission, took steps that made the New Orleans newspapers praise him even more. On January 21 acting chief of police Colonel J. H. French ordered his lieutenant to arrest all African Americans found without a pass after 8:30 in the evening. Military authorities detained between three hundred and four hundred blacks in the streets of New Orleans that night. The incensed free black community of the city then petitioned Banks for redress, but it is unclear what became of their pleas. When an abolitionist visiting New Orleans tried to free one of the arrested, the army's provost marshal general told him that the woman had been arrested "to prevent her from being a vagrant about the streets." He added, "It is perfectly proper." This seemed odd to the abolitionist, who wrote to a friend that most of the people likely to become public charges in New Orleans were white. So he pressed the case further. The provost marshal then threatened him with arrest as well. He appealed to a provost court judge, who directed him to Banks. Saying he had no knowledge of the order, the general sent the man back to Clark. The abolitionist left the city with the woman still incarcerated.[7]

This incident rightly supplied northern critics with support for their charges of tyranny, but it also revealed the extent to which concerns about vagrancy pervaded Banks's developing labor policy. On January 29, 1863, his birthday, the general issued orders explaining the Emancipation Proclamation and establishing a labor system. These rules, the basis for Union army policy in Louisiana for the next three years, rested firmly on northern prewar assumptions about the relationship between labor and poverty. "The public interest peremptorily demands that all persons without means of support be required to maintain themselves by their labor," Banks proclaimed. "Negroes are not exempt from these laws." African Americans who left their employers would be compelled to labor on public works for the support of themselves and their families. "Under no circumstances whatever" would blacks be "maintained in idleness, or allowed to wander through the parishes and cities of the State without employment." "Vagrancy and crime will be suppressed by enforced and constant occupation and employment." To institute actual legal relationships of labor, Banks had Butler's Sequestration Commission meet with planters and others to arrange a yearly program of labor that would provide fixed wages or shares as compensation, would ensure for proper treatment, and would secure provision of food, clothing, and medical care. Upon reaching such an agreement, the army would enforce "all the conditions of continuous and faithful service, respectful deportment, correct discipline and perfect subordination." Payment of wages rested on a lien against the crops by the laborer. Banks admitted that this was not the best system, but he declared that it was the only "practicable" arrangement and predicted that under this "voluntary system of labor" Louisiana would increase its production threefold.[8]

Early in February, Banks and the Sequestration Commission met with planters at the St. Charles Hotel in New Orleans. After negotiations, Colonel E. G. Beckwith, president of the commission, issued an order setting monthly wages at three dollars for mechanics, sugar makers, and other skilled laborers, two dollars for able-bodied male field hands, and one dollar for able-bodied females. Contracts for shares were fixed at three, two, and one for the previous categories. Planters were to provide food, clothing, and education. The status of former slaves under these agreements was far from clear, for the commission stipulated that planters did not give up their property rights in slaves by signing them. Moreover, these "contracts" hardly constituted free labor even under the most conservative of northern definitions because workers had not been a part of the wage bargain. Still, the commission was not in the business of reinforcing plantation slavery; instead, it intended to enforce work generally. Beckwith closed the order with another warning about vagrancy: "All negroes not otherwise employed will be required to labor on the public works, and no person capable of labor will be supported at the public expense in idleness." The planters present assented to these terms, though, the *New York Tribune*'s correspondent reported, they "made the best of what they consider[ed] a compulsory bargain." In the coming weeks, planters expressed their dissatisfaction, especially about their decrease in personal power. Freedpeople also hated the settlement, in particular the vagrancy section's restriction of their freedom of movement.[9]

As the justification for the labor system, Banks used the terminology employed by poor-law reformers. Vagrancy meant unemployed people wandering about or becoming a financial burden on the government. Promulgating this order, Banks applied a language developed as a projection of class power under very different circumstances to a situation in which the interested parties operated from a language of race instead. Although his system separated blacks as a group for almost compulsory labor, he reached that point from assumptions about the nature of unemployed, unskilled workers rather than from those about slave labor. Reliance on poor-law concepts appeared in the way in which Banks and the Sequestration Commission carried out their threat of forcing vagrants to labor for the government. The commission acquired control of several abandoned plantations from the Quartermaster's Department. These plantations, the "home colonies," which lasted until 1866, operated as "a sort of general poor farm," Freedmen's Bureau chief Oliver Otis Howard later wrote. They also served as a labor bureau after the organization of the Bureau of Negro Labor under Hanks in February 1863.

Like antebellum local governments that auctioned off paupers, the home colonies funneled workers to private plantations as well as employing them on government lands.[10]

While Banks and many of his later supporters acted from these predilections, former slaveholders saw freedpeople in purely racial terms and desired a much stronger apparatus of racial control. After the January 29 orders, the *New Orleans Picayune* praised the general's "determination . . . not to permit swarms of 'contrabands' to be any longer a tax upon the government and a vicious prey upon society." Yet the paper also played an instrumental role in bringing about another planters' convention at the St. Charles on February 19–20. This well-chronicled, yet vague, event has become central to historians' investigations of Union intentions.[11]

After an organizational meeting at noon on the 19th, about sixty planters from parishes within federal lines assembled in the rotunda of the St. Charles that evening, observed by a buzzing crowd gathered in the gallery above. At about 8 P.M. they retired to the "oppressively warm" gentleman's parlor. Two or three took seats at the table, and the remainder formed an irregular circle around the room. Three and a half hours of heated debate about the future of plantation labor in Louisiana ensued. The group promptly appointed a committee to find out from Banks whether assenting to the agreement of the 5th meant that the military would bind blacks to work. The meeting next resolved to see if police juries could be formed to enforce patrols for "all strange slaves in the parish." A Dr. Knapp then proposed that while they should thank Banks for arresting "black vagrants," they would like the return of all civil authority. After considerable discussion, the motion was tabled. Another man then offered a resolution authorizing planters to hire laborers from other plantations, but the group shouted him down with cries of "No! no! never!" and "Shame! shame!" Finally, the meeting resolved to contact Banks and request him to meet with them.[12]

The next evening the meeting resumed. A committee reported that it had received Banks's pledge that he and the state would "do everything in their power to facilitate the planters in carrying out the arrangements that had been entered into." Upon hearing these assurances, the assembled planters agreed to support Banks and the Sequestration Commission. At 8 P.M. the general entered the hall to "a tolerably good imitation of applause." The president of the group expressed their "high respect for [him] as an officer and a gentleman" and thanked him for the "many favors" he had bestowed upon them. Unmoved by flattery, Banks said he had not come to interfere and that he was there reluctantly. He claimed he had published what he thought to be his "duty to do as an officer of the government" and concluded his speech with what the correspondent of the *New York Tribune* called "amiable Fourth-of-Julyism." That same correspondent, from one of the leading radical papers in the nation, drank to Banks's health in the hotel bar five minutes later.[13]

What actually happened at the St. Charles meetings appears hazy. The planters thought they had received Banks's guarantee that slavery would be all but reinstated in the loyal regions of Louisiana. Yet they did not achieve agreement between themselves or with the general on their more extreme demands. Neither could representatives of northern radicals agree on what was going on in Louisiana. Another correspondent of the *Tribune* at first thought the meeting of February 19–20 intended to "criticize and reform the orders of the commanding general," but after hearing Banks's speech he exclaimed that the commander "talked of peace with all the fervor of a Copperhead Democrat of the Middle or Western States." Banks "was willing to be turned from his purpose by any suggestions" the planters might make. George Denison, an agent and correspondent of Treasury Secretary Salmon P. Chase, believed that "slavery, abolished by Gen. Butler, [had been] completely re-established."[14]

Perhaps the most confused person of all was not one of the planters or one of the radicals but David Hunter Strother, a Virginia Unionist and sketch artist traveling with Banks. He recorded the meetings earlier in the month with some consternation. After speaking with Banks on February 2, he felt confident in notifying planters that "their servants would be returned to them and forced to make a living." Yet the next day Banks said he "had no intention or authority to force the slaves back to their masters." A disappointed Strother complained that his "efforts to reconcile the Massachusetts idea of the Negro with the planter's practical knowledge was a total failure." They had agreed while dealing in generalities, but now a "vast gulf" had developed, Strother believed. Promising to return slaves "without contemplating a resort to physical force" was like doing *Hamlet* with Hamlet left out. Yet Strother must have been even more amazed when Banks disapproved of a proposal by Captain W. Sturgis Hooper, whom Strother described as an abolitionist, to require African Americans' assent in being returned. He finally concluded that "the General seemed solely interested to accomplish a good result within the limits of his authority and willing to let it take its chance with the public."[15]

In his description of these events, Strother inadvertently mentioned the key to the confusion about Banks's program—reconciling the "Massachusetts idea" with that of the planters. The northern view of slaves being freed by the war was not as singular as Strother assumed, but in forming his system Banks drew on the general ideas of Bay State labor and poor-law reformers and on his own prewar experience. As the state's prewar governor, he had been involved in the treatment of vagrants. In 1859, boys at the Westborough Reform School set it on fire several times, destroying at least two-thirds of the structure. Banks discharged all the board members except the son of the founder and appointed a new board that instituted a "school-ship" for the "discipline of the older and more vicious boys." [16]

Banks's reliance on previous labor law became clearer when he issued a new set of regulations on February 3, 1864. In part a response to criticism of the previous year's program, these more explicit rules fixed the hours of labor at ten in summer and nine in winter, stipulated payment for overtime, established a schedule of wages, rations, shares, and fines for disobedience, and gave provost marshals the authority to adjudicate all labor disputes. They outlawed flogging but also required passes for plantation hands to travel from place to place. The new rules restricted the labor market further by incorporating the terms of northern farm labor contracts. Freedpeople could choose their employers, but they would be "held to their engagement for the year, under the protection of the government." Workers feigning sickness or refusing to labor could be turned over to the provost marshal for employment on the public works. Banks declared that these rules supported the "encouragement of independent industry" and that they aimed to "prepare the laborer for the time when he [could] render so much labor for so much money." Besides the labor laws, he also initiated a free-labor bank and a freedmen's school system. [17]

This time Banks stated explicitly why he was acting in this manner. The regulations were "based on the assumption that labor is a public duty, and idleness and vagrancy a crime." Civil and military authorities were not exempt from this law, he continued. "Every enlightened community has enforced it upon all classes of people by the severest of penalties. It is especially necessary in agricultural pursuits." Those people "identified with the cultivation of the soil" should not believe they had been "relieved from the necessity of toil, which is the condition of existence of all children of God." The revolution of the war had not altered basic social arrangements, Banks declared. "This universal law of labor will be enforced upon just terms by the

Government, under whose protection the laborer rests secure in his rights." [18]

Again, the general saw freedpeople not only as former slaves but as unemployed agricultural laborers. Banks's rules and his arguments for them
were well in line with the legal and social principles of his home state. Massachusetts's courts had been instrumental in establishing the legal rule that
agricultural laborers must be encouraged, if not coerced, to honor long-term
labor agreements. Northern courts had assumed these contracts had been
the product of a free bargain in the marketplace. Banks and other federal
officials in the South intervened in the labor market at the inception of these
agreements, but they expected normal rules to apply once contracts were
signed. Moreover, they knew, and northern courts had explicitly recognized,
that the seasonal nature of nonmechanized agriculture required workers to
be available to labor at specific moments in the crop cycle. Whether intentionally or not, the legal and social assumptions of northern farmers and
courts fit all too comfortably with the needs of southern planters. The same
fit between northern ideas and southern needs occurred with regard to vagrancy. For Banks, vagrancy laws were an earmark not of oppression but of
"enlightened communities." It was not only African Americans who possessed a duty to work but "all children of God." The role of the state in this
political economy was to enforce both the rights of workers and the duty
to labor. [19]

The Reverend Thomas W. Conway, who headed the renamed Bureau of
Free Labor after Hanks departed, summarized the point the system had
reached in 1864. Banks's labor order, he believed, had notified fifty thousand
freedpeople "that they were free to labor as freemen, protected by the government which had broken their chains; that they were to have schools for
their children, and pay for their services, and redress for their grievances."
While federal regulations had restricted freedpeople, they had also protected
them by compelling planters to give laborers all the benefits they deserved.
The reverend also noted that one-fourth of workers held the status of "first-
class hands" and received eight dollars per month plus board, medical care,
schooling for their children, and one acre of land. At this level, their wages
were "as a whole, more remunerative than those which ha[d] ordinarily
been paid to Northern farm hands who worked by the year." [20]

Conway had enumerated most elements of the evangelical version of free
labor—lack of literal bondage (self-ownership), protection, education, and
paid labor. Moreover, he acknowledged specifically the northern legal stan-

dard of year-long farm contracts. Conway clarified the use of vagrancy law when he testified before the Smith-Brady Commission. He had not forced individual workers to work with individual planters, he stated. Rather, he had counseled them in wage bargaining and let them make the ultimate decision. Nevertheless, he compelled the idle to work for wages "with parties whom [he] knew to be suitable" or to go to the home colonies and work without pay. In his policy toward the latter group, he explicitly imported the gender distinctions of northern law and thought. If whole families were taken to the army's poor farms, those who could were permitted to work for wages elsewhere, "while the vagrant,—the head of the family,—would be taken alone to the farm." If such men were eventually hired by planters, Conway sent their families with them and required their employers to support them and their dependents in return for wages. Trying to establish a semblance of northern material culture, Conway required planters to house such workers in a single-family dwelling. Similar to Tuckerman and other prewar writers, he wanted "vagrant" men to learn both work and domestic discipline.[21]

Banks's program was not the only effort to organize labor in wartime Louisiana. For a short period in mid-1863 and then for a longer duration in late 1864 and 1865, part or all of the Union labor program in the Mississippi Valley came temporarily under the Treasury Department. In July 1864 Treasury agent William P. Mellen issued a different set of labor rules for lessees of abandoned plantations. The central benefit of this arrangement was that it set wages much higher than previously and at almost twice the prewar rate for farmworkers in the North. Nevertheless, these regulations incorporated northern law. They required work of all able-bodied people over the age of twelve and continued the home colonies. In addition, they employed both apportionment and entirety. For workers who failed "to labor as contemplated in the contract," the superintendent could cancel the contract after the employer paid wages due. Such a provision instituted specifically jurists' suggestions about the role of apportionment in labor discipline. Yet the rules also allowed lessees to reserve half of workers' pay until the end of the season, a formalization of prewar payment procedures, and they used wage forfeiture for workers who "quit voluntarily." Half the remaining wages went to the planter, half to the government.[22]

When Mellen reissued these orders in February 1865, the half-pay sections caused critics to fear that workers would slip back into dependence on planters. Partially in response to these worries, President Lincoln returned the labor program to the army a month later, and Major General Stephen A. Hurlbut issued a new series of labor regulations. Hurlbut's system required rations, clothing, and medical attention and established a graduated wage scale that recognized a superior value for skilled labor. Drawing heavily on both the entirety rule and antebellum vagrancy concepts, Hurlbut advised freedpeople that they might choose their employers; but once hired, they would not be permitted to abandon the contract. If they did so, they would "forfeit all wages earned to the time of abandonment and be otherwise punished." Those refusing to work would be employed at public works without pay. "The laborers must understand," Hurlbut declared, "that it is in their own interest to do their work faithfully, and that the Government, while it will protect and sustain them, cannot support those who are capable of earning an honest living by industry." In response to criticism from New Orleans's free black community, the general stressed that the regulations guaranteed paid labor, kept the family together, provided education, and allowed freedpeople to bring suits for redress. Further progress would have to come through a slow process of education to eradicate entrenched prejudices. As 1865 progressed, these cheery predictions faced the realities of white Louisiana's growing backlash against emancipation. Beginning with Opelousas in July, towns reenacted the curfews and pass laws of slavery. In response, Conway and General E. R. S. Canby, who had taken command of the Department of the Gulf, voided these ordinances and declared that laws must not discriminate racially.[23]

By the summer of 1865 authority over free labor passed to the Freedmen's Bureau. Having headed the Union army's Bureau of Free Labor, Conway set up the Louisiana Freedmen's Bureau and became its first assistant commissioner. In doing so, he ordered that freedpeople must "in all cases enter into free and voluntary contracts with employers of their own choice," contracts that could "not be broken by either party except for just and sufficient cause." Conway assured freedpeople that they would not be forced to work for unsuitable employers, but his orders contained the ambivalence the vagrancy concept produced. Bureau agents were to explain to the freedmen that they were "entirely free to work where and for whom they please[d], and that at the same time that a life of idleness [would] not be allowed or encouraged." While Conway pursued a policy similar to that of Banks, he did interfere with local laws and often ordered the release of blacks arrested for vagrancy. This moderate course prompted Louisiana planters to lobby President Andrew Johnson for Conway's removal. In October 1865 Johnson pressured bureau commissioner Howard into relieving Conway from duty. Although Howard appointed Brevet Major General Absolom Baird as assistant commissioner for Louisiana, travel delays prevented his arrival, and General Joseph S. Fullerton took over during October 1865.[24]

Whether from naïveté or from a more conservative stance, Fullerton began immediately to dismantle Conway's moderate administration. Fullerton tried to close all orphan asylums supported by the Freedmen's Bureau and to apprentice the children to private citizens. When a group of citizens complained to him about black vagrants in New Orleans, he allowed the chief of police to arrest them and bring them to the bureau's provost marshal, who was to "secure for them employment and means of support during the coming winter." On October 27 the authorities arrested hundreds of African Americans under this order, both employed and unemployed. By November 1 Fullerton modified this policy to make the existing state vagrancy law applicable to blacks as well as whites. Fullerton's administration lasted only a month, and by November 1865 Baird had arrived.[25]

From its inception through the permanent organization of the Freedmen's Bureau, federal policy in Louisiana had followed the general outlines of the free-labor ethic and the concepts of antebellum labor and poor law. The free-labor indictment of slavery had predicated the new southern society merely as slavery's negation. Laborers would be protected at home, educated in schools, and freed from *physical* compulsion at work. Yet they would be subject to the *legal* compulsion embodied in the system of laws that enforced free labor. Although freed from specific coercion to work for a master—the antebellum definition of *involuntary* servitude—workers were not free from a general duty to labor and to perform contracts fully. For many northerners, including many abolitionists, emancipation itself merely implied this transition in forms of labor discipline. It did not mean the advent of an unregulated labor market.

Although set within this general discourse, the specifics of emancipation were an open issue, and northern commentators expanded the meanings of legal regulation of labor. Their discussions voiced the fluidity of free-labor law between 1863 and 1865. As might be expected, conservative northerners expressed almost unqualified support for the stringent rules governing labor. Perhaps more surprising, most moderates and even some abolitionists upheld certain elements of Union policy. Only radical abolitionists, the core of an emerging group of liberals, challenged dominant themes about labor law's place in emancipation.

LOUISIANA IN THE NORTH

The version of free-labor law implemented by Nathaniel Banks and others in Louisiana engendered heated discussions of the meanings of freedom in the Civil War North. The inchoate state free-labor law had reached by 1860 made this outcome quite likely, but the combination of law's fluidity with the centralizing demands of the state bureaucracy present in the Union army made it all but inevitable. In Louisiana, the Union army had made law in a centralized, administrative fashion almost unprecedented in the nineteenth century. Consequently, army officials had combined elements of law kept separate in the prewar period, unveiling the legal system that had undergirded the emerging capitalist wage system of the North. When heightened by the intensity of emancipation's social crisis, this exposure led commentators in the North to consider directly the place of law in a free-labor system. In the course of this debate, three positions on free-labor law crystallized. Conservatives praised the use of state power to regulate labor, and they usually employed the language of poverty that reform writers had developed. Liberals, on the other hand, argued for a free market in labor and sometimes eschewed the more strident elements of prewar social discourse. Moderates, as the label implies, sought to steer a middle course, borrowing the main principles of free-labor law while placing limits on their application.

If adherence to the language of poverty established perimeters for Banks, it also acted as a measure of acceptance for his system. Conservative organs quickly rallied to his program in 1863. *Harper's Weekly* commended Banks's labor regulations and reminded its readers of the universality of laws for the idle. "Those who regard the unwillingness of the negro to work as evidence of his inferiority to the white," the editors wrote, "will do well to remember that every civilized nation in the world has vagrant laws on its statute books, and that time was when our ancestors needed the gentle stimulus of the law to compel them to earn their living." The *New York Times* ran numerous editorials praising Banks's every step, concentrating especially on his vagrancy laws. The restrictions on idleness were "capable of much wider application," the editors suggested. Linking emancipation to the general question of controlling the unemployed, the paper suggested, "It should be distinctly understood that emancipation is from *Slavery*—not from *work*. No community can safely have any portion of its dependent population unemployed. . . . Every State has its laws concerning vagrants—compelling them to work for the public if they depend on the public for support, or punishing them for their refusal to do so." Like those who argued for harsh vagrancy laws before the war, these conservative writers believed that the unemployed owed an obligation of labor for their support and that all dependent groups must be compelled to labor. The rhetoric they applied to freed African Americans seems mild in comparison to what would appear in the industrial crisis of the 1870s.[26]

While conservatives gave unqualified support, radical abolitionists outlined an emerging liberal position on labor law that criticized Banks sharply for his system of labor as well as his general tone of conciliation. "Under Gen. Banks method," railed the *New York Principia*, "our government, the government of the United States, is as truly a slave-trading government as that of the Confederacy." Although William Lloyd Garrison supported Banks, another editorialist in the *Liberator* declared that Banks substituted serfdom for slavery and that he used his military authority to enforce his vagrancy orders against "the poorest and weakest class only." The *Christian Watchman and Reflector* implied that Banks deliberately delayed enforcing the Emancipation Proclamation and then "published it with a general order that seem[ed] designed to make its effect as little as possible." The *New York Tribune* charged that Banks formulated his 1863 regulations with a "complete disregard for the welfare of the negroes and the authority of the President." Banks had "yielded without hesitation or reluctance to every demand which the grasping avarice" of the Louisiana planters had wanted.[27]

A persistent liberal critic was radical abolitionist Wendell Phillips. "'Banks's freedom' . . . is no freedom to me," he stated flatly. Phillips charged that provost marshals were in the service of planters and that whipping was "undoubtedly practiced" on Louisiana plantations. For Phillips, the "Idea of Massachusetts liberty is, a man competent to sell his own toil, to select his own work, and when he differs with his neighbor, a jury to appeal to." Banks, he claimed, denied all these privileges: "Gen. Banks's liberty for the negro is, no right to fix his wages; no right to choose his toil, practically no right; having once chosen his place, no right to quit; any difference between employer and employed tried by a Provost Marshal, not a jury." Phillips did not share Banks's assumptions about poverty and explained pauperism as the result of intemperance rather than a refusal to labor. By the middle of the war, he had come to accept the central tenets of the liberal position: the right to quit, the cash nexus as the only acceptable form of labor discipline, and the need for an unregulated labor market.[28]

Perhaps the most thoroughgoing criticism of Banks's system came from American Freedmen's Inquiry Commission member James McKaye. If allowed to become permanent, he warned in 1864, the Union program would "differ very little from the workings of slavery itself." In part, McKaye worried about the actual administration of the program. Planters co-opted assistant provost marshals and convinced them to allow whipping and other forms of corporal punishment. McKaye also singled out year-long contracts as a problem. He conceded that former slaves must be taught the general obligations of contract and "should be held to the just fulfillment of such as he ha[d] voluntarily entered into." Still, long-term agreements were open to abuse.[29]

McKaye was more concerned with the general nature of the Union regulations and their restriction of African American workers as free agents in the labor market. The program allowed assistant provost marshals and planters to classify hands and fix the wage bargain, leaving laborers out of a process in which they should be central. If the wage bargain had to be fixed, McKaye suggested that the Treasury Department's program would be better. He praised its classifications and claimed (wrongly) that its wage rates were nearer the market level. His central point was that the Union program undermined freed slaves' sense of self-reliance. "If the only object to be accomplished was simply 'to compel the negro to labor' in a condition of perpetual subordination and subjection, this arrangement would be appropriate enough," McKaye observed. "But if the object be to make the colored man a self-supporting and self-defending member of the community, then he must be placed in a position where he can determine the value of his own labor, and be left to take the responsibility of his own existence and well being, as well as that of his family." If self-mastery could not be secured, he predicted, not only would the freedpeople be hurt, but "the great industrial interests dependent on their voluntary, enlightened, and justly compensated labor, [would] be seriously, if not fatally, jeopardied." McKaye wanted a free market in labor, and like Joel Parker, Jesse Holman, and other northern jurists who had advocated adoption of apportionment, McKaye thought that legal controls on labor actually hurt work discipline.[30]

Liberal critics voiced what might appear to be dominant nineteenth-century themes about political economy and labor relations. Their view of the "Idea of Massachusetts liberty" rested on self-ownership. In line with classical economists, they envisioned a laissez-faire market in labor, in which workers selected their occupations, bargained away their labor power as free agents, protected their interests by leaving undesirable employers, and sought protection in the civil courts. As labor reformer Robert Dale Owen advised in the AFIC's final report, labor should be hindered by no compulsory contracts, no "statutory rates of wages," and no restrictions on movement except those relative to the war. "The natural laws of supply and demand should be left to regulate rates of compensation and places of residence," he concluded. Other liberals, such as Carl Schurz, expected the wage relation itself to contain the means of work discipline. The willingness to work depended on the reliability of wages, he argued, and northern employers managed free labor by firing undependable employees, not whipping them. Such ideas aligned well with formal principles of political economy, but they did not match most northern states' legal rules regarding the employment relation. As such, liberals existed as a community with a language outside antebellum legal discourse on poverty and work, yet they provided a path toward the future.[31]

While liberals could accept little or nothing of what was happening in Louisiana, many northern reformers reacted to Banks's program with some reservations about the particulars but with wholehearted support for the assumptions on which it was based. The *Christian Examiner,* a Unitarian social reform journal, responded to Phillips with a lengthy defense of Banks and the general principles of his system. W. H. Allen, a Massachusetts educator and member of the American Freedmen's Aid Commission, worried that freedpeople as well as white refugees would be thrown upon the nation's charities. Consequently, Banks's "principle of compulsory labor, harsh as it appear[ed]," seemed wise. To Phillips's point that freedpeople were bound to their positions, Allen responded with a rhetorical question: "If I hire an Irishman for a year, has he a right to stay with me through the winter at high wages, and then go elsewhere to get still higher for the summer?" In other words, strict enforcement of contract must apply to freedpeople as well as whites; legal agreements superseded an open market. Additionally, African Americans rendered indolent by slavery had to be taught to become self-reliant workers. "This mass of needy freedmen must either be supported by charity, or work must be found for them," Allen believed. If they were to secure land, they had to achieve it through wage labor first. "Why," he asked, "should a worthless vagrant, because he is a negro, receive the gift of a farm, the value of which a hard-working farmer's son in New England would think himself fortunate to acquire in ten years?" Allen's argument carried the ideologies of free labor and equality before the law to their logical extremes. He would apply reform principles despite the situation or outcome.[32]

Other reformers also supported Banks. E. E. Hale, a political economist and social critic, noted that Banks faced uncertainty because of the parishes exempted from the proclamation. Considering these difficulties, Hale believed Banks had used his opportunities the best way he could. Though Garrison withheld open praise, he approved the assumptions on which Banks's program was based. The system constituted a temporary remedy "to adjust matters in the midst of a disorganized state of society, where masters no longer ha[d] power to enforce authority, and where the unemployed and uncoerced [were] liable to be a burden to the government, or to become vagabonds." Such comments have usually been taken to indicate that Garrison modified his stance on race as emancipation approached. Yet they also show how some abolitionists could be or could become radical about racial equality while maintaining class-based assumptions about poverty that undermined their radicalism.[33]

Several people who had worked with Banks in Louisiana also came to his defense. James Bowen, provost marshal general for a time under Banks, claimed that the regulations assumed that the able bodied were to labor for support and that restrictions were placed on both races. "Vagrancy was held to be a public misdemeanor with one race as with the other," he affirmed. Through Banks's system "the black was taught that freedom was not idleness, and that with his newly acquired right he was still subject to the inexorable law, that in the sweat of his brow he should earn bread." E. M. Wheelock, a self-proclaimed "John Brown abolitionist" who favored land confiscation, also stressed the suppression of "idleness, insolence and vagrancy." The "famous Free Labor System" intended to "supersede the lingering remnants of chattel slavery on the one hand, and on the other the idleness, misery, and vice with which the Department [of the Gulf] was filled." The Reverend Charles Hepworth, who with Wheelock helped implement the regulations, reproduced documents showing that passes were issued in cases where freedpeople had been evicted and that blacks were returned under an agreement promising fair treatment. Calling himself a "warm abolitionist," Hepworth echoed reform writers' concerns about material culture, describing the labor system as a humanitarian response to the conditions of dirt and degradation existing in the contraband camps. The system would "elevate the black man to the position of the white laborer," teaching him the value of money. It would also protect the crop and save government funds. Overall, it would prepare former slaves for freedom. While these men had a personal interest in defending the system, they all employed a set of terms that saw the former slaves first as poor people and only second as black poor people. Especially for Wheelock, truly radical ideas such as land redistribution need not preclude adherence to a conservative belief in the need for controlling vagabonds.[34]

The Louisiana labor system illustrates the mixture of racial and class ideologies that influenced the developing course of Reconstruction during the war and after. Although conciliation might have been the general motive and the general result, it was not the main determinant of the emerging labor system's content. As inheritors of the poor-law reform movement, Union officials saw suppressing vagrancy through forced labor as a perfectly normal action. They perceived emancipation as the sudden appearance of four million unemployed, unskilled agricultural laborers. This is not to argue that race did not enter their minds. Even though they claimed to be applying rules equally, they only did so in the most general sense. Still, they *did* view former slaves primarily as impoverished people, and their policies grew from that assumption. Radical abolitionists and southern planters, on the other hand, did not act from these bases. Planters, of course, saw the problem as racial control, though at times they mimicked reformers' language about the poor. Ironically, the radical abolitionists who voiced the liberal position also used a language of race, but one that posited an a priori equality between blacks and whites. More important, their laissez-faire views removed the restricting role of law. As such, they denied the prewar conception of free-labor law more than they affirmed it, and they prefigured the coming changes in civil law in the postwar North.

THE THIRTEENTH AMENDMENT

While the debates of wartime Reconstruction in Louisiana caused northerners to consider the meaning of free-labor law, so too did the debates in Congress over the Thirteenth Amendment. On the floors of the Senate and the House, congressmen struggled to find the legal definitions of free labor. For supporters of the amendment, this discussion took place within the context of free-labor ideology as it had developed in the antebellum North. Most members of Congress could agree on what a free-labor society looked like, but they had less success describing its system of law. The death of slavery forced congressmen to discuss law in two complementary ways. On the one hand, they defined free labor by trying to understand what was not slavery. On the other, they sought to conceive of what was free labor.

The experience of free labor in Louisiana had prompted widespread discussion about the role of law in free-labor society, an issue primarily confined to the courts, legislators, or reform community before the war. Similar concerns informed the simultaneous debate over the Thirteenth Amendment. As events in Louisiana unfolded in 1864, support for a constitutional amendment banning slavery grew in the North. On February 9, 1864, a petition lay on the table of the U.S. Senate. Bearing the signatures of one hundred thousand men and women, it prayed that Congress would "pass at the earliest practicable day an act emancipating all persons of African descent held in involuntary service or labor in the United States." As Senator Charles Sumner remarked, no reason was assigned for abolition. The petitioners' prayer, Sumner claimed, spoke for itself, and it asked "nothing less than universal emancipation; and this they ask directly at the hands of Congress."[35]

The amendment was debated for the first time in the spring of 1864, having been introduced by James M. Ashley of Ohio in the House and Lyman Trumbull of Illinois and John B. Henderson of Missouri in the Senate. It passed the Senate in April 1864 but failed to receive the required two-thirds majority in the House. Reintroduced in the House in January 1865, the amendment passed on January 31 after lengthy debate. Republican members of the House "instantly sprung to their feet, and regardless of parliamentary rules, applauded." The male spectators in the crowded galleries "waved their hats and cheered loud and long, while the ladies, hundreds of whom were present, rose in their seats and waved their handkerchiefs, participating in and adding to the general excitement." The Thirteenth Amendment was on its way to the states for ratification, but neither the petitioners nor the congressmen were certain about what sort of social and legal change they had wrought.[36]

In framing the Thirteenth Amendment, congressmen not only brought constitutional force to the struggle slaves had waged against slavery since the beginning of the war; they also sought to establish free-labor society and, more important, its system of labor law in the postwar South. As was the case elsewhere for Union army officers and Freedmen's Bureau officials, the Republicans in Congress who passed the Thirteenth Amendment drew heavily on free-labor ideology, but to define exactly what they were prohibiting in the amendment, they imported concepts of labor law common to the ante-bellum North. Because the amendment was framed broadly, it contained a latent potential to revolutionize labor in the North as well as in the South by overturning, or at least refining, labor law, especially laws relating to vagrancy, apprenticeship, and labor contracts. The debates over the amendment forced lawmakers to consider these ill-defined areas of northern law and consider what the end of slavery meant in a practical, legal sense. Ultimately, Republicans in Congress found themselves unwilling to face the amendment's legal implications. Consequently, inherited conceptions of free labor and labor law limited the amendment's meaning and the nature of freedom in the postwar era.[37]

As Foner has made clear, the ideology of free labor and its pronouncement of a slave power conspiracy sketched broadly what abolition meant for most Republicans, and during debate on the amendment, many congressional Republicans envisioned emancipation within this context. In analyzing the causes of the rebellion, Lyman Trumbull of Illinois, the Senate co-sponsor of the amendment, pointed to the clash between "the slaveholding aristocracy, who made the right to live by the toil of others the chief article of their faith, and the free laboring masses of the North, who believed in the right of every man to eat the bread his own hands had earned." Based on this distinction, the dignity of labor had been almost invariably touted as a right in the North. Consequently, the amendment's supporters hoped to fulfill this goal, which the Republican Party had held since its inception. James M. Ashley of Ohio, the radical manager of the bill in the House, laid out this aim clearly in his major address on the measure, describing it as "a pledge that the labor of the country" should thereafter "be unfettered and free."[38]

In 1864 and 1865, Republicans believed that their vision of a free-labor society and the political and social rights that it produced could be easily established in the postwar South. What might appear as naïveté occurred in part because antislavery discourse often imagined slavery not as a social, labor, or legal system but as a personality. While some speakers described the "Slave Power" as an aristocratic class in the South, many others reified "slavery" as a powerful motive subject in itself. Ashley employed such rhetoric in his address for reconsideration: "It has bound men and women in chains. . . . It has silenced every free pulpit within its control. . . . It has denied the masses of poor white children within its power the privilege of free schools, and made free speech and a free press impossible within its domain." The "it" in this case was the neutral person of slavery. In the Senate, Republican

Daniel Clark of New Hampshire gave slavery a gender, substituting "she" for "it" and reeling off a list of abuses similar to Ashley's.[39]

This transformation of slavery in radical discourse had significant implications, for it limited, momentarily at least, the need to establish positive safeguards against servitude's return. Because many Republicans both reified and personified slavery, they assumed that destroying the evil eradicated its effects. A basic faith in freedpeople and their ability to undertake free labor strengthened this view and united Republicans during 1864 and 1865. For example, Republican Glenni W. Scofield of Pennsylvania claimed that under the various border state abolition acts, former slaves were demonstrating their worth: "The slaves . . . are leaving their old masters, forming new associations, seeking education, earning new homes, learning self-reliance, and thus creating barriers to the revival of slavery stronger than legislation itself." Reports such as this verified Republican assumptions about what should happen when the institution of slavery was removed. In short, slavery's removal would automatically call forth the morally virtuous system of free labor. Consequently, Scofield's scenario of emancipation was no mere list. Instead, it described a progressive process in three steps. First, slaves threw off the chains of bondage; next, they became virtuous citizens through voluntary associations (contracts by implication), education, and the establishment of home and family; finally, as the outcome, they became self-reliant. Thus, black men (but not women) achieved independence, which in republican ideology allowed access to political and civil rights. In essence, Scofield's hierarchy of rights harkened back to what reformers had asserted since at least the 1830s. Work and domesticity must precede political participation.[40]

As a result, the amendment's proponents spent more time talking about the negative aspects of emancipation, those that removed laws, rather than the positive ones, those that enacted them. One part of the negative half of freedom meant the abolition of such "badges" or "incidents" of slavery as interference with marital, parental, and property relations as well as civil rights such as testifying in court. Equality before the law supplied the means to this end. Based on this precept, Charles Sumner introduced an alternative amendment that read: "All persons are equal before the law, so that no person can hold another as a slave." The first clause operated as a conditional; equality before the law by itself produced emancipation. While Sumner may have had other ends in mind (such as women's rights), slavery, not servitude or service in general, was the object being operated on in the text. Yet, while equality before the law could be revolutionary for radicals like Sumner, for others it could be conservative and carry no implication of change. Simultaneously invoking a commonplace of the northern language of poverty and garbling a passage of Scripture, Godlove S. Orth, a Republican from Indiana, declared the amendment would "leave both classes [in the South] in the hands of God who created them, and giving each equal protection under the law, bid them go forth with the scriptural injunction, 'In the sweat of the face shalt thou eat bread [*sic*].'"[41]

Harmonizing southern society with northern law by ridding it of positive support for slavery or a similar system of forced labor was a main goal of the amendment's supporters. Yet they found concrete description of this goal difficult. In part, they envisioned application of the *Somerset* doctrine, the British decision that had been the basis of abolitionist legal challenges to slavery. Freedom was national; slavery had to be supported by positive, local law. If northern laws were made national and applied equally, slavery could no longer exist. Still, if the negation of slavery through equality of law was sufficient, why did Republicans retain the "involuntary servitude" clause, a staple of antislavery language since the Northwest Ordinance?[42]

In part, the meaning of the prohibition rested on the distinctions between "slavery," "servitude," and "service." Recently elected Republican congressman John A. Kasson of Iowa outlined the basic difference between servitude and service. Speaking during House reconsideration of the measure in January 1865, Kasson quoted James Madison: "The former [*servitude*] being thought to express the condition of slaves, and the latter [*service*] the obligation of free persons." Elijah Ward, a Democrat from New York who spoke against the amendment but eventually voted for it, provided further clarification. Servitude would exist in all societies, he avowed, but "servitude rendered necessary by circumstances the servile party [could not] control, [was] bondage." In other words, compulsion, not subordination, constituted slavery. Other congressmen followed similar lines. For Union Party representative Thomas T. Davis of New York, slavery consisted in personal ownership of labor, while Radical William Kelly described slavery as a "system of unpaid labor and property in human beings."[43]

These definitions were not used clearly or consistently, but they did contain a common theme. Both Republicans and Democrats recognized slavery and "involuntary servitude" as separate from servitude or service generally. In debating emancipation, congressmen were unwilling to examine the imbalances of power in labor contract bargaining. Unequal relationships of power were acceptable as long as entered with the knowledge and consent of the unequal party. Such definitions of workers' position in free society echoed prewar comments made by conservative jurists such as Maine's Ether Shepley, who had dispensed with the concept of mutuality with ease in Almeda Harmon's 1853 labor contract case. Moreover, they followed the definitions of popular writers such as Catherine Beecher, who included the relationship of "employer and employed" within those "involving the relative duties of subordination." "Every domestic, and every artisan or laborer, after passing from parental control," Beecher had written in 1847, "can choose the employer to whom he is to accord obedience, or, if he prefers to relinquish certain advantages, he can remain without taking a subordinate place to any employer." Though compatible with northern laws and ideas, these principles of subordination were far from adequate for the needs of emancipated African Americans.[44]

Viewed another way, the Thirteenth Amendment's restrictions revolved around the connotations of "involuntary," and here drafters probably had something more specific in mind. During debate on the amendment, Republicans seldom discussed examples of "involuntary" labor. Still, outside commentators did, and the amendment's supporters must have imagined something similar. One thing that advocates of constitutional emancipation hoped to prevent was freedom on the British West Indies' model of apprenticeship. In its final report, the American Freedmen's Inquiry Commission had cautioned that emancipation could not set up apprenticeship as a halfway house between the dependence of slavery and the self-reliance of freedom. In July 1865, H. R. Brinkerhoff, a lieutenant colonel in the Fifty-second U.S. Colored Infantry, suggested that Mississippi planters intended to initiate "a system of apprenticeship, or some manner of involuntary servitude." In 1867 U.S. Supreme Court chief justice Salmon P. Chase drew from the amendment the power to strike down a Maryland law holding an African American woman in a long-term apprenticeship. More salient was the example of Mexico. German émigré and Radical Republican Carl Schurz warned of planter plots to institute peonage, as did W. B. Stickney, a Union army officer in the Bureau of Free Labor in wartime Louisiana. Treasury agent John H. Pilsbury in Charleston, South Carolina, worried that state legislation could place African Americans "in a state of actual peonage and submission to the will of the employer" and consequently "restore the former slave to, as nearly as possible, the condition of involuntary servitude." In the end, concerns about peonage pushed Congress to outlaw the practice in New Mexico in 1867.[45]

Given these definitions, the involuntary servitude clause proscribed any positive law that would interfere with the voluntary act of wage bargaining. Individual workers must be free to choose individual employers, and the parties' negotiations over remuneration and conditions of employment must be unfettered. Once a contract had been *voluntarily* entered, however, the doctrine of entirety presumed it could not be broken without penalty, no matter what conditions of labor it subsumed. Ultimately, the critical word in the phrase was not "servitude" but "involuntary."

Destruction of slavery and its incidents through equality before the law represented only one-half the policy question in the Thirteenth Amendment. The question of positive policy creation opened issues that ranged far beyond slavery or its incidents and helped to clarify the amendment even more. Democrats charged that the amendment would effect a broad social revolution. "Mere exemption from servitude is a miserable idea of freedom," declared Democrat William S. Holman of Indiana. Holman speculated that the radicals had more in mind, that they planned to gratify their "visionary fanaticism" through "the elevation of the African to the august rights of citizenship." Willard Saulsbury, a cantankerous Democrat from Delaware, spoke for many congressmen when he claimed the amendment would grant the power to interfere with marital and parental relations and with all species of property. During both debates in the House, opponents reiterated these charges. Chilton A. White, lawyer and Democrat of Ohio, took the argument to its extreme. The amendment was "a leveling principle," he proclaimed. "It is agrarian in its character, and once entered upon there is no telling when to stop."[46]

Social leveling was not the intention of the Thirteenth Amendment. Many of the resolution's supporters did not even envision it securing civil and political rights for African Americans, much less changing social relations for whites. John B. Henderson, the conservative Republican from Missouri who first introduced the resolution in the Senate, flatly denied that it offered blacks the right to vote. House Republican John F. Farnsworth of Illinois answered the charges by claiming rights rested on merit. "If, as a race, they shall prove themselves worthy [of] the elective franchise . . . they will enjoy the right," he predicted. "They will demand it and they will win it, and they ought to have it." However, to say the Thirteenth Amendment granted such a right appeared absurd to Farnsworth. "If political rights must necessarily follow from the possession of personal liberty, then all but male citizens in our country are slaves," he (rightly) pointed out. Even Kelly, a man who proclaimed freedom to be a permanent and universal institution, saw nothing new stemming from such an action. He would "trust the freed negroes to the care of God, under [the nation's] beneficent republican institutions."[47]

Although the amendment's supporters did not intend revolutionary outcomes, they did intend for legal changes to take place. With regard to labor, Radicals such as Sumner or Henry Wilson focused on equality of law and envisioned a radically free market in labor, as did many former abolitionists. For them, the ending of slavery meant establishment of the right to quit, and by implication, the nationalization of the *Britton* doctrine. Other supporters, however, followed the line of law being adopted simultaneously by army officials such as Banks. Although neither side often voiced their views about labor law openly, Senator James Harlan of Iowa in a major speech on the amendment did uncover northern assumptions about the legal side of free labor.[48]

Harlan started by asking a deceptively simple question: How does one person obtain a property right to the labor of another? In classical political economy, rights to the product of labor lay with its producer. For support, Harlan invoked the labor theory of value, noting that "the increased value of possessions growing out of labor and skill on the part of the possessor belongs to the person who has applied the labor." The key issue was how this right, or title, transferred to another. Harlan outlined two basic methods. The first involved contracts. "[Property rights in the labor of another] may be applied to the title or right of individuals to the service of another, whether claimed under an express or implied contract. That property may exist in the services of others will hardly be seriously questioned." Obligations under an express contract became void only if they lacked a consideration. Here was one kind of allowable servitude, when a laborer sold his or her rights in the marketplace. Harlan, and other senators, had no intention of striking down contract law, the basis for the northern economy.

The second basic method of acquiring service in another rested on a much older conception, mutual obligation. Harlan cited first the example of parent and child. "[The child was] under obligation to serve his father and mother until he shall have restored to them the equivalent for the labor and means they have applied to him for his welfare during the period of his inability to serve and protect himself." Confined to parent-child relationships, this principle said little about servitude, or at least about a kind likely to be challenged. However, Harlan continued, "The same principle, I think, is involved in the title of the community to the service of paupers and vagrants.

Having provided him with shelter, food, raiment and protection, the community acquires a right, a just title to the service of a pauper or the vagrant until it shall have received in return a just equivalent for the means applied for his benefit." Harlan thus connected vagrancy laws and contract doctrines.[49]

Harlan's analysis represented a frank exposition of the northern legal system's suppositions about both labor and poverty. If the laborers maintained independent status, they retained the rights of labor in full. If they bargained it away through contract, these rights transferred to another and the laborer took on a justified position of dependence and servitude to that *individual*. If laborers ignored the duty to work, they incurred an obligation to the *state*, which then had a right to their labor. The worker was again in a dependent relationship of service that elite and middle-class northerners took for granted.

How deeply embedded these ideas were in northern ideology can be seen in Harlan's summary of the outcome of emancipation. From the activities of free blacks in the North and from soldiers' reports from the South, Harlan assured himself and his fellow senators that "a vast majority" of the potential freedpeople were "capable of providing for their own wants." In other words, if freedpeople became independent laborers, they would be entitled to the rights of independent labor. If they slipped into dependent relationships, Harlan believed no new policies need be invented. "If any considerable portion of [freedpeople] would probably become paupers or vagrants, society can protect itself from danger by applying to them the same laws which are applied to paupers and vagrants in the white race." Every state in the Union, he continued, had laws that could "secure the application of the proceeds of the pauper or vagrant's labor for the promotion of his welfare or those legally dependent on him. This could not possibly occasion any shock to society, or endanger its peace or prosperity." Such assumptions ran so deeply in northern society that Harlan believed poor and vagrancy laws to be a virtual answer to all the problems of emancipation. "All will be made secure," he promised, "by applying to paupers and vagrants of African descent the same principles and laws now in force and applied in every State of the Union to paupers and vagrants of Caucasian origin."

Harlan's address went a long way toward exposing ideas about the nature of servitude in northern thought. Service to another individual was not servitude so long as it involved the voluntary obligations incurred from a contract. Service to parents or to the community as a vagrant or pauper was not a form of servitude because it also involved a forfeiture of rights and the assumption of an obligation. All of these areas assumed either a *voluntary* servitude, as in a labor contract or as in a vagrant's willful neglect of the duty to work, or a servitude based on the dependency of the child or the pauper. None constituted an *involuntary* servitude, which was what the amendment prohibited.

In republican ideology, independent labor and independent relationships formed a social basis for rights. The right to work and the right to undisturbed family relationships laid the foundation from which all other matters of society and politics must proceed. The key was the absence of a dependent state of being. Harlan pointed to the inverse of this scenario, the right to the service of another that originated in some sort of dependent relationship. The dependence of women, children, and the poor fell under this category. So too did the dependence of vagrants who, according to social thinking, refused willingly to establish necessary home and labor relationships. Finally, labor contracts for unskilled and semiskilled workers involved a voluntary surrender of independence.

Regulation of these dependent relationships by a legal system formed an integral part of free labor. In theory, free labor rested on geographic, occupational, and social mobility. Paradoxically, for the ideology to work in practice, it needed both the operation of all three types of mobility and, at the same time, the control of all three types. Laws that restricted mobility underlay Republican and northern definitions of *slavery* versus *service*. Both were systems of social control and labor discipline based in dependent relationships. The crucial difference lay in the means. Ultimately, regulation of slavery depended on physical compulsion; regulation of service rested on subtle social and cultural constructs and on racially blind laws. Free labor as it was defined by antebellum northerners could not have existed without this legal system.

All of this is not to say that the Thirteenth Amendment *should* be read a certain way. Indeed, as Lea VanderVelde has rightly pointed out, the amendment can and should be used as a constitutional basis for the expansion of worker rights. Certainly, some members of Congress envisioned this outcome. Yet as a historical interpretation, such an approach is of limited benefit, for it lifts the amendment out of its antebellum and wartime contexts. Seen in these lights, the amendment must be viewed more narrowly. Most congressmen did not intend to release workers from their contractual obligations, nor did they intend to disestablish the general societal duty to labor as expressed in vagrancy laws. If the Republicans intended any positive policy statement in 1864 and early 1865, they meant to establish free-labor society and free-labor law as the starting points for inclusion of freedpeople in the social and political institutions of the Union. These same concerns motivated Freedmen's Bureau officials, who would attempt in the months and years after passage of the Thirteenth Amendment to transform its promises into realities.[50]

The Mutation of Free-Labor Law

"The sudden emancipation of four millions of illiterate people, who had hitherto been slaves—a people without property, money, or book-learning—required some change of legislation," Texas Unionist lawyer George Washington Paschal remarked in 1867. The shock of the Civil War and the Thirteenth Amendment, he continued, distracted southern planters and "caused inventions, as to how labor should be controlled for the benefit of the old masters." These "inventions" were embodied by southern legislators in laws known collectively as the Black Codes. Enacted in 1865 and 1866, some of these statutes restricted the civil rights of freed slaves, while contract, vagrancy, apprenticeship, and enticement laws defined the conditions of their labor. Southerners protested that their laws were modeled on northern examples, but northern newspapermen and Radical Republicans soon claimed these provisions constituted a return to slavery in all but name. In 1867 Freedmen's Bureau commissioner Oliver Otis Howard declared that these laws would "occasion practical slavery."[1]

The bureau Howard headed, the first federal agency of its kind, has become central to the history of emancipation and Reconstruction. Established by Congress in March 1865 with a one-year mandate and renewed in 1866 over President Andrew Johnson's veto, the Bureau of Refugees, Freedmen, and Abandoned Lands through its state assistant commissioners, district sub-assistants, and local agents aimed to define and implement a capitalist system of labor. Scholarly evaluations of the bureau's success or failure in this mission have varied widely. Some have seen the bureau as an ineffective instrument of social change or as a tool of planter domination. Those interested in the origins of sharecropping emphasize pure market forces, compromises between freedpeople and planters, or class domination. Newer works are more sympathetic to the bureau and sometimes blame the ambiguities of free labor itself.[2]

Many of these more recent scholars see the bureau's central aim as the establishment of capitalist labor relations in the postwar South. Measured against this goal, bureau labor policy appears ambivalent at best because officials established regulations that restricted the wage bargain and the labor market. These regulations appear contradictory because they are compared with prevailing bourgeois constructions of the free-labor ethic, especially the abolitionist view that advocated the right to quit in an unfettered market. As noted, however, northern jurists had only begun to translate this idea into law before the war. Though challenged by wartime experiences in Louisiana and elsewhere, many northerners kept their faith in labor contracts and vagrancy laws. Still, the particulars of that faith varied because of the divergent constructions of work established by antebellum courts and legislatures. Bureau officials promulgated their labor codes without consistent or fixed models on which to draw. In addition, Howard headed a loose hierarchy that allowed local agents considerable discretion in carrying out general directives. As a result, the bureau's success often hinged on its numerous participants' levels of commitment to rights for former slaves and abilities to use received notions of labor law either to help or to hinder African American workers. In some places and at some times, assistant commissioners used inherited legal precepts in both traditional and creative ways to secure labor's rights. Ultimately, the success or failure of the assistant commissioners' programs rested on the ideological commitments possessed by their field agents. Even when bureau officials applied northern labor law faithfully, the vagaries of emerging labor relations in the postwar South forced them to search for solutions beyond received concepts. Yet free-labor law had left them ill prepared to do so.[3]

As with northerners during wartime Reconstruction, then, Freedmen's Bureau officials employed popular notions of free-labor law and social discourses about work and poverty. In other words, most were not practicing lawyers with direct knowledge of the juridical debates of the antebellum period. Nor did they read law books or consult judges. Nonetheless, as they used their own varied understandings of the functions of law in a free-labor society, they did act in ways consistent with the prewar controversies going on within the "law." Like their wartime counterparts, bureau officers also failed to resolve the tensions present in the prewar debates. However, their places in a centralized bureaucracy created by a national state gave them

administrative control over the immediate social reality of four million freedpeople. In turn, this power required bureau officials to implant free-labor
law into a social environment ill prepared for its reception. Such a turn of
events generated the volatile potential for change and produced a legal outcome perhaps best described as mutation. When Freedmen's Bureau officers
engrafted their own notions of northern legal principles onto the divergent
social and legal environment of the South, they often reconfigured free-labor
law into forms that retained original elements from the old law but combined
them in new ways. Still, these men followed the directions in which free-
labor law had been evolving during the antebellum period and during the
war. Some produced the liberal strain that led to a free market in labor, while
others clung closer to the old conservative stock that demanded state control.
Most generated a moderate middle variety that synthesized elements from
both sets of parents. For some at least, received principles ultimately failed
to meet social conditions, and they abandoned the project of remaking
southern labor and law in a northern image.[4]

LABOR AND THE STATE AT THE STATE LEVEL

The altered strains of free-labor law that evolved during Reconstruction appeared clearly at the state level of the Freedmen's Bureau. Indeed, the actions of state assistant commissioners, the top position in each part of the
bureaucracy, differed considerably. Theoretically, such an outcome should
not have happened, for policy directives originated in the central office of
Commissioner Howard in Washington. As noted, however, Howard did not
seek tight control over bureau policy. Moreover, as historians of the modern
state in the twentieth century have pointed out, administrators often pursue
their own agendas within larger policy directives. The dynamics of state bureaucracies explain only a part of the reason for the legal modifications undertaken by bureau officers. More important, the uneven legal legacies of
the prewar North provided multiple possibilities. So, too, did the various
strains of the received bourgeois language of poverty and work. Uncertain,
then, of what central directives meant and facing a hostile social environment, bureau officials used their own notions of free labor and free-labor
law. On this basis, "law" in any particular part of the bureau apparatus became what a particular administrator thought it was based on popular notions of labor law. Understanding the history of bureau involvement in labor
relations, consequently, requires close attention to the language in which

particular bureau officers imagined the actions they took. Viewed this way, these men become people with complex intellectual histories of their own. Their words reveal how the somewhat arcane discourse of the antebellum legal system came to influence social relations in the postbellum South.

Although historians have often charged bureau officers with helping to implement the planter program of labor repression, many of the bureau's early state commissioners followed the liberal line sketched during the war by radical abolitionists. These men tempered or rejected free-labor law and moved toward a free-labor market. One of the most obvious examples of this type was Rufus Saxton in South Carolina. Saxton fought vigorously for the rights of black workers and lost his position because of it. In doing so, he placed less emphasis on northern labor law than many of his colleagues, envisioning instead a free-labor society based on petty proprietorship. A career officer and son of a Massachusetts lawyer, Saxton had headed the Port Royal experiment with free labor during the war. When he began operations of the bureau in July 1865, he did not structure labor as many of his contemporaries did. He saw the bureau as experimental, acting with "no past experience to guide [bureau officers] in the performance of the peculiar and delicate duties which pertain[ed] to it." Saxton regarded the simple enforcement of emancipation as one of the bureau's foremost tasks. "The Freedmen should understand their status as freemen at once, and must be protected in their newly acquired rights," he wrote to the acting assistant commissioner of Georgia. "The former owner must be informed that slavery is not recognized by the U.S. Government." Beyond this notification, Saxton considered settling the freedpeople on forty-acre tracts as the key. Landholding was tantamount to citizenship and a first step toward future progress. Ideally, Saxton hoped to skip the intermediate step of wage work that the free-labor ethic envisioned and proceed directly to its end benefits, as did other radicals.[5]

When Saxton did set up a labor program, he made it as open as possible. He preferred agreements on shares split in half and advised bureau agents to make contracts that were "fair and liberal," remembering the familiar biblical (and Republican) phrase that "the laborer is worthy of his hire." After President Andrew Johnson's pardons of former Confederates made land unavailable, Saxton issued a short, simple form for "equitable contracts" that required planters to supply quarters, fuel, food, medical attention, and other necessaries and to pay monthly wages. Although he did not preach the sanctity of contract like many of his contemporaries, Saxton did counsel South Carolinians that "where fair and equitable contracts" were made, they were to be kept "by both parties." Moreover, he believed work to be the duty of all. "Bear in mind that a man who will not work should not be allowed to eat," Saxton intoned, echoing Paul the apostle. Still, his labor vision remained anchored in the free-labor ethic. "Labor is ennobling to the character," he avowed, "and if rightly directed, brings to the laborer all the luxuries and comforts of life." Freedpeople, he continued, should prove that free labor was more productive than slavery, not only for the country but for themselves. They needed to form a "plan and object in life" that would allow them to take care of the present by growing corn and potatoes while looking to the future by cultivating cash crops like cotton and rice.[6]

Throughout his short tenure as assistant commissioner, Saxton's labor program aimed to carry out a free-labor vision that tempered the harsher effects of northern law. He suggested that ten dollars per month was the lowest acceptable pay, but he refused to fix the price of labor, preferring to "leave it to seek its own value in the market." With regard to apprenticeship, the assistant commissioner reminded agents to protect the rights of orphaned blacks and that "the guardianship of these defenceless ones" was a "sacred trust." While he believed that "all well-regulated communities" discouraged vagrancy, Saxton cautioned agents to see that "no injustice [was] done to the freedmen who [were] idle from necessity and inability to find employment, and not from choice." Like other liberals, he recognized structural unemployment and refused to allow prevailing law to become oppressive: "No penalty involving the re-enslavement, even for a time, of any freedmen, will be recognized." Saxton followed this belief in daily practice as well. When Colonel J. J. Upham, an agent in Lawtonville, informed Saxton that he would arrest all freedpeople not under contract after January 1, 1866, as vagrants, the assistant commissioner suggested that he wait longer before enforcing the order. Saxton even supported the "river traders," peddlers who came up South Carolina's tidal waters to barter cheap goods with freedpeople in return for their crops. "In many cases the freedmen would probably be imposed upon by dishonest and unscrupulous men," he admitted, "but as freedmen they must be taught self-reliance."[7]

Saxton's willingness to go beyond received legal notions originated in a racial vision that placed trust in freed African Americans. He informed Howard that no danger of insurrection existed among the freedpeople: "At the slightest show of kindness they seem to forget all their past grievances. . . . If but simple justice is done to them, a more orderly, peaceful people could not be found than this same 'barbaric race.'" Even when the freedpeople learned that they would receive no land, Saxton maintained, they would "submit with the same patient resignation that they [did] to their other disappointments." While Saxton's language could be read as paternalist, he still worked in favor of freedpeople. This stance and his unwillingness to enforce Johnson's land policy placed Saxton in conflict with the president and with Howard. On October 19, 1865, Howard visited the Sea Islands of South Carolina and issued two special field orders that returned land to the former owners and enforced plantation labor. Even before then, Saxton had worried about the safety of his job, and in January 1866 he was replaced by Brevet Major General Robert K. Scott.[8]

If Saxton represented one end of a spectrum of policymaking, Joseph Barr Kiddoo in Texas symbolized the other. Kiddoo provides an example of the conservative position that had emerged during the war. Conservatives such as Kiddoo indulged the more repressive elements of northern labor law and, in effect, forged an alliance with planters to control black workers. Replacing Edgar M. Gregory, whose exit Texas planters and politicians secured in 1866, Kiddoo took over operations in Galveston on May 14, 1866. Having entered the Union army as a private, he had worked his way up to a brevet major general, receiving a spinal injury along the way. Although he inherited an office that had fought for payment of wages and other benefits for freedmen for almost a year, the new assistant commissioner displayed a greater willingness to use legal means to force freedpeople to labor. Kiddoo insisted that blacks be taught the inviolability of contracts and the need to be industrious, and he hoped to reassure planters that his office would aid both planters and freedpeople. His more conventional views on race diminished restraints about using compulsion to achieve this goal.[9]

Kiddoo toured the state soon after arriving in Texas and concluded that contracts were being violated. Freedpeople distrusted planters and remained unwilling to sign agreements. Their intransigence bothered Kiddoo, who believed firmly that the freedpeople's path to improvement lay directly through labor. Examining the contract system, he concluded that one of its central problems was that planters enticed workers to break their labor agreements. To Kiddoo, enticement was "not only dishonourable and a flagrant violation of the law of contracts, but also destructive to the energetic system of labor the bureau desire[d] to establish, and detrimental to the agricultural interests of the state." Whatever the effect of enticement on the bureau's labor system or the state's agriculture, this statement either ignored or wilfully misread the common law of labor contracts. Although an occasional case or comment appeared on the subject in English and American law, no American body of law on enticement existed in the 1860s.[10]

Nevertheless, the assistant commissioner prevented the practice. Planters who enticed laborers to break contracts with better wages or with claims that a bureau-approved contract was illegal were fined from one hundred to five hundred dollars. Bureau agents could put a lien on crops or other property to force payment. Freedpeople who allowed themselves to be enticed faced a penalty of five to twenty-five dollars. A lien could be placed on "the future wages of the freedman, garnished in the hands of the employer." This part of the order fell equally on freedpeople and planters, but Kiddoo added a section aimed squarely at African American laborers. The problem was "a prevailing disposition on the part of the freedmen to disregard, and in many instances, to violate their contracts to labor by abandoning without cause their plantations and engaging themselves to others at the critical period in the progress of the crop." To stop this behavior, Kiddoo ordered a fifty-dollar fine for any freedman who voluntarily left an employer who had done nothing to annul the contract. The fine could be collected as a lien on wages. To make his intent clear, Kiddoo reiterated the sanctity of contracts. "[Freedpeople must] maintain inviolable the provisions of so solemn a legal document as a written contract. If the employer fulfils [*sic*] his portion of the contract as to wages, rations, and treatment, the laborer must fulfil his portion as to time and labor."[11]

Though probably based mainly on exigency and the demands of planters, Kiddoo's orders revived a part of labor contract law long since dead. Though still available in England in the nineteenth century, direct penalties for enticement had not been used in the United States since the eighteenth century. In ways far more direct than many used elsewhere, Kiddoo invoked labor law nearly forgotten in the North for the purpose of assisting the planter class. During the summer of 1866 he guaranteed that these regulations were carried out. Continual rains fell in June and July, fields became clogged with grass, and Kiddoo worried again about freedpeople absconding. To secure their labor, he ordered bureau agents to explain "the justice of the [enticement] order, the nature of a contract, and the importance of fulfilling it in good faith." Kiddoo claimed this action made the planters see "that the bureau was working in their interest as well as that of the freedmen." When rain threatened the harvest, he repeated this measure.[12]

Even though Kiddoo used force against former slaves, he did make motions to aid them. Because he had more troops to back him than had his predecessor, Kiddoo prosecuted violent crime against freedpeople more actively. He also tried to make sure planters paid for the labor they received. In August 1866, he made unpaid wages a first lien on planters' crops and other property and stipulated that wages had to be paid in specie. In the fall his office directed agents to review share contracts, determine the amount of crop due, and help laborers market it. However, he qualified this order by advising agents not to interfere in "private agreements or book accounts, except in extreme cases." An agent's "legitimate duties" pertained only to written, bureau-approved contracts. Once again, the general allowed planters more leeway than freedpeople in controlling the employment relation.[13]

By the summer of 1866 Kiddoo had placed the bureau in Texas on a path that empowered planters at the expense of African American laborers. Kiddoo's conservative policies had their roots in his views about the meaning of free labor, the law, and race. Rather than a means of social mobility, Kiddoo conceived of labor as an end in itself. He intended to teach African Americans that "the highest enjoyment of their freedom [was] through the means of labor, diligence, industry, frugality and virtue." Although Kiddoo suggested that freedpeople had a better chance of acquiring land in Texas than elsewhere, he did not actively advocate landholding. He meant that getting land would keep African Americans working within the state, not that it would lead to property ownership. As a result, he did not put much effort into circulating Homestead Act information among African Americans. By keeping them working, the assistant commissioner maintained, he was helping the freedpeople, who shared a common interest with planters. "It has always and will be my policy," he wrote, "to give all the legal and moral force of the Bureau to advance rather than retard the agricultural and industrial interests of the state." He reiterated that he would do so because freedpeople's best chances lay "in the immediate channel of labor and industry." Similar to conservative reform writers such as Edward Everett, Kiddoo saw freedom *in* work, rather than *through* it.[14]

Even though he upheld equality before the law, Kiddoo took a conservative position on the use of legal compulsion. Like most people of his day, Kiddoo sustained a solid faith in the sanctity of contracts. Unlike legal writers, however, he did not even pretend to view contract as an egalitarian tool. As his use of criminal penalties suggests, Kiddoo saw contracts primarily as a means to guarantee freedpeople's faithful labor, confessing that he "found it necessary to restrain [freedpeople] by every means in [his] power from shifting from one other employer to another on flimsy pretexts." He judged that he was successfully reproducing free labor in Texas, but he reported that it had required "much exertion on the part of the planters and the Bureau to induce the freedmen to work." Nonetheless, Kiddoo did apply legal compulsion to planters, requiring them to pay wages and insisting continually that "no distinction in color be made in legislation." In other words, he saw his role and the role of law as enforcing both sides of the employment relation, while openly recognizing the power disparities it contained. Without the limiting force of egalitarian discourse, Kiddoo took extraordinary measures against both planters and laborers to attain his goals.[15]

While he believed in a rough functional equality of blacks and whites before the law, Kiddoo possessed many of the racial stereotypes of his time. To him, African Americans were "as a class, perfect children, intellectually" and were "too often restless, shiftless and suspicious of all restraint." Following the environmentalism of the mid-nineteenth century, he blamed these characteristics in part on slavery; nevertheless, he saw African Americans' destiny as fixed in agriculture. "The Free Negro, unlike the North American Indian, is agricultural in his propensities," Kiddoo declared. "He is a tiller of the soil. . . . His status as an industrial being is a decree by God, and hence irrevocable." This status did not mean Kiddoo was unwilling to protect African Americans. "I grow *sick at heart*," he wrote, "and wonder at the war power of the government leaving this unfortunate race of people whom it liberated by force to the violence of chagrined and live-long enemies." If the general's views did not hinder his duties, they did block a course toward civil and political equality. Combined with his conservative position on work and the law, Kiddoo's beliefs on race let him deny African Americans genuine freedom of choice in labor and helped clear the way for greater use of legal compulsion. Texas legislators took these suggestions to heart when they passed the Texas Black Codes.[16]

By October 1866 the Eleventh Texas Legislature had begun to act on labor and race issues. Although the general was in Washington when the laws passed, he monitored lawmakers and tried to influence their actions. He informed the sponsor of a guardianship bill that "all laws pertaining to apprenticeship, vagrancy, paupers and guardianship [were] to be recognized and enforced by the Bureau provided they [made] no distinction of color." Some legislators may have taken the assistant commissioner seriously, for an early draft of the contract law required contracts for "all common laborers." Kiddoo also recommended to Governor James W. Throckmorton that the legislature pass laws protecting African Americans from violence by lower-class whites.[17]

The laws approved in Austin tightly controlled labor and race. A contract law regulated agricultural work and gave planters wide authority to deduct from pay for offenses including sickness, abuse of animals, breakage of tools, and even indecent language. The enticement law adapted parts of Kiddoo's order and added a provision for a certificate proving contract fulfillment, mimicking the "line" required of northern textile workers. Legislators also sanctioned apprenticeship for children not supported by parents. Another law defined freedpeople's civil rights and required nondiscrimination in criminal matters. This act stipulated, however, that African Americans' civil rights did not include interracial marriage, jury duty, public office holding, voting, and testimony in cases involving whites. The vagrancy act empowered the county court, justice of the peace, mayor, and town recorders to arrest a variety of offenders. The law granted broad powers to both planters and whites in general. Warrants could be issued by a county judge, or a magistrate plus a mayor or recorder acting together. More important, the law allowed citizen's arrests: any "credible person" who filed a formal complaint could also obtain a warrant, and such citizens could serve warrants "if no peace officer [could] be conveniently procured." Convicted vagrants faced fines of ten dollars plus costs. Local authorities could regulate convict labor and compel prisoners to work for one dollar per day to pay the fine.[18]

In theory, the Texas Black Codes did not recognize distinctions of color, but these laws affected freedpeople almost exclusively. Kiddoo realized as much and tried to void the contract law. The Texas district commander, General Samuel P. Heintzelman, supported the codes and tried to remove Kiddoo while the assistant commissioner was in Washington. Kiddoo returned to take command, but he resigned in early 1867 after Congress combined the offices of district commander and assistant commissioner. The editor of the *Galveston Daily News* believed the departing general "had managed the Bureau rather satisfactorily." The editor's claim rested on a sound basis, although Kiddoo did not please all the state's planters, politicians, and publishers. Assumptions about free labor and law motivated Kiddoo, but he occupied a far more conservative position. The elements of free-labor ideology that he emphasized and especially his views on race made him tolerable to Texans and to the Texas legislature.[19]

Historians critical of the Freedmen's Bureau have often implied that assistant commissioners such as Kiddoo typified northern efforts in the postwar South, yet Kiddoo represented only one, extreme resolution to the problem of free labor and its legal system, just as Saxton exemplified the other extreme. In between lay most assistant commissioners who tried to make law for their states in ways that comported with both free-labor ideology and free-labor law. These officers tried to maintain the prewar balance between free-labor ideology and free-labor law. Yet within this moderate middle, there was also divergence, as the examples of Edgar M. Gregory in Texas, Wager Swayne in Alabama, and Robert K. Scott in South Carolina illustrate.

General Edgar M. Gregory, the first assistant commissioner for Texas, struggled to implement a radical vision of free labor, yet he did not reject its legal basis so thoroughly as Saxton had. An abolitionist, Gregory started bureau operations in Galveston in September 1865. Until he was removed in May 1866, he combined military orders and personal persuasion to generate a system of free labor. He initiated the labor contract system, issued a vagrancy ordinance, and sent troops to force planters to pay wages and refrain from violence. Throughout his service, Gregory remained genuinely committed to freedom of choice for former slaves, though he would tolerate no idleness on their part.[20]

The assistant commissioner introduced regulations for labor contracts on October 12, 1865. The freedpeople, he assured planters in this circular order, would "be enjoined to work," but they would labor under contracts entered into freely, approved by bureau agents, and breakable solely for "sufficient cause." Gregory instructed his agents to be sure the freedpeople understood their right to choose. "In all cases," he stipulated, "give the freedmen to understand that they are entirely free to contract to work where, and for whom, they please, and at the same time that a life of idleness will not be encouraged or tolerated." The lash, he declared, "must give way to law and moral power; man must learn to govern himself before he can govern others." Self-discipline plus legal restraint would bring about a free wage system. For those not swayed toward self-control, Gregory issued a vagrancy order five days later. Such regulation was needed, the general said in preface, because "many persons [had] not learned the binding force of a contract and that 'freedom' [did] not mean 'living without labor.'" The order empowered local authorities upon an employer's oath to arrest any employee missing work two consecutive days or five in one month. Local authorities could put vagrants to work on roads or other labor or turn them over to the bureau.

Like his colleagues elsewhere, Gregory was willing to combine openly the civil and criminal elements of northern law, at least at this initial stage.[21]

Orders from Galveston notwithstanding, the contract system was still not functioning in Texas by late fall 1865. Continuing rumors of a year-end land distribution and poor treatment had prompted African Americans to adopt a wait-and-see attitude. Fearing the demise of free labor in its infancy, Gregory left Galveston on November 10 to exhort the freedpeople. Traveling more than seven hundred miles into the interior, Gregory estimated he met with more than twenty-five thousand planters and freedpeople. In tiny villages, often at night in conjunction with religious services, the assistant commissioner intoned the virtues of free labor. He urged freedpeople to make contracts for the coming year and supplied them with a sample form. He suggested that they settle on a plantation, preferably near where they were born and raised, near "all their family ties and associations." To make official these suggestions, Gregory issued a circular on December 9 recommending that freedpeople enter contracts for the coming year by January 1.[22]

The effectiveness of Gregory's labor program is open to question. The assistant commissioner's reports to bureau headquarters described success. In December 1865 he sent word of the good crop produced by free labor. Like congressmen who trumpeted statistics about northern versus southern productivity, the assistant commissioner deemed free labor to be more productive. Although he admitted that in some counties forced labor still existed, Gregory believed that planters were recognizing that free labor could increase their wealth and "infuse a spirit of enterprise, industry and thrift." In January 1866 he noted that high cotton prices had stimulated the demand for labor, and freedpeople were willing to work if the bureau enforced promises made to them by the planters. Furthermore, Gregory contended, he was winning the battle against idleness. Never before had "inducements to labor" been higher. "As a result," he claimed, "in the more orderly portions of the State, theft, idleness and vagrancy have almost become things of the past." He asserted that 90 percent of the freedpeople worked under contract. I. J. W. Mintzer, the surgeon in chief for Texas, seconded Gregory. Mintzer maintained that in the small towns there was "not an idle freedman to be found." The inducements to labor had "swept all clean." Violence against freedpeople continued, but equality under the law would eventually bring peace to the state.[23]

Gregory's reports were overly optimistic, for Texas remained in turmoil.

Inspector General William E. Strong, who had visited the northern and eastern parts of Texas in November, recounted a starkly different state of affairs.
Although the cities showed improvement, Strong described "a fearful state
of things" in the interior with frequent acts of violence against the freedpeople. Planters had little faith in free labor, thinking the freedpeople "idle
and worthless" with "no dispensation to work." In the planters' eyes, blacks
were "wandering around the country utterly demoralized . . . plundering and
stealing indiscriminately from citizens." Strong disputed this description,
noting a good harvest, but he added that the planters had only paid about a
third of their laborers, those wages being disbursed over bayonet points. In
the worst areas, freedpeople were still held in slavery but without the institution's constraints on violence by whites. Probably a more accurate description of Texas in late 1865, Strong's report reveals how Gregory's assessment
was an exercise in wishful thinking. Gregory did not understate the facts; he
merely made them fit his ideology.[24]

The belief system that underlay Gregory's reports and his labor regulations
rested on his views of free labor, law, and race. Gregory's reports constantly
vaunted central tenets of the free-labor ethic. Ideally, labor sprang from an
internalized spirit of industry, a work ethic. Material incentives aided this
spirit's development, and freedpeople would respond like humans every-
where. Correctly assessing the immediate goals of many former slaves, Gregory believed they wanted social mobility through the avenue of landowning
or small proprietorships. The general hoped that eventually northern society
could be reproduced in the South. What Texas needed was "a change in the
system of industry." "The spirit that has made the great states of the Northwest [i.e., the modern Midwest] must be at work in Texas, and villages and
small farms, the steam engine and the water wheel, the school house and the
church shape its society."[25]

Law and the doctrine of contracts also formed that society. Gregory worked
hard to establish workable contracts and to make planters and freedpeople
accept them as inviolable. Law would replace pain to enforce these agreements. "The lash and corporal punishment," Gregory reported enthusias-
tically in October 1865, "are fast giving way to law and moral power in
controlling and regulating the conduct of the freedmen." He affirmed the
harmony of capital and labor through the means of voluntary association in
contracts. "[If freedpeople] settle down and enter into contracts with the
planters . . . labor is applied to capital, future want and its attending evils will
be driven from our midst, and the freedmen will become an educated and

prosperous and happy race." Gregory maintained that the bureau's only real goal was equal protection under the law, but equality of law meant application of northern laws that upheld free labor. In response to a complaint about vagrant freedpeople in Panola, the general advised: "Apply the vagrant and criminal laws of the state to blacks and whites alike, and meet out [*sic*] to each offender the stern discipline of justice." Legal compulsion was justified if applied evenly.[26]

Gregory's views on controlling the unemployed of both races through equal laws formed part of a general commitment to racial equality, at least if conceived in nineteenth-century terms. Though not thoroughly radical, the assistant commissioner's views on race were certainly advanced for his time. Although he believed blacks "particularly adapted by nature and training as a tropical race" for agriculture, he openly professed a "friendly spirit for the freedmen." Gregory stressed genuine freedom of choice in labor and deemed freedpeople capable of social and economic mobility. Moreover, he recognized the depths of white racism. "I sometimes think that long after the oppressed race shall rise into rights, duties and capacities so haughtily denied, the dominant class will not have overcome the contempt for the Negro," he wrote. "Its roots will even then exist and trouble the land." For all his paternalist preaching, he took his duty to help freedpeople seriously, and his efforts to aid African Americans brought his mission to an end.[27]

Because Gregory championed equality and used the military to force payment of wages, Texas planters and politicians engineered his removal. Complaints poured into the Galveston office, and Commissioner Howard began to investigate them. David G. Burnet, former president of the Republic, fueled the controversy in a *Galveston Daily News* article in January 1866. Burnet charged that Gregory's speeches to freedpeople were inciting rebellion. Gregory requested a rejoinder, and Burnet wrote another article in March asking for the assistant commissioner's removal. President Andrew Johnson learned of Burnet's charges, notified Howard, and Gregory was promoted into an inspector general's position on April 2, 1866.[28]

Gregory represented assistant commissioners who clung to an evangelical vision of self-ownership and self-reliance but saw free-labor law as a means to these ends. In his views of free labor, he had much in common with Saxton and other liberals, yet he was not willing to go all the way to a labor market completely unrestricted by law. Without legal training, Gregory implemented one type of a popular vision of free-labor law, one that focused on the sanctity of contracts and the general social duty of labor bequeathed by the doctrine of entire contracts and the prewar reformist vision of vagrancy. For assistant commissioners with legal training, implementing free-labor law was much more of a technical matter, as the example of Swayne in Alabama demonstrates.

Brigadier General Wager Swayne became the head of the Alabama Freedmen's Bureau in July 1865, replacing the Reverend Thomas Conway, who had overseen both Louisiana and Alabama based on his wartime tenure. The son of Supreme Court justice Noah Swayne, he grew up in Ohio, where his father had settled after leaving Virginia to escape the ideological burdens of slavery. Wager graduated from Yale, read law in Cincinnati, and entered his father's practice. Commissioned a major in the Forty-third Ohio Infantry, Swayne received a lieutenant colonelcy after the Battle of Corinth and rose to the rank of brigadier general in the Army of the Tennessee. Near the end of the war he lost his right leg after being hit by a shell. When he became assistant commissioner, he had not yet reached the age of thirty.[29]

The bureau operated under Conway's program until Swayne issued a set of labor regulations in late August 1865. They required written contracts with heads of families to provide food, quarters, medical attention, and "such further compensation" as might be agreed on. These agreements constituted a lien on the crop, not more than half of which could be marketed before payment. On the one hand, Swayne saw this program as unexceptional, suggesting that the "usual remedies" of forfeiture of wages by laborers and suits for damages against employers would suffice for contract violation. On the other, he noted, "Many persons have not yet learned the binding force of a contract and that freedom does not mean living without labor." Consequently, he stipulated that freedpeople absent from plantations without leave for longer than a whole day or an aggregate of three days within a month could be proceeded against as vagrants and set to work on the roads by local authorities. Problems arose with this system almost immediately, prompting another order two weeks later. To deal with freedpeople driven off by their employers, Swayne forced employers to take them back until other work could be found and directed that crops could not be sold until planters concluded settlements satisfactory to bureau agents. In addition, Swayne had to remind agents to prevent corporal punishment.[30]

Many of these enforcement problems originated in one of Swayne's initial acts as assistant commissioner. In early August he had designated sitting local magistrates as bureau agents who would hold power as long as they enforced the laws of Alabama without distinction of color. He justified his action by declaring himself unwilling to set up courts in Alabama "conducted by persons foreign to her citizenship and strangers to her laws." Influenced by federalism, a desire for reconciliation, and perhaps the bureau's lack of resources, this decision created problems, for it precluded the "usual remedies" on which Swayne hoped to rely. Until the legislature amended or repealed them, local officials tried to control freedpeople by using the state's vagrancy, apprenticeship, and stay laws. Finally, in November 1867 Swayne issued an order giving labor a superior lien and allowing bureau officers to take possession of crops to settle contract disputes. About a year later the Reconstruction legislature passed a similar law. In the meantime, the bureau fought to protect freedpeople's interests from the depredations of the planters without ample legal or ideological power to do so.[31]

In 1865 and early 1866 Swayne endorsed strict enforcement of labor and poor-law policies. While he warned the mayor of Selma against assessing excessive fines and assigning freedpeople to chain gangs, he assured the sub-assistant commissioner in Tuskegee that he did not object to freedpeople being set to work as vagrants as long as they were not placed on half rations. His office also stipulated that it would not enforce payments where no contract had been made unless the freedpeople had labored faithfully and had been driven off without means to survive the winter. Moreover, his office stated straightforwardly, "The Bureau assists Employers who comply with the regulations of this office by giving Civil Magistrates authority to arrest and punish Freedmen for violation of contracts."[32]

Still, Swayne did not mean enforcement of contracts in the same way that the Alabama legislature had when it passed the state's Black Codes. He secured Robert Patton's veto of vagrancy and apprenticeship provisions in the Alabama Black Codes, and his office tried to terminate repressive local curfew and pass laws and to interdict corporal punishment on plantations. His office also interfered with the detention of black families and the apprenticeship of African American children whose parents objected or who were old enough to support themselves. In one such case, Swayne told a plantation mistress that if she did not release two freedpeople's families, he would send an armed force to free them and charge her for the expense.[33]

These apparently contradictory policies originated in Swayne's peculiar formulation of free-labor ideology and its relation to the law. Having found rural freedpeople taking a "lawless holiday" when he arrived in the state, Swayne explained his labor regulations as a response to idleness, which was "extremely prevalent." Like many of his contemporaries, Swayne would not abide freedpeople dropping out of work completely. Still, he did not try to enforce plantation labor alone, and on at least one occasion he helped employers find freedpeople willing to labor on railroads. Swayne contended that his regulations did not compel anyone to contract, nor did his vagrancy order commit anyone to jail; it simply initiated investigations. His purpose, he claimed, was not to bind freedpeople to the land "but simply to be present during the hours of labor." Swayne intended to enforce work, not peonage or involuntary servitude.[34]

Ideally, Swayne hoped that the "makeshift" contract system would fade away, leaving wages and working conditions to be regulated by the market, by material conditions, and by the common law. "The true *incentives to labor* in the free States are hunger and cold," he declared. If laborers found themselves abused, they had two remedies: common-law suits for damages, or quitting. Swayne connected the "right to quit at pleasure" with the existence of money wages and found it to be the ultimate remedy. "The true *security of labor*, also, in the free States is that whenever the laborer finds himself ill treated, or his wages insufficient or unsafe, he can quit without having to account to anybody," Swayne maintained. "This is more and better than all laws." The assistant commissioner's assertion of a *right* to quit embodied a central tenet of the liberal position on free labor. Yet he could make this bold declaration only because his fears about idleness had been allayed. "I have no further fears of the wandering propensities of the negro," he assured Howard. "The removal of forced restraint was naturally followed by a jubilee; but that is now over." For Swayne, the right to quit an employer did not imply the right to quit the labor force. Moreover, he still believed that common-law penalties for forfeiture and remedies for damages would regulate this seemingly free market in labor.[35]

Combining this wider belief in a free market with his training in law, Swayne began to secure freedpeople's rights more forcefully by fall 1866, discovering a source of authority in the Civil Rights Act of 1866. As soon as news of the congressional override of President Andrew Johnson's veto reached Alabama in late April, Swayne's office tried to stop the use of the chain gang as in violation of the law. By September the general condemned the Alabama vagrancy law as operating "most iniquitously upon the freedmen": "In terms the law makes no distinction on account of color, but in practice the difference is invariable." In October he made good on his new position by ordering the subassistant commissioner in Demopolis to investigate the case of a woman "sold as a vagrant" by a justice of the peace. He directed the agent to give the woman and her husband transportation to bureau headquarters and to collect information that would convict the justice of the peace under the Civil Rights Act. In early 1867 Swayne's office again instructed the Demopolis bureau to hire local attorneys to sue a Justice Taylor for false imprisonment. The case involved two freedpeople arrested as vagrants after they had left work to be witnesses in a case of assault by a planter against one of his laborers. When a U.S. commissioner had been appointed in the area, the office was to proceed against Taylor under the Civil Rights Act. Swayne also used the Civil Rights Act to release three African American apprentices.[36]

In late 1866 and early 1867 Swayne protected freedpeople's rights by other means. His office found a contract submitted for review to be "an unjust one, if not a deliberate attempt to swindle the freedmen," and Swayne directed the agent to contact attorneys in Mobile to attach the planter's cotton "that the rights of the freedmen [might] be established." In another case, bureau headquarters nullified a contract made by a drunken freedman and noted that he had "a perfect right to contract again with whoever he please[d]." By late 1867 Swayne's office regularly authorized subassistant commissioners to set aside unjust contracts and effect an "equitable settlement" in cases in which laborers had been driven away without pay. In January 1867 the office used a ruling of the Alabama Supreme Court against itself. The court had declared that all cases coming before a justice of the peace had to be capable of appeal. Because the state's vagrancy law contained no appeal provision, Swayne's office pronounced it unconstitutional. Later that month, the assistant commissioner tried to convince the mayor of Montgomery to stop city police from threatening freedpeople with arrest as vagrants in order to compel them to contract. By February 1867 Swayne had obtained repeal of the vagrancy law, and in April he ordered, "Attempts which are still made to put it into execution will hereafter be the subject of *military cognizance*."[37]

Although he made some progress with these actions, Swayne believed the situation warranted an expansion of federal authority. To do so, he returned to the Civil Rights Act. The assistant commissioner argued the act was deficient because it allowed involuntary servitude for crime but lacked a clear definition of what constituted an illegal act. "Thus," he noted, "in Alabama to violate a labor contract, a purely civil matter for which the proper remedy is in damages at law, is punishable as a *crime*." So too was enticing away a laborer, "not rightly punishable at all." Florida, he noted, had passed a law against freedpeople teaching school, and Mississippi had forbidden them to bear arms. As a remedy, Swayne suggested amending the Civil Rights Act to make it applicable to such cases. Doing so, he believed, "not only would itself be of great benefit" but would allow future amendments "with a convenience and celerity that might match the ingenuity of wickedness upon the other side."[38]

By 1867 Swayne had moved considerably beyond the position he maintained in 1865, finding regulations his own office had established a year earlier to be detrimental. His rather tortured journey toward more forceful promotion of freedpeople's interests illustrates the limiting effect of contemporary ideas about labor, poverty, and, in his case, federalism, but it also demonstrates the creative potential inherent in free-labor law.[39]

While Swayne learned to use the common law creatively to protect worker rights, his counterpart in South Carolina, Robert Kingston Scott, ultimately came to rely on equitable remedies that by implication extended apportionment to its potential legal conclusion. Although Scott remained anchored in free-labor ideology, he did not reject free-labor law as his predecessor Saxton had done. Scott's experiments in equity resulted in part from his lack of legal training. Unlike Swayne but like Gregory, Scott drew primarily on a popular version of free-labor law.

Even before Scott took over, the labor program in South Carolina came more in line with typical northern principles under an order issued by district commander Major General Daniel E. Sickles. Born in New York City, Sickles had graduated from City University, studied law with Attorney General B. F. Battle, and gained admission to the bar, all in 1846. During the 1850s, he built a political career that culminated with his election to Congress in 1857. With the outbreak of the war, he helped raise New York's Excelsior Brigade and won fame at Gettysburg, losing a leg during the second day of fighting. Though he would later become a radical, in 1865 and 1866 Sickles occupied a stance more aligned with moderates or conservatives. He had been a friend of South Carolina governor James Orr since their days in the U.S. House. Sickles and Orr corresponded in December 1865 on the newly passed Black Code and reached an agreement about replacing it with rules that established color-blind laws.[40]

As commander of the Department of South Carolina, Sickles became involved in setting up its labor program. In December 1865 he informed the freedpeople that the government had no land to give away and that no rations would be issued to those who could work. Consequently, he directed officers to help freedpeople arrange "fair contracts to labor" while admonishing all concerned that cultivation must proceed if they were to "avoid the losses, privations, and sufferings, which must follow idleness on the one hand, and harsh and unreasonable exactions on the other." Any officer preventing or discouraging employment of the freedpeople would be arrested and punished. On January 1, 1866, Sickles issued a more comprehensive list of regulations, spelling out clearly his reasons for doing so: "to the end that civil rights and immunities may be enjoyed; that kindly relations among the inhabitants of the State may be established; that the rights and duties of the employer and the free laborer respectively be defined; that the soil may be cultivated and the system of free labor undertaken; that the owners of the estates may be secured in their possession of their lands and tenements; that persons able and willing to work may find employment, that idleness and vagrancy may be discountenanced and encouragement given to industry and thrift; and that humane provision may be made for the aged, infirm and destitute." In specific, the rules ordered equal protection of the law and equal use of testimony, opened all occupations to all races, prevented combinations to suppress wages, provided for the old and infirm, and allowed planters to evict freedpeople who refused to work or who were "rightfully dismissed or expelled for misbehavior." Establishing civil rights and immunities and protecting free labor went hand in hand with suppressing vagrancy. Sickles warned officers not to encourage idleness when dispensing relief rations and empowered them to arrest and employ vagrants on public works with the proceeds going to orphan children. Vagrancy laws of South Carolina "applicable to free white persons" would apply to former slaves, but these statutes would not be enforced on persons who were without employment, if they could prove that they had been "unable to obtain employment after diligent efforts to do so." In effect, Sickles tried to erect the northern labor and poor-law system with one military order while tempering its potentially severe effects.[41]

Scott adopted these rules as one of his first acts in setting up the bureau's labor program. Unlike Sickles, however, Scott had not been trained as a lawyer. Born in Pennsylvania in 1826, Scott was a third-generation American of Scotch-Irish descent. He went to the common schools in Pennsylvania, attended Central College of Ohio, and studied medicine at Starling Medical College. In 1850 Scott emigrated to California and engaged in real estate intrigues in Mexico and South America, returning in 1851 and settling in Ohio. For a few years he practiced medicine and then dabbled in real estate and merchandising. In 1861 Ohio governor Dennison appointed Scott a major in the Sixty-eighth Ohio, and he took part in action at Fort Donelson, Shiloh, and Corinth. He was later taken prisoner at Atlanta but was exchanged in Charleston in September 1864 and accompanied Sherman on his march through Georgia. By the time he took over the assistant commissioner's office in January 1866, he had been breveted major general. Although he expressed an aversion to politics, he resigned his command in July 1868 to become Reconstruction governor of South Carolina, gaining reelection in 1870. Surviving charges of fraudulent issue of state bonds, Scott left the governorship in 1872 to deal in real estate in South Carolina. In 1877 he returned to pursue the same occupation in Ohio, where he died in 1900.[42]

Scott came to the office of assistant commissioner in 1866 as a political moderate, and his labor policies followed the paths taken by others of that designation. He supported gradual abolition, believing it "would have educated and prepared both classes for the new regime and enabled the civil authorities to have anticipated the requirement of the new condition by appropriate and timely legislation." Yet Scott was not devoid of some advanced sentiments, for in 1867 he praised the president of the Charleston Rail Road Company for opening its cars to blacks. Still, he felt that the war had "suddenly disarranged" social, industrial, civil, and financial interests and had "induce[d] antagonism of feeling between the two classes" in the South. Moreover, Scott was a devotee of free-labor ideology. When he assessed his year's work in November 1866, he used a common standard. "That free labor is a success," he wrote, "there can be no doubt in every instance where it has been tested by practical and fair minded men, who were willing to treat the black men as laborers are treated at the north and in other parts of the country." Lacking the liberal views of Saxton and the legal training of Sickles, Scott tried to deal with what he saw as a social crisis by drawing on a vague concern for "equity" and a lay reading of northern state constitutions and laws.[43]

In February 1866 he began by issuing an elaborate form for yearly labor contracts. The sample agreement envisioned work compensated by a one-third share in the crop and performed as tasks or a ten-hour day. Not unlike the Black Codes, Scott's contract enumerated numerous rules and fines to govern plantation life. Planters could deduct for time lost as well as for injury to farm animals. In addition, planters could select a foreman from among the hands. This worker would then report "all abuses, refusals to work, and disorderly conduct of the employees" to the employer and read this list to the laborers weekly. Although these provisions practically revived rules under the slave codes, Scott did import the idea of apportionment, stipulating that discharged laborers be paid five dollars per month for the time they had worked. Moreover, contracts with specific regulations did not entirely contradict northern conceptions of free labor. After all, mill hands had worked under such tight control for decades, and northern courts had allowed employers considerable control after the wage bargain.[44]

During 1866 Scott took further measures to enforce labor. In April he republished Commissioner Howard's orders that charity must be given to extreme cases only. In a June circular letter he noted that the season when uninterrupted labor was "absolutely necessary for the salvation of the crops" had arrived and numerous freedpeople were coming to bureau headquarters with small matters that could just as easily have been brought by a representative. With such problems in view, he ordered officers to "discountenance any such proceedings on the part of the freedpeople, and enjoin upon them the necessity of steadiness of purpose" and to "advise them of the folly of litigation in trivial matters which they could settle themselves." Importing directly the concerns of northern farmers and jurists about agricultural seasonality, Scott readily approved of using the state to control the labor market if production required it.[45]

At the end of 1866 Scott considered the outcome of this system. Where free labor had failed, he believed, it was due to "unfair contracts" that provided "small recompence [sic]." Scott claimed this proved that "a contract unfair to the laborer [was] unprofitable to the planter." More important, Scott blamed the failure on both the planters' and the freedpeople's misunderstanding of proper social relations. "Mutual distrust between the planter and the laborer has also contributed, the principle that the interests of capital and labor are identical, having been ignored by both contracting parties." More problems had come from "misunderstandings concerning the requirements and stipulations of contracts." Denying his own form of a year earlier, Scott claimed that the simplest contracts were the best. Although the lack of capital might require recourse to a system of shares, Scott advised South Carolinians "to follow as nearly as practicable the labor system of the agricultural districts of the North and West paying each laborer fair compensation for his services by the day, week, or month as . . . agreed upon." In addition, fines and penalties should be abolished because they did more harm than good and were not adaptable to free labor. Fired workers should be paid in full at the time of dismissal. Among the points that Scott tried to communicate in such statements was that "justice and equity" provided a more effective form of labor discipline than did compulsion. Scott advised planters that "consideration and respect for the rights of those employed by him [would] in no way impair or detract from his own; while acts of kindness [would] endear him to them and ensure a more faithful performance of labor than [could] be obtained by acts of coercion." Although Scott understood quite clearly the eventual results of the North's legal system, he continued to search for ways to implement it.[46]

During 1867 and 1868 he issued several more orders defining the bureau's labor program. His 1867 form of contract provided for both shares and wages and removed the system of fines, though it retained deductions for time lost and provided for payment of wages upon discharge. In January 1867 Scott again ordered that no relief be granted to Sea Island freedpeople not under contract. Echoing this concern for uncontrolled relief, Scott directed officers making contracts to make sure workers received enough pay to keep them from depending on government aid after their contracts expired. In June he suggested that agents allow political meetings only in ways that would not interfere with farmwork. Harsh as these provisions were, Scott also notified planters in September that he would bring charges against those who fired freedpeople in order to deprive them of their wages.[47]

Scott's generalization from the principles of "equity" appeared in the somewhat contradictory daily operations of his office as well. In early February 1866 he directed an agent to divide the crops on a plantation by halves and, if he deemed the contract unjust, to give the whole crop to the laborers. But a few weeks later he ordered an officer to "make the 4 Freedmen who contracted with D. McCauley return to his plantation and live up to their agreement," and in March 1866 he stopped the enticement of laborers. In May 1866 the assistant commissioner allowed a black man to practice medicine, yet a month later he ordered that watermelons being grown by freedpeople among the cotton be destroyed. On many occasions Scott ordered the investigation of freedpeople discharged without cause, and more than once he directed a local agent to seize crops and property to pay laborers. Like many of his counterparts, Scott had not yet discarded the idea of a right to security. Contracts might be used to limit both employers and employees.[48]

While Scott struggled to make the contract system work, he became increasingly skeptical of it. By early 1867 he suggested to an agent, "In cases where the Freedpeople are inharmonious and, perhaps from want of knowledge and understanding, unsettled and Stubborn, prejudicial to their future welfare; all circumstances considered, where the terms of the Contract may not meet with your approval, insofar, that other inducements of many who have no capital or means to work their lands . . . you need not either approve or disapprove the contract leaving the matter open." In advising such a course, Scott was careful to note that all agreements should not "work in any manner but that of Equity between the parties."[49]

Scott's partial retreat from contract derived from his general goal of bringing "equity" to his labor program. He recognized quite clearly that a central problem of Reconstruction was the conflict "between the landowner and the laborer, the former struggling to retain absolute control, and the latter determined to maintain his newly acquired freedom to its full extent." Equity provided Scott with a solution to this conflict. In fact, he reported, he had often voided contracts approved by local agents because they were "inconsistent with justice and the principles of free labor. . . . It was evident that the contracts were made by the planter with a sole view to *their* interests, and without reference to those of the freedmen." For Scott the "principles of free labor" implied a looser construction than one derived directly from the doctrine of entirety, and he easily abandoned strict adherence to contract when called for by circumstances. He assured Governor Orr that he did not send agents to plantations "for the purpose of annuling [*sic*] equitable contracts or creating disaffection among the laborers but for the purpose of securing strict justice in the settlement of *all* contracts."[50]

FLUIDITY AND FAILURE IN THE FIELD: THE CASE OF SOUTH CAROLINA

The fluid nature of free-labor law during Reconstruction was not confined to the state level. Although some uniformity might be expected of local agents in a particular state, the case of South Carolina suggests that no such consistency appeared. Having left a relatively complete set of records, local officials in South Carolina offer a way to investigate how free-labor law and ideology interacted in the agency's daily operations. Looking at the ways in which local agents interpreted and implemented northern ideas about free labor illuminates two important themes in the history of free labor and its laws. First, their stories reveal how thoroughly the conflicted legal language of the prewar North had penetrated the consciousness of white middle-class northerners and the ways in which that language influenced Reconstruction at the ground level. Although judges, legislators, and reformers had not created a unitary set of principles for free-labor law, they had fashioned ways to think about the role of the state in establishing and maintaining a capital-ist labor market. Bureau agents' words and actions demonstrate that these imaginative constructs had not remained confined to the rarefied realms of formal legal theory and bourgeois reform. Rather, they had become part of the discourse bureau agents would use to envision emancipated labor. The nature of the bureau as a modern state apparatus required agents to trans-form imaginative constructs into lived reality. In effect, the considerable lati-tude available within the bureau hierarchy obliged bureau agents to com-plete a cycle. They now took popular conceptions about labor and the state and turned them back into regulations that had the force of law. Second and more important, their ideology helps explain in part the program and the ultimate failure of the Freedmen's Bureau. While Scott fought for equity through his office, many of his officers pursued other courses. They, too, transformed received legal concepts when they tried to apply law developed in one social setting to an environment that was quite different. In this time of social upheaval, "law" became particularly malleable.

As these field officers used popular legal discourse to make positive law, they followed the same basic lines laid out by wartime Reconstructors and by state assistant commissioners. Liberals clung to the free-labor ethic, while often remaining antagonistic to, or unaware of, the legal system. Conserva-tives often supported coercive labor discipline without any belief in or even real understanding of free-labor ideology. The moderate majority tried to combine the two, seeing legal labor discipline as one of the best ways to achieve the ultimate result of social mobility.[51]

Yet while much of the policy developed by local agents in South Carolina mirrored what occurred in assistant commissioners' offices across the South, a new and critical dynamic also appeared. In general, local agents followed general concepts of contract, vagrancy, and poor law. Often they connected these sets of rules explicitly in ways that had only been implicit in the ante-bellum North. By 1867, however, social conditions in the state led some bu-reau officers to question and then reject the central principles of the ante-bellum legacy. Along with the mutations that had already occurred, this internal breakdown of free labor contributed to the ultimate failure of both the bureau's mission and the victorious Union's ambition to build a free-labor world on the ruins of a slave-labor society. As such, this intellectual transfor-mation demonstrates how the failure of the Freedmen's Bureau resulted not only from the rejection of its program by southern whites and blacks. It also came from the inadequacy of mid-nineteenth-century poor and labor law to confront a large-scale social crisis.[52]

At one end of the ideological spectrum stood conservatives, who accepted a legal system of work discipline as normative while remaining opposed to the promises of the free-labor ethic. Often acting from racial predilections as well, conservatives saw law as a tool to help employers reestablish plantation discipline. Like one group of prewar jurists and reformers, they envisioned a way to capitalism that used a high degree of state power. For them, labor markets would remain relatively constricted, under the direct control of the state.

E. R. Chase, who was stationed in Barnwell and Aiken in the western part of the state, offers a clear example of a conservative. Instead of relying on free-labor ideology as many agents did, Chase perceived freedpeople almost exclusively in racial terms. Viewing the prevalent violence against blacks during 1866, he placed the blame on freedpeople's "insolence," theft, and neglect in fulfilling contracts. Moreover, he filled his daily records with racial references, recording faithfully planter charges of freedpeople being "saucy," "insolent," or "unruly." While most other agents usually referred to former slaves as "freedmen," "blacks," or "Negroes," Chase took down the words of a planter who alleged his hogs had been "killed by Mr. Duncan's niggers." Chase seemed especially disposed to believe in theft by freedpeople. His reports complained of "petit thefts" by blacks, and he dismissed a freedman's claim for wages after the man's employer charged him with theft. This obsession with petty theft also led Chase to invoke a series of premodern shaming punishments. He compelled a group of boys to march in front of the guardhouse wearing placards marked "thief," and he forced another detainee to stand on a barrel for six hours a day for five days and to have his head half shaved.[53]

Chase's racial ideology, in addition to making him ill disposed toward freedpeople, encouraged him to use labor law to compel plantation discipline. In a July 1866 report, Chase made it quite clear that he did not believe in a free market in labor. Freedmen, he disclosed, were "under the impression that they [were] only to make and save the crop." With the crops laid by, freedpeople believed they were "entitled to leave until harvesting to go where the[y] please and work for whom they chose." Chase attributed much of the dissatisfaction between planters and freedpeople to "this evil." For him, contracts bound workers to stay at work and to do all the work that employers expected them to do. As such, he followed the path laid down by prewar jurists, especially with regard to agricultural contracts.[54]

For Chase, the way to remedy the evil of free movement in a labor market lay in the power of the state. Chase arrested freedpeople for nonperformance of contracts in order to elicit promises "to do better in the future." He arrested and returned workers after employers claimed they had been enticed away. When planters requested it, Chase sent troops out to drive off workers for "insolence" or for being a "bad example" to other workers. In one instance, he sent a guard out to make an example of a freedwoman, threatening her with arrest and lecturing the others on the place to "be faithfull [sic] and fulfill *their contracts*." Chase imagined such actions as enforcing the concept of vagrancy. In one case, he arrested a freedman named Jim Duncan under a vagrancy charge, holding him in the guardhouse in Aiken for more than two weeks until Duncan was released "promising to do better."[55]

Chase turned the bureau into a labor police little different from the slave patrols. Although not as cruel, Chase's colleague, A. J. Willard, also used the bureau to institute the harsher side of the prewar legal legacy. Willard bemoaned the "moral condition" on the plantations and advised Saxton, "It is certain that the freedpeople have an exhorbitant [sic] idea of the amount that they ought to receive, and have no just sense of the importance of persistent labor." In November 1865 Willard issued a circular of regulations for his Georgetown district. He informed officers that "the object of visiting plantations [was] to preserve order, prevent violations of law and to assist as far as practicable in enforcing the provisions of the existing contracts and inducing the Freed people to contract for another year." Willard's "Rules Relating to Work" all intended to help owners maintain plantation discipline. Officers were instructed to tell freedpeople they could be fired if they did not work in accord with their contracts and that if they refused to obey the owner or bureau agent they could be evicted. To quell possible resistance to these harsh orders, Willard counseled officers that "care should be taken not to have too many people, at one time, removed from the plantation for disobediance [sic] of orders." Willard's "Rules as to Plantations" went even further. They required anyone remaining on a plantation at the end of the season to work or leave. While that might have seemed sensible under a strict application of trespass laws, Willard also proscribed the visiting of plantations for hunting or trading and ordered that any firearms used for hunting without permission or during work hours would be confiscated. Willard was willing to compel adherence to his rules. In December 1865 he reported blithely that "where misconduct [was] general upon a plantation," he rounded up two or three of the "leading spirits" and dealt with them on his own, "trusting the force of such an example to secure obediance [*sic*] to lawful authority on the part of the rest."[56]

A third conservative, Brevet Major Edward O'Brien, did not turn to the extreme measures followed by Willard and Chase, but he nonetheless adopted the prewar model of a legal control. Unlike Chase, however, O'Brien's ideology was not based so thoroughly in race. For example, his office rebuked a planter who had allowed the foreman on the place to act as a slave driver. "[Blacks had] equal rights with one another and they must be protected in them," the letter declared. "No white man or black has any right to abuse another." Moreover, O'Brien believed much more firmly in the bourgeois vision of commodified labor and the cash nexus, and he pictured people who did not inculcate such values as vagrants. Unfazed by the fact that African Americans in his area subsisted on green corn, pond lily beans, and alligator meat, O'Brien reported in September 1866 that the freedpeople of Christ Church Parish were (presumably as a whole) "idle, vicious vagrants whose sole idea consist[ed] in loafing without working." Being close to Charleston, these characters could obtain transportation to the city, where they became "idlers and [then] return[ed] to this parish only to plunder for the purpose of indulging their vicious practices." A month later O'Brien was no more sanguine. At first he contended that freedpeople were "naturally improvident, having no foresight," echoing the racial ideology of southern and many northern whites. Then he reverted to the method of payment and finally back to the metaphors of poverty. "I find that there is not the same amount of diligence among the freedmen when they work on shares as there is amongst those who are working for monthly wages," O'Brien wrote. "Always accustomed to look upon freedom as immunity from labor, the majority prefer to wander about hunting and fishing neglecting everything that they ought to attend to and becoming idle worthless vagrants."[57]

For O'Brien, the solution to such problems lay in law. Like Chase and Willard, O'Brien took an expansive view of contracts. In late 1866, he advised a planter to inform workers that they were "bound by their contract to perform all labor necessary for the preservation of the plantation" and that the employer could withhold their entire share in order to get them to do so. Yet, unlike Chase and Willard, O'Brien did not give planters unrestricted power. In another case at about the same time, Willard threatened to send a guard if the planter did not give workers their share of the crop. Without a violation

of the contract, he noted, workers must be paid. More important, the power
to decide such disputes had now passed to the state. "You have no authority to decide what is a violation of the contract and therefore no power to
discharge or punish," O'Brien declared. That power lay only with bureau
officials.[58]

Bureau conservatives, then, followed the side of antebellum law that had
underlain the older right to security. Some, like Chase, applied vagrancy law
strictly and revived enticement and specific performance of contracts to aid
planters and compel plantation discipline. Others acted more like O'Brien,
using law somewhat more equally. All relied at least partially on the shrill
racial and class language of the prewar period to imagine freedpeople and
free labor. Most of all, they believed in a role for the state far from the laissez-
faire views of liberals. For them, the power vested in the bureau as an agency
of the national state should decide the terms of freedpeople's labor. Willard
put the matter most bluntly by informing his agents to "instruct the people
that the government ha[d] the right to decide what work they [were] bound
to do under the contract."[59]

Conservatives, however, represented only one perspective on free-labor
law. At the other end of the spectrum were liberals, agents who relied for the
most part on the cultural ideology of free labor and abolitionist desire to
assist freedpeople. Unlike many of their colleagues, they were not overly concerned with northern labor or poor law or with reconciling it to social conditions in the Reconstruction South. Rather, they identified with the daily
problems of freedpeople and tried to find the best expedients for easing their
conditions. Consequently, they generally advocated a free market in labor
with little place for legal compulsion.

The liberal faction did not gain numerical superiority, but it did contain
two of the most prominent agents in the state, Martin R. Delany and John W.
De Forest. Stationed on Hilton Head Island, Delany was one of the few black
agents of the bureau in South Carolina. An émigré from the North, Delany
had been an editor, physician, and amateur naturalist before the war and
had assisted Saxton in raising black troops. When Delany came to Hilton
Head as a special agent of the army, he arrived with a well-developed free-
labor vision. In late 1865, he announced through a local newspaper his
"Triple Alliance" between land, capital, and labor. White southern land-
owners should make the soil available to former slaves to buy or rent, while
northerners would provide the capital necessary to establish agrarian capitalism. Delany believed freedpeople needed such a system to learn the "self-

reliance" denied to them by "the barbarism of the system under which they had lived." Productive property along with civil and political rights would turn freedpeople into contributing members of society and consequently initiate "a great market, . . . a new source of consumption of every commodity in demand in free civilized communities." Freedpeople, Delany predicted, would become "great consumers," who would purchase new houses and farm implements. They would replace their meager diets with "the luxuries, as well as the general comforts of the table," while their "osnaburgs and rags would give place to genteel apparel becoming a free and industrious people." Whether Hilton Head planters believed in this program or not, Delany used it as a way to imagine the agreements he did conclude. When a Colonel C. J. Colcock wrote to the major about contracts with workers, Delany saw the letter as a request for labor "on the basis of copartnership of capital, land, and labor, or what [he termed] the domestic triple alliance."[60]

As Delany sought to implement this bourgeois vision, his policies moved from a liberal reliance on a free market to a more radical advocacy of intervention on the side of workers. In July 1865 he urged freedpeople on the Sea Islands to refuse low-wage work and seek instead to rent land on shares. "I tell you slavery is over, and shall never return again," the major declared. Initially, he adopted a contract form with restrictions like those in Scott's 1866 model but also with protection for workers in the form of third-party settlement of disputes and a provision for workers to keep accounts to ensure "that no advantage be taken by incorrect charges." As agricultural labor became inevitable after the restoration of lands to whites, Delany attempted to ensure that freedpeople working on shares got a fair settlement for their crops. By October 1866 he had established a cotton depot where freedpeople on the islands could bring cotton to be sorted, ginned, and bagged. Delany set up this project as an experiment in black mutualism, assembling local freedpeople who had foot gins to work under one roof and be paid out of the proceeds of their labor. Delany's efforts brought a rebuking letter from Scott and a scolding: "The people must be free to sell when they think proper." After his tenure with the bureau, Delany continued to assist black workers through the South Carolina Bureau of Agricultural Statistics, a commission established by the Reconstruction legislature.[61]

Although Delany was clearly the most liberal of the South Carolina agents, John W. De Forest also pursued a liberal course. Born in Connecticut into a family descended from seventeenth-century Dutch settlers, De Forest traveled widely in Europe and the Levant before the war as part of his literary career. During the war as captain of the Twelfth Connecticut Volunteers he continued his writing, contributing articles to journals such as *Harper's Monthly*. As he later made clear in his memoir, *A Union Officer in the Reconstruction*, De Forest preferred an open labor market: "My advice was to pay weekly wages, if possible, and discharge every man as fast as he got through with his usefulness." Such sentiments echoed the wartime vision of liberals who saw emancipation as bringing commodified labor power to the South. Seeing freedom in this manner might have led men like De Forest to favor planters, and indeed, De Forest attended numerous social events at the homes of South Carolina whites, all the while recognizing his "native infamy as a Yankee." While some officers were co-opted by being feted by prominent planters, De Forest upheld freedpeople's power as free agents in the market. As the time to contract for 1867 approached, De Forest advised freedpeople to contract for monthly wages instead of shares and to emigrate to other states if such terms could not be secured. Apparently, De Forest came to the bureau completely unaware of the concept of wage forfeiture. He later labeled as a "prevalent fallacy" the idea that a farmer could "withhold all or part of the laborer's pay if he left the farm before the expiration of his contract." Out of step with older northern law but foreshadowing the coming postwar system, De Forest apparently advised planters that the only recourse for contract abandonment was a suit for damages. De Forest acknowledged that he could have "sent for the delinquent and ordered him to return to his work" but that doing so would have undermined his "main duty" in "educating the entire population around [him] to settle their differences by the civil law." [62]

De Forest's course of action suggests that his idea of what "the civil law" contained about labor varied a great deal from the ideas of many of his colleagues. He followed the liberal line emerging from *Britton* instead of the still prevalent belief in state intervention embedded in older parts of the common law. In fact, De Forest apparently took little action of any kind regarding contracts. His letter books, unlike other local records, did not record correspondence discussing contracts. Mainly, he concerned himself with the poor, seeking admission for freedpeople to local poorhouses and advocating the apprenticeship of black children under existing state laws. Although De Forest's views on poverty, both during and after the war, contained conventional class and racial language, he thought the conduct of blacks better than "the idleness, shiftlessness and begging habits of a large part of the 'low down whites.'" Not an unqualified liberal like Delany, De Forest nevertheless worked to secure the broader cultural vision of free labor for blacks without strict adherence to its legal system. In addition, he applied the language of poverty to whites in equal, if not greater, measure.[63]

Other agents not so noteworthy as Delany or De Forest also pursued a liberal course in their districts. Stationed in the Edgefield district, one of the most violent parts of the state, Brevet Brigadier General Benjamin P. Runkle described the anarchic conditions that ensued with the return of civil law and removal of the army. Local citizens, he wrote, seized the opportunity to exhibit "a spirit of utter lawlessness and to show their hatred of the institutions established among them by the Govt and to wreak their vengeance upon the freedmen for no other reason than that the fate of war has made them free." Sensitive to the dire conditions under which freedpeople lived, Runkle also realized that many of their economic problems resulted from the actions of whites who cheated them out of their share of the crops. Freedpeople "thrust out and unjustly deprived of their earnings, destitute and desperate," resorted to stealing and thus gave ground "for complaint against them." Still, Runkle did not blame freedpeople for their destitution and like De Forest refused to view them as vagrants: "There are few vagabond negroes thru the country and if the employers would do but fair justice, much of the evil would be remedied at once. After all the blame of the existing state of affairs may be equally placed at the door of their former owners who seem to be utterly ignorant of the manner in which free labor ought to be managed and treated."[64]

Runkle's comments suggested some affinity with the dominant discourse in that he still used vagrancy as a measure and saw fair treatment as a way to "manage" free labor. Yet he also took a narrower view of labor contracts than many of his fellow officers, one that pointed toward a more fully capitalist labor market. He believed that freedpeople could not be forced to do extra work, such as clearing land, not connected with cultivation in the contract year. "While I believe freedmen should be compelled to fulfill their contracts in every particular," he opined, "it would be unlawful and unjust to compel them to perform labor not contemplated by them nor provided for in the contract and which can only benefit their Employers." Like liberal jurists before the war, Runkle believed that a contract represented the sale of a definite amount of labor that must be recompensed, and when settling contract disputes, he compelled planters to pay. When four freedmen working for a William Kemble complained of being discharged without pay, Runkle warned the planter that he would arrest him or seize his property if he did not pay for all the time they had worked for him.[65]

Runkle's insistence on cash payment for a set amount of labor under a confined contract brought him in line with other liberals who had acquired a more thoroughly capitalist imagination of work. For men like De Forest, these views suggested a labor market with little state intervention. During early Reconstruction, most liberals wanted a free market in labor along with at least some protection for workers. Indeed, Delany's move toward a stronger role for the state suggested one way out of liberal discourse. Most, however, could not reconcile their belief in waged self-reliance with effective legal protection for workers. Apparently unaware of the potential right to security embedded in northern law, they tried to assist workers without the intellectual resources to do so.

While agents of the conservative or liberal stripe create the appearance of a Freedmen's Bureau that worked exclusively for planters or solely for freedpeople, their actions were not typical. Most agents in South Carolina were like Scott, moderates who mixed parts of the free-labor ethic with its legal constructs. Yet even these moderates fell into different categories. Some were more like conservatives, tempering their class and racial rhetoric only slightly. Others operated from a fairly equal balance of interest in the welfare of freedpeople and adherence to dominant ideals about free-labor law. Still others followed a more liberal line, but one that was nevertheless restricted within the language of poverty.

A good example of those who leaned toward the conservative side is J. E. Cornelius. With jurisdiction over part of the Sea Island lands, Cornelius found that freedpeople there stuck jealously to the idea that these lands were theirs under General William T. Sherman's Special Field Order No. 15, which had granted fleeing slaves abandoned lands in the low country. Cornelius complained to Scott, "They have been preached to about '*their rights*' until they are persuaded that nobody else has any rights, and until they learn better no dependence can be placed on them as laborers." Because of this, Cornelius believed, Sea Island freedpeople refused to contract, "asserting that they were now *free* and would work for no one but themselves and could not understand the relation between capital and labor." Cornelius drew from the free-labor ethic its conservative conclusion, that the proper relationship between labor and capital was class subordination and disciplined work without protest. In fact, he contended that free labor could only be a success in places where "the owner had entire management of the crop and control of the labor." While these may have been euphemisms for collusion with whites, they suggest that agents such as Cornelius perceived the labor question in the postwar South in class terms as much as in racial ones. Moreover, although Cornelius believed in strict labor discipline, he did not slide completely into the conservative camp. He did not conjure the violent imagery often employed by conservatives, and neither did he call for an unqualified application of the criminal law. If law were applied strictly, he warned, it would be "a persecution," for offenses such as adultery and theft would require punishment. In some ways, Cornelius sounded the racial tropes of the proslavery argument. Yet he did not see the behaviors he described as inherent. Rather, they resulted from "a long course of degrading servitude," and he felt certain that freedpeople were "rising rapidly above this condition but [could not] be raised at once."[66]

While Cornelius remained close to conservatives, other agents maintained a basic mixture between a free-labor vision and the use of law to promote it. Garret Nagle in Summerville sought to use contracts as a way to inculcate whites and blacks with the market values of a free-labor society. In part, that meant establishing the cash nexus. As Nagle observed planters in his district, he became increasingly irritated at their treatment of laborers. "The pestilential avarice of some of them has led them beyond the limits of ordinary cheating," he observed in November 1866. While planters feigned concern for the freedpeople, Nagle felt that their conduct bore "a direct refutation to their hypocritical pretensions." Nagle described the discharge of hands without pay at the end of the crop season as "an act of great injustice to the laborer." Yet he also lectured freedpeople about their responsibilities under contracts. Former slaves, he reported, believed contracts meant "so much work per day in the field and when the crop [was] harvested to have their share." Unable to embrace this liberal position, Nagle explained to freedpeople that "if they failed in the performance of their agreement, it would be unjust to compel the planter to fulfill his with them." Nevertheless, Nagle worked to teach planters and former slaves the meaning of commodified labor. Like liberals, he believed contracts obligated workers to labor only on the growing crop. Consequently, he advised a group of freedmen "to keep a strict account of their time they [were] employed on work not legitimately connected with the crop" so they could "charge" it against their employer.[67]

Similar to bureau liberals, then, Nagle had moved toward a capitalist conception of labor, but like conservatives, he saw a considerable role for law in establishing such a labor market. When a planter complained that his hands were not working properly, Nagle threatened to annul the contract and have the workers arrested and evicted. In another case, he arrested a freedperson for "non-fulfillment of contract," openly combining the entirety concept of the common law with the vagrancy concept of the criminal law to reinvoke legal enforcement of specific performance. Additionally, he upheld discharges for workers who "did not work agreeable to contract" and for displaying "insubordinate conduct," and he allowed planters to deduct for "lost time." While these actions might make Nagle appear as a conservative, he used law equally against planters. In one case, he threatened a planter with arrest for the "injustice and outrage" of dismissing a worker without pay. In another, he brought charges against a planter for refusing to take a worker back. In general, he reported that he had pointed out to the planters "the injustice of discharging their hands" without cause and "intimidated" them to take workers back.[68]

While Nagle steered a position in the middle, several moderate agents took a more liberal path. George A. Williams, a native New Yorker and career soldier, combined a desire to achieve equity and fairness in labor settlements with concerns about the influence of vagrants. Williams presents a complex case. He clearly supported free labor but at the same time thought measures should be taken to punish voluntary unemployment. Williams came to such positions because he believed "labor must be controlled by the same laws that regulate[d] it at the North, before any permanent advance [could] be secured." Although he was probably referring to the "laws" of the market as well in this remark, Williams saw the enforcement of vagrancy laws as one of the means through which labor was "controlled" and progress "secured." Moreover, while Williams decried the freedpeople's "ignorance of the common duties of citizens," he also warned that if the government withdrew protection from the freedpeople, "their condition in a short time, would be much worse than under the old system of slavery." Free labor could be made "a perfect success," he argued, if "the Government retained sufficient authority . . . to restrain the disposition on the part of many whites to reduce the blacks to a condition as near that of slavery as possible."[69]

Part of that government authority, for Williams, concerned unemployment. When the prospects for a crop under free labor looked dim in the fall of 1866, Williams put the problem down to a mix of freedpeople's migration, the weather, the system of shares instead of wages, and unscrupulous planters who took advantage of freedpeople. But he placed much of the blame on "the influence of a large vagrant class, who, having no other idea connected with the word Freedom than that of immunity from labor, refused to contract with anyone, squatted upon deserted rice plantations and in the woods, and spend their time hunting, fishing and stealing from both Whites and Blacks." At the close of the year Williams recommended measures "to prevent the gathering of idle vagrant hands on the deserted plantations in Colleton District, as they [were] a source of terror to the citizens, and being without means of subsistence, live[d] by depredation of the surrounding country." In 1867 Williams continued to complain about unemployed people gathering in Charleston and refusing to go to work in the country. Later that year, partly at the urging of Scott, he refused all aid to able-bodied workers. In trying to explain the failings of free labor, Williams utilized familiar imagery, but he also exhibited sensitivity to the exigencies facing freed slaves. In the same report in which he condemned "idle vagrants," Williams sounded a note of class analysis in regard to the operation of the law. In his district, the civil law was "merely a source of power and oppression in the hands of the wealthy few, it being in this state an expensive luxury." He concluded, "There is no justice for poor whites or freedmen."[70]

As Williams's application of northern poor-law principles exhibited considerable fluidity and some affinity with a more liberal position, so, too, did his views on contracts. Unlike liberals such as De Forest who sponsored migration by freedpeople, Williams decried emigration plans that had "tended to excite a restlessness among the people." To prevent widespread labor market movement, he enforced enticement by holding anyone "inducing hands to leave the party with whom they ha[d] contracted" liable for losses sustained by contract abandonment. Even as Williams restricted the labor market with this order in early 1867, he appears to have been losing faith in contracts as he issued it. At about the same time, he reported that many freedpeople in his district signed contracts under which they "rented" lands in exchange for two days' labor per week. In such cases, he ordered officers to refuse approving such agreements, notifying the parties that "in case of difficulty" they would divide the crop by thirds.[71]

Another agent who followed such lines of thinking was the Prussian-born Frederick W. Liedtke. Starting the war as a private in the Ninety-seventh Pennsylvania Infantry in August 1862, Liedtke rose to the rank of captain by March 1865. More than many other agents, Liedtke strove to implement the principles of antebellum poor laws he had apparently imbibed in his adopted home. In order that old and infirm freedpeople might contribute to their own support, he put them to work at handicrafts, making baskets, ax handles, and horse collars. When freedpeople contracted to work in groups and some of the parties refused to perform, Liedtke punished them with extra work on plantations because they "impair[ed] the interests of the others." However, Liedtke's hatred of idleness was relatively color-blind. While he reported the presence of "many idle and worthless people" among the freedpeople, he also accepted that they were "like the white population." Reviewing the destitution in his district, he stressed the existence of "a very low class of white people, male and female," who had "intermixed with Negroes and Indians and who themselves as well as their offspring [were] so unwilling to work that charity expended to them would be the very inducement to make them lazy." Because of them, he recommended that no aid be given to anyone who had not contracted to do "reasonable work." In his district, he contended, there was "plenty of work for everyone willing to earn his bread honestly." Liedtke put these ideas into action as well, arresting freedpeople for "repeated breach of contract and theft" and compelling them to work on the public roads or perform hard labor at his headquarters. By doing so, Liedtke did not revive specific performance as such but rather invoked the prevailing bourgeois notion that the paternalist state could establish a social duty to work.[72]

Holding firmly to the principles of mid-nineteenth-century poor relief, Liedtke nevertheless tried to protect the wages of those freedpeople who did labor under contracts. In one case, he ordered a planter to allow a worker to remain after an "unjust dismissal." He arrested a planter for "refusing to make a contract" and another for "breach of contract," ordering him to turn over half the crop to his workers. Throughout early 1867, his complaint registers recorded case after case of using the power of his office to force divisions of the crop. Moreover, Liedtke took the liberal position regarding the meaning of contracts, rejecting the idea that freedpeople had signed on to anything a planter wanted. When a Dr. Dwight complained about a freedman who refused to perform work not stipulated in a contract, Liedtke informed him that he must pay more for extra labor. When the planter tried to convince the officer that "plantation" meant land and all work connected to it, Liedtke informed him that "plantation" merely signified land under cultivation and that no amount of land could make one man wiser than another. Dwight grew agitated at these remarks, and Liedtke threw him out of the office. Based on this incident, Liedtke explicitly rejected entirety and suggested an order forbidding the dismissal of freedpeople for absence without leave except in "aggravated instances." It was "unjust to take from any freed-man his whole year's work, for absence without leave for three days." Such an order would "frustrate the designs of some evil disposed men whose hearts [were] set 'to keep the nigger down.'" Bringing these ideals into prac-tice, Liedtke sponsored the case of Cuffy Glover, who had a claim of more than one hundred dollars against his employer, Nathan Guyton. The case eventually resulted in an order from Scott that confiscated property to rec-ompense Glover for his time worked.[73]

Like Williams, Liedtke combined the concepts of poor relief with a con-cern for laborers. In addition, he sounded one of the shibboleths of the cul-tural free-labor ethic. In the winter of 1865–66 Liedtke visited plantations in his district around Moncks Corner, "explained to the freedpeople their position as free men, and . . . endeavored to impress upon their minds, that by honest, industrious and peaceable labor they would gradually become able to buy homes for themselves and become good citizens." Such state-ments presented the assembled freedpeople with an exact precis of the ar-guments of more prominent northerners about the genius of their society. For people like Liedtke, this formula produced individual upward mobility and general social progress. But similar to his counterparts in the North, Liedtke believed the general social ethic worked best when wedded to law.[74]

Although moderates such as Williams and Liedtke stayed fairly firm in their commitment to free-labor ideology and its laws, others began to go be-yond it. Either in their administration of poor relief or in their operation of the contract system, they began to diverge from received concepts. One of these officers was Daniel T. Corbin, one of the few agents who entered Re-publican politics in South Carolina. By as early as April 1866, Corbin found it "difficult to see how the contracts [were] to be lived up to and great suffer-ing avoided" in cases in which planters could not supply provisions. In such cases, he reported, he "found it necessary to inform owners . . . that if they could not advance provisions, their laborers could not, and would not be required to fulfill the contract." Believing that free labor depended on pro-viding adequately for workers, Corbin became increasingly disenchanted with the prospects of the system as planters organized in 1867 to depress wages and freedpeople responded by refusing to contract. He decided that when "so much an organized antagonism between capital and labor existed it was considered best to allow the opposing elements to work out their own salvation, or at least to attempt it." In reaching such a position, Corbin drew on the free-labor ethic's prescriptive principle of the mutual interest of employers and laborers. But in the face of "organized" opposition to free labor's legal system, Corbin was willing to open the wage bargain and its results to the market. In other words, Corbin followed free-labor ideology to a rejection of the contract constituents of its legal system.[75]

James Durell Greene of Massachusetts followed it to an alteration of its vagrancy elements. Greene complained on more than one occasion about the problem of vagrancy in his district. In October 1866 he tried to explain its prevalence in terms that combined both the ideological and legal components of free labor. "A difference of opinion in regard to the contract system" had arisen between planters and freedpeople, he observed. Planters refused to bind themselves to contracts from "a want of confidence in the freed-people," and freedpeople avoided contracts because they were "under the impression that justice could not be done there by the employer." Greene then tied this legal conflict over labor directly to the problem of poverty. Such conflicts "encouraged idleness, vagrancy, and theft, and [were] the main cause of half the destitution" in his district. By 1867, however, Greene had begun to realize that poverty might arise from sources other than conflicts over contracts. He reported that destitute blacks and whites included "those who [were] industrious and those who [were] exerting themselves to their utmost to raise their crops." In the growing famine of the summer of 1867, many people of both races were forced to leave growing crops to search for wage work. In the face of these conditions, Greene pleaded to go beyond regulations that denied aid to able-bodied persons in order "to relieve temporarily the wants of the working class."[76]

Greene and Corbin stretched the edges of mid-nineteenth-century discourse about labor and poverty. Ironically, they both used class analysis to undermine and go beyond received bourgeois notions. A final moderate, G. E. Pingree, tried to do the same despite doubts about approaching new ideological territory. Pingree perhaps best exemplifies the complicated position of moderates who tried to combine adherence to free-labor ideology and law in the face of social conditions radically different from the ones in which those concepts were grounded. Stationed at Darlington, Pingree came to the bureau with typical bourgeois sentiments about work. In May 1867, for example, he instructed freedman Ford Parker, "The harder you work, the larger crop you will make and the more money you will have at the end of the year." In addition to these conventional words about hard work, Pingree possessed typical views on charity and relief. Reporting on rations issued to impoverished whites, he noted that he endeavored "to discriminate justly and to issue rations" to those only who were "really destitute and worthy."[77]

As he tried to issue policy directives based on these notions, he drew on a number of the available elements of free-labor law. Invoking directly the language of northern vagrancy laws, Pingree blamed a wave of thefts on "ignorant 'Poor Whites'" who were "lying about with no intention of working and with no visible means of support." To remedy the problem, he recommended a law for "the arrest of vagrants both black and white." In addition to urging vagrancy laws, Pingree enforced contracts strictly against both sides, drawing on the general notions embedded in the antebellum concept of entirety and in the prewar law regarding discharges. He used the army's power to return freedmen who had left their employers and, at the same time, forced planters to take back workers they had driven off. He upheld discharges of workers he believed "lazy and insolent" or guilty of "general worthlessness," while he compelled planters who discharged workers without cause to pay for the time worked. Like many other agents, his complaint books recorded many orders sent to force a division of the crops. "Wrote to Haselden," he jotted down in early 1868, "ordering him to settle at once, or take the consequences."[78]

Although Pingree attempted to use free-labor law throughout his tenure, like some other moderates he began to reject received ideas. As he wrestled with prevailing notions about free labor and its laws, he adjusted his thinking to the social realities of emancipation South Carolina. In the spring of 1867 he noted that freedpeople were leaving verbal agreements "often without cause" but that he refused to send them back without written contracts. When planters fired laborers, Pingree compelled them to take them back, and if they had worked more than six months, he disallowed such discharges "unless it ha[d] been proved by black witnesses that the laborer [was] insolent and unworthy." In such cases, Pingree apportioned the contract, making planters pay six dollars a month for the time worked. Although that was a low rate of wages, that Pingree allowed compensation at all to workers he deemed "insolent and unworthy" was out of step with his colleagues and with northern common-law requirements for entirety.[79]

Pingree struggled as well when he tried to apply poor-law concepts. As food shortages increased in 1867, Pingree became more and more distressed about the prospect of widespread relief to the able bodied. "In issuing rations this year I have fed many who are able bodied," he disclosed, "but only because they had neither money or credit, their crops would have been aban-

doned without help, and I believed it to be better to assist them in making a
crop that they might not be objects of Charity next year. There is no doubt
that I have been swindled in issuing in spite of all my efforts to prevent it,
and idleness and lazyness [sic] has been the result[;] the people here have
no pride in the matter, and will beg rather than work." When faced with
massive human need, Pingree managed to go beyond the discourse of poverty in action but continued to justify his actions within its language.[80]

Pingree's confusion and its causes can be illustrated by a complicated case
he handled in the fall of 1867. The dispute involved three freedmen, George,
Henry, and Armstead Terry, who worked for J. S. Coker. Sometime in late
October, the three freedmen appeared in Pingree's office and reported having been fired by Coker for attending a Union League meeting. Henry Terry
considered it "his duty according to [his] Oath" to attend the meeting.
George Terry explained the matter in a more veiled manner, saying he had
recently been in prison, his wife had nothing to eat, and the meeting had
been a church gathering. At least George Terry appears to have wanted his
job back, for he told Pingree that he did not know Coker would "prevent
a man from going to church"; he added, "And as my family is perishing I
thought it would be best for me to stay and gather the crop." Coker claimed
he fired the men not for actually attending the meeting but for not seeking
his consent. Coker testified that he had told George Terry that he "did not
think any society had the right to take them away from the work they had
contracted to do on that farm, that they could attend the society on their
own time, or when the business would not suffer by their absence." He requested that Pingree provide someone "to compel the performance of their
duties."[81]

Pingree's record of the case indicates that he felt overwhelmed by the conflicting views of free labor that lay embedded in the dispute between Coker
and the Terrys. The Terrys had come to Pingree to see if they could be fired
for attending the meeting. Originally, Pingree marked the case "charge not
sustained," but he then added, "Coker was ordered to retain the Terry freedmen on his place by Gen'l Scott." When Pingree transferred the case file to
Scott's office, he appeared noticeably irritated. Coker, he believed, had been
"wronged in the matter." His hands had been "angry and malignant" since
the Terrys were fired and had "conspired together to cause Mr. Coker all the
trouble" they could. Reflecting on the case, Pingree cast it as a dispute over
the legal rights of free laborers. "It rests with the Asst. Commr.," he concluded, "to announce whether laborers have a right to leave the plantations

of their employers whenever they see fit, without regard to whether their services are indispensable on the plantation."[82]

In raising questions about the right to leave, Pingree probably meant only whether workers could be absent during working hours and then return, but the quandaries created by disputes like the Terry case pointed to larger questions about the role of free labor and the law. By focusing on the right to leave, Pingree had found the heart of conflict over free labor in the Reconstruction South. Pingree and his colleagues had come South at a time when the rights available to workers under labor contracts were in flux. As a result, bureau officers could draw on numerous popular notions about the role of labor law in a capitalist society. Like many agents, Pingree tried to implement free-labor law as he knew it. However, the social conditions onto which such men grafted northern ideology denied them success. Many experienced considerable intellectual dissonance when faced with a situation such as the liberal De Forest recounted when describing white poverty. After castigating poor whites for their "low down" condition, De Forest had to admit that the war had caused "much honest and worthy suffering" among them. De Forest's comments betrayed the grinding poverty that by 1867 had forced at least some South Carolina agents to doubt the capability of their intellectual and legal system to deal with the social and economic conflicts of freedpeople and planters. This doubt suggests that blacks and whites did indeed work out their own arrangements, but that development occurred in part after bureau officials began to lose faith in prewar northern conceptions of labor, poverty, and law.[83]

In the end, the tenure of the Freedmen's Bureau exposed both the power of free-labor law to shape emancipation and the internal elements that led to its ultimate failure. If applied with enough force by assistant commissioners such as Gregory or Wager Swayne or by liberal local agents, labor law could do more than oppress. Even if used ambiguously, as it was by moderate local representatives or top officials such as Robert Scott in South Carolina, legal control of labor might afford some positive benefit to African American workers through the enforcement of equitable principles of contract or, more important, through the right to security embedded in entirety. In the hands of officers such as Kiddoo or conservative bureau subassistant commissioners, labor regulations became little more than a powerful mechanism of planter domination. The actions of this final group presaged what would happen in the Redeemed South, when states enforced draconian contract, vagrancy, enticement, and convict labor laws. They also prefigured one-half of the synthesis that free-labor law would reach in the postbellum North as the power of the state to enforce a general duty to work expanded. By 1880 the vagrancy laws of the Freedmen's Bureau would look mild by comparison. The other half of that synthesis came from liberals, who believed in an almost unqualified right to quit. Although not numerous in the bureau, they, too, foreshadowed what would happen in the Reconstruction of the North.[84]

None of these groups, however, had resolved the confused strains of free-labor law by the time Freedmen's Bureau operations wound down in 1868. In fact, their failure to resolve northern labor law's internal contradictions helps explain why the bureau could not implement a coherent labor program in the emancipation South. Northerners could not agree if the state should even have a role, much less what that role should be. Their inability to construct a legal system of free labor arose because northern law itself contained competing principles on which to draw. Their failure also occurred because they tried to apply a body of law from a market society increasingly embedded in bourgeois values to a social and legal structure decidedly more agrarian. Yet, even as northern whites fumbled with competing versions of free-labor law, southerners, both white and black, followed their own agendas, helping to shape the postwar legal system.

Southern Reactions and Reformulations

In April 1865 the Reverend Thomas W. Conway, superintendent of freedmen in the Union army's Department of the Gulf, assumed authority over Alabama as interim Freedmen's Bureau assistant commissioner for the state. In May he adopted a set of labor regulations he had drafted for Louisiana under the authority of Major General Stephen Hurlbut. Conway considered these regulations essential to establishing order and assisting the freedpeople. He noted that when he arrived in Montgomery he found "a perfect reign of idleness on the part of the negroes." Conway blamed this state of affairs on planter violence, which "chill[ed] and dishearten[ed] the freedmen." He assured the planters that "the freedmen must work" but warned that they "not be persecuted and murdered" because they were free. While Conway found fault with planters, Charles W. Buckley, Conway's assistant in Montgomery and later head of the bureau's educational program in the state, was more worried by former slaves themselves. Speaking with men from the city's African American churches, Buckley informed them that "they were *not* free to be insolent, to be idle, to pilfer, to steal, or do anything contrary to good order. They were free to come under the *restraints of law*; free to toil and claim the fruits of their own industry." He preached the binding nature of contracts and the need to seek employment. Reporting these sermons to Conway, he assured himself that black leaders had "received it all with joy" and that his discourse had quieted the city, cleared the streets of idlers, and created "mutual confidence" between planters and freedpeople. Just to be sure, Buckley sent armed guards to plantations to secure order and diminish vagrancy.[1]

Conway and Buckley represent, again, the divergent ways in which northerners imagined labor law in the emancipation South, but their perspectives also suggest that legal change depended on how southerners, black and white, received northern principles. As the experience in South Carolina showed, the northerners who carried antebellum principles southward encountered a legal and social milieu quite unlike the one they left behind. In turn, the southerners who formed that social world found themselves confronted with a legal system that was put in place before the social relations of free labor had crystallized into established patterns. As a result, planters, free blacks, and freedpeople reacted to northern labor law differently. Planters aimed to maintain class, racial, and labor control; middle-class blacks looked for ways to help black workers but simultaneously maintain the language of northern bourgeois culture; and African American workers strove for control over the legal conditions of their own labor and that of their children. In short, none of the southern recipients of free-labor law accepted it totally, nor did any reject it completely. Along with the internal change and decay in free-labor law, this southern resistance and alteration ended the northern project in the South.

PLANTER RESISTANCE AND ACCOMMODATION

One point often forgotten in investigations of northern policy during Reconstruction is that seemingly restrictive Union army and Freedmen's Bureau policies aimed to control planters as much as they did former slaves. As emancipation proceeded, planters sought to control black workers as much as possible. In doing so, they sometimes sought to maintain the legal system that Old South lawmakers had produced for nonslave workers, one that undermined the right to security and curtailed the right to quit while establishing vagrancy as an offense against personal and class honor punishable by forced labor. Yet they also took up elements in northern discourse that proved serviceable for establishing labor, class, and racial control.

The most daunting obstacle to the implementation of free-labor law in the postbellum South came from planters' desires for labor control. In part, planters embodied this goal in informal arrangements to control the movements and power of workers in local labor markets. Although the planter attempts to control labor varied somewhat from state to state, the experience in Alabama represents a typical planter response to free labor.[2]

In the summer of 1865, whites in Alabama acted as if slavery still existed and took numerous informal measures to restore labor discipline. Whites whipped refractory laborers and terrorized African American communities in organized raids by local "militia." Near Tuskegee, bands of white men dressed in women's clothing or in blackface and intimidated African Americans, young and old, men and women. In part this violence was intended for racial control as an end in itself. But in some parts of the state, armed bands of whites in 1865 and 1866 used violence to force freedpeople to sign labor contracts. At least one freedman was shot for refusing. Other planters formed unions to control both laborers and other employers. Some made agreements that forbade offering work to African American laborers found more than ten miles from their former masters. In Tuscaloosa County, planters agreed to pay freedpeople no more than one-eighth of the net proceeds from the crop. When a local planter offered his hands one-sixth, the combination, or union of planters, formed a committee that coerced him and his employees to accept their agreement.[3]

Still employing these extralegal measures, Alabama whites also turned to legal coercion in late 1865. As during wartime, planters sought direct legal intervention in the labor market and hoped to use law to enforce specific performance. Passed in December 1865 and February 1866, the Alabama Black Codes created new laws governing vagrancy, enticement of labor, and apprenticeship. Although these acts were color-blind, the motive of labor coercion was unmistakable. The vagrancy law established a system of poorhouses, but its text made it clear that these were not to be benevolent institutions. The legislature sanctioned chain gangs, stocks, solitary confinement, and "such reasonable confinement as a parent may inflict on a stubborn refractory child." A vagrant was defined as "a stubborn or refractory servant; [and] a laborer or servant who loiters away his time, or refuses to comply with any contract for any term of service without just cause." Such persons could be fined fifty dollars and sentenced to the house of correction for up to six months, but that was not the law's primary object. In lieu of this sentence, offenders could be hired out for cash, the sale to be announced with three days' notice and the proceeds to go into the county treasury for support of the helpless in the poorhouse. Vagrancy arrests would thus control reluctant adults; the apprenticeship law would supervise their children. It allowed the apprenticeship of orphans and, more important, children who judges of the probate court determined could not be supported by their parents. While the law included nominal requirements for education, it gave enormous powers to masters. They could inflict corporal punishment, carry their wards to other states, and capture runaway servants, who would then be punished as vagrants if they refused to return. In addition, the law gave preference to former masters when making indentures. Finally, to regulate stubborn planters, the state enticement law made hiring a laborer under contract to another master punishable by fines of fifty to five hundred dollars.[4]

While similar in name to some northern laws and bureau regulations, the Alabama Black Codes enforced labor even more directly than their southern predecessors. Vagrants were not members of an undifferentiated underclass in general but individual plantation workers who refused to accede to plantation discipline. The laws did not coerce a general duty to labor. Instead, they reinstituted compulsory performance of contracts, the very legal principle that Jesse Holman had rejected in Mary Clark's case and that most northerners had abandoned in the first two decades of the century. The hopes the planter class placed in these particular statutes came abruptly to an end when Alabama governor Robert Patton vetoed the bills and the legislature failed to override him. However, the antebellum vagrancy law remained in effect, and Alabama whites used it to procure convict laborers until it was repealed by the legislature in 1867.[5]

Though they retained hope for a new slave code, Alabama planters slowly accommodated to the contract system then being implemented by the Freedmen's Bureau. In the fall of 1865, before their attempt at legislation, planters expressed a desire either for indentures that would bind laborers for two to three years or for no contracts whatsoever, which would free them to dismiss laborers at will. When they were forced to adjust to bureau policies, one recourse was to secure restrictive contracts. In the Eufala area in 1867 planters obtained various agreements that required freedpeople to pay for all lost stock, half the land tax, $12.50 per year for use of mules, and three to four times the values of work time lost. Near Huntsville, planters engineered an ingenious double-lease arrangement whereby freedpeople paid rent to a sublessor who then refused to pay rent to the owner, after which the owner attached the freedmen's crop to cover his "loss." As late as 1868, contracts in the Demopolis area contained clauses stipulating forfeiture of wages for disobedience.[6]

Although these sorts of agreements intended to bind labor to the plantation, planters took the opposite action even more frequently, violating their agreements with African American laborers. In 1865, 1866, and 1867, planters commonly drove laborers from their plantations when the heavy work of summer hoeing was done. On a Talladega plantation, freedpeople were driven off for going to town to celebrate Independence Day. In early 1868, planters across Alabama discharged laborers who voted in state elections.

Dismissing laborers might seem to contradict the desire for labor control, but as one bureau agent reported, planters could hire women and children at harvest time at lower wages. When freedpeople sought redress for unjust discharges, planters sometimes disregarded orders to appear for settlement.[7]

MIDDLE-CLASS BLACKS AND AMBIVALENT CRITICISM

While planters such as those in Alabama sought to resist or manipulate northern law, black leaders in the South occupied a much more ambivalent position. They did not, as Charles Buckley hoped, receive Freedmen's Bureau programs "with joy," yet neither did they reject them completely. In fact, the responses of African Americans to free-labor law were just as complex as the ones taken by white northerners and southerners. From the beginning of emancipation, African Americans steadily resisted the pressures for labor discipline contained in the Black Codes. Perhaps more important, former slaves and free blacks discovered ways to turn existing law to their own benefit and to make labor legislation more amenable to their needs. Elite and middle-class blacks who were within this general framework of resistance sometimes reverted, however, to the dominant cultural discourse about law and work. They voiced sentiments compatible with those held by moderate and conservative commentators in both parts of the country and sometimes admitted a desire for legal control of freedpeople's labor.[8]

One of the clearest and most constant African American voices on post-emancipation labor law came from the South's tiny freeborn elite. No organ communicated this viewpoint more effectively than the *New Orleans Tribune*, the leading black newspaper of the city and the South. Initiated in Union-occupied Louisiana in 1864, the *Tribune* was primarily the work of three men, Dr. Louis Charles Roudanez and Paul Trévigne, members of Louisiana's prewar freeborn elite, and Jean-Charles Houzeau, a Belgian émigré. The *Tribune*, which published in both French and English, drew on European radical thinkers and political economists. It developed a philosophy of labor that diverged significantly from the free-labor ethic and from free-labor law. Throughout the evolution of federal labor policy in Louisiana under Major General Nathaniel P. Banks and subsequent Union officials, the editors of the *Tribune* carried on a dialogue with Union policymakers and fought an emerging labor system that they saw as a poor replacement for slavery. "Slavery is dead," they noted in April 1865, "but 'free labor' still lives and has yet to be killed." By criticizing federal policy, the editors of the

Tribune helped define the meaning of freedom and offered alternatives to both the free-labor ethic and free-labor law. Yet at crucial points, their ideology remained within the bounds of mid-nineteenth-century thinking.[9]

In general, the *Tribune* objected to federal policy because it represented guardianship for former slaves. Analyzing the Treasury Department's short-lived labor program in December 1864, the editors commended its more liberal elements but lamented the planners' lack of consultation with freedpeople. Reviewing a report from the wartime Bureau of Free Labor two months later, the paper argued that the government had given the freedpeople "protectors, a special code, special rules, and special obligations." When Major General Stephen Hurlbut's labor orders appeared in March 1865, the editors of the *Tribune* published them with "a deep sentiment of sorrow," claiming that the Bureau of Free Labor was "now pushing [their] brethren into a disguised servitude." The editors organized former slaves, free blacks, and white radicals in protest, and at a mass meeting at Economy Hall on March 17, 1865, they adopted a series of resolutions denouncing the new policy. James Ingraham, a black captain in the Corps d'Afrique, denounced Hurlbut's labor regulations as a halfway measure between slavery and freedom. "No system of gradual elevation is required to make us men," he declaimed.[10]

Although the free black elite rejected guardianship, its position on protection was complex. The *Tribune* constantly advocated removing all restrictions on labor. "Let the laborer alone!" Houzeau exclaimed in April 1865. "We denounce every plan calculated to keep him from moving about, in order to compel him to work for low wages." Yet the editor also called for federal intervention as the only way to secure the rights of labor and blacks generally. Rejecting Hurlbut's suggestion that a slow learning process could cure racism, the paper averred that prejudice had never been rooted out by education: "All injustices against races, classes, or sets of individuals had to be removed by the strong arm of power."[11]

Two more specific labor policies often drew the paper's attention: vagrancy orders and labor contract regulations. When put into practice, Banks's doctrinaire adherence to vagrancy concepts resulted in arbitrary arrests. The *Tribune* decried summary detention of unemployed workers. But, unlike some northern antislavery radicals, it did not oppose the general concept of vagrancy laws. Houzeau and Roudanez merely wanted equal application to both races. "A good law on vagrancy, equally applicable to the whole population, giving power to set to work the man who has no honest means of existence," Houzeau wrote, "will effectively protect the general interests of society." Yet for both free blacks and white radicals, a "good law on vagrancy" meant something different than it did for federal officials. For the men at the *Tribune*, idleness constituted a punishable vice only when it was "habitual and voluntary." Unlike most mid-nineteenth-century political economists, Houzeau recognized the existence of structural unemployment. "It is the very nature of trade," he noted, "that men be sometimes unoccupied and have to pass from one shop to another and to look for employment elsewhere." Thus, the *Tribune* again retained some aspects of the free-labor ethic while rejecting others. Vagrancy itself could be voluntary, but to be punishable it had to indicate a pattern of outright refusal to work, for at times employment might be beyond the control of the laborer.[12]

Adopting an increasingly radical position, New Orleans's free blacks rejected northern versions of freedom completely with regard to the inviolability of labor contracts. In response to Hurlbut in March 1865, the paper submitted, "Liberty of contracts is the essence of industry and the characteristic of freedom. Permit our brethren to try themselves that way." With action on contract law pending in the Louisiana legislature by late 1865, the paper claimed that through contracts, planters "intended . . . to renew a servitude or bondage." Freedpeople, the editors counseled, should agree only to short-term contracts because the only way to "escape the injustice and exactions of a bad master, [was] to remain free to leave the plantation and go elsewhere." Later, the paper recommended the outright rejection of contracts.[13]

Similar to sentiments voiced by other liberals, the *Tribune*'s position on contracts originated in its desire for a free-labor market. The paper criticized fixed wage rates and demanded the removal of government from wage bargaining. It cautioned planters that they must negotiate fairly with freedpeople, who knew that they could do better as casual laborers on the New Orleans Levee. When a labor shortage developed in the fall of 1865, the editors advised freedpeople to take advantage of their power and work only for good employers. If allowed to do so without government interference, they would receive justice. "As soon as [the freedpeople] will be permitted to freely discuss, with their employers, the terms of the agreement of contract," Houzeau predicted, "they will obtain . . . just remuneration for their labor, according to the natural law of supply and demand." Drawing explicitly on European political economists, the paper argued in 1867 that laborers must be free to leave their employers at any time and look for better wages elsewhere.[14]

Though facing glaring power disparities in Reconstruction Louisiana, the liberals at the *Tribune* retained an extremely laissez-faire conception of the labor market. Yet they did not mean to leave laborers entirely unprotected. Houzeau, Roudanez, and Trévigne advanced several novel approaches to the challenge of achieving justice for former slaves. Some of the paper's most significant departures from dominant conceptions of labor law came in its suggestions for legal remedies to labor disputes. In the fall of 1864, the paper identified the central problem of labor contract law: who would judge whether the terms of a contract had been fulfilled. If planters were allowed to do so, Houzeau pointed out, "every bad man [would] be empowered to bring the laborers to his own terms, irrespective of any right of contract clauses." Consequently, the paper suggested creating courts of arbitration based on the French *counseils de prud'hommes*. These labor courts would consist of a government-appointed chair and two representatives each from employers and employees. They would adjudicate disputes over labor agreements by use of both contract law and equity. In arguing for such an institution, the *Tribune* explicitly rejected the free-labor ethic's belief in the harmony of capital and labor. The editors declared that these courts had been instituted in places "where capital had taken sway over labor and had to be safely counterpoised" and that they would protect "the rights of labor against the invading propensities of moneyed men." Protesters who met at Economy Hall in March 1865 suggested such a system to Hurlbut, but he rejected it out of hand as impractical. The *Tribune* continued until 1867, however, to advocate special labor courts as the best means of protection.[15]

Then, no longer sanguine about their adoption, the paper advanced a new idea: free legal counsel in Louisiana. Charging that the planters had co-opted most agents of the Freedmen's Bureau, the editors claimed that the civil courts remained out of reach to freedpeople because of the cost of attorneys. If a laborer tried to pursue his case, he would be "crushed at once, on account of his ignorance of the law, by his opponent's lawyer." The paper also claimed that northern states such as Pennsylvania had lowered fees so poor mechanics could gain access. The editors did not want the state to lower fees in this manner, but they did believe lawmakers in the upcoming constitutional convention should establish a system of free counsel. "Injustice should not triumph because a man is poor," the editors declared. These suggestions contradicted the paper's adherence to a completely free labor market. By 1867, the editors had begun to realize that to remedy power discrepancies, government intervention was needed, as they had believed it was in general civil rights for some time.[16]

Over time, members of Louisiana's established free black elite spoke for the African American community in numerous ways. In forswearing contracts and in their calls for establishing labor courts, they advocated radical departures from northern conceptions of free labor and legal labor discipline. Yet they could not escape their position in the economic elite. They held most firmly to the principles of free-labor law when discussing vagrancy and the general duty to toil for support. Moreover, whether they spoke of a radically open labor market or special courts to protect freedpeople's interests, the goal remained self-reliance. Their positions illuminate the power of the legal assumptions of free labor, even on individuals trying to leave them behind.

The inability to escape received language about law and labor was not confined to the editors of the *Tribune*. Elite and middle-class African Americans meeting in conventions in the postwar period also voiced commonly accepted ideas about work and poverty. In its 1865 preamble, the National Equal Rights League proposed litigation to protect the rights of African Americans, but it also pledged to "encourage sound morality, education, temperance, frugality, industry, and to promote every thing that pertains to a well-ordered and dignified life." In an address to the convention, William Nesbit, one of its vice presidents, called on the league to cultivate "industry, frugality, and sobriety" and "domestic virtues." In 1865 members of a committee appointed by a Virginia convention of African Americans suggested that the nation should take some responsibility for alleviating the poverty of those who so recently answered its call for defenders, but they also assured their listeners, "The colored man knows that freedom means freedom to labor, and to enjoy its fruits." To those who claimed that freedpeople would not work, the committee responded that "fair wages and fair treatment [would] not fail to secure" labor. In addition to recommending savings and acquisition of land, the business committee of a North Carolina meeting advised freedpeople to refrain from coming to town. The committee suggested that freedpeople instead seek "employment at fair wages, in various branches of industry" and that they educate themselves and their children "in a high moral energy, self-respect, and in a virtuous, Christian, and dignified life." One of the most striking uses of the dominant discourse on labor and poverty came from a black convention that met in Baltimore, Maryland, in January 1866. Along with the usual suggestions about virtue, dignity, and industry, the convention issued an "advisory address" to freedpeople that asked them "to use [e]very exertion to contradict the predictions of [their] enemies, which were uttered previous to the emancipation of the States, that if the slaves were freed they would become a pest to society and paupers dependent on public charities." A Georgia meeting in 1866 added to the voices demanding "fair and impartial enforcement of contracts." Yet in an address to the state legislature, the conventioneers accepted the claim that freedpeople had fled their homes to "lounge"—a word commonly applied to vagrants—in the state's towns, entertaining "false ideas" about the advantages to be gained there. No need to worry, the letter continued: these wanderers would soon "become a little tempered to freedom," and already thousands were returning to their former masters or taking new homes and preparing to cultivate Georgia's red clay in the upcoming season.[17]

Although conventioneers often mouthed the words of conservatives from both the North and South, they also advocated equal rights and fair treatment for African American workers. The Virginia committee decried the growth of planter combinations that prevented free choice of employers, the violent detention of workers who tried to leave plantations, the widespread refusal to pay wages to freedmen who faithfully fulfilled their contracts, and the grant of power to county courts to apprentice children as the courts saw fit. The committee encouraged black workers to form "Labor Associations" to oppose planter unions. These organizations would strive for fair wages, set up an employment bureau, and seek enforcement of all contracts made with black workers. In 1865 a Tennessee meeting resolved to form committees that would seek just compensation and fair treatment of workers. A group in Arkansas meeting the same year acknowledged that black people would continue cultivating cotton in the state but insisted that Arkansas "deal justly and equitably with her laborers." In 1869 a national convention urged Congress to provide homes for homeless black people, and the Reverend Charles H. Thompson proposed a National Freedmen's Mutual Aid Company to help former slaves defrauded by their employers. Almost all black conventions, it should be noted, sought equality of law and suffrage as the ultimate guarantors of black rights.[18]

The conflicting positions maintained by the *Tribune* and by African American conventions also appeared at the local level in the wake of emancipation. While trying to maintain dominant standards about homelessness and poverty, the African American community in southern towns attempted to establish autonomous institutions to deal with jobless freedpeople. In Mobile, Alabama, a freedpeople's association established schools and churches and helped the unemployed find jobs. In September 1865, however, a committee of African Americans in the city helped the Freedmen's Bureau clear Mobile's streets of about sixty idle freedpeople by supplying them as workers for a railroad project. These actions expressed a concern for order on the part of some African Americans, but other organizations lobbied bureau agents to relieve freedpeople forced into harsh labor arrangements. In Selma, a group of African Americans who were "well-settled in business" complained to the bureau about local officials who arrested freedpeople for using abusive language, badgered them into pleading guilty, and put them on chain gangs when they could not pay the one-hundred-dollar fine. In Louisiana, New Orleans's black community drafted a "Prospectus for a Farming Association" and made it available to freedpeople at the city's Third African Church. The prospectus called for families to farm together in "associations" or collectives. While the formal proposal for these associations embodied a spirit of mutualism contrary to the free-labor ethic and the *Tribune*'s laissez-faire position, it also contained the assumptions of free-labor society about work discipline. "All persons going to work on this plan must agree not to abandon it until the expiration of the year," the document stipulated. "Any one party failing to do his just proportion of work shall be deducted in his share of the crop, and any member who is idle and will not work shall be expelled and reported to the authorities as a vagrant." [19]

AFRICAN AMERICAN WORKERS AND DIRECT ACTION

While middle-class blacks clung to many received notions, African American workers had few such pretensions. Instead, they fought for the right to security and for the right to control their own families' labor. As elite and middle-class spokespeople struggled with the tensions of inherited language, African American workers and their allies challenged labor law directly in the fields and in the courts. Focusing special attention on apprenticeship, they were remarkably successful in resisting the harsher powers of law and in shaping the legal contours of labor in the early postemancipation South.

As numerous historians have argued, former slaves sought autonomy from planter control above all else. Some former slaves fought planter power by seeking opportunities for land. Across the South in late 1865, individual freedpeople refused to contract for 1866 in the hope that the U.S. government would grant land as it had promised. African Americans also took collective action to acquire land and autonomy. For example, Horace King, a master mechanic from Russell County, Alabama, organized a settlement company for emigration to Georgia. His group planned to take subscriptions, obtain land, improve it, and divide it among heads of families. Apart from seeking independence through land, African American laborers resisted planter control in several ways. Some resistance came on the plantation, reminiscent of the sort of quiet defiance practiced by slaves. African American men kept their wives from field work, precipitating conflicts with planters unwilling to support nonproducing freedpeople. Other freedpeople asserted their power to control work rhythms and the amount of work performed.[20]

Freedpeople also engaged in collective labor actions. At contract time in every year from 1866 to 1868, freedpeople in some parts of Alabama participated in informal "strikes" against planters. In 1866 African American labor in Lowndes County held out against a local planter combination and eventually pushed up the wage level. African American workers in the Eufala area informed planters in 1867 that they must have higher wages or larger shares or they would not work. A year later, freedpeople in several areas of the state withheld their labor in the hope that elections would usher in a new government more amenable to their interests.[21]

Organized labor resistance was relatively rare, however; many African American laborers simply left their jobs to work for other employers or quit the labor market altogether. In Alabama, for example, a relatively small proportion of freedpeople actually abandoned contracts, for bureau agents often reported that few violations had occurred. However, numerous freedpeople found new employers at the beginning of 1866, asserting their separation from old masters. Even after they signed new agreements, some freedpeople refused to stay on plantations when they faced abuse or when they could achieve better living conditions elsewhere. Although many freedpeople accepted the contract system in 1866 and 1867, by 1868 disaffection became widespread. Frustrated with their inability to collect wages, many African American workers refused to contract. Economic hardship eventually forced most back to plantations, but in 1868, as in previous years, large groups of freedpeople withdrew from the labor force. Some lived under brush arbors in the countryside, some subsisted on garden plots, and others resorted to stealing and killing farmers' livestock. Although the bureau ventured to find steady employment for freedpeople, many continued to congregate in towns as casual laborers.[22]

Working conditions were not the only reason for abandonment of legal labor discipline. Reacting to the bureau's program, at least some African American workers openly rejected the time rhythms of market discipline, as did their counterparts in the northern working class. For example, freed-people in coastal South Carolina usually completed assigned tasks by early morning and took the rest of the day off, as they had done under the task system in slavery. While these actions continued work rhythms inherited from the antebellum period, A. J. Willard, a South Carolina bureau agent, relayed a more telling example, one that demonstrated the clash of industrial and agricultural work rhythms that, in part, underlay the labor conflict. A sawmill owner who had contracted for twenty-five dollars per month plus rations came to Willard to resolve a dispute. The two workers in question, "very intelligent and good laborers" in Willard's opinion, claimed an hour off between 8 and 9 A.M. for breakfast and another between 12 and 1 P.M. for lunch. Trying to resolve the situation, Willard explained to them that "labor-ers at the North got less wages and worked from sunrise to sunset, this season of the year, only having an hour at noon." The workers' answer was, "'We want to work just as we have always worked.'" Looking back at this incident, Willard confessed that "the two parties of the contract [were] so widely sepa-rated in their ideas on this subject as to offer little encouragement than an early solution [would] be arrived at." Willard was a staunch conservative, so his comments must be taken with caution; but this incident does illustrate how freedpeople in the early emancipation period often preferred agricul-tural work rhythms to those proffered by the bureau.[23]

All these nonlegal forms of opposition to planter control set the stage for resistance in the courts, where African American workers won their most important victories during the Reconstruction period. Neither the abroga-tion of the Black Codes nor even the coming of Republican governments ended the planter's desire to control labor. As a result, black workers fought hard during Reconstruction to establish the most basic of the labor rights. Using the Freedmen's Bureau, they sought fair enforcement of contracts and payment of wages. Seeking to maintain custodial rights over their children, they took their cases to the courts at the local, state, and, on one occasion, federal levels. African American workers often won these suits, and in doing so they actively shaped the legal outcome of emancipation.

At the local level, the Freedmen's Bureau was one of the most common forums of redress. According to an Alabama bureau official, freedpeople filed "thousands" of complaints about unfair contracts in early 1866. Another common action involved settlements for wages at the end of the contract year. The Freedmen's Court for one district in north-central North Carolina was deluged with such claims in late 1865 and early 1866. Captain Benjamin Evans reported having heard 46 cases in Franklin County, 187 in Warren, and 410 in Granville County in January and February 1866. At least in this district, freedpeople secured some compensation for their labor during all of 1865. Evans usually made planters grant either one-fourth of the crop or cash payments from ten to forty dollars; he occasionally instituted in-kind settlements in corn or winter clothes, usually for children. A third common suit involved freedpeople who had been fired. From the fall of 1867 through the summer of 1868, for example, various bureau agents in Montgomery, Alabama, heard twenty to thirty unjust discharge cases per month. The disposition of such cases depended almost completely on the inclinations of local agents. Some agents denied compensation altogether, some apportioned the contract, and others set a prevailing monthly wage.[24]

Release from apprenticeship might have been the most common legal action undertaken by African Americans. Here again the bureau became a first forum for redress. Black workers carried hundreds of cases to the bureau, often achieving at least some success. In Alabama, freedpeople plied the office of Assistant Commissioner Wager Swayne with requests to recover their children. Even though Swayne had returned the civil courts to local control, his office often answered these requests by dissolving apprenticeships, first under the authority of the bureau and later under the 1866 Civil Rights Act. Although some entreaties ended successfully, others did not. Swayne upheld some indentures, as did commissioners in other states.[25]

Before a state supreme court ruling curtailed apprenticeship in North Carolina, a freedman named Daniel Bagley used a slightly different tactic in Freedmen's Court to resist being indentured. To command Bagley's labor until he reached the age of twenty-one, his employer, Benjamin M. Richardson, had secured an apprenticeship. When Bagley tried to leave, Richardson tied him to a chair and beat him repeatedly with a leather strap, all the while trying to get Bagley to agree to stay until the apprenticeship was up. After Bagley had left the farm once and then returned only to face renewed violence, the bureau intervened and brought assault charges against Richardson. Richardson's defense rested on the claim that he was not trying to force the apprenticeship on Bagley. In response, Bagley argued that if a person whipped a table, told it to say something, then repeated the process over and over again, it would surely look like that person was trying to get the table to say what the person doing the whipping had said. The court accepted this argument in its opinion and passed a verdict that included five hundred dollars in damages for Bagley. Bagley's suit illustrates the ways in which freedpeople used legal remedies against whites who wanted to control their labor. The fact that the court explicitly accepted his reasoning as a basis for its decision also suggests the formative role that African Americans sometimes played in the emerging labor law of the postwar South.[26]

Although the bureau and its courts offered freedpeople some relief, in most states local tribunals recovered their powers relatively quickly. As a result, black families who hoped to break indentures encountered numerous obstacles. First, they faced the daunting task of litigating in unfriendly arenas. Local pressures for labor discipline and racial control, many bureau agents and freedpeople learned, could overcome the best intentions. In addition, as the *Tribune* had pointed out, litigation was a difficult undertaking for freedpeople without resources for counsel. And even if they obtained an attorney, the legal grounds for suits were weak. Judges could rely on the long line of antebellum acts codified in states' revised statutes or on the language of the Black Codes, especially after pressure from federal authorities made the laws color-blind. Moreover, a body of antebellum case law, both northern and southern, affirmed the power of local courts to bind out as apprentices the children of the poor, be they black or white.

But the greatest obstacle might have come from the nature of legal emancipation and the ways in which it prevented constitutional challenges to apprenticeship and other forms of oppressive labor law. The constitutional fruits of slaves' struggle for freedom, the Thirteenth Amendment and the various state constitutions abolishing slavery, proved to be weak sources of power to oppose the laws that followed the destruction of slavery. By failing to define clearly the involuntary servitude clause, Republicans left the door open for courts to narrow the power of the amendment to slavery alone.

Events in the Union slave state of Maryland confirmed Republicans' fears even before the amendment had acquired approval by the number of states needed for ratification. In October 1865 the Maryland Supreme Court considered the appeal of Adeline Brown, an Anne Arundel County planter convicted of enticing apprentice George Brown to run away from Lancelot Warfield Jr., his master. Sentenced to pay a fine and serve time in the county jail, Adeline Brown based her appeal on the Declaration of Rights in the 1864

Maryland constitution, which prevented "special laws" and, more important, outlawed involuntary servitude. Apprenticeship, Edward Gantt argued for Brown, "ignore[d] the essentials of a common law contract, and sanction[ed] 'involuntary servitude' contrary to the [state] constitution."[27]

Gantt, however, was in a shaky position. The state's attorneys, William Schley and William S. Waters, quickly pointed out that because the state code contained a similar law for white apprentices, no "special law" existed. Furthermore, they maintained, the Maryland Declaration of Rights used language substantially identical to that of both the Northwest Ordinance and the antislavery constitutions of northern states. "In all the Northern and Northwestern States, and in England, all the features claimed objectionable in the negro apprentice system in this state prevail," they argued. "Indeed, the most of them prevail in the white apprentice system of this State."[28]

The Maryland law authorized binding black people to whites but not the opposite. Cheerfully ignoring the fact that the law treated blacks and whites differently, the court accepted the state's argument and engaged in an extended discussion about the distinctions between slavery, involuntary servitude, and apprenticeship. It also addressed the merits of indenturing. Maryland law, Justice Daniel Weisel wrote for the court, had always considered slaves and free negroes as two distinct groups. Neither black nor white apprentices had been considered slaves. Weisel then attempted to distinguish apprenticeship from involuntary servitude, but his explanation was unclear and had little coherence. In the Northwest Ordinance and other manifestations, involuntary servitude had traditionally embraced not only slavery but "all other modes of servitude imposed upon white and black, against the will" of either the servant or the master. Weisel argued that the traditional exception for criminal convictions explained the meaning of involuntary servitude: punishment through hard labor was involuntary servitude, and it would be prohibited for all but the exception. Relatively unsuccessful with logic, Weisel turned to social utility. Parents had a right to the labor of their children and could bind them out. But often children became either orphans or "in such a condition by reason of the 'indigence of the parent, or his vagrant or dissolute character, or other circumstances.'" In such cases, the legislature could act for the good of society and the children and bind them to masters who would raise them in the "habits of industry," educate them, and prepare them for citizenship. The laws of England and the northern states allowed these actions, and so long as any living parents were consulted, such laws could not "be regarded as imposing involuntary servitude."[29]

Although no evidence exists that Weisel's opinion influenced later decisions, he and the state's attorneys had summarized the hurdles facing constitutional challenges to apprenticeship and other harsh labor laws. For several decades, northerners and northern courts had approved of statutes and common-law rules not unlike those contained in the South's Black Codes. Such laws clouded the meaning of the involuntary servitude clauses in both the Thirteenth Amendment and state constitutions and rendered them almost useless as tools for litigation. Since Congress envisioned the Civil Rights Act of 1866 as enabling legislation for the Thirteenth Amendment, this law labored under the same disabilities. As Wager Swayne had pointed out, the act was deficient because it allowed involuntary servitude for crime but lacked a clear definition of what constituted an illegal act.[30]

Lacking a solid constitutional basis, legal challenges to apprenticeship became a matter of arguing about the specifics of the statute or obtaining a writ of habeas corpus to secure the release of apprentices held illegally. Such litigation often required the court to consider a complex set of relationships between former slaves, their former owners, and the families of each. As both Barbara Fields and Richard Fuke have argued for Maryland, apprenticeship disputes involved both labor control and family conflicts. This characterization is borne out for the rest of the South in the cases that reached state supreme courts between 1864 and 1868.[31]

Basically, apprenticeship litigation represented disputes between planters and freedpeople over the control of African American child labor. In many instances, former owners kidnapped the children of their former slaves, dragged them before local authorities, and had them bound. In early 1866, for example, Frances G. Jones of Russell County, Alabama, seized twelve children from two different families and presented them to probate judge James F. Waddell. One couple failed to satisfy the court of its "ability to support and provide" for its children; the other, Nathan and Jenney Cox, refused to appear. Both families found their children bound to Jones, the girls until sixteen and the boys until twenty-one. In Mississippi, the sheriff of Copiah County used the 1865 apprenticeship law to report a freedman named Jack as an orphan under eighteen years of age. Upon this act, the county probate judge, M. H. Peyton, bound Jack to his former owner, Jesse Thompson, until he reached twenty-one with compensation set annually but paid at the end of the term.[32]

Many actions of this kind involved not only the use of law but its abuse as well. In Copiah County, the sheriff might have misrepresented Jack's age, claiming he was under eighteen when actually he was nineteen. Although the Coxes' appeal did not state the specifics, they, too, believed their children had been "procured by fraud and misrepresentation." The most striking example of trickery comes from a case slightly later. In July 1870, Milly Cutts was working at fifty cents a day for W. A. Hatcher in Calhoun County, Georgia. Apparently Hatcher did not find this arrangement advantageous enough. When her former master, a man also named Cutts from nearby Sumter County, obtained a warrant that charged Milly Cutts with stealing six hundred dollars, Hatcher saw an opening. When the sheriff came to haul Milly Cutts to jail, Cutts asked Hatcher if he would care for the children in her absence. He agreed but asked her to sign a document he had obtained from the ordinary of Calhoun County. Milly Cutts, unable to read or write, then unknowingly affixed her mark to an indenture, which Hatcher promptly returned to the ordinary. Hatcher claimed Cutts could not care for her children because she was in jail. Believing that Hatcher had obtained the consent of Milly Cutts as the law required, the court official approved the apprenticeship.[33]

Although the desire to control labor motivated the establishment of most apprenticeships, the family relationships that had developed because of slavery made the conflicts more complex. In several cases, apprenticed children appear to have been living as parts of extended families, staying with grandparents, uncles, or aunts. In other cases, the children lived with one or both of their parents, but kinship ties had been complicated in some manner. While bound as a slave in Georgia, for instance, Jacob Comas married a woman owned by a neighbor. The marriage produced five children, including a boy named Henry. Comas then abandoned Henry's mother for another wife, Henry's mother died, and Henry was transferred to Isaiah Reddish. Henry stayed with Reddish until September 1865, when he went to live with his father in Appling County. By claiming deceitfully that Henry had no parent living in the county, Reddish then received an indenture for Henry from the ordinary of Appling County, who had jurisdiction in such cases.[34]

The family relationships involved in Samuel Adams's attempt to recover custody of his children, Tucker, Francis, and Zachariah, were even more elaborate. Enslaved in Baker County, Georgia, Adams married a woman on the nearby Thomas Pearson plantation. He visited his wife on most Saturday nights but at the same time cohabited with the mother of the children in question, who was also a slave of Adams's owner, William H. Adams. After Tucker and Francis were born, their mother married a man named Taylor, who subsequently died. While married to Taylor, she continued to sleep with Adams. Then, Samuel Adams's "real wife" was sold out of the region, and he wed a woman named Frances, living with her until she gave birth to a mulatto child. Samuel Adams then abandoned Frances and married his children's mother, having three more children by her.[35]

During the last marriage, the family stayed with William Adams after emancipation. By claiming that Samuel Adams was not their legal father and that he had disowned them, William Adams "frequently" tried to wrest control of the children from their parents. In the summer of 1866, the children's mother died, and William Adams took control of the three youngest. In December Samuel Adams moved his remaining family to Robert A. Dykes's place, where Adams hired out the three older children to Dykes for $120, plus their board and clothing. William Adams might have evicted Samuel Adams and his children; he claimed that in late 1866 Samuel Adams had been "running about in violation of his contract." In early February 1867, William Adams obtained an indenture for the three older children by stating they were orphans. He then kidnapped them from their father.[36]

The apprenticeships detailed in these narratives might have occurred in any case, but the broken nature of these families certainly gave prospective "masters" an opportunity. And as Samuel Adams's hiring out of his children suggests, family reconstitution merged with a desire on the part of freedpeople to pool resources in the family economy. Given such motives, some former slaves sought to use labor law to reclaim children from former spouses and to secure legal arrangements that would provide security for the proceeds of children's work.[37]

The best example of the interrelationships of family economy and labor control appears in the extensive record preserved in a Texas Supreme Court case, *Timmins v. Lacy.* Decided in April 1867, the case involved three families in northeastern Texas, and it reveals the plasticity of the seemingly rigid labor laws of presidential Reconstruction. In this case, the litigants exploited the laws and the courts to structure work and family. *Timmins v. Lacy* arose as a test of an October 1866 apprenticeship statute. In its first section, the act retained family control by allowing parents to bind out their minor children over age fourteen. A second provision empowered local officials to apprentice "all indigent or vagrant minors" within their jurisdictions. The law required masters and mistresses to furnish food, clothing, and medical attendance, to treat their charges "humanely," and to teach them some trade or occupation, but it also authorized them "to inflict such moderate corporeal punishment as [might] be necessary and proper." Servants who ran away could be chased and captured. Although apprentices could receive a discharge for "good cause," lawmakers sanctioned punishment of runaways as vagrants until they agreed to return. The law was also linked to an enticement statute, which stipulated fines of five dollars per day, paid directly to the master or mistress, for anyone luring away an apprentice. Because the statute made no specific reference to race, Texas Freedmen's Bureau officials approved it.[38]

The political and intellectual debates about labor carried on by elites during the early emancipation period focused on free-labor ideology and formal law, but rarefied theory meant little to the three families involved in *Timmins v. Lacy*. Their concerns centered around work discipline and family economy. The suit encompassed the Timmins, Pope, and Lacy families. The plaintiff, Mary B. Timmins, and her son Robert operated a plantation in Cherokee County about thirty miles from Tyler in northeastern Texas. Prior to the war, Harry Pope had been her slave. In the early 1850s, Harry Pope married Sarah Lacy on Timmins's plantation "after the usual fashion of slave marriages." The couple had three children, including Elkin—the child in question in the case—another boy, Chuff, and a girl, Leney. Eight or nine years after the marriage, Harry abandoned Sarah because she had a child by another slave. Both Harry and Sarah remarried, Harry to a woman not named in the record, and Sarah to Moses Lacy, with whom she had three more children.[39]

At the end of the war, both black families still lived in the vicinity of the Timmins plantation, although Harry had been separated from his children by sale. After emancipation, he returned to Mary Timmins and contracted to labor for her in 1866. He also contracted with her to keep his three children for 1866, 1867, and 1868, if she approved of the arrangement year by year. Moses and Sarah Lacy had also contracted in advance to work for the Timmins family in 1866, but in December 1865 they abandoned the agreement and worked instead for Harmon Carlton, hiring out Elkin and Chuff to G. W. Pearson. The day after the latter agreement was concluded, Robert Timmins rode to Pearson's farm and used a double-barreled shotgun to repossess the boys.[40]

By the end of 1866, the Lacy family had accumulated property worth fifty to sixty dollars, and they sought to increase their earnings by using a mixed family economy. Moses Lacy contracted with William Parks to work for ten dollars per month, plus a house and food. The agreement permitted Sarah to work for herself, and the couple believed they could, with the help of their children, "take care of themselves." Following this intention, Sarah hired Elkin to Harmon Carlton for forty dollars per year, Chuff to E. Morgan for thirty dollars, and Leney to John T. Murray for thirty-five dollars. The contracts required each child's employer to supply food, clothing, and medicine.[41]

Once again, the Timmins family disrupted the plans of the Lacy family. In January 1867 Mary Timmins obtained an order from the Cherokee County Court authorizing her to hold Elkin and Chuff until the last Monday in January, when the county court pertaining to estates would consider their case. Robert Timmins again seized the boys and carried them back to his mother's farm. This time the Timmins family had the power of the state's new apprenticeship law on its side. On December 27, 1866, Mary and Robert had persuaded Harry Pope to bind Elkin, Chuff, and Leney to them until each child reached twenty-one. One condition of the agreement probably convinced Harry Pope to return his children to his former master. Mary Timmins had agreed to give each child one hundred acres of land upon his or her majority.[42]

This narrative depicts complex relationships between work, family, and the law in the immediate aftermath of emancipation. In late 1865, members of the Timmins family believed they still had the right to use physical force to exact the labor of freedpeople. By late 1866 they had learned to use the law instead. The Popes and especially the Lacys also assimilated the use of law to control their economic futures and their family lives, and their stories demonstrate that African Americans were not always passive victims in the legal process. Sarah Lacy and Harry Pope both followed the familiar pattern of freed slaves who tried to reestablish family life and provide for the future. The Lacys attempted to do so by using the contract system set up by the Union army and the Freedmen's Bureau. By operating a planned family economy, in a way suggestive of urban-ethnic working-class families, they hoped to live free from the control of their former masters. Harry Pope, on the other hand, was willing to manipulate the Black Codes to his and his children's benefit. Aspiring to obtain land, Harry Pope took advantage of the Timmins family's desire for labor and full control. In doing so, he acted in accord with other freedpeople. Ironically, Pope was willing to reconsign his children to short-term servitude to gain a chance at long-term independence.[43]

The conflict began its journey to the Texas Supreme Court when Mary

Timmins applied to the Cherokee County Court on January 14, 1867, to make the apprenticeship binding under state law. On January 29, the Lacys, probably with the aid of Leney's employer, John Murray, filed a bill of exceptions. They claimed Harry was not Elkin's legal father. They also portrayed themselves as residents with a "comfortable home," who could earn two hundred dollars a year "if they [could] be let alone and [were] permitted to have the management and control" of their children. If Elkin had to be apprenticed, they requested that it be to a different master of their choosing. During its January term, the county court overruled the exceptions. The Lacys then obtained a writ of certiorari that removed the case to the Ninth District Court of Reuben A. Reeves, where it was tried de novo. Reeves was an unlikely source of aid for the Lacys. Born in Kentucky, he was a former slaveholder who had been a secessionist and a captain in the Confederate army. Nevertheless, Reeves found Sarah Lacy to be the children's natural guardian, revoked the county court's order, and returned them to her care.[44]

Mary Timmins appealed to the Texas Supreme Court, but Sarah Lacy retained control of her children. That she did is surprising enough, but that her victory was not an isolated case is even more astonishing. Indeed, African Americans seeking to break apprenticeships usually won if their cases reached the highest state courts. In the lone federal case of this type, an October 1867 U.S. circuit court decision in Maryland, Chief Justice Salmon P. Chase used the Thirteenth Amendment and the Civil Rights Act of 1866 to release freedwoman Elizabeth Turner. Perhaps the most effective action at the state level occurred in North Carolina. There, freedpeople filed a petition on behalf of Harriet and Eliza Ambrose, two teenage girls who, without parental notification, had been indentured to a man named Russell. The case led the North Carolina Supreme Court to narrow the definition of the state's apprenticeship statute, which in turn enabled Freedmen's Bureau officials to annul numerous indentures sealed since emancipation.[45]

The *Turner* and *Ambrose* cases probably had the most far reaching effects, but freedpeople in several states found redress in their particular situations. Because these litigants usually argued their cases before jurists unlikely to be sympathetic, their achievements require some explanation. In part, the temporary nature of apprenticeship might underlie their success. Barbara Fields suggests that planters used apprenticeship to come to terms with emancipation and to force labor and that the practice slowly faded in the late 1860s when it proved a poor means to meet either end. Yet the appearance of apprenticeship cases into the mid-1870s conflicts with this interpretation. Clearly, white landowners in some states continued to use indentures through Republican Reconstruction and Democratic Redemption. This turn of events is not startling; apprenticeship remained anchored in the poor laws and continued to be practiced occasionally in a few northern states as well. Something other than the uselessness of apprenticeship must explain why courts would listen to the entreaties of African American workers.[46]

Some jurists acted on antislavery sentiment or a grudging acceptance of emancipation. Hatred of slavery obviously motivated Chase, a man whose political career had been built on opposing the institution. In his *Turner* opinion, Chase declared Elizabeth Turner's indenture to be involuntary servitude under the meaning of the Thirteenth Amendment. But some southern judges also opposed apprenticeship, or at least certain types, as bound labor. In the case of Jack, the freedman in Mississippi, Justice William L. Harris upheld the general concept of apprenticeship but argued that local courts must take care that apprentices "not be deprived of [their] freedom" when their apprenticeships ended. In the Georgia suit of Jacob Comas, Justice Iverson L. Harris of Milledgeville went much further. Harris read the state's 1866 apprenticeship act as applying equally to both white and blacks. Consequently, public functionaries were to "be vigilant in preventing any one, under the name of master, from getting the control of the labor and services of such [a] minor apprentice, as if he were still a slave," Harris declared. "It should be borne always in mind, and at all times should regulate the conduct of the white man, that slavery is with the days beyond the flood." Prohibited by both the state and national constitutions, slavery's *"continuance [would] not by any honest public functionary be tolerated, under forms of law or otherwise, directly or indirectly."*[47]

Although southern jurists were willing to uphold the general use of apprenticeship as part of the poor laws, some would not allow the legal vestiges of slavery to continue. Indeed, formal application of the law represented a second reason why African Americans won their appeals. Most of the cases presented to southern courts involved gross violations of statutory procedures. In Delaware, for example, the Court of Errors and Appeals released apprentice Mary Cannon under habeas corpus because her mother, Julia Cannon, had neither been notified of the indenture nor given time to find a home with "some respectable white person" and because she had not been allowed the statutory five-day period to indemnify the county against her daughter becoming a public charge. Yet formalism could also prevent African American successes. In *Cox v. Jones*, the Alabama court dismissed the family's appeal by relying on antebellum precedents and on the fact that the Coxes had proceeded under the wrong statutory provision.[48]

Arguably, formalist decisions simply undergirded the hegemonic power of the legal system, and this was certainly true in some instances. In *Beard v. Hudson*, an 1867 case, North Carolina Supreme Court justice Edwin G. Reade admitted as much. Having urged "prudence" already in his *Ambrose* opinion, Reade now commended John Beard for carrying his attempt to reclaim Nicey Hudson's son to the courts instead of tracking him down alone. "It is best that the colored population should be satisfied that they are liable to no unlawful impressments, and that they should see that what is required of them has the sanction of law," Reade stated with astonishing frankness. "It may then be hoped that they will be contented, and will cheerfully submit to what they might otherwise mischievously resist."[49]

Given such a bald statement about the utility of the law to suppress dissent, all of this litigation could easily be dismissed as hegemonic. But doing so would ignore a third major reason for African American victories: nineteenth-century assumptions about the sanctity of the free family and its domestic relations. The most common reason voiced for breaking indentures was that allowing them would disrupt families. With a sympathy never allowed slave families, southern jurists insisted that, within certain limits, free families had a right to control the labor of their own children.[50]

The limits concerned the level of kinship and the "moral character" of the family. In most cases, courts were willing to return children to their parents, stepparents, and grandparents. But other kin relationships might have been less certain. In an 1868 Kentucky decision, for example, Justice Brevard J. Peters refused to break the indentures of Henry and Wesley Lamb. Their parents had died, leaving them in the custody of an uncle and an aunt's husband. Here the court looked into domestic relations and found them wanting. Although the relatives who claimed custody of Henry and Wesley were "men of good character and industrious habits," the court found, "one of them ha[d] a large family of children, and [did] not own a residence, and neither of them [was] shown to be as competent to take charge of the boys as the man to whom they [were] bound." In *Beard v. Hudson*, which involved a young man apprenticed before the war who ran away to live with his mother in May 1865, Reade said courts could regulate the "domestic relation" of apprenticeship when it had been "wantonly broken, or grossly abused" as it had by young Hudson's "idle and disreputable manner."[51]

Although the Lambs and the Hudsons lost their cases, people with closer

kinship ties or those with "reputable" families found the courts more amenable. After reviewing the web of family relationships in Samuel Adams's
case, the Georgia Supreme Court decided that he was the legitimate father
of the children and gave him custody. In Kentucky, Justice Mordecai R.
Hardin remanded Sam Thomas, age twelve, to the care of his grandfather,
who swore "that he was qualified and willing to bring up the boy in moral
courses" as required by the apprenticeship law. Relying on this decision,
Hardin then released Washington Small from his indenture to James Small,
who formerly might have been his owner. Hardin declared that more than
"the mere poverty and orphanage of the infant" was required for the court
to act and that Washington Browder, the boy's grandfather, was a man who,
"although poor, [was] shown to be of good moral character."[52]

The power of Victorian domestic sentiment appeared strongly in Eliza and
Harriet Ambrose's case. Judge Robert B. Gilliam of the Lumberton Circuit
Court noted in his record of the case that Harriet and Eliza were "industrious, well behaved and amply provided for in food and clothing." They resided with a mother and stepfather who possessed "good character" and
could be considered "well to do." Perhaps because the young women were
so clearly anchored in middle-class respectability, Gilliam was reluctant to
take them from their homes. "What interest had society in having these relations broken up, and themselves put under the care of strangers, with no
affection for them, nor any other interest, except gain from their services,"
he asked. Gilliam went on to say that courts should bind children only when
it would improve their lot. He then recounted a story, presumably from the
antebellum period, when three or four "neat and clean" fatherless children
appeared before the Granville County Court. Their mother "cried much but
did not say a word" as the proceedings to bind the children took place. When
asked about her situation, she replied that "she was an honest, industrious
woman and widow, who had labored hard for her children, and that just
when they could begin to help her the rapacity of some bad man sought to
take them away." In the end, some "gentlemen of the bar" took up a collection for the woman that enabled her to keep her children. Gilliam used this
narrative to emphasize the point that courts must inquire into parents' lives
and "hear their own simple story" before making decisions. Justice Reade,
who would soon deny Nicey Hudson's appeal, agreed with Gilliam that there
was "no propriety in taking [the children] from the society and services of
their parents and friends."[53]

The *Ambrose* case illustrates the hold nineteenth-century notions of domesticity and class respectability had even on such hardened southern judges as Reade. Yet the best example of the role of middle-class domestic ideals in helping African American families secure custody appeared in *Timmins v. Lacy*. The Texas Supreme Court heard arguments in the case during its April 1867 term in Tyler. Timmins's attorney contended that the county court retained exclusive jurisdiction over apprenticeship and guardian cases, that the law of guardian and ward gave preference to the father, and that the apprenticeship law intended to cover precisely this type of case. The Lacys' brief was not preserved, but somewhere in the judicial process they had retained the services of one of the state's prestigious law firms, Bonner and Bonner.[54]

In a strange twist of events, Chief Justice George F. Moore, a former officer in the Confederate cavalry, examined the law of black marriages under slavery and freedom and found the authority to place Elkin with his mother. He rejected the argument that Harry Pope's authorization of the apprenticeship was enough to keep Elkin with the Timmins family. Because all slave marriages were unrecognized by law, Elkin was legally a bastard, and it was "a universally recognized principle of the common law, that the father of a bastard ha[d] no parental power or authority over such illegitimate offspring." Moore cited a previous decision that manumission granted civil rights to a slave and validated any marriage existing at that time. On these grounds, emancipation legitimated the marriage of Moses and Sarah Lacy, and they became Elkin's legal guardians. Moore was unwilling, however, to let his opinion close on such a narrow, formalist basis. In his search for a broader one, Moore informally imported a principal element of New England's vagrancy laws, one that punished fathers who abandoned homes, wives, children, and domestic responsibility. Even if the father were legitimate, he declared, it would be unreasonable to construe the apprenticeship statute so "that this child could be taken from its mother against her consent, and apprenticed solely at [the father's] will and pleasure." The law intended to give control of children to their rightful parents. Moore reiterated the point: "Surely it is not to be supposed that merely because the father, when discharging his duties as such, is regarded as the head of the family, [that he] may, after years of desertion and abandonment, during which he has left his wife to struggle unaided for their support, rob her, by means of this law, of the society of her children, and thus add to the injury already done her the severest blow which can be inflicted upon a woman, whatever may be her condition or sphere of life." Ironically, he combined part of a law designed for labor and social control—vagrancy—with the ideals of domesticity and motherhood and thereby denied the authority of a black father, a white plantation mistress, and a state labor law.[55]

Timmins v. Lacy illustrates how formal labor laws could function in action. For Cherokee County planters, the Black Codes provided a way to govern former slaves, but for two black families, the legal arrangements set up by the Freedmen's Bureau and the state legislature provided different paths by which to escape planter control and establish domestic relations. To jurists in Texas and other states who lived middle-class family lives themselves, invocations of domesticity were powerful. Whether knowingly or not, freedpeople and their advocates used gender-based arguments that allowed jurists to strengthen opinions that rested on either formalism or antislavery sentiment.

In a broader sense, the Texas case points to the ways in which southerners reacted to the northern project to bring capitalist labor law to the South and the ways in which that resistance ultimately undermined the northern endeavor. By 1868, as many historians have pointed out, sharecropping and tenancy had begun to take hold as the dominant labor system. This outcome originated in the complex class struggle carried out between southern landholders, merchants, and workers. Still, as the work of Harold Woodman has made clear, sharecropping and tenancy also called forth a new system of law. The landlord-tenant and lien laws under which sharecropping developed presented a markedly, though not completely, different legal path than the one blazed in the South by the bourgeois northerners who peopled the Freedmen's Bureau. They had followed the legal discourse of the antebellum North, with its uneasy tension between a premodern right to security, an emergent capitalist right to quit, and a growing bourgeois desire for a paternalist state that imposed a societal duty to work.[56]

The social realities of emancipation prepared neither southern whites nor blacks to accept capitalist free-labor law fully. Planters, of course, wanted nothing to do with a broad right to quit. Nor had their experience with contracts led them toward support for the right to security; in fact, the only widespread investigations of labor contract law in the antebellum South, those involving overseers, had predisposed planters to expect the state to countenance the effortless discharge of unwanted servants. Antebellum vagrancy laws in the South had let the planter class use the state to assert class-based standards of respectability and to compel labor directly for individuals. Based on this legal heritage, planters hoped for a legal system quite different from the one proffered by northerners through the bureau. Initially, the planter class strongly oppposed northern attempts to bring capitalist labor relations to the South through law. However, as time wore on, planters learned how to resist free-labor law or use its nebulous areas to their advantage. That some Freedmen's Bureau agents shared their assumptions made this outcome all the easier.

The daily realities of slavery also implanted the potential for resistance to free-labor law on the part of southern blacks. As a result, African Americans also shaped the development of labor law in the immediate postemancipation period. Elite newspaper editors, local community leaders, and workers scraping to make ends meet all contributed to this process, though often with somewhat contradictory intentions. While elite voices, such as those in the *Tribune,* wrestled with labor law as a matter of political economy, African American laborers worked out their own means to resist legal oppression and attempted to devise a decent life for themselves and their children. As most accounts of emancipation make clear, freedpeople wanted productive property, not the cash nexus. Moreover, decades of life under a system where law controlled labor directly meant that former slaves prized autonomy from the state in labor and family relations. As Freedmen's Bureau agents of all ideological stripes pointed out repeatedly, freedpeople often saw any legal restriction on labor as an imposition on their hard-won freedom and their desire for autonomy from white control. Still, former slaves' resistance to law did not mean that they wanted the laissez-faire labor market proffered by liberals. If they wanted anything available in free-labor law, it was the right to security, which would, in turn, help them secure the fruits of their own labor and an eventual release from the market altogether.

Part of controlling their own labor involved command of their children's services. Consequently, they took their cause to the courts, first to the Freedmen's Bureau offices and then to local tribunals across the region. With its conflicted and contradictory policies, the bureau proved eventually to be a weak reed, but black workers' insistence on their wages or shares prompted bureau agents across the South to act. The flood of cases that blacks carried into local bureau offices led agents to enforce the right to security inherent in entirety in a way neither northern nor southern courts in the antebellum period had even been willing to do, especially for farm laborers. Until the federal government ceased bureau operations, African American workers made significant progress in securing the fruits of their labor. In the early years of emancipation, black families also proved successful in southern courts, where they successfully opposed bound apprenticeship in a way the Freedmen's Bureau, with its qualms about federalism, had not been able to accomplish. Even though Redeemer governments undercut many of the rights of black workers, it should not be forgotten that workers did establish securely basic rights to self-ownership, custodial control of children, and some form of payment, rights that were by no means certain in 1865. As African Americans in the South fought for these gains, they helped erect barriers to planter designs, but they also shaped the legal system brought South by northerners. As this southern legal transformation came to an end in the early 1870s, workers, employers, reformers, and jurists in the North and West finished the reformulation of the antebellum system of free-labor law that had begun in the postwar South.

The Northern Reconstruction of
Free-Labor Law

At two o'clock in the afternoon on June 5, 1879, Mrs. Alfred Winegar latched the front door of her farmhouse near Millerton, New York. A "very estimable woman" between sixty and seventy years of age whose husband had recently passed on, she and an eighty-year-old friend had been spending the afternoon talking as men worked the fields nearby. Moving to the back entrance, Mrs. Winegar was affronted by "a man of advanced age with long, gray whiskers." The stranger yanked her from the entrance and pushed her toward one of the farm's buildings. Roused by the commotion, her friend ran from the house and chased the scoundrel from the premises, but she was too late to save Mrs. Winegar. "The fright and over exertion so affected her that she died instantly," the *New York Times* informed its readers the next day. Mrs. Winegar's death was clearly a case of "Death from a Tramp's Violence."[1]

Whatever the man's intentions or Mrs. Winegar's medical condition, this narrative formed part of the pervasive fear of tramps that had developed by the late 1870s. A product of the depression that started with the Panic of 1873, industrial tramping created a period of crisis for free labor and free-labor law in the post–Civil War North. While northerners tried to implement antebellum legal principles in the Reconstruction South, they tested, altered, or discarded them at home. During the Reconstruction of the North, jurists, reformers, and lawmakers finally found a synthesis for the competing principles within antebellum free-labor law. For the most part, jurists established the right to quit and curtailed the right to security for workers. Simultaneously, the social crisis of industrial tramping led reform-minded legislators to increase state power to punish failure to participate in the labor market.[2]

By 1880 northern labor law had reached an oddly paradoxical stage. The prewar doctrine of entirety eroded, diminishing the role of binding contracts in governing the conditions of labor, while simultaneously northern legislatures enacted criminal tramp laws with the potential to constrict workers' movements severely. In part, growing intellectual criticism of entirety's ability to oppress led to its diminution, but in a broader sense its decline resulted from the simple fact that employers no longer wanted binding, long-term agreements. Farm mechanization increasingly made them unneeded for farmers, and they had never proved especially useful for craft or industrial work. Now, both employers and the courts invented new ways to secure labor discipline, but ways that did not significantly restrict workers' movement in the labor market. At the same time, tramp laws directly limited industrial mobility by establishing penitentiary terms for not working. A departure from prewar vagrancy statutes, these laws nonetheless drew on prewar roots in reform discourse about work, gender, and class. Spurred by fears of downward mobility in an uncertain economy and by growing antimodernist longings for release from the restraints of industrial and domestic life, reformers secured laws that were considerably harsher than their antebellum or Reconstruction antecedents.

THE RIGHT TO QUIT COMES OF AGE

Since the 1830s, the developing capitalist economy of the United States had been aiming toward a market in which individuals were nominally free to sell their labor power without legal incumbrance. By 1880, courts had established this ability much more firmly by enhancing the "right" for workers to quit and the power for employers to discharge them. Courts began to back away from entire contracts, while increasingly supporting employment at the will of either party. The remaining restraints on job seeking fell most heavily on agricultural workers or on those in similar occupations, as they had in the antebellum period. To be sure, courts did not allow collective actions that interfered with the wage bargain, nor did they countenance workers' control of the shop floor. Nevertheless, judicial action increasingly "freed" laborers to circulate in the labor market. This "right" was at best a limited gain for employees, for as it commodified labor, it also undermined security. In essence, the liberals who lost during the Reconstruction of the South had won during the Reconstruction of the North. The laissez-faire vision of men such as Wendell Phillips and James McKaye, which had met so much resistance in the South, came to fruition in the postwar North.

Entire contracts, the hallmark of the right to security in prewar law, continued to find some use in the postwar economy, but their importance became increasingly confined to farm labor or to work that resembled agricultural employment. Like their southern counterparts, northern and western farmers used contracts in the postwar period to bind agricultural labor. In common with prewar practice, Frank Halsey signed on at Axle Weaver's place in Illinois from March 1, 1877, "until after corn picking." Jeremiah Baker contracted with Solomon Duncan to work for seven months at fifteen dollars per month on Duncan's farm in southeastern Kansas. William Thrift paid William Payne twenty dollars per month for work on his Macon County, Illinois, farm from March through November. Payne's job also indicates that some seasonal laborers were not simply a rural proletariat, for he gained permission from Thrift in late September to gather a hay crop of his own.[3]

Although farmers were still using these sorts of arrangements, their need for bound labor decreased after the Civil War. The most important reason for this change was the growth of agricultural mechanization. Long-term arrangements had always been used primarily to hold laborers for the harvest. Now farmers relied increasingly on contract harvesters like Azariah Huls, who owned a threshing machine that he took around Kane County, Illinois, working at the rate of two dollars per bushel of seed separated. By employing men like Huls, farmers could get the crop in without supporting workers for the whole year. As a result, the minor sons of other farmers seem to have replaced the adult farmworker of the prewar period. Adult farmworkers who remained were not the bound servants of the premachine age. Some were like William Payne, who used his wages to supplement the income from his own farm. Others worked out informal agreements, such as the one between Thomas McComber and Frank G. Parcell, to avoid waiting until the end of the season or the year for payment. Although McComber and Parcell agreed to a price of $195 for a year's work, Parcell testified that McComber "had been working for [him] before, and he drawed money whenever he wanted it."[4]

Some industrial employers also continued to use entire contracts to limit workers, but when they did so, the nature of their labor process had more in common with the agricultural world than the industrial one. Two cases involving litigants on the edge between the craft and industrial worlds illustrate both the influence that the character of work had on contract and the ambiguity with which jurists still approached industrial discipline in the 1870s. In the spring of 1878 a Chicago hat dealer corresponded with a Peoria milliner about employing her for the season at fifteen dollars a week plus travel expenses. Thinking she had been hired from April through July, the milliner went to Chicago, brushed up on the recent innovations in the trade, and sought her prospective employer. Because he had not received a definite reply, the dealer had since traveled to Peoria and hired another worker. Finding herself in Chicago without employment, the milliner sued, claiming the hat dealer had made a special contract with her. In upholding the lower-court decision in favor of the dealer, the high court noted the urgency of the season. Given the lateness of the year and the danger to the dealer's business, Justice John Scholfield argued, the dealer had not acted improperly when he engaged another milliner. In dissent, Justice T. Lyle Dickey called for a strict application of contract in the milliner's favor, stressing that "she kept her promise" and that the dealer could not be released from his agreement.[5]

In another Illinois case, the superintendent of a children's clothing factory had been detained in jail twelve days during the company's January busy season. Again, the Illinois court faced the question of whether a servant's unavoidable absence during a busy time released the master. In the usual manner of late-nineteenth-century judges, the court tried to erect a "reason-ableness" standard. Scholfield asserted that whether the worker was gone for "an unreasonable length of time" depended "on the nature and necessities of the business in which the servant" was employed. Scholfield made it clear that employers would determine what those necessities were. The question to be asked was, "Does the delay so affect the interests of the master that the performance of the residue of the contract by the servant would be a thing different in substance from what the master contracted for[?]" These two cases were on the margins of industrialization, in a trade that had experi-enced the decline in skill and status common to all artisan-based labor. As such, the courts were not forced to deal with litigants who were truly indus-trial workers.[6]

Most industrialists did not want restrictions on the market anyway; in-stead, they wished to control the labor process or the wage bargain. Such goals did not fit easily with common-law precedents, nor with the emerg-ing laissez-faire doctrines of the late nineteenth century. As a result, judges found it difficult to respond to industrialists' demands. Nonetheless, they did grant industrial employers some legal means of direct control over the wage bargain and the labor process by resurrecting the old doctrine of enticement and by strengthening the notice-of-leave clauses that had appeared in the antebellum period.

The common-law tort of enticement offered a potential avenue for controlling workers' actions in the labor market by restricting the wage-bargaining abilities of competing employers. Enticement had been suggested by Freedmen's Bureau officials in the South and continued to be used by southern planters to control the labor market after the departure of federal authority. In addition, enticement had a basis in English law. Similar to the antebellum period, however, industrial employers used enticement only occasionally. More commonly, enticement concerned domestic servants. Even then, it seemed to contradict the very basis of free labor, for it hindered a worker's freedom of movement. In a New Hampshire litigation in the early 1870s, the defendant's attorneys made precisely this point. Albertina Larson of Gottenburg, Sweden, had been brought to the United States as a domestic by a labor agent. When the agent placed her with a different employer than the one for whom she was intended, the latter man sued for enticement. Not only was such a contract void because it lacked mutuality, the defense argued, Larson also "had the right upon her arrival here to go where and engage with whom she pleased." Still, the court found Larson's employer liable.[7]

Domestic servants fit readily into English and American master-servant discourse, but industrial workers did not. When the Massachusetts Supreme Court heard a rare enticement action against a shoemaker in 1871, it ruled the suit legitimate, but only after a tortured discussion. The plaintiff, Samuel Walker, operated a shoe and boot factory in Milford, Massachusetts, and in January 1869 his competitor, Michael Cronin, induced several factory operatives and about forty-five outworkers to leave Walker and work for him instead. When the superior court accepted Cronin's defense, the Massachusetts Supreme Court had to decide whether this sort of competition in the wage bargain was actionable. Justice John Wells, who wrote the opinion upholding Walker's claim for enticement, went to great pains to harmonize enticement with an open market. "Everyone has the right to enjoy the fruits of his own enterprise, industry, skill, and credit," Wells wrote, echoing one of the shibboleths of the free-labor ethic. Still, no one had the right to protection against the vicissitudes of the competitive market. Harm that resulted from free competition would be *damnum absque injuria*, damage without wrongdoing, a staple of laissez-faire legal doctrine. Entrepreneurs did have a right to protection against harm from wanton acts that did not result from competition or from some valid purpose. Nevertheless, Wells was not willing to base the action solely on this older idea, nor on the master-servant relation itself. Instead, he reverted to contract language, arguing that "everyone has an equal right to employ workmen in his business or service" and that no harm was done by inducing workers to leave—unless a contract existed. Only then might employers sue.[8]

While Wells sought a consistent basis for the litigation, he overlooked Walker's purpose in bringing it. The Milford shoe manufacturer was not concerned with his general rights in the market but with more specific elements of his business. When his workers went over to Cronin, Walker lost several "who were skilled in the art of bottoming boots and shoes." Apparently, Walker wanted control over this particular type of worker and this particular segment of the labor process. More important, the workers' action had disrupted Walker's wage agreement with his other employees. Because Cronin had offered the workers "greater than the usual market price for such work," Walker's remaining employees forced him to raise their wages as well, presumably under the threat of walking out.[9]

Although they might prove useful to industrialists such as Walker, enticement litigations were an extreme measure. By the post–Civil War period, northern employers had developed a standard practice to meet the same ends Walker sought in his claim for damages. In textiles and iron, and perhaps elsewhere, employers required between ten days' and two weeks' notification before leaving. Workers who did not "work out their notice" forfeited wages due them. This practice worked well because of the manner in which workers were paid. Although they might be employed at daily wage or a piece rate, many workers received a pay packet only once a month. In addition, some companies left a gap between the end of the pay period and the time they gave workers their pay envelopes.[10]

Notification had originated in the Massachusetts textile mills during the 1830s and 1840s; thus by the 1870s the courts had considered the question several times. Consequently, judges were willing to legitimize the practice but not without some reservations. As in most prewar labor contract litigations, the courts recognized sickness as a valid excuse for being absent from work, the reason being that acts of Providence could not be foreseen. In an astonishing decision, the Massachusetts court in 1865 declared that an arrest and conviction for adultery also fell under the same general rule. Notification clauses, Chief Justice George T. Bigelow wrote, implied a right to leave work, and the only way the forfeiture provisions could operate was by "some voluntary act of imprudence or carelessness" that led directly to abandonment of the contract. Bigelow admitted that adultery might be viewed in this light but maintained that it was the arrest that caused the abandonment, not the sexual indiscretion. In another surprising opinion, the New Jersey court in 1881 decided that a weaver's skipping work to "go down to the river on a pleasure excursion" did not constitute abandonment without notice. Even though the company's attorneys argued that one day's absence was as detrimental as permanent abandonment, the court found notification provisions to cover only the latter contingency. In a broad sense, decisions such as these sustained the general liberal discourse of contracts. The key was whether the worker's act had been either voluntary or intentional, whether the worker had disregarded the supposed mutual agreement in the original contract. Nevertheless, the workers did receive their wages, and the companies did not achieve their goals.[11]

This concern about lack of mutuality in employment contracts was also the central doctrinal issue in more standard litigations in which a worker left voluntarily. As they did in antebellum courts, workers' attorneys argued that lists of rules containing notification clauses did not constitute a contract, especially if the employee had no knowledge of the rules. Furthermore, a weaver's lawyer suggested in an 1876 case, a company's notification rule imposed "a penalty unequal and uncertain in extent, and therefore [could not] be enforced as a contract." In 1874 the Massachusetts court accepted the first part of this argument, that a worker had to know about the rule before forfeiture could apply. Such a decision was in line with prewar principles on notification and was almost inevitable under contract doctrine. To accept the company's logic that an individual assented to a penalty simply by continuing to work would have baldly exposed the fiction of equality in contract.[12]

Knowing the rules was the crux, for two years later the same court denied recovery to a weaver who knew of the notification requirement, even though he had signed no contract to that effect. Justice Charles Devens Jr. accepted the employer's contention that assent could be found in silence or in the act of continued work. Devens went considerably further, however, rejecting want of mutuality as fatal to the contract. Echoing the rationale of Senator James Harlan during the Thirteenth Amendment debates, Devens suggested that equality could be bargained away: "It is competent for either party to give to the other the right to terminate the contract abruptly while he himself agrees only to do so upon notice." When faced with a direct challenge to liberal discourse, jurists such as Devens made no real attempt to mystify power structures. They had accepted unequal bargains before the Civil War, and they continued to do so afterward.[13]

As with enticement, these doctrinal questions were not employers' main concern. Notification had several purposes, but the relatively short time requirements confirm that its overall purpose was not to restrict the labor market in the broader sense, as was the case with farmers. One main function was preventing disruption in the labor process. When the Fall River Iron Works lost Daniel Naylor in 1873, it claimed damage because of the loss of his skill. Naylor's job "consisted in taking the iron as it came through the furnace and passing it through the rolls, and . . . this could not be done by a green hand." The Massachusetts court accepted this reasoning, "considering the nature of the work and its relation to the other operations in the defendant's business." Continuous-process industries such as iron and steel required some skilled workers, and their loss could disrupt the entire operation. In some ways, preventing interruption resembled the farmer's worry about harvest, but in the latter case, the employer wanted to bind unskilled workers for long periods to ensure their presence at a specific moment as well as to avoid paying higher day wages in the end. An iron and steel company intended to secure skilled workers for their role in ongoing production; it wanted only to stabilize the supply of skilled labor on a daily or weekly basis and did not want to interfere with the individual wage bargain.[14]

In some instances, however, notification regulations were aimed at breaches of shop-floor discipline or collective action by workers. Some New England textile mills tied notification requirements to "honorable discharges" as they had done in the prewar period. The gentlemen's agreements between company supervisors not to hire an operative without such an endorsement continued in the late nineteenth century. As the century progressed, some companies also considered notification a direct antistrike tool. In 1887, the Pennsylvania Supreme Court upheld a wage forfeiture on this basis. Requiring two weeks' notice constituted "an entirely proper and reasonable means of protection against wanton and ruthless injury" caused by "a sudden and extensive strike of the men."[15]

During and after the Civil War, many northern courts retreated from the doctrine of binding labor contracts, adopting instead the equitable remedy of apportionment laid out by Joel Parker in *Britton v. Turner*. At the level of legal doctrine, this slow change represented the ultimate triumph of market relations in free labor. Removing the penalty of wage forfeiture allowed workers to leave contracts and circulate freely. In the broader sense, however, the decline of entirety went hand in hand with the rise of the at-will employment doctrine, which helped employers secure more power in constructing the employment relation. At least in some cases, courts had previously upheld the sense of obligation and job security for workers inherent in entire contracts. Apportionment left both workers and employers almost completely free of court interference, a situation not advantageous to a weaker party.

Although on the wane, entirety still had its supporters in the postwar North. One of the most fervent defenses came from Horace Gray Wood, who published an American treatise on the law of master and servant in 1877. Wood represented the antebellum school of thought about labor contracts, freely adopting English master-servant discourse on the employment relation. English writers confined "servant" to menials and domestics, Wood wrote, but Americans conceived of it as any employee. Wood argued that the master-servant relationship arose from contract, but he spurned the fiction of equality in bargaining. Servants were defined as people "subject to the direction and control of another in any department of employment or business." Wood advocated application of full performance of fixed contracts without deviation, even after one day's absence from work. While he noted that *Britton* had been adopted in some places, he asserted that it was not favored generally and that most states had adopted entirety. For Wood, entirety stood as "sound public policy, and in the industrial interests of the country." If workers could depart at will, "the interests of employers would be constantly at the mercy of employees." Wood argued that entirety was not detrimental to workers, but not in the usual way of asserting the employer's mutual obligation. Instead, he pointed out somewhat ruefully that in England the criminal law enforced contracts.[16]

Entirety found supporters in the courts as well. The New Jersey court in 1870 disallowed a maid's suit for a month's wages, claiming that because her contract was for a fixed period it was "not apportionable either in law or in equity." In 1876 the Wisconsin Supreme Court denied recovery to a farmworker and his wife, who had worked as a maid, even though her pregnancy was what prevented fulfillment of the contract. Wisconsin's judges faced the question again in *Diefenback v. Stark* (1883) with the same result. A minor farmhand had left a six-month contract after four months because his employer refused to pay in installments, as the boy had understood the agreement. Acknowledging the growing number of decisions in favor of *quantum meruit*, the court nevertheless declared the remedies suggested in *Britton* to be "against the current authority in this country and in England, and certainly against reason" as well as "quite inadequate to indemnify the employer under the ordinary rule of damages." As in the prewar period, the nature of employment influenced the terms of the contract and the outcome of the case. If the farmer had wanted only a month-to-month worker, he would not have stipulated a six-month term and would have paid less wages, the opinion argued. In other words, if the employer had no desire to control his employee's participation in the labor market, he would not have offered an entire contract. Moreover, the contract was not apportionable because several months of work on a farm was likely to have "very different benefit and value." Farmwork (or other nonindustrial labor) did not possess the constant value intrinsic to the industrial labor process. The employer supported the laborer through slack times to ensure his or her presence when needed.[17]

Even though entire contracts continued to find favor among some jurists, juridical support for constricting workers' movements in the labor market was on the decline by the 1870s. The declining need for agricultural labor control helped the courts weaken entirety, but it was not the only reason for the changing construction of labor contracts. After the Civil War, jurists and law writers rejected both the formalist and functional arguments of entirety's supporters and advocated the adoption of *Britton* because of its equity. In his treatise on damages, George Washington Field noted that *Britton* had been adopted in several states and that "in view of its manifest justice," it was "likely to grow in favor until it [became] universally recognized." Iowa justice John F. Dillon declared in 1864 that though inconsistent with "the more technical and more illiberal rules of the common law found in the older cases," the New Hampshire rules were "bottomed on justice and right on principle." George and Joseph Chandler, attorneys for farmworker Jeremiah Baker, also saw apportionment as equitable: "This rule wrongs neither party. The best reason approves it. It does exact justice to both."[18]

In particular, advocates of apportionment rejected distinctions based on the labor process or the nature of work, valuing all labor as Parker and other prewar liberal jurists had done. The issue arose because of the prevalence of *quantum meruit* and other equitable remedies in cases involving craft workers. As Wisconsin judge William P. Lyon maintained in a case involving a boilermaker, "no arbitrary rule of law . . . in violation of every principle of natural justice" could allow an employer to enjoy the fruits of his employee's labor and then not be bound to pay for it. Conservative judges admitted that apportionment might be allowed in such cases because the labor product (house, mill, etc.) had been accepted voluntarily, with an implied promise to pay. Echoing Parker's reasoning in *Britton*, judges and attorneys desiring equity rejected this voluntary acceptance test. Field asserted it was generally recognized that if employers accepted a benefit, "voluntarily or from the necessity of the case," then workers could recover for the work done. Considering Jeremiah Baker's case, Kansas justice David M. Valentine refused to accept that this rule applied only to building cases. Employing an analogy that would fit into rural life in Kansas, Valentine pointed out that if a person contracted to haul a thousand bushels of grain but delivered only five hundred, the recipient still received some value and was bound to pay for it. As long as some benefit accrued, he concluded, personal service contracts should be treated the same way.[19]

As before, supporters placed themselves in the van of progress. Dillon admitted that *Britton* had been repeatedly criticized as "good equity, but bad law" but claimed it was gradually gaining acceptance by judges and lawyers. Valentine admitted that entirety was certainly undergirded by the bulk of older decisions, but he maintained that most recent cases supported apportionment. Nebraska Supreme Court justice Amasa Cobb went a step further, declaring that apportionment was a settled principle in the western states. Cobb also hinted that popular pressure prompted changes in the law of labor contracts. Apportionment had gained so much support from the profession and from the people, he averred, that it "would be unsafe to adopt" the arguments for entirety.[20]

Cobb was correct in his assessment of trends in labor contract law. By 1880 most western states had adopted *Britton,* and several eastern and midwestern states had either followed the same course or had diluted entirety in some manner. In other words, the courts were finally beginning to create the true conditions of free labor. In states where wage forfeiture crumbled, the last barrier to free movement in the market fell along with it, for employers no longer possessed a direct, legal means to bind workers for long periods of time. In the important sense of day-to-day survival, workers certainly benefited from this development, but employers gained as well. Now they were no longer shackled with any contractual obligation to pay their workers or keep them on during a period of business decline. This outcome was certainly not the intention of equitable jurists in apportionment cases, but it was the aim of judges and law writers who developed another doctrine out of entirety: at-will hiring.[21]

Although the basic idea of at-will employment could be found in some prewar farm contracts, in southern overseers' agreements, and in early litigations such as *Costigan v. Mohawk Railroad,* the concept is usually attributed to Horace Gray Wood. In his 1877 treatise, Wood declared that general, indefinite hirings were "at will" and could be terminated by either party at their pleasure. Adopted definitively by the New York court in *Martin v. New York Life Insurance Co.*, the at-will employment rule became a common element of U.S. labor law in the twentieth century. As Jay Feinman has argued, the new rule concerned primarily the emerging class of middle-level managers. Although they may not have had the grand designs on owners' power that Feinman attributes to them, these accountants, clerks, superintendents, and others presented the immediate problem of using entirety to seek damages or compensation after being dismissed from their jobs. The at-will doctrine solved this problem, and it aided industrialists another important way, allowing them to dismiss any sort of laborer when an economic downturn or a problem of shop-floor discipline dictated it.[22]

Whatever the ultimate intention, the practice of at-will hiring vastly strengthened capitalists' powers over managers and others, and it radically undermined the security of their employees' lives. As Wood noted, a yearly salary was not the same thing as a yearly contract, and under such agreements, this "mere hiring at will" could be "put to an end by the master at any time." By the 1870s employers such as the Kansas Pacific Railroad Company saw this sort of arrangement as normal. The company employed its agents "so long as they gave satisfaction or their services were required." Such terms of contract left middle-class employees in a precarious position. As a Philadelphia judge noted in 1863, they would not easily give up one situation for another without the assurance in contract that it would continue. A Pittsburgh judge put the matter more succinctly a year earlier in *King & Graham v. Steiren,* a case involving the superintendent of the chemical department at a soda ash company. Professional or scientific labor could not always find a purchaser, the judge wrote. "A man of this class may go unemployed for many months, notwithstanding the most untiring efforts to procure a place." Without the guarantees of entire contracts and decisions following *Costigan,* middle-class professionals could easily slip into the ranks of the poor. Eventually, Edward Steiren recovered his nine-hundred-dollar salary, but a decade or two later he may not have been so lucky.[23]

The decline of entirety and the rise of at-will employment represented the fruition of the vision proffered by wartime liberals. Workers must be absolutely free to circulate in the labor market. Thus, labor would become a more movable commodity, sustaining capitalist development. Free labor, in the sense of self-ownership and self-marketing, did not, however, imply the decline of employers' powers in the workplace. As in the antebellum period, postwar courts continued to grant employers control over their workers' actions on the job. Yet also as before, judges did not grant these powers without restrictions, and they continued to tailor employers' legal prerogatives to the means of production.

Often, employers sought legal support for more than one means of labor control, but the courts did not always oblige them effortlessly. The complicated role of the courts in contract-based management appeared in a series of litigations involving Illinois coal miners. Although coal production had burgeoned in Pennsylvania in the 1840s, miners opened Illinois fields only in the 1870s and after. With increasing production, owners sought greater control over their workers and turned to the courts for support. One way mine owners exerted labor discipline was through pit bosses, much like prewar slave owners had done through overseers. In October 1877 the DuQuoin Star Coal Mining Company fired its pit boss, John Thorwell, and then sued him for $2,500 in damages for his poor performance. When the case came before the Perry County Circuit Court, sixteen miners trooped in to support the company, "several of them showing much feeling in the manner." In what the company must have viewed as a perverse turn of events, the jury granted Thorwell $330 in wages due. In 1879 the Fourth District of the Appellate Court of Illinois overturned the decision, finding in the colliers' testimony "overwhelming" evidence of just cause for the discharge. In an odd turn of events, the judges vindicated the company, but in doing so, they relieved the workers of an apparently despised boss.[24]

Two other industrial cases considered the contracts of actual colliers employed by the Wilmington Coal Mining and Manufacturing Company in Will County, about fifty miles south of Chicago. In governing their miners, the owners invented an ingenious contract that incorporated both entirety and the emerging at-will doctrine. The contract stipulated service from June to May, but it also contained a clause stating that any employee could be discharged without notice and that any employee could leave "in good faith" without notice. Signing the agreement also bound the miner not to be absent from work except for sickness, to abide by all company regulations, and to "keep his roadway properly brushed down, and his room in good working order." Most important, the contract employed the yellow-dog clause. Anyone wanting work at the Wilmington Mining Company had to agree to "not stop work, join any strike or combination for the purpose of obtaining or causing the company to pay their miners an advance of wages, or pay beyond what [was] specified in the contract; nor [would] he in any way aid, abet or countenance any such 'strike,' combination or scheme, for any purpose whatever, during the time specified in the first clause of said contract." In constituting the employment relation, the company had used every means at its disposal.[25]

The different conceptions of worker rights contained in entire, at-will, and yellow-dog contracts clashed when Wilmington's miners pressed claims for wages in court. The company wanted to construe the contract both ways, dismissing unruly or organized workers at will but then withholding their wages as if they had signed a special contract. However, when John Barr quit the company, the circuit court granted him $140.02 in wages due. On appeal to the Appellate Court of Illinois in June 1878, the panel upheld Barr's right to leave under the at-will clause. Nevertheless, it remanded the case because the circuit court judge had refused to allow the company's attorneys to investigate whether Barr had participated in the May 1877 Braidwood miners' strike. Striking, the court suggested, could be seen as a bad faith violation of the contract.[26]

When an identical suit reached the state's high court in September, Justice Alfred M. Craig went even further. The mine owners may have been damaged when the collier abandoned the contract, he acknowledged, "but when the contract gave him the right to leave at any time he saw proper, the damages could not be set off against the amount which was due [him]." In this case, an ambivalent supreme court confronted directly the issue of industrial work discipline and disallowed use of a contract set up to control workers. Of course, it could be argued that this decision came easy for the court, for there was "no proof that [the miner] quit in bad faith or for any evil-disposed purpose." In other words, he had no connection to organized labor. Moreover, such occasional decisions can be seen as solidifying the hegemony of liberal law by demonstrating its supposed equality and thus further shrouding power structures.[27]

In any event, such decisions demonstrate that expressions of class power in labor contract cases were not uncomplicated. By the late nineteenth century, extractive industries depended on a mobile proletariat, but industrial work discipline more often involved regulation of the workplace itself. Within certain limits, the courts legitimized the rules set up by particular industries, but in doing so they paid attention to the means of production as much as to contract doctrine. Even then, the effect of these decisions was often limited, for state legislatures began to redress the power imbalance in the wage relation. By 1920 about thirty states had adopted some statutes

mitigating notification requirements. Some gave workers the right to demand wages due when they quit, and others penalized employers who fired
workers without notice.[28]

In the broader sense, the 1870s saw the decline of common-law doctrines
that had been in place since the early part of the century. The intellectual
attack on entirety, the rise of the at-will doctrine, and even some elements
of industrial cases all signaled the courts' retreat from enforcing contracts
for fixed periods. In many cases, judges took these actions in opposition to
the demands of industrialists. Nevertheless, these common-law decisions did
release workers from many of the remaining vestiges of English master-
servant law and created a laissez-faire market in labor. At the same time, they
relieved employers of any legal obligation to workers, be they steelworkers
or chemical plant managers. Individual workers could now sell their labor
power without legal interference, but they did so in an atmosphere of uncertainty about the employment relation. As the right to quit triumphed, the
right to security fell.

TRAMPS AND THE TRIUMPH OF THE BOURGEOIS STATE

At the same time northern courts emancipated workers to seek employment,
northern legislatures more severely punished the failure to do so. By 1875,
the economic crisis generated by the Panic of 1873 led bourgeois northerners
to enact new and harsher laws to chastise workers who left the labor market
altogether to join the growing numbers of industrial tramps. In doing so,
reform writers continued to invoke the same cultural language they had employed to describe vagrants in the antebellum period and in the emancipation South. Now, however, this language came to support more drastic measures as the class tensions that had produced it grew stronger. Although the
tramp laws of the 1870s drew on prewar roots, they differed markedly, for
they surpassed in severity both antebellum vagrancy laws and war-era codes
of the Union army and the Freedmen's Bureau. Here, the wartime conservatives triumphed.[29]

Combined with the right to quit, the tramp laws represented a more settled
synthesis for the conflicting system of free-labor law that had been growing
since the early antebellum period. At first glance, this outcome might seem
to be the triumph of the moderate position present in the Reconstruction
South. However, the moderates during Reconstruction had simply tried to
hold together the right to quit and the duty to work without resolving the

ambivalence created by a belief in the right to security. The legal changes of the 1870s represented a true synthesis, for the changes in both the civil and criminal laws compelled labor market participation without any certain outcome. With this formulation, the state now undergirded the unrestricted commodification of labor needed by a more fully developed capitalist economy and bourgeois culture.[30]

By 1880, most states in the North and some elsewhere had adopted new criminal laws controlling unemployed workers who tramped on foot or rode the rails in search of work. Although grounded in the prewar language of poverty, the tramp laws of the 1870s went considerably beyond their antebellum or wartime antecedents. As detective Allan Pinkerton pointed out in 1878, the need to tramp in search of work had been common a century earlier, but seeing tramping as in need of restrictive laws was new. Pinkerton was essentially correct. Most of these new laws were passed in a compressed period between 1876 and 1880, yet some of the groundwork for their enactment had been laid in the years since the end of the war.[31]

In the same year that former abolitionists decried the Black Codes and Congress passed its first Civil Rights Act, Massachusetts lawmakers enacted the state's first separate vagrancy code. Central to reform of the state's poor laws was Samuel Gridley Howe, the third member of the American Freedmen's Inquiry Commission. During the war, the governor of Massachusetts had appointed Howe to head a State Board of Charities, the first of its kind and a model for other states. Howe professed belief in the hereditary sources of poverty, decried the congregation of paupers in large state-run almshouses, and warned that vice could not be conquered by the "social ostracism of the vicious." Howe encouraged other reformers to take the pauper's point of view, but his suggestions contained little real empathy: "The pauper is to be legislated for and about, and he is to be disposed of and treated, as seems best from the class above pauperism; and this should be so mainly, but not entirely." Howe reached this position because of the firm faith in self-reliance and personal agency that had undergirded the AFIC's reports. He supported paupers' rights to work and enjoy the fruits of their own labor, but he acknowledged a role for the state in securing this end. A central goal of his program was "a better classification of the dependent and criminal classes, to diminish their number, and to secure a better means for their restoration to the ranks of industrious life." Howe occupied the ambivalent position of wanting to classify the poor, while at the same time fretting about the severance of social ties through institutionalization.[32]

It is unclear how much direct influence Howe and the State Board of Charities exerted on the legislature, but when it passed its new vagrancy act in 1866, the effect was to implement part of Howe's program of classification. Although prewar Massachusetts had been home to some of the more strident poor-law reformers, it does not seem to have split vagrancy completely from the general system of poor laws. The new law enumerated clearly what constituted vagrancy. Gone were the antiquated British definitions; in their place was a description of underclass life, probably copied from New York's prewar statute. In addition to the usual idlers and beggars, the law denominated "all persons wandering abroad and visiting tippling shops or houses of ill fame, or lodging in groceries, out-houses, market places, sheds, barns, or in the open air, and not giving a good account of themselves" to be guilty of vagrancy. Equally important was the provision that these offenders should be sent to houses of correction, workhouses, or houses of industry. Whether legislators had heard from Howe specifically or not, they agreed with his general desire to categorize the poor.[33]

The Massachusetts law was not a tramp act, but it did move toward the more specific definitions employed a decade later and toward the separation of a clear class of offenders. Lawmakers in Pennsylvania pursued a similar course, even as they clung to the state's relatively benevolent tradition. Acting in ways similar to Massachusetts, the legislature altered the state's hundred-year-old vagrancy law by extending coverage specifically to public places such as railroad depots, steamboat landings, banks, restaurants, taverns, and gambling houses. It created a special constable's office to police these areas and authorized these officers to conduct searches of vagrants' luggage and other belongings if they suspected such people were thieves, gamblers, burglars, or pickpockets. Evidence produced from these searches could lead to a one-hundred-dollar fine and three months in the county jail. A local law two years later indicated that the incidence of vagrancy continued to increase in the immediate postwar era. Its preamble noted that the number of "vagrants and wanderers" requiring support in Northampton County had "largely increased" and that no uniform rule existed for supplying their needs. "Justice requires that the rule should be uniform," the legislature added. To meet this need, lawmakers enjoined the county to "take care" of these wayfarers by providing food and lodging. It also prohibited summary convictions for vagrants unless they were drunk.[34]

Caring for wayfarers in Pennsylvania constituted part of the response to the upsurge in vagrancy and begging caused by the war itself. The war created a large group of disabled veterans who begged subsistence in the streets of northern cities. Despite organized efforts to assist them, they and other homeless people clogged northern relief agencies even before the depression overburdened social welfare providers. By the early 1870s northern police stations initiated the practice of lodging and feeding homeless people, much to the dismay of charity reformers.[35]

The war had also orphaned numerous children, and reformers took steps to assist them and separate them from the rest of the paupers. Pennsylvania headed the postwar relief effort, providing both support and education. State boards of charity and other organizations also removed children from what they saw as the demoralizing effects of adult dependents. In New York this culling process drew on antebellum roots. In 1862, the state allowed local magistrates to drain juvenile delinquents into the House of Refuge that had been established in 1824 by the Society for the Reformation of Juvenile Delinquents in the City of New York, an offshoot of the New York Society for the Prevention of Pauperism. In 1867 it transferred to houses of refuge teenage prostitutes who were arrested or who appeared voluntarily, "professing a desire for reform." Finally, in 1878 lawmakers outlawed placing children in the poorhouses, moving them instead to orphan asylums and reformatories. New York legislators also tried to remove able-bodied adults from the poorhouse on a local basis. In 1862 the legislature authorized justices of the peace in Ontario County to convey any "improper person to be sent to the poor house" to Syracuse's workhouse in neighboring Monroe County.[36]

Yet legal developments during the 1860s were not accompanied by the extreme rhetoric of a decade later. Before the mid-seventies, existing charity organizations seemed able to take care of the problem. In 1865 the New York City police found the streets filled with vagrant children "in training to recruit the fearful armies of vice and crime." The report was noticed, but it did not spark great anxiety. "We have most confidence in the existing voluntary institutions which need only to be liberally supported and enlarged to sweep the city clean of childish vagrancy and poverty," the *New York Times* commented. Four years later the paper declared that the city's eight thousand ragpickers were industrious souls. They lived in "very neat" houses, stayed free of vice and disorder, and aided the economy. As late as September 1873 the paper remained convinced that distribution was the chief problem with poor relief and that the system could be improved easily.[37]

By 1874 opinion was changing. In that year Boston passed an ordinance to require vagrant children to produce proof of school enrollment, and New

York City considered a similar regulation to implant "the love of industry and self-respect" in its truants. Municipalities across the nation discovered "a vast fringe of destitute humanity" that hung "on the edge of the busy, bustling, and industrious life" that constituted "the heart of the City." In New York the police classified between 10,000 and 15,000 persons as vagrants. Boston logged 58,000 homeless lodgers at station houses in 1874. The secretary of the Chicago Relief and Aid Society reported an astounding 150,000 lodgers in 1874, many of them "rounders," repeat visitors. The police chief of San Francisco raided the city's wharves, arresting vagrants who endangered hay bales with their pipe ashes.[38]

These concerns, however, did not always produce immediate action. In 1876, the same year that the wave of tramp laws began to pass northern legislatures, Pennsylvania reformed its poor laws in a manner out of step with the general trend. A series of two laws separated the poor law from the vagrancy law, but both stressed provision over punishment. The poor-law act, which aimed for uniformity in poorhouse erection, began with a general injunction to benevolence. "It is the duty of society to make provisions for the comfortable maintenance of those upon whom fortune has frowned who are found to be destitute and void of the means of support," the preamble read. The act retained many of the features of earlier laws, including the binding out of poor children as apprentices and the discretion to grant outdoor relief as long as it did not exceed the cost of indoor support. In trying to enact humanitarianism, the legislature commanded poorhouse directors to visit poorhouse apartments monthly, "see that the inmates [were] comfortably supported," listen to inmates' complaints, and see that they were redressed.[39]

The vagrancy law passed on the same day preserved and in ways extended Pennsylvania's benevolent tradition. It retained the 1767 definitions but changed the administration significantly to incorporate increasing demands for work in return for support. The act required vagrants to labor at county farms, on roads or highways, or in workhouses, poorhouses, houses of correction, or common jails for one to six months. Unlike laws in some other states, this statute aimed to meet specific needs by stipulating that labor should be "suited to the proper discipline, health and capacity" of offenders. Lawmakers required local officials to house vagrants in "comfortable lodging" and feed and clothe them "in a manner suited to the nature of the work engaged and in the condition of the season." Custodians who neglected this duty could be fined one hundred dollars and jailed for up to three months.

Another section allowed local officials to assist offenders in paying their own way back home by finding private employment for them. In addition, the law allowed time off for good behavior, provided certificates exempting a released offender from arrest for five days, and authorized officials to give money to aid vagrants in leaving the county.[40]

For the most part, the enactments of the late 1860s and early 1870s diverged little from antebellum vagrancy laws. Yet they also represented the last manifestation of the prewar conception of the offense. During the latter half of the 1870s, state legislatures throughout the North passed new and harsher tramp laws to augment or supersede antebellum statutes. By 1880, when the tramp scare began to subside, states' powers under older vagrancy statutes had been extended through the new tramp acts. These laws restricted movement by making misdemeanors like loitering into felonies when committed by a tramp and provided for long terms of incarceration at hard labor. New Hampshire led the way with a revised vagrancy statute in 1875; New Jersey came next with the first real "tramp" act in 1876. Although these laws varied in their particulars, they employed similar definitions and punishments and can be considered as a group.[41]

In the narrow, legal sense, a primary purpose of these laws was to define a tramp as something different from the vagrant or sturdy beggar of colonial and antebellum days. The principal attributes were mobility, homelessness, and reliance on public or private charity. Representative of other states, Pennsylvania formulated this definition of a tramp: "any person going about from place to place begging, asking or subsisting upon charity, and for the purpose of acquiring money or a living and who shall have no fixed place of residence or lawful occupation in the county or city in which he shall be arrested." Legislators took pains to say who was *not* a tramp. Nearly all states exempted females, minors, and the blind. Some added people who were disabled. Lawmakers intended to restrain a particular problem: adult, able-bodied males who had rejected work and home for the open road.[42]

In addition to this "common tramping," most states added sections punishing severely a specific list of behaviors. The New Hampshire law, similar to those in other states, imposed a maximum two-year confinement at hard labor in the state prison for any tramp who entered a house without permission, lit a fire in the roadway or on private property without consent, carried a weapon, or threatened to injure people or their property. For tramps who did "willfully and maliciously" harm people or their real or personal property the maximum penalty rose to five years. With varying precision, other states copied these harsh provisions. Some went even further. Wisconsin, for example, added a novel clause that allowed two years' imprisonment for "any five or more tramps" who assembled or congregated together for "encouraging vagabondage."[43]

While intent and definition were similar in most states, administrative practices were more diverse. Though longer than those for antebellum vagrants, terms of incarceration and the use of fines varied widely. So too did the power to arrest. In some states, citizens were authorized to haul in tramps. In others, the legislature mandated the creation of special tramp constables. Still others left capturing the offenders up to established local officials, some of whom received a fee for each tramp they cuffed. Punishment usually remained tied to local enforcement. Only in New England did the matter become entirely the function of the state. Many states employed some mix of local and state action. Common tramping was more often treated at the local level, whereas those committing the enumerated offenses were sent to the state penitentiary. Some states, most notably New York, provided state funding for local administration.[44]

These generalizations describe the tramp laws of the industrial Northeast and Midwest, but at least five states in the South and three in the West also enacted similar legislation. The southern laws are deceptive. They all used the word "tramp" and employed some of the same restrictions of definition used in the North. In addition, the Tennessee and Alabama statutes confined punishment to fines or incarceration in jail or the workhouse. Mississippi, however, was more vague. It prescribed imprisonment and fines but stipulated that the offender, when committed, would "be dealt with as other convicts." Perhaps this clause was intended to sanction hiring out. North Carolina acted most peculiarly of all. In 1879, the state passed a tramp act that was a near replica of northern laws. Yet at the same time, it affirmed the vagrancy statute that had been voided by the Freedmen's Bureau in 1866. This section proscribed general idleness, neglect of family, and "sauntering about without employment." The fines and prison terms were lower in this section, but it also allowed other punishments that were "not to exceed the above mentioned."[45]

Phrases used in these statutes suggest several explanations for the southern tramp acts. In part, they were the product of Redeemer governments' desire to control African American labor. Still, the southern enactments had some connection to the social crisis in the North. Some tramping laborers went south in the winter in search of work and shelter. Southern editors complained about this onslaught bitterly. "Louisiana is too poor to feed tramps and vagabonds from the Western and Northern States," the *New Orleans Picayune* protested. "We have no surplus for the Communists and vagabonds of other states." Transient laborers within the South might also have been the target of the laws. Young, male laborers, especially later in the century, moved across the South, following the labor market. A final possibility is that southern lawmakers passed "tramp" laws in response to the Black Exodus of the late 1870s. Working through organized colonization societies, thousands of African Americans left the South for Kansas and other western and northern states. Peaking in 1879, their movements may have been the "tramping" to which southern lawmakers reacted.[46]

The western laws, enacted over the course of the decade, resembled older vagrant statutes. Definitions included common drunkards, common prostitutes, gamblers, loiterers, and rowdy boys. Penalties included fines and hard labor at the county level. Conspicuously absent were the specific offenses and exemptions of northern and midwestern statutes. In the West, legislators used traditional vagrancy rules to bring order to mining camps and the frontier towns that supported them. As easterners went west, they took the regulations of urban life with them.[47]

While southern and western states enacted tramp laws, then, the significant change occurred in the industrial Northeast and Midwest. This period of rapid legal change stemmed from numerous sources. The bourgeois reformers who had pushed for stronger vagrancy laws during the antebellum years voiced the strongest support for harsher punishments, but now they and others used a wider array of arguments. Moreover, support for new legislation came from sources outside elite reform circles.[48]

Occasionally, advocates of new laws located the source of tramping in the Civil War. Cut loose by the war, a writer in *Scribner's Monthly* claimed, demoralized men had become "rovers, nominally looking for employment but really looking for life without it." They threatened to become "a huge brood of banditti who [would] ultimately become as monstrous and as disgraceful to [the] country and to Christian civilization as the banditti of Greece or Southern Italy."[49]

"Crimes" perpetrated by tramps presented another stimulus for restriction, and they seemed to be occurring on all levels of society—individual, municipal, corporate, and interstate. Reports about women and girls being attacked by tramps flooded the press. In a typical story, Carrie Roberts, a servant girl in Cincinnati, discovered a tramp trying to lift a box of her mistress's jewelry. Carrie turned out to be the heroine, scaring the intruder off with shots from a revolver. Others, like Mrs. Winegar, were not so lucky. So, it appeared, tramps were attacking individuals; they were also raiding villages. In January 1876 "eighteen of these Bedouins of civilization . . . joined together in a raid upon the unsuspecting town of Belvidere, [New Jersey]," probably prompting the first true tramp act. After this event, the *New York Times* predicted "a very little effort would collect in almost any part of the Northern States a body of tramps large enough to capture and sack any of [their] smaller villages." In July 1878 the *Baltimore Gazette* reported that a band of fifty tramps boarded a Baltimore and Ohio Railroad Company train and threw the freight off to waiting companions. In the summer of 1878, a group of tramps commandeered a train in Iowa and rode it to Wisconsin.[50]

Political considerations also figured in the tramp panic and the push for laws. After a group of reformers convened in Ohio to consider legislation, the *New York Times* predicted wryly that the tramps would respond in kind by organizing a political party. Five months later, in April 1876, the paper detected a convergence of tramps on Cleveland for said convention, suggesting that the alleged conference would adopt a "broad platform of more greenbacks and fewer large housedogs." Tramps were becoming associated with paper money reformers. By October of that election year the *Times* was convinced that tramps were traveling in to cast their votes "to exert their influence for Tilden and Reform." A midwestern novelist seconded these fears, asserting that proper laws controlling tramps could not be passed "as long as political tricksters [were] permitted to profit by the votes of this element of venality." After the rail strikes of 1877 tramps became increasingly linked to labor radicalism, syndicalism, and Communism.[51]

Social scientists also sought to clarify the problem by turning to heredity and environmentalism. The New York Board of State Charities, headed by Charles Hoyt, provided statistical data on the nature of tramps, finding them to be primarily young, male immigrants. John V. L. Pruyn, who collated the data, concluded that the "army of tramps" was growing and becoming permanent. "All these young and vigorous men will transmit to their children their own debased habits and character of life," he warned. Charity reformer C. S. Watkins of Davenport, Iowa, contended that pauperism originated and spread in degraded households, and this state of affairs justified "the forcible entry into the domestic sanctity of even such a home" to protect its children. The most influential argument for environmentalism and heredity came from Richard Dugdale. Visiting a rural jail in Ulster County, New York, in

1874, Dugdale noticed a high prevalence of poverty and crime among a family he called "the Jukes." Investigating the family's history, he found it had been dominated by paupers, criminals, and prostitutes for five generations. Dugdale's conclusion, readily accepted by his readers, was that degeneracy was hereditary.[52]

Some writers pushed these conclusions to the extreme. One constructed an elaborate racial theory, describing tramps as a "tribe." As civilization proceeded, some people resisted, "retaining their old instincts and propensities, a residuum as it were of the older savage type." In the past the state had simply exterminated these "failures of civilization," thereby contributing an "essential factor of progress." Humanitarian concerns had prompted the abandonment of this "weeding out" and had left social scientists searching for the best way to reinstate the process. Based on Dugdale's and Hoyt's reports, the writer concluded that a new "thoroughbred" strain of the "predatory tribe" had developed, and he stated further, *"This tribe must be throttled, or—it will throttle us!"*[53]

Occasionally, more perceptive social observers blamed the depression on industrial growth itself. One *New York Times* editorialist claimed that New England tramping grew from "the social change that ha[d] taken place in that region within the memory of the past generation." Manufacturers had introduced "a new element in the population" that differed from the former inhabitants of the "Land of Steady Habits." Edward Everett Hale, speaking to the Conference of Boards of Public Charities in 1877, also associated tramping with industrial changes. An "oversupply of labor," he noted, could "remove many unskilled laborers from the places where they had made their homes." In a more radical vein, Montgomery Blair, president of the Maryland Prison Aid Society, suggested that "the wealth of the Stewarts and the Astors" set men to tramping. Pinkerton believed the main cause for the tramp crisis was the Panic of 1873. It had turned people out of work and made tramping the only way to subsist outside the poorhouse: "Their rapid increase, which is so alarming to certain kid-gloved social scientists, is the direct result of unprecedented hard times and conditions which a great and protracted war has left us as a legacy." When economic prosperity returned, tramping would subside.[54]

Support for measures to punish tramps was widespread. Clearly, bourgeois reformers, now organized throughout the North into charity societies, took the lead in calling for and sponsoring new legislation. They now lobbied actively for laws to help cement the distinction between worthy and unworthy poor. The charge of some historians that the New York Tramp Act was almost a plot by charity organizations is surely oversimplified, but these organizations did wield considerable influence in Albany and in other state capitals. They wanted legislation that would help remove charity from localities to the state and that would define clearly who deserved help and punish those who did not. In the end the charities got less than they wanted, but their members helped shape the bills that finally became law. In a general sense also, organized charity's goal of classifying the poor helped secure the more precise definitions of "crime" contained in tramp laws.[55]

Prominent politicians as well as lawyers and jurists added their backing. Horatio Seymour, Democratic nominee for president in 1868, warned in a *Harper's* article in December 1878 that tramps were coalescing into a "kind of organization" and developing a "system of brigandage." After a tortuous explication of the possible benefits of public whipping, Seymour recommended harsh punishment to rid the country of "a dangerous and growing class of wanderers." In December 1877, Montgomery Blair, who had served as Lincoln's postmaster general, organized a conference on tramps that called on the Maryland legislature to pass more stringent measures. Seymour D. Thompson, legal editor and later a justice of the Missouri Court of Appeals, recommended "stringent vagrant laws" under which persons who went about the country begging would "be arrested and *put to work*."[56]

Newspapers also called for restrictive legislation. "Benevolent country and city folk in the Eastern states begin to believe that they must repress in some manner this odious and steadily increasing nuisance," the *New York Times* editorialized in February 1875. The *New York Tribune* kept a steady watch on vagrancy and tramp bills in the state legislature and featured frequent editorials in support of suppressing tramps in one way or another. Still, the paper remained less strident than the *Times*. When Pennsylvania passed a draconian tramp law in 1879, the *Tribune's* editors warned that such "iron measures" would drive many of the needy poor to "absolute starvation." Such laws, they believed, must distinguish between "imposture and actual suffering." Press coverage extended beyond metropolitan areas as well. Farm magazines took a keen interest in the tramp crisis. For example, the *American Farmer*, a Baltimore publication, reported on the convention organized in the city by Blair and published a guest editorial entitled "The Tramp Nuisance."[57]

Charity societies, politicians and jurists, and national newspapers all suggest solid bourgeois support for tramps laws, but the new legislation should not be seen as coming wholly from the elite or middle class. Luther Stephenson Jr., chief of Massachusetts detectives, sent two men to investigate tramps in the western part of his state. Based on their research, Stephenson reported to the governor: "Instances have been brought to my notice where people who live in the outskirts of towns are compelled to leave their homes to avoid the dangers and troubles from this cause." Vigilance committees formed to patrol railroads and scare off hoboes. The Lima, Ohio, city council initiated a state convention that met on December 8, 1875, in Columbus. Attended by seventy-eight delegates from twenty-five towns and cities, the conference considered the power to arrest vagrants and commit them to the workhouse. In New Haven, Philadelphia, and Detroit, local charity organizations issued relief tickets on the prewar model of the New York Association for Improving the Condition of the Poor. Portland, Maine, instituted a registry for the poor, and Lowell, Massachusetts, set up a "Ministry-at-Large" to beggars.[58]

Popular suppression was in keeping with the general American tradition of extralegal violence. Still, grassroots efforts were not always successful, sometimes leading toward assistance instead of repression. In Boston, local officials helped an Italian family who begged start a fruit stand business. One telling incident involved an attempt in Montgomery County, Pennsylvania, to establish a local vigilance committee to arrest tramps along the Pennsylvania Railroad. In calling the meeting, local citizens responded to tramping laborers who congregated at a deserted building outside the Montgomery County village of Bryn Mawr. At the time of the meeting in July 1877, this group of tramps numbered near fifty and included a barber, a tailor, and a carpenter, as well as common laborers. These men intended to make money in the summer's harvest and then return to their usual occupations. Ultimately, the move for a Citizen's Protective Association failed as the president of the meeting argued that "all tramps were not habitual vagrants" and that the depression had thrown many out of work. The local committee, he believed, could devise a plan to protect the town's citizens "but also to rescue the tramp from the degradation which was consequent upon his unfortunate position."[59]

Tramp laws, then, arose from a variety of sources. Nevertheless, all of this argument and agitation should not be confused with the causes of legal change. The genuine tramp acts of the North and Midwest came from deeper cultural roots, and they represent the fruition of a process begun during the antebellum period. While not without criticism or opposition, the tramp laws originated in a complex interaction between emergent bourgeois ideals about the paternalist state, the labor market, the construction of gender, and the insecurity of the bourgeoisie itself.

Since the antebellum period, bourgeois reformers aimed for a paternalist state that legitimated a social duty to work in a capitalist labor market. Nonetheless, not everyone in the 1870s was prepared to accept a modern bureaucratic state, even in the atmosphere of "crisis" generated by tramping. Pinkerton, for example, criticized legal punishment as a way to deal with the problem: "If you throw a man in prison as a vagabond, you leave the prison taint upon him, and forever he is embittered and at war with his fellows." Both the Ohio and New Hampshire tramp laws received criticism as being too stringent, and in Cleveland, the Ohio act was nearly a dead letter because of it. Such qualms notwithstanding, advocates of new measures still hoped to erect a modern state with powers far surpassing the local justice of the past.[60]

For the state to carry out its task, however, required legitimation of its administrative power in contravention of common-law rights. As with antebellum vagrancy proceedings, legal argument about the state's powers during the postbellum period focused on summary arrest and conviction. In 1873, the Illinois Supreme Court upheld an award for damages under a trespass writ to a Chicago tent and flag maker who had been arrested without a warrant by the Chicago police. When the state passed its tramp law in 1877 to overcome this decision, a Chicago Criminal Court judge denounced the new legislation as "villainous" and "the most atrocious statute that was ever placed upon the statute books in this State." The law, he declared, set up a "one-man-power-system" that left the liberties of poor Chicagoans "actually and practically at the mercy of the police force of the City of Chicago." The law abrogated the right to trial by jury reaffirmed in Illinois's 1870 constitution, and it exposed "honest poverty to be contumed and punished as a crime." In short, the judge believed, the statute had been "conceived and planned . . . by those who had nothing else in view than to subject all the poor classes of this community to the power of the police." These Illinois jurists were not alone. As late as 1883, a Luzerne County, Pennsylvania, judge dismissed a tramp act detention because it involved summary conviction. The judge relied on the 1876 vagrancy act to argue that "no person [could] be convicted of vagrancy unless he ha[d] committed some act forbidden" under that law.[61]

The clearest judicial opposition to the administrative power of the state came from the Maine Supreme Court. In an odd twist of events, the same court that had upheld the state's paternal power in Nott's case struck it down in an 1876 decision. The opinion in *Portland v. Bangor* is remarkable not only because it upheld common-law rights in the face of the modern state but also because it linked events in the North directly to the Reconstruction of the South. Judge Charles W. Walton declared that summary commitments to the workhouse by overseers of the poor under the state's poor laws violated the Fourteenth Amendment by depriving people of liberty without due process of law. While liberty could be restrained, the judge averred, the matter had to be investigated and the accused had a right to be heard. If these rights were not upheld, then Reconstruction was a sham. "If white men and women may thus be summarily disposed of at the north," Walton pointed out, "of course black ones may be disposed of the same way in the south; and thus the very evil which it was particularly the object of the fourteenth amendment to eradicate will still exist." [62]

By 1876, opinions such as Walton's were clearly out of the mainstream of bourgeois thinking. Since the late antebellum period, courts and legislatures had been headed in the direction taken by the Ohio Supreme Court in an 1869 case about the state's power to commit boys to its reform farm. *Prescott v. State* involved a boy who had burned down the barn of a Van Wert County farmer. His attorneys argued that the summary nature of the commitment undermined the right to due process under the Fifth Amendment and his right to trial by jury under the Ohio constitution. What is important about the case is how the state's attorney and the court found their way around common-law rights. State's attorney James L. Price argued, and the court accepted, that these rights did not adhere because, in fact, the commitment did not involve an indictment, charge, or punishment. The statute was "intended to subserve the *public good*" and cause "*no individual injury.*" Through the law, the state aimed to "protect itself and promote the public weal." [63]

The quasi-judicial power of a modern state embodied in *Prescott* prefigured what bourgeois advocates of new laws during the tramp crisis hoped to achieve. Horatio Seymour voiced this desire most clearly. He suggested that magistrates be given the power to bind out tramps and to force parents to discipline their children. Beyond this odd stricture, Seymour hoped to erect something like a legal caste for tramps. Local authorities, he believed, needed "the same right of control over vagrants, disorderly persons, and habitual offenders which parents or guardians ha[d] over their children or wards." He added, "The fact that they belong to these classes should be judicially decided after a certain number of convictions." Once they were declared to be second-class citizens, the loss of other rights would naturally follow. "When they are enrolled in these classes," Seymour concluded, "they should have no right to vote at any election." [64]

Seymour's desire for legal classes represented an extreme, but only an extreme. The summary powers inherent in older vagrancy laws and augmented in the new postwar tramp legislation provided one of the links to a modern state that was both bureaucratic and paternal. The reformers who won this victory hoped to use the state for a number of ends. At the first level, they expected the state to assert and legitimate the social duty to work in a capitalist labor market.

Work itself, then, constituted the starting point for reformers' discussions. As Daniel Rodgers has noted, the tramp scare represented a crisis in the work ethic, but arguments about tramps and work went beyond the moral dimension of free labor. The key for reformers was that tramps had *willfully* rejected the social duty to work. The tramp's profession was indolence; he had "deliberately planned to live without work." Nothing could be offered that would induce tramps to return to labor, for "every month of idleness confirm[ed] them in their vagabond life, [made] them more unfit for useful labor, and increase[d] the danger to the community because of their presence." The Reverend A. P. Peabody of Harvard spoke for many when he declared, "The major part of these people are, no doubt, idlers by choice." *Scribner's* stated the case more bluntly: "If anything is notorious now, it is that ninety-nine tramps in a hundred . . . would not work at any wages if they could. . . . They scorn work and scout the idea of engaging in it. They coolly propose to live upon the community, and to 'eat their bread in the sweat of other men's faces,' and to do this *in perpetuo.*" Indiscriminate alms added to the problem by removing the incentive to work, these commentators believed. If tramps could survive without work, declared New York State Board of Charities member Martin Anderson, "more and more [would] join them until vagabondage [grew] to be an unendurable nuisance." [65]

For many reformers, tramps had not just rejected work in general but the steady, rationalized toil of industrial life, and these writers feared a general breakdown of society as a result. Levi L. Barbour, president of the Detroit Association of Charities, believed that although insufficient demand for labor sometimes caused unemployment, vagrancy usually came from "the inability or unwillingness of the person to adapt himself to any kind of labor *steadily.*" Investigating New York's workhouse on Blackwell's Island, William H. Davenport described what he called "the Work-house spirit." If allowed, inmates "rested at once from their toil, and, collecting in small groups, lazily smoked and talked." Davenport suggested that part of the problem was lack of wages, for without pay no one could be expected "to work with much gusto." Still, he believed, steady work should come naturally: "An energetic man could not from habit refrain from being industrious in the task given to him." For Davenport and others, tramps simply had not internalized the routines of a capitalist system of wage labor. Vagrants had no regard for the future, nor did they realize the value of money. If their number continued to grow, predicted C. W. Chancellor, secretary of the Maryland State Board of Health, "the result would be general impoverishment, and if they continued to increase, general ruin." [66]

Nearly all the conservative commentators agreed on one element of the solution: the state should put tramps to work. The opinion of E. L. Godkin, editor of the *Nation*, was typical. "The spectacle of a goodly number of professional vagrants being promptly arrested and made to work, and work hard, for their board and lodging," he wrote in 1878, "will greatly encourage the rest to efforts at voluntary and honest labor." Praising the 1879 Pennsylvania tramp act, Pennsylvania charity organizer Diller Luther suggested establishing district workhouses for "a system of compulsory labor" to be placed "under State control." As a last resort, Barbour contended, "The strong arm of the law [must] be invoked and this persistent blot on the face of society be placed perforce where he shall be compelled to work, and the community relieved from the incubus of his presence." Based on these general suggestions, states, charity organizations, and municipalities started various programs to compel labor in return for support. Stephenson, the Massachusetts detective, supported a system of registration for vagrants. *Scribner's* proposed that "a standing commission of vagrancy should be instituted in every large city, and every county of the land; and institutions of industry established for the purpose of making these men self-supporting." [67]

Given statements such as these, it would be appealing to see tramp acts as directly enforcing labor contracts through the criminal law. But just as in the Reconstruction South, adherents of these ideas did not speak with one voice. Support for compulsory labor was almost universal, but when charity reformers tried to justify these schemes, unanimity broke down. Some reformers saw work in return for support as a path to market discipline. Pruyn in New York made this basis explicit: "When 'tramps' throughout the State are obliged to work, and to render an equivalent by their labor for the aid they receive, it is believed that they will take measures to provide for themselves, preferring to work on their own account rather than to labor, under compulsion, for the public." Others simply wanted tramps to go away. Massachusetts authorities posted the tramp acts in towns and along roadways in the hope of scaring tramps off. Brooklyn reformer Seth Lowe also suggested that tramp acts effectively put the nuisance out of sight. When subjected to the work test, "the number of tramps and vagrants diminished almost as rapidly as the snow-banks of winter before the suns of spring." Francis Wayland Jr. of Yale upheld compulsory labor for various reasons: "[Tramps] should be placed in a situation which will provide for their necessities, compel them to perform useful work, prevent them from committing crime, render it impossible for them to propagate paupers." [68]

Like their antebellum counterparts, reformers based arguments about work in different assessments of its social value. Those who saw charity as a contractual relationship envisioned labor as a commodity and clung to the prewar concept of self-ownership. Others, even some of the most conservative, emphasized skill as the value of labor. Henry Pellew, vice president of the New York Association for Improving the Condition of the Poor, argued that a main cause of tramping and pauperism was that young men no longer acquired a skilled trade. For Barbour, one problem was that a vagrant had "no trade, no business, no aim in life, but to satisfy his daily wants at the expense of the public." Connecting ironically with artisanal criticisms from earlier in the century, people such as Pellew and Barbour recognized the relationship between deskilling and poverty, although not following it to its conclusion. Yet the idea of value in work itself had not been abandoned. Sounding like Edward Everett or Joseph Kiddoo, Anderson suggested that humans needed physical labor to live: "Man is constituted, bodily and mentally, that happiness is found only in connection with constant systematic labor." [69]

Fear about rejection of industrial work discipline was one central motivation behind the transformation of vagrancy laws into tramp acts, but these arguments about work usually did not appear outside the context of gender. Seymour located part of the problem of juvenile vagrants in an excess of masculinity. He hoped that increasing magistrates' powers would "put an end to the bravado and swagger of disorderly boys which [were] so much admired by their weak or youthful companions." For most reformers, however, the problem was not brash manliness but a lack of it. Tramps defied nineteenth-century middle-class gender roles, especially with regard to masculinity. Moreover, they evaded the force of domestic discipline, which middle-class northerners viewed as the ultimate basis of social order. Already available in antebellum discourse, these concerns about gender and domesticity came to the fore in the postwar period. [70]

Work played a central role in mid-nineteenth-century constructions of masculinity, and tramps' lack of it deeply troubled social critics. Anderson explicitly linked work to gender, ironically harkening back to Jacksonian artisanal language. Labor created a sense of well-being because as the worker witnessed his crops or manufactures taking shape each day, he knew he created something useful. In doing so, he became "conscious of a new accession of manhood" and developed "a desire to provide for himself, to be his own master." In other words, self-reliance and personal mastery constituted central elements of masculinity. Viewed this way, those dependent on handouts or public support appeared to be its antithesis. As the *New York Times* put it, "The tramp slouches through life, a continual reproach to the inscrutable Providence that has permitted him to exist, yet has not made him a crawling thing. . . . He does not lift his feet and set them down again as a man does." For the Iowan Watkins, "Pauperism is the last stage on the downhill journey of manhood, and when once reached, the victim is then and thenceforth *sans* pride, *sans* self respect and *sans* ambition." [71]

Masculinity was not only a product of labor; it was also defined by its supposed opposite. As in the story about Mrs. Winegar, charity reformers placed degraded male tramps in opposition to weak women. C. D. Warner of the *Hartford Courant* boasted that through its tramp law his state had rid itself of "the hordes of worthless vagabonds who made their living without work by preying on the community, robbing and assaulting defenceless women, and being a continual terror on the rural population." Similarly, the *New York Tribune* worried about tramps' impostures upon "the rural feminine soul" and about their assaults on the homes of "tender-hearted women folk." Wayland made a similar point: "Indeed, [the tramp] seems to have wholly lost all the better instincts and attributes of manhood. He will outrage an unprotected female, rob a defenseless child, or burn an isolated barn, or girdle fruit trees, or wreck a railway train, or set fire to a railway bridge, or pilfer an umbrella with cruel indifference, if reasonably sure of equal impunity." Such images had a double value. They helped portray tramps as outside the bounds of manhood, and they established respectable middle-class males as protectors of women. [72]

The situation of female tramps was more complicated. Though not numerous, women did take to the road. Although they often performed domestic roles in tramp camps, their freedom placed them well outside Victorian constructions of femininity. Female tramps as well as female vagrants presented particular problems of explanation for middle-class writers. Upon seeing a female vagrant on Blackwell's Island, Davenport exclaimed, "Can this brutish monster, casting malevolent side-glances as it sluggishly and painfully descends from its den, be or have been a woman? Not only that, but once, a beautiful and lovely one." Davenport seemed particularly concerned with the ways in which the workhouse disrupted regular gender roles. At one point, he observed two "stalwart females" unloading a cart on the steamboat dock and found the scene unsettling. "The odd situation of these Amazons, as they 'chaffed' with the men around, their bold and confident looks, their apparent delight in their masculinity, fastened them securely in my memory," he disclosed. Josephine Shaw Lowell, like her male counterparts, connected poverty to the breakdown of gender roles. Jails and almshouses degraded women "until the last trace of womanhood" had been destroyed. Lowell cited numerous examples of unwed mothers living in poorhouses with several illegitimate children. Some appear to have been prostitutes, but most were not. Dr. Elisha Harris, corresponding secretary of the New York Prison Association, reversed the imagery, seeing women vagrants as weak victims, open to ridicule and rape by sheriffs and their deputies. Yet these images could not overcome vagrant women's working-class status. Anderson envisioned training child vagrants in ways that would remake the Jacksonian social structure that was beginning to fade. Boys should be taught a skilled trade or farmwork, and girls should be trained in sewing, cooking, and other housework with a view toward becoming domestics. Lowell believed vagrant women had a "deep-seated repugnance to labor" and that they needed to be taught to work. As might be expected, she wanted them to learn housekeeping skills, but she also hoped they might be trained in outdoor chores such as gardening or milking.[73]

Worries about tramps and the destruction of gender roles gained force because they originated ultimately in fears about domestic discipline. Domestic ideology provided a way for the Victorian middle class to adjust to the rigors of modernity. Supposedly it would provide a respite from cruel competition and uncertain fortune and would rein in the independence and excess of Americans, especially of men. Joseph Dacus, who chronicled the 1877 strikes, asserted that most Americans would not accept anarchy because they had homes or expected to get them. People with domestic connections upheld social order, "but neither government nor social order [could] be maintained when the majority of the people [were] homeless and hopeless." According to Luther, "Home influences may reclaim the prodigal wanderer."[74]

To reformers, tramps had abdicated domesticity. By legal and popular definition, they were the homeless. The mendicant, Chancellor noted, "has no fixed place of abode, and when darkness overtakes him, he begins to look about him at random for lodging and shelter." Courts were likely to agree with the definition. In Pennsylvania, the Cumberland County Court of Common Pleas released a man named David Warner from a tramp act arrest because he certified that he lodged with his mother within his home county.[75]

Beyond legal terms, the tramp's homelessness meant that he had severed the cords that bound him to society. Pinkerton described a group of tramps encamped along the Boston and Albany Railroad as "utterly homeless": "In the wide world [they] have no spot that they may go and claim an interest in." According to an editorialist in the *New York Times*, the tramp had escaped from one of the controls over that "American recklessness" that had been "justly charged with so many of [the country's] vices." In short, the tramp was truly independent. He had released the bonds of middle-class life. "Other people have someone more or less dependent upon them, in one way or another," the paper declared. "The tramp has not even the responsibility which binds the sparrow to its mate."[76]

For this reason, the re-creation of domestic roles and emotions was essential. Lowell suggested that vagrant women should be placed in reformatories, but these institutions should not be prisons. "They must be *homes,* — homes where a tender care shall surround the weak and fallen creatures who are placed under their shelter, where a homelike feeling may be engendered, and where, if necessary, they may spend years." Among other things, reformatory inmates must "be induced to love that which is good and pure, and to wish to resemble it; they must learn household duties; they must learn to enjoy work." *Journal of Social Science* editor Franklin Sanborn hoped tramp laws would "convert the modern tramp into a home-keeping citizen, or a fast prisoner."[77]

Reformers' focus on the home also helps explain their obsession with tramps' apparent refusal to accept middle-class material culture. Over and over again, reformers indicted tramps for the way they dressed, walked, and especially smelled. In the words of the *Times,* a tramp was "foul to the eye, loathsome to the nostrils, revolting the moral senses of all decent people" who beheld him. Robert Givins, author of a novel about tramping, placed intemperance within these images as well. One of his characters, a former journalist reduced to tramping, had worked in slaughterhouses, drank beer, and slept with his dirty working-class companions because his "sense of pride" would not allow him to reveal his drunkenness and "disgusting appearance" to men with whom he would usually associate. Barbour decried beggars who sent "dirty, ragged, half-naked children through the streets from door to door to beg even for castaway food."[78]

The middle- and upper-class supporters of tramp laws, then, found the tramp reprehensible on a deep cultural level. He rejected both sets of values, home and work, that blended independence and dependence at the vital core of late-nineteenth-century culture. Hatred for tramps' inversion of dependence and independence sometimes appeared in the same text. Barbour's description of vagrants was an especially clear embodiment of these tensions. For him, vagrants were dependent to the point of disgust: "What a life, to filch each mouthful of food from a stranger's hand by means of a whining lie, through cowardly servility to obtain each garment, to cringe and crawl for each necessity of life, which with the least leaven of manhood could be as readily had as a swallow of water or a breath of air! . . . Can there be drawn a more revolting caricature on God's noblest creation; a more cutting satire upon civilization than that it has produced such a being?" Yet Barbour believed vagrants could not just be ignored because of their "vicious desire to be let alone." Pinkerton recounted the case of a Chicago newspaper business manager who lost his job through a change in the paper's ownership. The last time he saw the man, Pinkerton reported, he was "shuffling" in "animated degradation" yet seemingly cheerful and content, "as though he derived some satisfaction from the reflection that he could go no lower."[79]

Nowhere was the relationship between the loss of home, the rejection of work, and the attendant social ills illustrated better than in *The Man Who Tramps*, probably the earliest tramp novel to appear in the United States. Published in 1878 by Lee O. Harris, an obscure midwestern writer, the story reveals many of the deeper fears that underlay the severity of tramp legislation. *The Man Who Tramps* narrated the adventures of Harry Lawson. Orphaned as a boy, he was taken west by a charity organization to live with a farm family. John Shannon, his adopted father, was kind and gentle, but his mother, Jane, possessed a "naturally petulant and tyrannical disposition." She beat and scolded the boy constantly. Finally, he ran away, not because of any "antipathy to labor" on the farm but because of Jane's "petty tyranny." His natural mother dead, his adopted mother a moral failure, Harry left the protection of the home.[80]

Finding himself alone on the road, friendless and hungry, he found a day's work with a wheat farmer, who took him for a vagabond and warned him that nine times in ten boys who left "comfortable homes" became tramps. As they worked in the fields, the farmer lectured Harry on home and work:

"Whatever may be the troubles at home, it is generally better to bear them than to throw yourself upon the world, without resources, to depend upon charity or chance for your support. Quit the tramping. . . . If you have a home, return to it at once. If not, get into some employment, however humble, at the very first opportunity. Do not wait for work to suit you, but make yourself suit the work." After Harry left the farm, he concluded that the farmer may have been right. "I am travelling almost aimlessly," he reflected. "I shall be compelled to sleep out of doors."[81]

Farther down the road, Harry met another man, called Black Flynn. Flynn made no excuses for his position. "I am a tramp," he boldly proclaimed. "And my business is to beat the world out of a living, but I take from those who are able to give." Flynn was not bound by the regimen of industry: "When I'm weary I rest." Flynn professed that tramps were "content with what they eat and wear, without troubling themselves about the source from which it comes." And one day, all the world would be like this. "[Tramps] are the beginning of the new order of things," Black Flynn prophesied. "And the time will come when they no longer will be vagrants but rulers in the land. Then out of this will come the equality of all men in all things." If the lesson was not clear, Harris interjected the author's voice bluntly later on. The labor unrest of 1877, Harris alleged, did not come from true workingmen but from "the irresponsible floating populace," who had "no home ties to bind them to society."[82]

Many themes in *The Man Who Tramps* were familiar. The relationships between poverty, work discipline, gender, and domesticity had antecedents in the language of antebellum reformers. However, Black Flynn's sense of contentment outside industrial discipline suggested a newer element of the postwar discourse, the fragility of middle-class status itself. On the one hand, the new industrial bourgeoisie felt threatened by the emergence of a working class, a class for whom tramps provided a ready symbol. On the other hand, the new middle class faced fears about its own internal dissolution. Some prewar commentators had edged toward this latter position, but with the depression, both trepidation about downward mobility and the desire to escape middle-class restraints became more prominent.

Bourgeois fears about tramps as a dangerous underclass sometimes appeared directly. As noted, middle-class commentators linked tramps to industrial action and radical labor organizations. "Reluctantly we are obliged to admit," the *New York Tribune* editorialized in 1876, "the advent of a class, which, if not yet dangerous, may speedily become so." Noting Blair's conference in Maryland a little more than a year later, the *Tribune* also exposed candidly the role of law in creating class lines by criminalizing the life of the tramp: "The advantage of treating him like a criminal is, that it makes his immethodical method of life disreputable, and may thus keep the yet uncontaminated from embracing it."[83]

At times, tramps also prompted middle-class commentators to reflect on the top of the class structure. When a pauper accepts public support, an Iowa reformer pointed out, "he acknowledges himself beaten in the game of life, willing to accept the crumbs that fall from the rich man's table." If they recognized their own delicate class position, members of the middle class could have easily viewed this situation as potentially theirs as well. At least one reformer expressed middle-class hatred of the elite by turning to the image of tramping. Anderson comforted his readers (and himself) by pointing out that people who subsisted on investments and trust funds were in actuality the unhappiest of all people. Because they did not work, the idle rich became "whining hypochondriacs" or traveled about "with no well-defined purpose except to kill time." Because of such behavior, these sections of the wealthy were "the analogues respectively of the chronic grumbling pauper and the professional tramp."[84]

More often, though, revelations of class fear appeared in the literary conventions of bourgeois discourse about tramping. Throughout the tramp "crisis" of the 1870s, the metaphorical language created by antebellum reformers found widespread use as a way to talk about poverty. Moreover, this language increasingly came to emphasize the supposed power possessed by tramps, vagrants, and beggars. Barbour saw vagrants as "pirates" on public charity and warned his listeners to be wary of the "cunning" of beggars. To Anderson, paupers were "swindlers," who took the taxes of honest working people. Another image, which became common after the 1877 strike, rendered tramps into an "army." Dacus portrayed tramps and the idle in general as a major force behind the strikes of 1877. In Chicago, tramps came "Marching in by Hundreds." In general, the strikers were aided by "a nondescript class of the idle, the vicious, the visionary and the whole rabble of the Pariahs of society." Because the nation lacked a standing army, "these classes absolutely controlled the country." In the nation's cities, thieves, vagrants, and tramps stayed "on the alert, ready to plunder, burn, and cut throats at the slightest provocation." After the strike, Wayland declared that "large detachments of [the country's] standing army of professional tramps," not the strikers, perpetrated destruction of property. Tramps, *Scribner's* noted, stood "waiting, a great multitude to join in any mob that [would] give them the slightest apology for pillage."[85]

For the most part, these images of collective power were linked to the strike and the fears of social revolution it generated. The military metaphor portrayed middle-class anxiety about working-class consciousness and activism, but it also embraced a subtext of admiration for the alleged power of tramps acting together. Other common images also conveyed an embedded fascination with power. As in prewar discourse, reformers again transformed poor people into animals, diseases, or forces of nature. As noted above, Lowe compared tramps to snowbanks. Luther defined tramps as the pests of society and as wandering predators, who preyed on the community. Wayland and Sanborn recommended strict enforcement of tramp laws, "for tramps, like other migratory creatures, will again return." Harris warned that, with tramps around, the homes of respectable people were no safer than the abodes of the pioneers, which were "surrounded by a wilderness, harboring ravenous wolves and skulking savages." Even Pinkerton, who defended tramps, noted that vagabond beggars had so increased in numbers that they now "travel[ed] in herds."[86]

Tramps and vagrants were also seen as a disease or carriers of it. Although the state controlled infectious diseases such as smallpox and diphtheria, Mrs. W. P. Lynde of the Milwaukee Industrial School believed, its laws did nothing to stop the spread of moral vice by the female vagrant (presumably a prostitute). Instead, the legal system "sent the contagious pestilent forth to exercise her baneful influence wherever—poor, hunted, wounded animal,—she [might] hide or flee." Barbour also employed medical analogies, counseling that "heroic remedies are sometimes as necessary in the suppression of vagrancy as in surgery and medicine." His "heroic measures" included breaking up families, sending fathers and mothers to workhouses and children to reform schools.[87]

The richness of these tropes suggests the considerable uneasiness that had seeped into bourgeois visions of class by the postbellum period. These images of tramps' potency served complex purposes in postwar language. On the most visible level, they turned relatively powerless people into a revolutionary social force that could be controlled outside the American tradition of civil liberties. In addition, like their antebellum counterparts, they dehumanized the poor so harsh remedies would not contradict humanitarianism directly. Reformers' qualms about falling into poverty themselves, however, complicated the matter. The Jacksonian class structure had fostered considerable mobility in both directions; now, in the uncertain economic and legal world of the 1870s, the potency envisioned in tramps and their poverty became an expression of the power potential pauperism held over middle-class reformers.

In reality, most tramps came from the working class, but reformers and social critics often focused on members of the middle class slipping into poverty. In Givins's novel, *The Millionaire Tramp*, several characters had elite or middle-class origins. As noted above, one was a journalist; he had been educated at "a leading university" and had held jobs as a foreman, bookkeeper, and manager. The main figure of the story was an English aristocrat who, after he thought he had killed a man on his estate, fled to America and lived a tramp's life. His main companion, Old Tom, was born into a wealthy New England farm family. Trained as a clergyman, he worked at many jobs throughout life. When he considered his tramping life, Old Tom compared himself with people of higher station: "*This is a period of the world's history when millionaires become paupers;* when the tide of adversity runs against rich as well as poor. I am no worse off, never having had anything, than the man whose income of hundreds of thousands has been depleted to a pittance."[88]

Old Tom was not alone in his assessment. Chancellor of Maryland also realized as much. "Nothing is so generally dreaded as poverty," he wrote. It exposed people to contempt, obscured personal virtue, and left its victims without a clear way out. Pinkerton expressed these fears without evasion. If readers combed their minds, he submitted, they could think of "men and women . . . at one time enjoying a good position or good social standing, [who had,] by some fault of their own, perhaps, but still oftener through ill-fortune, been bereft of their means of support, and, as a consequent, their friends, and in due time became wanderers and vagrants of the road." He continued, "It is also quite true that the growth of tramps has been by no means confined to men and women of the working classes. . . . Men occupying the highest of positions have in some way fallen." To middle-class observers, tramps presented an unpleasant reminder of what "decent people" might become if their fortunes fell.[89]

Some writers were undoubtedly repulsed by the specter of downward mobility and class dissolution, but others seem to have been drawn irresistibly toward the alleged contentment and irresponsibility of tramping. These texts revealed what historian Jackson Lears has called a deep "ambivalence" about industrialization, urban life, and modern culture among the elite.

Pressed too strongly by the tension between the work ethic and the nurturant values of the home, members of the elite rebelled. This allure also suggests the role of an unstable class structure in calling forth new legislation.[90]

Though Lears locates this antimodernist impulse a few decades later, it first surfaced in the 1870s. Both Lowe and Barbour alleged that beggars made a better living than those who worked. Barbour claimed he knew of a Detroit man who had begged $2.50 worth of quarters in a few evening hours, when he could have earned only between $1.25 and $1.50 at prevailing daily wages. The inevitable conclusion was: "Mendicancy is a business, that, viewed in a certain light, pays." Even though Harris hated tramps as much as the next person, he portrayed Flynn as contented. Givins's Old Tom admitted that times were bad in the winter but confessed that summer tramping had its temptations: "There are times when I rather enjoyed myself strolling around the country breathing the fresh air, scenting the clover from meadows, and sleeping soundly under the pine trees," he told his English comrade. "Why, sir, there is a world of freedom in certain phases of a tramp's life in summer." This liberty, some reformers conceded, could not be given up easily. As one New Yorker put it, once a person entered the tramping life, he or she seldom left it.[91]

A *New York Tribune* editorial in 1880 summarized many of the supposed attractions of tramping but went further by connecting it to racial tropes that invoked preindustrial life. A tramp was a tramp, the paper averred, because he did not desire "a competency dull and honest": "He has the vagabond-blood which makes him delight in the risk, the triumph even, the adventurous misery of his life." Not necessarily a criminal, the tramp simply found "the ordinary American money-making career tedious." What tramps rejected was the commercial heart of bourgeois culture, but, the editors continued, the tramp did something more. He chose, "with the Indian and the negro, to supply the lacking picturesque element" in the country's social life. Here, tramps became almost quaint, a kind of throwback to a life gone by in the increasingly commodified world of the industrial capitalist North. Dubbing tramps as "picturesque" undoubtedly marginalized them, but the editors' insistence on the "delight," "triumph," and adventure of the tramping life suggests a nagging longing for the imagined liberation tramps had achieved.[92]

The most open acknowledgment of the benefits of tramping came from Pinkerton, whose entire account constituted an apologia. Although he paused occasionally to protest that he did not mean to defend the bad variety of tramp, he did just that. Pinkerton sang the praises of walking for pleasure, of journeyman tramping, and of historical tramps, who included Abraham, Jesus, Sir Walter Scott, Charles Dickens, and Ben Franklin. He penned a hymn to the sheer adventure of the road, to the joy of seeing people in their everyday lives, and to the pleasures of discovering which hayracks offered a safe bed or which dogs were friendly. He intimated that tramping offered an almost instinctual feeling of satisfaction: "No person can ever get a taste of the genuine pleasure of the road and not feel in some reckless way, but certainly feel, that he would like to become some sort of tramp." He also declared flatly that departing middle-class life was one of the main reasons for wandering. One example was the case of a successful criminal lawyer who suddenly and inexplicably left everything behind for a career of vagrancy. More important, Pinkerton suggested that the lawyer's action was not atypical. When "business adversity" overtakes men, he asserted, "they naturally turn to the road and discover its pleasures, its freedom from care of any grave character, and the utter absence of responsibility, that they have found an easy solution to all their difficulties." [93]

Such antimodernist feelings arose ultimately from tensions within the middle class and its culture. Pinkerton himself did not want antitramp laws, yet he had recently climbed into the middle class and did not appear particularly pleased with what he found there. In this respect, he spoke more plainly about feelings that his cohorts could only intimate. That neither Pinkerton nor other writers were accurate in their descriptions of middle-class tramps strengthens this point. They knew when they wrote that their portrayals were not correct. Available data from charity organizations, newspaper investigations, and social scientists identified tramping with the working class, yet these writers imagined its sources within their own social stratum. Their images belied their own worries about impoverishment and their hopes of release from the burdens of their own class and its culture. In the 1870s, they were not willing to express these feelings candidly, nor were they ready to act on them personally. Suppressing tramps offered one way to lay these emotions to rest. Journalist C. D. Warner perhaps said more than he realized when he wrote that the Connecticut tramp law had "added a feeling of security" far beyond its savings in money to the state. [94]

Explanations based on a collective unconscious can easily be pushed too far. Tramp "crimes" against person and property, popular pressure, labor unrest, and the work of charity associations and social scientists may have been enough to bring about restrictive legislation. In addition, the depression caused unemployment on a scale that the nation had not witnessed before. Huge numbers of men and women out of work and moving about the country on the rails confirmed the formation of an American industrial working class, precisely what prewar republican ideologues hoped to avoid. Still, the country had experienced widespread unemployment in 1819, 1837, and 1857. Elements of the imagery and language used by advocates of new laws had existed since at least the turn of the nineteenth century, but previous legislatures did not go further than amending existing statutes. Even the wartime vagrancy codes of the Union army and the Freedmen's Bureau had fit (although uncomfortably) within antebellum conceptions of free-labor law. Immediate causes account for neither the tramp laws' severity nor the state of panic in which they were enacted. Ultimately, deeper hopes and fears about the modern state, the labor market, gender, and class underlay these new laws, and in particular, their timing.

In the decades after the Civil War, the relationship between work and law underwent a major transition. Farmers and some other employers still clung to the idea of binding laborers in entire contracts, but workers and the courts successfully destroyed the remainders of master-and-servant law that limited the right to quit. Apportionment gave workers their wages, while at-will hiring let capitalists rid themselves of unwanted employees without incurring legal penalties. In addition, industrialists developed new means of legal labor discipline with notification clauses and yellow-dog contracts. These measures diverged considerably from the concerns that characterized labor law at the beginning of the century and even in 1865. In the postwar years, the courts, employers, and employees used the civil law to legitimize a free market in labor. At the same time, however, the criminal law moved in the opposite direction. The tramp acts resurrected the centuries-old use of law as a direct means to compel labor. More important, the laws designated the tramp as an important figure in late Victorian culture, creating a social persona that inherited some traits from prewar vagrants but achieved considerably more explanatory power. With these changes, most of which were complete by around 1880, the antebellum system of free-labor law had become altered beyond recognition.

Conclusion:
Law and Social Change

By the late nineteenth century the bourgeois state had secured a capitalist market in labor. This process, which began about 1815, exerted a profound configurative force on the nature of emancipation and Reconstruction. The demise of slavery happened in the middle of the legal transition to capitalism. It might not even be too much to say that the northern project in the South centered on the creation of a national market in free labor. Whether emancipation occurred because of capitalist development or simply in the middle of it, timing was critical. The developing state of capitalist labor law in 1860 meant that the northerners who sought to create free labor in the South could draw on competing conceptions. Not knowing quite which ones were "law" in the sense of being fixed, they adopted and adapted various parts of legal discourse to fit southern society. In the end, bourgeois law could not prevail entirely in a region with considerably different social relations of production. At home, however, the bourgeois project continued apace, and by 1880 capitalist labor law had engendered the free market envisioned by Marx some thirty years earlier. The state, embodied in labor law, now thoroughly sanctioned a system of social relations in which workers toiled primarily for the means of subsistence. They could leave their employers with few restrictions, and employers could fire them with few restrictions. The state policed the boundaries of the labor market and, in doing so, legitimated the standards of bourgeois culture that kept workers looking for work.

The ways that capitalist labor law affected Reconstruction suggest numerous avenues for understanding other historical problems. First, Reconstruction and emancipation need to be connected more carefully to the general social and cultural history of the nineteenth century. Clearly, emancipation was a social revolution, but the outcome of that revolution depended on the larger social and economic changes of nineteenth-century America. Historians have long recognized this fact, but careful scrutiny of the ways in which antebellum society and culture influenced changes traditionally associated with "Reconstruction" is required.

Moreover, the ways in which law influenced Reconstruction suggest a closer look at how the state interacted with social development in the nineteenth century, especially with regard to class. Antebellum legal developments, as well as those that came later, were not merely a reflection of changes in American society. Rather, law interacted with structures of labor, domesticity, and class. Prewar employers, workers, and courts all sought to manipulate law in ways related to different modes of production, even in the South. Yet law retained some independent power in this process. Long-term labor contracts froze the employment relation, limiting individual agency in breaking work relationships. In much the same way, vagrancy laws crystallized new meanings of work, gender, and class. In regional perspective, these statutes did mirror the larger patterns of northern and southern society. Still, they had transforming effects in both regions; colonial transgressors against the poor laws became morally defined as nineteenth-century beggars.[1]

The autonomous power of law became clear as the nineteenth century continued. During emancipation, importation of northern ideas legitimated some options but foreclosed others. In the mid-1860s labor law still offered some means to protect rights of workers. Though constrained by the dominant language about labor and poverty, some army and Freedmen's Bureau officials realized as much and used apportionment, entirety, and other doctrines experimentally to produce equity. However, when used by conservatives or even by moderates casting about for new ways to organize work, contracts and vagrancy laws embraced assumptions about labor that diminished African American workers' chances of securing the promises of the free-labor ethic. At the constitutional level as well, the belief of moderate congressmen that voluntary servitude was compatible with freedom restricted the meaning and power of the Thirteenth Amendment.

Yet the autonomous power of law went only so far. As local bureau agents confronted the crisis of deprivation in the postwar world, the texts they had received began to lose their meaning. At least some agents searched for ways out of the dominant discourse. Although they were not always successful, that they did so at all should sound a cautionary note to historians who insist on the configurative power of legal culture. More important, African Americans of all classes pushed the edges of legal language and often moved beyond or around it. While the law may have shaped the larger contours of this struggle, black workers nevertheless resisted the harsher elements of labor law and fought instead for fair payment for the time they had worked in ways Joel Parker would have recognized. Their actions suggest the ways in which law as a language was always bounded by class, race, and gender.

In the postwar North the creative potential of law interacting with society was especially important. Changes in labor contract law occurred at least in part because of criticism from within the legal world itself, yet this legal development had considerable impact on the meaning of work and class. When coupled with at-will employment, courts left industrial workers, farmhands, and particularly the managerial class without confidence in their jobs. By 1880 the courts erased from labor contract law the last vestiges of mutual obligation, the hallmark of master-servant relations. For workers this change was a mixed blessing. They were now unrestricted in the market, but so were their employers. Connected to open labor market relations was egalitarian discourse, which posited an individual's unfettered agency. It, too, possessed ambivalent value. Although it did hide power structures, it also served workers well on occasion. As numerous contract litigations show, workers pressed for their rights as long as legal protection existed, and in many cases they won. Moreover, the actions of southern planters or conservative Freedmen's Bureau officials suggest what the employment relation might look like if stripped of both liberal-capitalist and master-servant constructions.

In addition, postwar changes show that the civil law's part in propagating a free market in labor should not be seen apart from criminal law. With regard to work discipline specifically, legislators used the tramp acts to augment the force of the state in defining the work relation at the very time that jurists were decreasing it. In part, the fluidity generated by the civil law might have prompted the tramp acts. Whatever the specific stimulus, the tramp acts allowed a middle class uncertain of itself to define its place vis-à-vis an emerging industrial working class and, simultaneously, to prop up Victorian constructions of gender and domestic discipline, both for the working class and for the middle class itself. Here, specific social groups used law as a way to constitute relations of power.

Finally, the story of free-labor law supports the need to examine more carefully the causal relationships between law, society, and culture. For too long, some historians have sought a definitive break between a "modern" liberal legal order and what came before. Perhaps it would be better to envision distinct periods of interaction between law and society, and even then, to accept that both "law" and "society" cannot be rarified into abstract motive forces. Moreover, these periods of interaction might be different depending on the issue under consideration. Looking at domestic law, for example, might suggest a different periodization of legal history. Whatever the example, "law" and "society" should be seen as representations of much more complex social realities and relationships of power. Close investigation will almost always reveal divergences not only between law and society but within them as well.[2]

Investigations of this sort of legal and social history need to pay much more attention to popular conceptions of law, especially if they deal with some part of the modern administrative state. The Freedmen's Bureau and its antecedents provide a useful example of one of the ways in which a modern state works. In the bureau, relatively "average" people with little or no formal legal training received a mandate to implement "law." To do so, they did their homework, but they also drew on their own popular notions of what constituted free-labor law. In doing so, they became part of legal culture, even though they possessed none of the mystified, internal knowledge of the legal profession. As such, their experience points toward the ways in which the modern bureaucratic state operates. People charged with carrying out state mandates may be trained experts in one sense, but they are not lawyers. They, and even people directly within legal culture, draw on popular notions of law as much as on formal statute or common-law precedent. To understand how law and the state function, then, requires attention to both the formation and reception of legal discourse. It means looking not only at what judges, lawyers, and lawmakers say but at what average people believe they say. Such an analysis requires careful attention to what Stephen Skowronek has called the "intellectual dimension" of state building. To do so means exploring the intellectual histories of the people who administer the state and, more important, locating them in social context. Removing judges or other administrators from their class or other affiliations seriously weakens the ability to understand them.[3]

Viewed in broader perspective, the career of free-labor law illuminates the inchoate nature of legal development across time. While the mid-nineteenth century's construction of law and work was transformed by around 1880, it did not die completely. In fact, the late-nineteenth-century changes in the criminal law were less conclusive than those in the civil law. The vagrancy acts of antebellum America and the tramp laws of the 1870s formed part of a long Anglo-American dialogue about legal control of the underclass. In the last two decades of the twentieth century, Americans have witnessed both an increase of homeless people and a reversion to nineteenth-century language and laws in public discussions of them. Living in a liberal legal world that affords little personal control over the terms of employment, many middle-class Americans remain anxious about the prospects embodied in the beggars produced by their society, and they continue to turn to law to ease their worries.

Notes

Introduction

1. Oliver Otis Howard, Circular Letter, October 14, 1865, Senate, *Orders Issued by the Freedmen's Bureau, 1865–1866*, 39th Cong., 1st sess., S. Exec. Doc. 6, 197–98. The best example of the argument that labor law contradicted the free-labor ethic is in Eric Foner's *Reconstruction: America's Unfinished Revolution, 1863–1877* (New York: Harper and Row, 1989), 155, 208. "Propertyless individuals in the North, to be sure, were compelled to labor for wages," Foner remarks, "but the compulsion was supplied by necessity, not by public officials, and contracts did not prevent them from leaving work whenever they chose." In regard to vagrancy laws, Foner contends that "Northern courts tended to view those without work as unfortunates rather than criminals, usually employing vagrancy laws only to discipline prostitutes and petty thieves."

2. For the most part, I have not discussed the specifics of the free-labor ethic itself. The starting point for understanding its influence on mid-nineteenth-century politics and ideology is in two works by Eric Foner: *Free Soil, Free Labor, Free Men: The Ideology of the Republican Party before the Civil War* (New York: Oxford University Press, 1970), 1–39, and *Politics and Ideology in the Age of Civil War* (New York: Oxford University Press, 1980), 34–76, 97–127. Foner has summarized many of his ideas in "The Meaning of Freedom in the Age of Emancipation," *Journal of American History* 81 (September 1994): 435–60. Another very good summary of what free-labor ideology meant in the Civil War era is Ira Berlin et al., eds., *The Wartime Genesis of Free Labor: The Lower South*, ser. 1, vol. 3 of *Freedom: A Documentary History of Emancipation, 1861–1867* (New York: Cambridge University Press, 1990), 2–6. The most comprehensive treatment of free labor as an ideological construct is Jonathan Glickstein, *Antebellum Concepts of Free Labor* (New Haven: Yale University Press, 1991). On these abstract formulations of free labor, see also David Montgomery, *Beyond Equality: Labor and the Radical Republicans, 1862–1872* (New York:

Alfred A. Knopf, 1967), 30–32; David Brion Davis, *The Problem of Slavery in an Age of Revolution, 1770–1823* (Ithaca, N.Y.: Cornell University Press, 1975), esp. 469–524; and Jonathan A. Glickstein, "'Poverty Is Not Slavery': American Abolitionists and the Competitive Labor Market," in *Antislavery Reconsidered: New Perspectives on the Abolitionists*, ed. Lewis Perry and Michael Fellman (Baton Rouge: Louisiana State University Press, 1979), 195–218.

The social changes that produced capitalist free labor are summarized in Bruce Laurie, *Artisans into Workers: Labor in Nineteenth-Century America* (New York: Hill and Wang, 1989), esp. chaps. 1–3. See also Paul E. Johnson, *A Shopkeeper's Millennium: Society and Revivals in Rochester, New York, 1815–1837* (New York: Hill and Wang, 1978), chap. 3. Most of these American historians follow the lead of E. P. Thompson's pathbreaking work *The Making of the English Working Class* (1963; New York: Penguin, 1968).

Richard B. Morris, *Government and Labor in Early America* (1846; New York: Harper, 1965), is still very useful on legal restraints on labor before the nineteenth century. See esp. chaps. 1, 4, 8.

3. Karl Marx, *Wage Labour and Capital*, in *Karl Marx: Selected Writings*, ed. David McClellan (New York: Oxford University Press, 1977), 250–51.

4. The works by Foner, Glickstein, and Berlin cited in note 2 above make the point about internalized market discipline. The classic formulation is, of course, Max Weber's *The Protestant Ethic and the Spirit of Capitalism*, trans. Talcott Parsons (New York: Charles Scribner's Sons, 1958), esp. chap. 5. Another near classic is E. P. Thompson, "Time, Work-Discipline, and Industrial Capitalism," *Past and Present* 38 (December 1967): 56–97. Also useful is Richard Stott, "British Immigrants and the American 'Work Ethic' in the Mid-Nineteenth Century," *Labor History* 25 (Winter 1984): 86–102. Stott suggests that U.S. workers in the early nineteenth century had internalized industrial work time far more than labor historians acknowledge.

Marx's classic comment about the state comes from Karl Marx and Friedrich Engels, *The Communist Manifesto*, in McClellan, *Selected Writings*, 223.

5. Stephen Skowronek, *Building the New American State: The Expansion of National Administrative Capacities, 1877–1920* (New York: Cambridge University Press, 1982), 3–35; Theda Skocpol, *Protecting Soldiers and Mothers: The Political Origins of Social Policy in the United States* (Cambridge: Harvard University Press, Belknap Press, 1992), 43. For another view of the state in the nineteenth century, see William E. Nelson, *The Roots of American Bureaucracy, 1830–1900* (Cambridge: Harvard University Press, 1982), 1–8. Focusing, in part, on abolitionists and Radical Republicans, Nelson locates the origins of the modern state in "the tension between the idea of majority self-rule and the concern for protecting individual and minority rights" (5).

6. For a further discussion of these points, see chaps. 1, 2, and 6 below.

7. Obviously, this definition is likely to meet with some opposition. Definitions of

"class" in American historiography, I have found, are many and conflicted. I am not attempting here to offer a definition for general use. I am only trying to summarize how I have used "class," and especially "bourgeois," in the pages below. I have not attempted a systematic definition of northern workers, southern planters, or African American slaves as classes, even though I occasionally use the term for them. In addition, I have not employed "bourgeois" rigidly throughout the manuscript, preferring instead for stylistic reasons to use "middle-class" or "elite and middle-class." I mean these only as stylistic devices. Whatever the myriad of social groups in nineteenth-century society, I believe along with the Marxists that a capitalist society, *at the structural level,* tends toward a two-class system. Yet I do not believe that such a Marxist prescription can be taken without a good deal of caution. In short, I believe American historians have a ways to go before they understand class. A promising synthesis that offers a Marxist analysis of the Civil War is John Ashworth, *Slavery, Capitalism, and Politics in the Antebellum Republic,* vol. 1, *Commerce and Compromise, 1820–1850* (New York: Cambridge University Press, 1995). Ashworth sees the conflict over slave and wage labor as central to the crisis, but more important, he offers an understanding of class that allows individual acts to be seen as class conflict. See pp. 13–15.

My thinking about class has been informed mostly by historians who use the concept in practice, not theorists who set up ideal types. For some discussions of class formation and class consciousness for the period under consideration here, see Alan Dawley, *Class and Community: The Industrial Revolution in Lynn* (Cambridge: Harvard University Press, 1976), 3–5; Sean Wilentz, *Chants Democratic: New York City and the Rise of the American Working Class, 1788–1850* (New York: Oxford University Press, 1984), 3–19; Stuart M. Blumin, *The Emergence of a Middle Class: Social Experience in the American City, 1760–1900* (New York: Cambridge University Press, 1989), 1–16; Allan Kulikoff, *The Agrarian Origins of American Capitalism* (Charlottesville: University Press of Virginia, 1992), 1–9; and Peter Way, *Common Labour: Workers and the Digging of North American Canals, 1780–1860* (New York: Cambridge University Press, 1993), esp. 2–7. Way offers a compelling critique of earlier works that focus on artisanal breakdown. His Marxist analysis of class as it applies to the experience of canal workers fits more closely the experiences of the workers I have discussed below.

Since the 1980s, historians have increasingly understood that class formation must be viewed within the context of gender and race as well. For examples of explorations of these issues, see Mary P. Ryan, *Cradle of the Middle Class: The Family in Oneida County, New York, 1790–1865* (New York: Cambridge University Press, 1981); Christine Stansell, *City of Women: Sex and Class in New York, 1789–1860* (Urbana: University of Illinois Press, 1982); and David R. Roediger, *The Wages of Whiteness: Race and the Making of the American Working Class* (London: Verso, 1991), esp. 43–95.

The definition of "class" I am using has some affinity with the Gramscian concept of hegemony. For a classic, yet still useful, example of how hegemony can be used to understand law, see Eugene D. Genovese, *Roll, Jordan, Roll: The World the Slaves Made* (1974; New York: Vintage Books, 1976), 25–49.

8. Kathleen Brown, *Good Wives, Nasty Wenches, and Anxious Patriarchs: Gender, Race, and Power in Colonial Virginia* (Chapel Hill: University of North Carolina Press, 1996), 5.

Chapter 1: The Right to Quit

1. For Breese's comment, see *Hansell v. Erickson*, 28 Ill. (18 Peck) 268 (1862).

2. The classic formulation of this argument is Morton J. Horwitz, *The Transformation of American Law, 1780–1860* (Cambridge: Harvard University Press, 1977), 186–88, 333 n. Wythe Holt, "Recovery by the Worker Who Quits: A Comparison of the Mainstream, Legal Realist, and Critical Legal Studies Approaches to a Problem of Nineteenth Century Contract Law," *Wisconsin Law Review*, no. 4 (1986): 677–732, rejects the focus on doctrinal idealism and calls for a return to traditional Marxist analysis focusing on dialectical struggle and class bias.

Robert J. Steinfeld, *The Invention of Free Labor: The Employment Relation in English and American Law and Culture, 1350–1870* (Chapel Hill: University of North Carolina Press, 1991), chap. 6, argues that free labor emerged with the decline of indentured servitude and the doctrine of specific performance. He sees this process as essentially complete by the 1820s. I would agree with his general formulation, but I would suggest that the process took considerably longer.

Christopher L. Tomlins, "The Ties That Bind: Master and Servant in Massachusetts, 1800–1850," *Labor History* 30 (Spring 1989): 193–227, and *Law, Labor, and Ideology in the Early Republic* (New York: Cambridge University Press, 1993), esp. 223–97, contends that labor contracts obscured power structures, but he also argues (correctly, I believe) that judges imported eighteenth-century master-servant discourse when structuring the work relation. Yet in arguing that the law became a "modality of rule" in the antebellum period, Tomlins seems to undervalue both the social context in which litigants were located and the ways in which labor law functioned differently depending on the type of work in question. Moreover, he locates alternative discourses only outside the law. An earlier version of Tomlins's thinking about law and labor in the nineteenth century can be found in *The State and the Unions: Labor Relations, Law, and the Organized Labor Movement in America, 1880–1960* (New York: Cambridge University Press, 1985), 36–44.

Peter Karsten, "'Bottomed on Justice': A Reappraisal of Critical Legal Studies Scholarship Concerning Breaches of Labor Contracts by Quitting or Firing in Britain and the U.S., 1630–1880," *American Journal of Legal History* 34 (July 1990): 211–61, argues that contracts often benefited service workers and that builders received no special treatment, as some previous historians claimed. Moreover, jurists often acted in ways contrary to their apparent class interests. This interpretation, it seems to me, moves rather far in the other direction. Certainly, at least some, if not most, nineteenth-century labor law decisions hurt workers. Karsten has incorporated these ideas into *Heart versus Head: Judge-Made Law in Nineteenth-Century America* (Chapel Hill: University of North Carolina Press, 1997).

For a view at the other extreme, see Karen Orren, *Labor, the Law, and Liberal Development in the United States* (New York: Cambridge University Press, 1991), 79–89. While her rejection of the crude functionalism of earlier accounts is warranted, her use of "feudalism" runs the risk of obscuring the real changes that took place in nineteenth-century labor law. Moreover, like Tomlins she does not see various strains of thought within legal culture. Although the common law might have suppressed these divergent legal arguments about labor contract law, workers and their lawyers continued to make them nonetheless.

For an excellent summary of workers' relationships with the state in the nineteenth century, see David Montgomery, *Citizen Worker: The Experience of Workers in the United States with Democracy and the Free Market during the Nineteenth Century* (New York: Cambridge University Press, 1993).

3. It is not my purpose here to probe the causes of this ideological shift. On the disappearance of indentured servitude and the emergence of free labor, see David W. Galenson, *White Servitude in Colonial America* (New York: Cambridge University Press, 1981), 179–80; Sharon V. Salinger, *"To Serve Well and Faithfully": Labor and Indentured Servants in Pennsylvania, 1682–1800* (New York: Cambridge University Press, 1987), 137–71; and especially Steinfeld, *Invention of Free Labor,* chaps. 5–6.

4. Collinson Read, *Precedents in the Office of a Justice of the Peace. . . .,* 3d ed. (Philadelphia, 1810), 3–4; Samuel Freeman, *The Massachusetts Justice. . . .,* 3d ed. (Boston: Thomas and Andrews, 1810), 12; John A. Dunlap, *The New-York Justice, or, A Digest of the Law Relative to Justices of the Peace in the State of New-York. . . .* (New York: Isaac Riley, 1815), 371–72.

5. Tapping Reeve, *The Law of Baron and Femme. . . .,* 3d ed. (Albany: William Gould Law Publisher, 1862), 339; Nathan Dane, *General Abridgement and Digest of American Law,* 8 vols. (Boston: Cummings, Hilliard & Co., 1823), 2:313. For similar analysis of these texts, see Tomlins, "Ties That Bind," 214–16. "Menial" originally meant "within the walls of the master's house." Jay M. Feinman, "The Development of the Employment of the at Will Rule," *American Journal of Legal History* 20 (April 1976): 123. On servants in the Puritan household, see John Demos, *A Little Commonwealth: Family Life in Plymouth Colony* (New York: Oxford University Press, 1970), 107–18; and Christopher Hill, *Society and Puritanism in Pre-revolutionary England* (London: Secher and Warburg, 1964), chap. 13.

6. Dunlap, *New-York Justice,* 371–72.

7. Dane, *Abridgement,* 2:315. *Commonwealth v. Baird,* 1 Ashm. 267 (Penn., 1831); *Matthews v. Terry,* 10 Conn. 457 (1838). Congress outlawed corporal punishment in

the navy in 1850. See Myra C. Glenn, *Campaigns against Corporal Punishment: Prisoners, Sailors, Women, and Children in Antebellum America* (Albany: State University of New York Press, 1984), 128–31.

8. For debate on specific performance in the colonial period, see Steinfeld, *Invention of Free Labor*, and Tomlins, *Law, Labor, and Ideology*.

9. *Respublica against Catharine Keppele*, 1 Yeates 233–37 (Penn., 1793).

10. *Negro Peter against William Steel*, 3 Yeates 250 (Penn., 1801).

11. Steinfeld, *Invention of Free Labor*, chap. 6. *In re Mary Clark*, 1 Blackf. 122 (Indiana, 1821). For Steinfeld, this case represents the dawn of free labor in itself, yet this seems a bit overstated. I have located only one citation to this case in antebellum courts, *Haight v. Badgeley* 15 Barb. 501 (N.Y., 1853), an enticement litigation. In addition, the *Clark* opinion affirmed, rather than established, a principle that had become commonplace by 1820.

12. *In re Mary Clark*, 1 Blackf. 124–25.

13. Ibid., 125.

14. *Cranmer v. Graham*, 1 Blackf. 158 (Indiana, 1825).

15. Theodore Sedgwick, *A Treatise on the Measure of Damages* 4th ed. (New York, 1868), 255. *Stark v. Parker*, 19 Mass. 267–76 (1824). *Britton v. Turner*, 6 N.H. 481–96 (1834). For this case as an equitable decision, see Peter Charles Hoffer, *The Law's Conscience: Equitable Constitutionalism in America* (Chapel Hill: University of North Carolina Press, 1990), 108.

"Labor contract" should not be confused with "contract labor." The latter term refers to importation of laborers as a group, as when nineteenth-century industrialists contracted with immigrant strikebreakers. On this matter, see Kitty Calavita, *U.S. Immigration Law and the Control of Labor, 1820–1924* (New York: Academic Press, 1984), 44–46. "Contract labor" has also been used to refer to debt peonage. Albion Guilford Taylor, *Labor Law and Labor Problems* (New York: Prentice-Hall, 1944).

16. The most prominent English case was *Cutter v. Powell*, 6 T.R. 320. The English and early colonial background of entirety is discussed in Karsten, "'Bottomed on Justice,'" 217–25. The New York cases were *McMillan v. Vanderlip*, 12 Johns. 165 (1815); *Thorpe v. White*, 13 Johns. 53 (1816); *Webb v. Duckingfield*, 13 Johns. 390 (1816); and *Reab v. Moor*, 19 Johns. 337 (1822).

For *Stark*, see 19 Mass. (2 Pick) 267–76 (1824). Tomlins, "Ties That Bind," 219; Holt, "Recovery by the Worker Who Quits," 680–81. For *Costigan*, see 2 Denio 609–16 (N.Y., 1846). For another example of the rule in *Costigan*, see Illinois chief justice John D. Caton's remarks in *Badgley v. Heald*, 9 Ill. 66–67 (1847): "Nor is there any hardship in this rule, as it might first appear. It is reciprocal, for if the employer turn off the servant before the expiration of the term of the time agreed upon, without any just cause, the latter may recover the full amount agreed upon, as if he had worked out his whole time."

17. *Larkin v. Buck*, 11 Ohio St. 561 (1860); *Miller v. Goddard*, 34 Me. 102 (1852);

Peters v. Whitney, 23 Barb. 24 (New York, 1856); *Badgley v. Heald*, 9 Ill. 66 (1847); *Olmstead v. Beale*, 36 Mass. (19 Pick.) 528 (1837).

18. *Olmstead v. Beale*, 36 Mass. (19 Pick.) 528 (1837); *Davis v. Maxwell*, 53 Mass. (12 Metc.) 286 (1847); *Larkin v. Buck*, 11 Ohio St. 561 (1860).

19. *Moses v. Stevens*, 19 Mass. (2 Pick.) 333 (1824). For the argument that minors were incapable of contracting, see ibid., 335; *In re Mary Clark*, 1 Blackf. 122 (Indiana, 1821); and *Forsyth v. Hastings*, 27 Vt. 646 (1853). In the last case, the Vermont court denied recovery because the plaintiff had become an adult during its terms. If he had sued before his majority, he could have recovered. *Fenton v. Clark*, 11 Vt. 566 (1839). On sickness as a defense, see also *Fuller v. Brown*, 52 Mass. (11 Metc.) 440 (1846).

20. R. S. Taft, "The Supreme Court of Vermont," *Green Bag*, March 1894, quoted in *Dictionary of American Biography*, 15:440. *Dyer v. Jones*, 8 Vt. 205 (1836).

21. *Cranmer v. Graham*, 1 Blackf. 158 (Indiana, 1825); *Olmstead v. Beale*, 36 Mass. (19 Pick.) 528 (1837); *Ripley v. Chipman*, 13 Vt. 268 (1841); *Miller v. Goddard*, 34 Me. 102 (1852); Illinois Supreme Court justice Richard Young made the same argument in *Eldridge v. Rowe*, 7 Ill. 91 (1845). *Lee v. Quirk*, 20 Ill. 395 (1858). For a much more complete discussion of the place of manual labor in Jacksonian social theory, see Glickstein, *Antebellum Concepts of Free Labor*, 3–11.

22. Edward Pessen, *Most Uncommon Jacksonians: The Radical Leaders of the Early Labor Movement* (Albany: State University of New York Press, 1967), 175; Frances Wright, *An Address to the Industrious Classes* (New York: Free Enquirer, 1830), 4. This tract and the ones cited below from Seth Luther, Edward Everett, and Joseph Tuckerman are taken from facsimile reprints in Leon Stein and Phillip Taft, eds., *Religion, Reform, and Revolution: Labor Panaceas in the Nineteenth Century* (New York: Arno Press, 1969); Seth Luther, *An Address to the Working-Men of New-England* (Boston, 1832), 5 (emphasis in original).

Skill dilution was a widespread phenomenon in this period in Europe as well. On France, see William Sewell, *Work and Revolution in France: The Language of Labor from the Old Regime to 1848* (Cambridge: Cambridge University Press, 1980), 161. For England, see Thompson, *Making of the English Working Class*, chaps. 6–9.

For an interesting general discussion of the relationship between producer ideology and legal development in the antebellum period, see Tony A. Freyer, *Producers versus Capitalists: Constitutional Conflict in Antebellum America* (Charlottesville: University Press of Virginia, 1994), 1–56.

23. Wright, *Address*, 4; Wilentz, "Artisan Republican Festivals and the Rise of Class Conflict in New York City, 1788–1837," in *Working-Class America: Essays on Labor, Community, and American Society*, ed. Michael H. Frisch and Daniel J. Walkowitz (Urbana: University of Illinois Press, 1983), 50; Commerford as quoted in Wilentz, "Artisan Republican Festivals," 65.

24. *Stark v. Parker*, 19 Mass. 267–76 (1824).

25. *Lantry v. Parks*, 8 Cow. 63; *Hayward v. Leonard*, 24 Mass. (7 Pick.) 180–86. For some scholars, the apparent contradiction between these "building cases" and those like *Stark* that concerned "service" contracts constitutes an important facet of the argument about the purpose of labor contracts. For example, Holt implies that the contradiction demonstrates "class bias," meaning that jurists and employers were of the same class. In contrast, Karsten argues that no contradiction existed. I would contend that *Stark* and *Hayward*, and the lines of cases that followed each, did contradict at the realm of doctrine but that they appear less contradictory if we look at the type of labor and the class of laborer involved, as I have done below. Holt, "Recovery by the Worker Who Quits," 683, 725–32; Karsten, "'Bottomed on Justice,'" 255–59.

26. *Britton v. Turner*, 6 N.H. 485–93. Holt, "Recovery by the Worker Who Quits," 683; Phillip S. Paladun, *A Covenant with Death: The Constitution, Law, and Equality in the Civil War Era* (Urbana: University of Illinois Press, 1975), 115. Although Britton's contract seems to indicate farmwork, the record of the case does not make this clear.

27. *Hartwell v. Jewett*, 9 N.H. 252 (1838). Connecticut followed this line of reasoning in 1856. See *Clark v. Terry*, 25 Conn. 395 (1856).

28. *Green v. Hutlett*, 22 Vt. 188 (1850). For a similar comment, see *Ryan v. Dayton*, 25 Conn. 188 (1856). J. C. Perkins, ed., *A Practical Treatise on the Law of Contracts not under Seal . . . by Joseph Chitty* (Springfield, Mass.: Merriam, 1851), 501a; Theophilus Parsons, *The Law of Contracts*, 2d ed. (Boston: Little, Brown, 1855), 1:523–24. For an example of the use of Parsons in a case, see *Clark v. Terry*, 25 Conn. 395 (1856).

29. *Ryan v. Dayton*, 25 Conn. 188 (1856); *Ripley v. Chipman*, 13 Vt. 268 (1841); *Fenton v. Clark*, 11 Vt. 561–62 (1839).

30. *Wolcott v. Yeager*, 11 Ind. 84 (1858); *Fenton v. Clark*, 11 Vt. 566 (1839).

31. Laurie, *Artisans into Workers*, 66. Edward Everett, *A Lecture on the Working Men's Party* (Boston: Gray and Bowen, 1831), 3–6, 17. On the last point, see chapter 2 below.

32. On the emergence of managers, see Alfred D. Chandler Jr., *The Visible Hand: The Managerial Revolution in American Business* (Cambridge: Harvard University Press, Belknap Press, 1977), 1–12. On suits for unjust discharge generally, see Karsten, "'Bottomed on Justice,'" 248–55.

33. *Singer v. McCormick*, 4 W.&S. 267 (Penn., 1842); *Heim v. Wolf*, 1 E. D. Smith 73 (N.Y. Sup. Ct., 1850); *Costigan v. Mohawk & Hudson R. R. Co.*, 2 Denio 609–16 (New York, 1846). For another opinion like Beardsley's, see *King & Graham v. Steiren*, 44 Pa. 101 (Penn., 1862), discussed in chap. 8.

34. *Gordon v. Brewster*, 7 Wis. 355–64 (1858).

35. Johnson, *Shopkeeper's Millennium*, chap. 3; Stephen J. Ross, *Workers on the Edge: Work, Leisure, and Politics in Industrializing Cincinnati, 1788–1899* (New York: Columbia University Press, 1985), xvii–xix.

36. *Thorpe v. White*, 12 Johns. 53 (N.Y., 1816); *Hair v. Bell*, 6 Vt. 35 (1834); *Winn v. Southgate*, 17 Vt. 355 (1845); *Nounenbocker v. Hooper*, 4 E. D. Smith 401–4 (N.Y. Sup. Ct., 1855). *Wyngert v. Norton*, 4 Mich. 286 (1856).

37. *Cobb v. Stevens*, 14 Me. 472–74 (1837).

38. *Durgin v. Baker*, 32 Me. 273–74 (1850); *Smith v. First Congregational Meetinghouse of Lowell*, 25 Mass. 177–78 (1829). For another time contract, see *Morris v. Redfield*, 23 Vt. 195 (1851). For examples of job contracts, see *Taft v. Inhabitants of Montague*, 14 Mass. 282 (1817); *Lord v. Wheeler*, 67 Mass. 282 (1854); *Veazie v. Hosmer*, 77 Mass. 396 (1858); *Veazie v. City of Bangor*, 51 Me. 510 (1853); *Cobb v. West*, 11 N.Y. Super. Ct. 38 (1854); *Pullman v. Corning*, 14 Barb. 174 (N.Y., 1853); *Camp v. Barker*, 21 Vt. 470–71 (1849); and *Bishop v. Perkins*, 19 Conn. 301 (1848).

39. *Tebbetts v. Haskins*, 16 Me. 289 (1839); *Waugh v. Shunk*, 20 Pa. 130 (1852); *McKinney v. Springer*, 3 Ind. 68 (1851). For other cases involving judgments of skill, see *Felt v. School District No. 2*, 24 Vt. 297 (1852); *Loundsberry v. Eastwick*, 3 Phila. 371 (Penn., 1859); *Goslin v. Hodson*, 24 Vt. 140 (1852); *Cole v. Clarke*, 3 Wis. 323 (1854); *Pullman v. Corning*, 14 Barb. 177 (N.Y., 1853); *Cobb v. West*, 11 N.Y. Sup. Ct. 38 (1854). For other direct statements on artisan adjudication, see *Efner v. Shaw*, 3 Wend. 547 (N.Y., 1829); *Holinshead v. Mactier*, 13 Wend. 276 (N.Y., 1835).

40. *Jewell v. Schroeppel*, 4 Cow. 566 (N.Y., 1825); *Clark v. Marsiglia*, 1 Denio 318–19 (N.Y., 1845); *Snow v. Inhabitants of Ware*, 54 Mass. 50 (1847); *Bassett v. Sanborn*, 63 Mass. 58 (1851).

41. *Pullman v. Corning*, 14 Barb. 179–81 (N.Y., 1853).

42. *Corbin v. American Mills*, 27 Conn. 274–80 (1858). The thousands of industrial accident cases under the fellow-servant rule also rested on this concept. Iowa Supreme Court justice George G. Wright believed severable contracts could be distinguished from entire agreements if the work consisted of "several distinct and separable items" priced individually. *Dibol & Plank v. Minott*, 9 Ia. 405–6 (1859).

43. Jonathan Prude, "The Social System of Early New England Textile Mills: A Case Study, 1812–1840," in Frisch and Walkowitz, *Working-Class America*, 17–24. *McMillan v. Vanderlip*, 12 Johnson 165. For New York's industrial development during this period, see David M. Ellis, *New York: City and State* (Ithaca, N.Y.: Cornell University Press, 1981), 96–117.

44. *Russell v. Slade*, 12 Conn. 455 (1835); *Thayer v. Wadsworth*, 36 Mass. 349 (1837).

45. Thomas Dublin, *Women at Work: The Transformation of Work and Community in Lowell, Massachusetts, 1826–1860* (New York: Columbia University Press, 1979), 58–60, 108–31. For a quite different reading of the following cases from Massachusetts, see Tomlins, "Ties That Bind," 221–25.

46. *Stevens v. Reeves*, 26 Mass. 198 (1829). On overseers' control of hiring, see *Bradley v. Salmon Falls Man. Co.*, 30 N.H. 487 (1855), and Dublin, *Women at Work*, 22, 112.

47. *Hunt v. Otis*, 45 Mass. 464 (1842).

48. *Rice v. Dwight Manufacturing Co.*, 56 Mass. 80 (1848).

49. *Harmon v. Salmon Falls Manufacturing Company*, 35 Me. 449, 451 (1853).

50. Ibid., 450.

51. Ibid., 452–55.

52. On this practice, see Dublin, *Women at Work*, 59, 70.

53. *Thorton & wife v. Suffolk Manufacturing Company*, 64 Mass. 377–82 (1852). Women often quit the mills after wedlock, but millwork was not just a short sojourn before marriage as once believed. Dublin, *Women at Work*, 23–57. Cassidy brought the suit *feme sole* and then married sometime during the litigation.

54. *Thorton & wife v. Suffolk Manufacturing Company*, 382–84.

55. Paul W. Gates, *The Farmer's Age: Agriculture, 1815–1860* (New York: Holt, Rinehart, and Wilson, 1960), 157, 196–97, 250, 271–79; Carville Earle and Ronald Hoffman, "The Foundation of the Modern Economy: Agriculture and the Costs of Labor in the United States and England, 1800–1860," *American Historical Review* 85 (December 1980): 1059–75; Jeremy Atack and Fred Bateman, *To Their Own Soil: Agriculture in the Antebellum North* (Ames: Iowa State University Press, 1987), 186; Winifred B. Rothenberg, "The Emergence of Farm Labor Markets and the Transformation of the Rural Economy: Massachusetts, 1750–1855," *Journal of Economic History* 58 (September 1988): 553; and especially David E. Schob, *Hired Hands and Plowboys: Farm Labor in the Midwest, 1815–1860* (Urbana: University of Illinois Press, 1975), 4–5, 67–110, 151–71.

56. *Brown v. Kimball*, 12 Vt. 617 (1839); *Olmstead v. Beale*, 36 Mass. 528 (1837); *Eldridge v. Rowe*, 7 Ill. 91 (1845); *Angle v. Hanna*, 22 Ill. 429 (1859); *Davis v. Maxwell*, 53 Mass. 287 (1847). Milking was considered degrading work by male antebellum farm laborers because it was often done by women. Schob, *Hired Hands and Plowboys*, 199–200.

57. *Stark v. Parker*, 19 Mass. 267–76 (1824); *Ryan v. Dayton*, 25 Conn. 188 (1856); *Swanzey v. Moore*, 22 Ill. 63 (1859). Winifred Rothenberg has found an increasing tendency of farmers in Massachusetts to hire by the month, season, or year rather than by the task, but Christopher Clark notes that five- to seven-month contracts indicated a decrease in duration from early year-long arrangements. Rothenberg, "Emergence of Farm Labor Markets," 544; Christopher Clark, *The Roots of Rural Capitalism: Western Massachusetts, 1780–1860* (Ithaca, N.Y.: Cornell University Press, 1990), 305. Given the long tradition of yearly farm contracts bequeathed by England, Clark's view seems more accurate. Thompson, *Making of the English Working Class*, 231–58. Based on wage data for 1866, Atack and Bateman calculate periods of actual employment for agricultural workers as ranging from 231 days in New Hampshire to 186 days in Wisconsin, in other words a period of seven to eight months (*To Their Own Soil*, 242).

58. *Peters v. Whitney*, 23 Barb. 24 (New York, 1856); *Hartwell v. Jewett*, 9 N.H. 249 (1838); *Larkin v. Buck*, 11 Ohio St. 561 (1860); Schob, *Hired Hands and Plowboys*, 224.

59. *Evans v. Bennett*, 7 Wis. 405–6 (1858). It is unclear whether this was a farm contract or not, although its terms of six to eight months from April 2 at fourteen dollars per month would indicate it was. *Sutton v. Tyrell*, 12 Vt. 79 (1835); *Whitcomb v. Gilman*, 35 Vt. 297 (1859); *Gates v. Davenport*, 29 Barb. 160 (New York, 1859), is not definitively a farmhand, but the circumstances point in that direction; Schob, *Hired Hands and Plowboys*, 224. For examples of opposing views regarding at-will contracts, see *Gates v. Davenport*, 29 Barb. 160 (New York, 1859), and *Seaver v. Morse*, 20 Vt. 620 (1848).

60. Rebecca A. Shepherd, "Restless Americans: The Geographic Mobility of Farm Laborers in the Old Midwest, 1850–1870," *Ohio History* 89 (Winter 1980): 28–35; Rothenberg, "Emergence of Farm Labor Markets," 553–54; *Eldridge v. Rowe*, 7 Ill. 91 (1845); *Davis v. Maxwell*, 53 Mass. (12 Metc.) 286 (1847); *Badgley v. Heald*, 9 Ill. 64 (1847). It is unclear whether Heald was a farm laborer or not, but I treat him as such because of the nature of the contract and because this case was often cited in other cases involving agricultural workers.

61. *Lantry v. Parks*, 8 Cowen 63 (N.Y., 1827); *Hansell v. Erickson*, 28 Ill. (18 Peck) 268 (1862).

62. *Angle v. Hanna*, 22 Ill. 429 (1859); *Swanzey v. Moore*, 22 Ill. 63 (1859). See also *Gates v. Davenport*, 29 Barb. 160 (New York, 1859); *Mullen v. Gullikson*, 23 Vt. 558 (1847); *Forsyth v. Hasting*, 27 Vt. 646 (1855); *Green v. Hutlett*, 22 Vt. 188 (1850); *Cahill v. Patterson*, 30 Vt. 592 (1858); and Schob, *Hired Hands and Plowboys*, 214–21.

63. *Brown v. Kimball*, 12 Vt. 617 (1839); *Sutton v. Tyrell*, 12 Vt. 79 (1835); *Marsh v. Rulesson*, 1 Wend. 515 (New York, 1828).

64. *Angle v. Hanna*, 22 Ill. 429 (1859).

65. *Stark v. Parker*, 19 Mass. 267–76; *Larkin v. Buck*, 11 Ohio St. 561 (1860). Biographical information on Lincoln is from *Dictionary of American Biography*, 11: 264–65.

66. *Cranmer v. Graham*, 1 Blackf. 158 (Indiana, 1825).

67. *Fenton v. Clark*, 11 Vt. 566 (1839); *Hansell v. Erickson*, 28 Ill. (18 Peck) 268 (1862). For other cases recognizing seasonality directly, see *Brown v. Kimball*, 12 Vt. 617 (1839), and *Peters v. Whitney*, 23 Barb. 24 (New York, 1856). Even in a case involving a professional employee, a Philadelphia court recognized that most contracts that had a fixed time were farm contracts intended "to endure until those operations ha[d] run through their accustomed course, and the revolution of the year ha[d] brought round seed-time and harvest in due succession." *Coffin v. Landis*, 5 Phila. 177 (1863). On farm laborers breaking contracts for higher day wages at harvest, see Karsten, "'Bottomed on Justice,'" 246. Karsten appears to defend the need for labor discipline, especially in societies with scarce resources.

68. On Breese, see Harold M. Hyman, *A More Perfect Union: The Impact of the Civil War and Reconstruction on the Constitution* (New York: Alfred A. Knopf, 1973), 341.

69. *Ranck v. Albright*, 36 Pa. 367. For other cases involving housekeepers, see *Bond v. Corbett*, 2 Minn. 248 (1858); *Hackman v. Flory*, 16 Pa. 196 (1851); and *Patterson v. Gage*, 23 Vt. 558 (1851). In the last case, the Vermont court held in 1851 that sexual harassment was a valid cause for abandoning a contract. On domestic servants generally, see Faye E. Dudden, *Serving Women: Household Service in Nineteenth-Century America* (Middletown, Conn.: Wesleyan University Press, 1983), 12–72, and Schob, *Hired Hands and Plowboys*, 193–206. Sharecropping was not uncommon in the antebellum North. Gates, *Farmer's Age*, 194; Schob, *Hired Hands and Plowboys*, 266.

70. Of the 153 southern labor contract cases I have examined, overseers were litigants in 72.

The only full-length study of overseers is William Kauffman Scarborough, *The Overseer: Plantation Management in the Old South* (Baton Rouge: Louisiana State University Press, 1966). Scarborough contends that overseers were not the rogues often pictured in older versions of plantation life. Three classes of overseers existed: sons of planters, a small band of "floaters," and a class of semiprofessional managers. An older book-length study is John Spencer Bassett, *The Southern Plantation Overseer As Revealed in His Letters* (Northampton, Mass.: Smith College, 1925). Genovese, *Roll, Jordan, Roll*, 12–25, is a useful discussion of the relationship between planter and overseer.

71. *Hays v. Marsh*, 11 La. 369 (1837). See also *Pettigrew v. Bishop*, 3 Ala. 440 (1842); *Roberts v. Brownrigg*, 9 Ala. 106 (1846); and *Whitley v. Murray*, 34 Ala. 155 (1859). In the few cases involving common laborers, southern courts usually upheld entirety as strongly as their northern counterparts. For example, see *Wright v. Turner*, 1 Stew. 35 (Alabama, 1827).

72. For examples of share contracts, see *Cochran v. Tatum*, 19 Ky. 405 (1826); *Anderson v. Rice, adm'x*, 20 Ala. 240 (1852); *Lambert v. King*, 12 La. Ann. 662 (1856); *Steed v. McRae*, 18 N.C. 57 (1836); *Dillard v. Wallace*, 1 McMul. 482 (S.C., 1837); *Graham v. Lewis*, 2 Hill 478 (S.C., 1834); *Hassell v. Nutt*, 14 Tex. 260 (1855); and *Rogers v. Parham*, 8 Ga. 191 (1850). See also *Southern Planter* 1 (April 1841): 58, and *Southern Planter* 3 (October 1843): 234. For contracts with supply clauses, see *Seal v. Earwin*, 2 Mart. (N.S.) 245 (La., 1824); *Walworth v. Pool*, 9 Ark. 395 (1849); *Nolan v. Danks*, 1 Rob. 332 (La., 1842); and *Coursey v. Covington*, 5 H.&J. 46 (Md., 1820). For examples of contracts with wages only, see *Wright v. Falkner*, 37 Ala. 274 (1861); *Johnson v. Gorham*, 30 Ga. 613 (1860); *Anderson v. Wales*, 22 Ky. 324 (1827); *McDaniel v. Parks*, 19 Ark. 673 (1858); *Hays v. Marsh*, 11 La. 369 (1837); and *Hendrickson v. Anderson*, 50 N.C. 246 (1858).

For a specific example over a long period of time, see Robert A. Jones Account Book, 1817–28, in the Southern Historical Collection of the Manuscripts Department, University of North Carolina, Chapel Hill, 129–30, 309–10, 341–42, 385–86.

For production bonuses, see *Hariston v. Sale*, 14 Miss. 635 (1846). See also *Nolan*

v. *Danks*, 1 Rob. 333 (La., 1842), and Sarah McCulloh Lemon, ed., *The Pettigew Papers*, vol. 2, *1819–1843* (Raleigh: North Carolina Department of Cultural Resources, 1988), 172. Such bonus arrangements were fairly common. Scarborough, *Overseer*, 30.

For rules, see *Roberts v. Brownrigg*, 9 Ala. 108 (1846); *Whitely v. Murray*, 34 Ala. 157 (1859); and Ulrich B. Phillips, *Plantation and Frontier Documents, 1649–1863*, 2 vols. (Cleveland: Arthur C. Clark Co., 1909), 1:112–30, quotation on 128. See also *Hariston v. Sale*, 14 Miss. 635 (1846); *Nolan v. Danks*, 1 Rob. 333 (La., 1842); Scarborough, *Overseer*, 68–70; Bassett, *Southern Plantation Overseer*, 24–32; John Hebron Moore, ed., "Two Documents Relating to Plantation Overseers of the Vicksburg Region, 1831–1832," *Journal of Mississippi History* 16 (January 1954): 35; Lucille Griffith, ed., "The Plantation Record Book of Brookdale Farm, Amite County, 1856–1857," *Journal of Mississippi History* 7 (January 1945): 23–27; and "Overseers' Rules," *Southern Planter* 18 (July 1858): 410–11.

73. *Craig v. Pride*, 2 Speers 122 (S.C., 1843); *McDaniel v. Parks*, 19 Ark. 674 (1858); Whatley and Jones contract reprinted in Bassett, *Southern Plantation Overseer*, 33; Scarborough, *Overseer*, 112–16, quotation on 114. See also *Steed v. McRae*, 18 N.C. 57 (1836); *Word v. Winder*, 16 La. Ann. 112 (1861); and Kenneth Stampp, *The Peculiar Institution: Slavery in the Antebellum South* (New York: Alfred A. Knopf, 1956), 38. Scarborough, *Overseer*, 20–47, discusses violability and many other factors in overseer contracts. On at-will clauses generally, see Feinman, "Development of the Employment of the at Will Rule," 118–35.

74. *Byrd v. Boyd*, 4 McCord 246 (S.C., 1827). It is unclear when the case was actually decided. It appears that it was in 1825. However, it was lost for a time and not reported until 1827. The court used this rule in several subsequent cases: *McClure v. Pyatt*, 4 McCord 26 (1826); *Eaken v. Harrison*, 4 McCord 249 (1827); *Saunders v. Anderson*, 2 Hill 486 (1834); *Suber v. Vanlew*, 2 Speer 126 (1843).

75. *Hariston v. Sale*, 14 Miss. 634–40 (1846); affirmed in *Robinson v. Sanders*, 24 Miss. 391 (1852); *Jones v. Jones*, 32 Tenn. 605–9 (1853); *Steed v. McRae*, 18 N.C. 435 (1836); *Meade v. Rutledge*, 11 Tex. 50 (1853). For the doctrinal development in Louisiana, see *Nolan v. Danks*, 1 Rob. 333 (La., 1842); *Youngblood v. Dodd*, 2 La. Ann. 187 (1847); *Lambert v. King*, 12 La. Ann. 662 (1856); *Kessee v. Mayfield*, 14 La. Ann. Reports 90 (1859). For Alabama, see *Martin v. Everrett*, 11 Ala. 375 (1847). Arkansas formed a similar rule, but it was not based on *Byrd v. Boyd*. See *McDaniel v. Parks*, 19 Ark. 671 (1858). South Carolina also passed an act in 1747 to regulate overseers' contracts, but it was not enforced. *Dillard v. Wallace*, 1 McMul. 484 (S.C., 1837). On knowledge of legal rules among overseers, see *Ford v. Danks*, 16 La. Ann. 119 (1861).

76. *Walworth v. Pool*, 9 Ark. 398 (1849); *Meade v. Rutledge*, 11 Tex. 52 (1853).

77. *Posey v. Garth*, 7 Mo. 97 (1841). See also *Wilson v. Bossier*, 11 La. Ann. 640 (1856); *Brunson v. Martin*, 17 Ark. 274 (1856); *Hendricks v. Phillips*, 8 La. Ann. 618 (1848); and *Kennedy v. Mason*, 10 La. Ann. 519 (1855). See also *McCracken v. Hair*, 2

Speers 258 (S.C., 1843); *Jones v. Jones,* 32 Tenn. 608 (1853); and *Miller v. Stewart,* 12 La. Ann. 170 (1857).

On allegations of sexual misconduct, see *Dwyer v. Cane,* 6 La. Ann. 707 (1851); *Fowler v. Waller,* 25 Tex. 697 (1860); and *Suber v. Vanlew,* 2 Speers 126 (S.C., 1843).

For more on treatment of slaves generally, see Bassett, *Southern Plantation Overseer,* 24; Phillips, *Plantation and Frontier Documents,* 1:113; Genovese, *Roll, Jordan, Roll,* 17–22; John Blassingame, *The Slave Community: Plantation Life in the Antebellum South* (New York: Oxford University Press, 1979), 273, 276; and Scarborough, *Overseer,* 120–21.

78. *Fly v. Armstrong,* 50 N.C. 340, 342 (1858). For other complaints about absence, see *McCracken v. Hair,* 2 Speers 258 (S.C., 1843), and *Martin v. Everett,* 11 Ala. 375 (1847). The latter case also involved cruelty to slaves.

79. *Meade v. Rutledge,* 11 Tex. 50 (1853); *Prichard v. Martin,* 27 Miss. 308 (1854); *Johnson v. Gorman,* 30 Ga. 613 (1860); *Harper v. Ray,* 27 Miss. 623 (1854); *Lane v. Phillips,* 51 N.C. 443 (1859); *Kessee v. Mayfield,* 14 La. Ann. 90–91 (1859); Scarborough, *Overseer.* In the last case, the planter wanted the black drivers or other slaves to perform the task, but the overseer flogged the slaves himself. See also *Dillard v. Wallace,* 1 McMul. 480 (S.C., 1837), and *Saunders v. Anderson,* 2 Hill 486 (S.C., 1834).

Agricultural reformers favored creating a professional class of overseers, as did those overseers aspiring to achieve such a status. See "Overseers," *Southern Planter* 5 (August 1845): 172; "Overseers," *Southern Planter* 5 (September 1845): 209–11; M. W. Phillips, "Domestic Economy–Overseers: A Few Thoughts on the Subject," *Southern Cultivator* 14 (November 1856): 339; and A. T. Goodloe, "Overseers," *Southern Cultivator* 18 (September 1861): 287.

80. Harris S. Evans, "Rules for the Government of the Negroes, Plantation &c. at Float-Swamp, Wilcox County South Alabama," *Southern Agriculturist* 5 (May 1832): 231–34, in *Advice among Masters: The Ideal in Slave Management in the Old South,* ed. James O. Breeden (Westport, Conn.: Greenwood Press, 1980), 292; Scarborough, *Overseer,* 112–16, 131–32. See also Little River, S.C., "Overseers," *Soil of the South* 6 (August 1856): 233–34, in Breeden, *Advice Among Masters,* 317; Charles S. Sydnor, "A Slave Owner and His Overseers," *North Carolina Historical Review* 14 (January 1937): 35; James C. Bonner, "The Plantation Overseer and Southern Nationalism as Revealed in the Career of Garland D. Harmon," *Agricultural History* 19 (January 1945): 1–2; Moore, "Two Documents," 33; and James Oakes, *The Ruling Race: A History of American Slaveholders* (New York: Alfred A. Knopf, 1982), 174–75.

81. *Byrd v. Boyd,* 4 McCord 246 (S.C., 1827); *Suber v. Vanlew,* 2 Speer 127 (S.C., 1843); *Talbert v. Stone,* 10 La. Ann. 537 (1855); *Nations v. Cudd,* 22 Tex. 551 (1858). On the honor ethic generally, see Bertram Wyatt-Brown, *Southern Honor: Ethics and Behavior in the Old South* (New York: Oxford University Press, 1982).

82. *Prichard v. Martin,* 27 Miss. 308, 313 (1854); *Boone v. Lyde,* 3 Strob. 78 (S.C., 1848); *Henderson v. Stiles,* 13 Ga. 136–37 (1853); *Youngblood v. Dodd,* 2 La. Ann. 187 (1847); *Darden v. Nolan,* 4 La. Ann. 374 (1849).

83. "Overseers," *Southern Planter* 16 (February 1856): 48–49; "Overseers," *Southern Planter* 4 (August 1844): 184; "Overseers," *Southern Planter* 5 (July 1845): 166. See also "Virginia Overseers," *Southern Planter* 5 (June 1845): 136–37; "Overseers: Their Duties," *Southern Cultivator* 12 (July 1854): 270.

84. The argument here affirms the conclusions of Hall and Ely about the relationship between modes of production and regional distinctiveness in law. See Kermit L. Hall and James W. Ely Jr., "South and the Constitution," in *Uncertain Tradition: Constitutionalism and the History of the South*, ed. Kermit L. Hall and James W. Ely Jr. (Athens: University of Georgia Press, 1989), 4, 7. It also supports Lawrence Friedman's suggestion that looking closely at southern legal history often complicates theories of legal, social, and economic change based on research primarily in northeastern sources. Lawrence Friedman, "The Law between the States: Some Thoughts on Southern Legal History," in *Ambivalent Legacy: A Legal History of the South*, ed. James W. Ely Jr. and David Bodenhamer (Jackson: University of Mississippi Press, 1984), 43. This latter argument is especially relevant with regard to the relationship between the law and capitalism. Southern courts started with the same English doctrines but derived a considerably different law of contracts. Yet they did so for essentially the same "capitalist" purpose that northern courts pursued in setting up the entirety doctrine: discipline of nonslave workers.

Chapter 2: The Duty to Work

1. Dane, *Abridgement*, 7:6. Many American legal historians have tended to conceptualize vagrancy laws that applied to whites as part of treatment of the poor, as part of the rise of modern police, or, at most, as a *response* to capitalist development, rather than as part of the *cause* of capitalist development. See, for example, Lawrence M. Friedman, *Crime and Punishment in American History* (New York: Basic Books, 1993), 101–4, and Kermit Hall, *The Magic Mirror: Law in American History* (New York: Oxford University Press, 1989), 168–69, 176, 185. These same historians have seen vagrancy laws in postwar Black Codes as restrictions on the labor market and tantamount to "involuntary servitude." Friedman, *Crime and Punishment*, 94; Hall, *Magic Mirror*, 146.

2. Historians of social welfare in Jacksonian America have often viewed this period of poor-law reform as a reaction to the postrevolutionary upsurge in poverty. Some accounts have envisioned this process as the triumph of liberal institutions; others have stressed the need to reimpose social control after the breakdown of community. A more current synthesis emphasizes the need for austerity, the desire to rid the social welfare system of the able bodied, and the imposition of the work ethic in light of classical political economists' claims that indiscriminate charity diminished industry.

Liberal-institutional accounts include Robert Bremner, *From the Depths: The Discovery of Poverty in the United States* (New York: NYU Press, 1956), chs. 1–3; and

Walter I. Trattner, *From Poor Law to Welfare State: A History of Social Welfare in the United States* 3d rev. ed. (New York: Free Press, 1984), v–xi, 47–76. The primary account to stress social control is David J. Rothman, *The Discovery of the Asylum: Social Order and Disorder in the New Republic* (Boston: Little, Brown, 1971), esp. chaps. 7–9. Another account of social control is John K. Alexander, *Render Them Submissive: Responses to Poverty in Philadelphia, 1760–1800* (Amherst: University of Massachusetts Press, 1980). Raymond Mohl, *Poverty in New York, 1783–1825* (New York: Oxford University Press, 1971), 159–70, also underscores the breakdown of colonial order and the turn to harsh moralism by 1825. For a synthetic treatment, see Michael Katz, *In the Shadow of the Poorhouse: A Social History of Welfare in America* (New York: Basic Books, 1986). On varied motives, see also Priscilla Ferguson Clement, *Welfare and the Poor in the Nineteenth Century City: Philadelphia, 1800–1854* (Rutherford, N.J.: Fairleigh-Dickinson Press, 1985), 20, who points to a mixture of "genuine concern," a desire to sift out the undeserving, and economy. An overview of basic ideas in early-nineteenth-century thinking on poverty can be found in Benjamin J. Klebaner, "Poverty and Its Relief in American Thought, 1815–1861," *Social Service Review* 38 (December 1964): 382–99.

In the large literature on the English debate, two of the better specific works are Anthony Brundage, *The Making of the New Poor Law: The Politics of Inquiry, Enactment, and Implementation, 1832–1839* (New Brunswick, N.J.: Rutgers University Press, 1978), and Peter Dunkley, *The Crisis of the Old Poor Law in England, 1795–1834: An Interpretive Essay* (New York: Garland, 1982). The best overall treatment of the problem of poverty in nineteenth-century Britain and its impact on the poor law is Gertrude Himmelfarb, *The Idea of Poverty: England in the Industrial Age* (New York: Alfred A. Knopf, 1984).

3. Thomas Haskell, "Capitalism and the Origins of Humanitarian Sensibilities," *American Historical Review* (1987): 339–61, 547–66. Haskell's argument is much more complex than this brief summary indicates.

4. Matthew Carey, *Appeal to the Wealthy of the Land, Ladies as well as Gentlemen, on the Character, Conduct, Situation, and Prospects, of Those Whose Sole Dependence for Subsistence Is on the Labour of Their Hands* (1833; reprint, New York: Arno Press, 1969), 6, 32; *Report of Select Committee Appointed to Visit Charitable Institutions Supported by the State and All City and County Poor and Work Houses and Jails: New York Sen. Doc. 8, 1856* (New York: Arno Press, 1976), 6 (hereafter cited as *Sen. Doc. 8*); John V. N. Yates, *Report of the Secretary of State in 1824 on the Relief and Settlement of the Poor,* in *The Almshouse Experience: Collected Reports,* ed. David J. Rothman (New York: Arno Press, 1971). This is a reprint of *Thirty-fourth Annual Report of the New York State Board of Charities.* The page numbers are from this last report.

5. Joseph Tuckerman, *On the Elevation of the Poor: A Selection of His Reports as*

Minister at Large in Boston (1874; reprint, New York: Arno Press, 1971), 28; Joseph Tuckerman, *Report of the Commissioners . . . on the Subject of the Pauper System of the Commonwealth of Massachusetts* (1833; reprint, New York: Arno Press, 1971), 34, 36, 38.

6. Yates, *Report*, 941–43, 952, 956.

7. Carey, *Appeal to the Wealthy*, 32.

8. *Report of the Committee Appointed by the Guardians of the Poor. . . .* (Philadelphia: Samuel Parker, 1827), 25 (hereafter cited as Philadelphia Committee, *Report*). A pesthouse was a public building for the quarantine of people with communicable diseases.

9. *The First Annual Report of the New York Association for the Improvement of the Condition of the Poor . . .* , in *Annual Reports of the New York Association for Improving the Condition of the Poor: Nos. 1–10, 1845–1853*, ed. David J. Rothman (New York: Arno Press, 1971), 17; Roy Lubove, "The New York Association for Improving the Conditions of the Poor: The Formative Years," *New York Historical Society Quarterly* 43 (1959): 311–13. Although based on a small sampling of the organization's leadership, Lubove's description of the social composition of the AICP seems correct. The demographic makeup of nineteenth-century poor-law reform organizations is an area that deserves more research.

10. *Fourth Annual Report*, 13 (emphasis in original).

11. Ibid., 16.

12. Ibid.

13. Stansell, *City of Women*, and Ryan, *Cradle of the Middle Class*; Philadelphia Committee, *Report*, 24, 27. On the incidence of vagrancy in antebellum Pennsylvania, see Priscilla Ferguson Clement, "The Transformation of the Wandering Poor in Nineteenth-Century Philadelphia," in *Walking to Work: Tramps in America, 1790–1935*, ed. Eric Monkkonen (Lincoln: University of Nebraska Press, 1984), 56–79.

14. Everett, *Lecture on the Working Men's Party*, 12–13; Joseph Tuckerman, *An Essay on the Wages Paid to Females for Their Labour* (Philadelphia, 1830), 21, 29.

15. Yates, *Report*, 957. E. Anthony Rotundo provides one of the best overall discussions of nineteenth-century middle-class masculinity in *American Manhood: Transformations in Masculinity from the Revolution to the Modern Era* (New York: Basic Books, 1993), 10–25. For discussions of the relationship between dependence, independence, and political rights, see Gordon Wood, "Interests and Disinterestedness in the Making of the Constitution," in *Beyond Confederation: Origins of the Constitution and American National Character*, ed. Richard Beeman, Stephen Botein, and Edward C. Carter II (Chapel Hill: University of North Carolina Press, 1987), 83–85; and Robert J. Steinfeld, "Property and Suffrage in the Early American Republic," *Stanford Law Review* 41 (January 1989): 335–76.

16. Both republicanism and the more specific point about dependence have

become staples in the historiography of the early Republic. See Drew R. McCoy, *The Elusive Republic: Political Economy in Jeffersonian America* (Chapel Hill: University of North Carolina Press, 1980), 107–19, 237; William B. Scott, *In Pursuit of Happiness: American Conceptions of Property from the Seventeenth to the Twentieth Century* (Bloomington: Indiana University Press, 1977), 53–93; Richard L. Bushman, "'This New Man': Dependence and Independence, 1776," in *Uprooted Americans: Essays in Honor of Oscar Handlin,* ed. Richard L. Bushman et al. (Boston: Little Brown, 1979), 76–96; and Rowland Bertoff, "Independence and Attachment, Virtue and Interest: From Republican Citizen to Free Enterpriser, 1787–1837," in Bushman et al., *Uprooted Americans,* 100, 117–18.

17. Tuckerman, *Report of the Commissioners,* 17, 19.

18. *Compend of Acts of Indiana* (Johnston, 1817), 189; *Code of Iowa* (1851), 462–63; *Revised Statutes of Maine* (1857), 252–53; *Laws of New Hampshire* (Metcalf, 1916), 5:691–93.

19. Gary V. Dubin and Richard H. Robinson, "The Vagrancy Concept Reconsidered: Problems and Abuses of Status Criminality," *New York University Law Review* 37 (January 1962): 104–7; William J. Chambliss, "A Sociological Analysis of the Law of Vagrancy," *Social Problems* 12 (Summer 1964): 72–73; P. Michael Lahan, "Trends in the Law of Vagrancy," *Connecticut Law Review* 1 (Spring 1968): 350–54; John T. Walsh Jr., "Vagrancy: A Crime of Status," *Suffolk University Law Review* 2 (Spring 1968): 160. English trends culminated in the 1824 Vagrancy Act, which divided vagrants into "idle and disorderly persons," "rogues and vagabonds," and "incorrigible rogues." The 1824 law and its interpretations based vagrancy on specific acts at specific times rather than on continuing status.

20. Forrest W. Lacey, "Vagrancy and Other Crimes of Personal Condition," *Harvard Law Review* 66 (May 1953): 1206. Chambliss, "Sociological Analysis," 75. Chambliss believes colonial and state vagrancy laws were primarily concerned with preventing crime and controlling undesirables. See also Douglas Lamar Jones, "The Strolling Poor: Transiency in Eighteenth-Century Massachusetts," *Journal of Social History* 8 (1975): 28–54.

21. Douglas Lamar Jones, "The Transformation of the Law of Poverty in Eighteenth-Century Massachusetts," in *Law in Colonial Massachusetts, 1630–1800* (Boston: Colonial Society of Massachusetts, 1984), 183–84; Linda Kealy, "Patterns of Punishment: Massachusetts in the Eighteenth Century," *American Journal of Legal History* 30 (April 1986): 171–72, 184–85; *The Colonial Laws of New York from the Year 1664 to the Revolution,* 5 vols. (Albany: James B. Lyon, 1894), 1:132, 238; 2:56–58; John Cummings, "The Poor Laws of Massachusetts and New York," *Publications of the American Economic Association* 10 (July 1895): 546–63; David M. Schneider, *The History of Public Welfare in New York State, 1609–1866,* 2 vols. (Chicago: University of Chicago Press, 1938), 1:149; Mohl, *Poverty in New York,* 44–47.

For a good example of a colonial vagrancy law, see the reprinted 1767 statute in

Session Laws of Pennsylvania, 1883, 35. This act defined vagrants as returnees after legal removal; persons living idly without visible means of support; beggars and wanderers; and immigrants who followed "no trade, occupation, or business," who had no visible support, and who could give "no reasonable account of themselves or their business." Such offenders could be committed to the workhouse or to jail at hard labor for up to a month.

For the best example of the trend away from corporal punishment, see the section on New York below.

22. *Session Laws of Pennsylvania, 1835–36,* 541–50.

23. This is drawn from a survey of Pennsylvania session laws from 1790 through 1900. The quotation comes from an enabling act for Westmoreland County passed in 1839, *Session Laws of Pennsylvania, 1838–39,* 2–9. This statute is a good example of these provisions. Other examples that I have drawn on specifically are Chester and Lancaster Counties: *Session Laws of Pennsylvania, 1797,* 202–3; Philadelphia: *Session Laws of Pennsylvania, 1827–28,* 170–76; Blair Co.: *Session Laws of Pennsylvania, 1848,* 324–25; Lawrence Co.: *Session Laws of Pennsylvania, 1856,* 352–55; Warren Co.: *Session Laws of Pennsylvania, 1864,* 438–43. By the time this last law passed in April 1864, workhouse provisions had begun to become more specific. The Warren County law stipulated separate cells for the paupers and for "the temporary confinement of refractory and insubordinate paupers." Idleness and drinking were to be discouraged and reading matter and religious instruction furnished. See also Guardians of the Poor, *A Compilation of the Poor Laws of the State of Pennsylvania* (1788; New York: Arno Press, 1971). On poor relief in Philadelphia, see Clement, *Welfare and the Poor,* 74–75. Clement sees a significant turn away from humanitarianism in this law and in this period generally.

24. *Revised Laws of Illinois* (1833), 201–2; *Compend of Acts of Indiana* (Johnston, 1817), 189; *Revised Laws of Indiana* (1831), 531; *Code of Iowa* (1851), 462–63; *Compiled Laws of Michigan* (Cooley, 1857), 1:493–94; *Digest of Laws of Vermont* (1808), 1:390; *Revised Statutes of Maine* (1857), 252–53; *Revised Statutes of Massachusetts* (Metcalf and Mann, 1836), 780; "Poor Laws," *American Quarterly Review* 14 (September 1833): 85; "Domestic Chronicle," *Niles Weekly Register,* March 18, 1837, 48.

25. *Revised Statutes of Massachusetts* (Metcalf and Mann, 1836), 780; *Laws of New Hampshire* (Metcalf, 1916), 5:693; *Code of Iowa* (1851), 462–63. See also *Revised Laws of Illinois* (1833), 201–2.

26. *Revised Statutes of Iowa* (1860), 772–74; *Revised Code of Illinois* (1827), 152; *Revised Laws of Illinois* (1833), 201–2; *Revised Statutes of Illinois* (1845), 175–76; *Statute Laws of Connecticut* (1821), 480; *Digest of the Laws of Connecticut* (Swift, 1822), 2:353.

27. These generalizations are drawn specifically from *Revised Statutes of New York* (1829), 79–80; *Revised Statutes of Maine* (1847), 217–20, 739–43; *Compiled Statutes of New Hampshire* (1853), 268–69; *Statutes of Connecticut* (1854), 738–44;

and *Compiled Statutes of the State of Vermont* (1851), 130–40, as well as from the other statutory sources cited above.

28. *Statute Laws of Connecticut* (1821), 480; *Revised Laws of Illinois* (1833), 202; *Revised Laws of Indiana* (1831), 531; *Revised Code of Laws of Illinois* (1827), 151–52; *Compiled Statutes of New Hampshire*, 268; *Statutes of Connecticut*, 743, 742.

29. *Session Laws of New York, 1785*, 81; *Session Laws of New York, 1788*, 643–46. The 1785 law had been passed initially in 1784, but it was vetoed by the Council of Revisions. Schneider, *History of Public Welfare*, 150.

30. Schneider, *History of Public Welfare*, 152–55; Michael Ignatieff, *A Just Measure of Pain: The Penitentiary in the Industrial Revolution, 1750–1850* (New York: Pantheon, 1978), 177. The wheel was employed in Britain until the 1870s.

31. Schneider, *History of Public Welfare*, 216–17. On the Yates report generally, see Schneider, *History of Public Welfare*, chap. 12; Mohl, *Poverty in New York*, 62–64; and Rothman, *Discovery of the Asylum*, chap. 7.

32. Yates, *Report*, 956–57; *Session Laws of New York, 1824*, 382–86.

33. *Revised Statutes of New York, 1827–1828* (1829), 632–33. *Session Laws of New York, 1833*, 9–10.

34. *Revised Statutes of New York, 1827–1828* (1829), 632–33. *Session Laws of New York, 1833*, 9–10. On the lack of funding, see Mohl, *Poverty in New York*, 63–64. On the persistence of mixing into the 1850s, see *Sen. Doc. 8*, 3–10.

35. "Chronicle," *Niles Weekly Register*, July 17, 1824, 336; "States of the Union," *Niles Weekly Register*, June 13, 1840, 229; *Commercial Advertiser* repr. in "Miscellaneous," *Niles Weekly Register*, August 31, 1844, 431; *County of Cumberland v. Holcomb*, 36 Pa. (12 Casey) 349–54 (1860). See also "Chronicle," *Niles Weekly Register*, January 20, 1821, 352; "Chronicle," *Niles Weekly Register*, May 18, 1822, 192; "Miscellaneous," *Niles Weekly Register*, March 4, 1826, 2; "Statistical," *Niles Weekly Register*, January 31, 1829, 366; "States of the Union," *Niles Weekly Register*, September 12, 1840, 19–20; *County of Northhampton v. West* 28 Pa. (4 Casey) 173–75 (1857); *County of Lancaster v. Brinthall* 29 Pa. (5 Casey) 38–40 (1857).

36. Dane, *Abridgement*, 7:46; Tuckerman, *Wages*, 46, 47. For a broader discussion of the relationship between wage work and political rights, see Judith N. Shklar, *American Citizenship: The Quest for Inclusion* (Cambridge: Harvard University Press, 1991), esp. 2–4, 72, 92–94. Shklar argues that Jacksonians, especially labor radicals, forged a new political language that envisioned dignity in labor and connected work to full citizenship. I think Shklar fails to recognize the earlier roots of producer ideology and she underestimates the differences in Jacksonian views on work. Nonetheless, her general point certainly applies to the bourgeois reformers and jurists discussed here.

37. *National Cyclopedia of American Biography*, 10:231; Glenn, *Campaigns*, 53, 61. New York abolished corporal punishment in 1847.

38. *People v. Phillips,* 1 Parker's Criminal Reports 95–98, 100–102 (N.Y., 1847).

39. Ibid., 107.

40. On Edmonds, see *National Cyclopedia of American Biography,* 10:231.

41. *Session Laws of New York, 1853,* 353–54; *Session Laws of New York, 1855,* 451–52; *People v. Forbes,* 4 Parker's Criminal Reports 611–12 (N.Y., 1860). Sutherland's remarks also demonstrate the prevalence of these sorts of arrests and convictions, for he prefaced his opinion by saying that he had "given most serious consideration" to the case because of its "great importance and public interest."

42. *People v. Forbes,* 612–15.

43. *People v. Gray,* 4 Parker's Criminal Reports 616–18 (N.Y., 1860).

44. *Byers and Davis v. Commonwealth,* 42 Pa. (6 Wright) 89–97 (1862); *County of Northhampton v. West* 28 Pa. (4 Casey) 173–75 (1857); *Commonwealth v. Sullivan, Same v. Daniels* (Mass., 1862).

45. The case report appeared in the *Cincinnati Commercial* and was reprinted in "Vagrancy in Cincinnati," *Western Law Journal* 2 (December 1849): 589–90.

46. *Adeline G. Nott's case,* 6 Me. 209 (1834).

47. Ibid., 211. Daniel T. Rodgers, *The Work Ethic in Industrial America, 1850–1920* (Chicago: University of Chicago Press, 1974), 1–30, discusses the meaning of the work ethic in this period.

48. *Adeline G. Nott's case,* 211.

49. Ibid., 212. Such "civic sanitation" applications of vagrancy became common in urban areas in the twentieth century. See Caleb Foote, "Vagrancy-Type Law and Its Administration," *University of Pennsylvania Law Review* 104 (1956): 631–33.

50. *Commonwealth v. M'Keagy,* 1 Ashm. 248 (Philadelphia, 1831).

51. Ibid., 250–53.

52. King referred to *Miles v. Oldfield,* 4 Yeates 423.

53. Ibid., 257.

54. Ibid., 258.

55. Hugh Jones, *The Present State of Virginia, From When Is Inferred a Short View of Maryland and North Carolina* [1724], ed. Richard L. Morton (Chapel Hill: University of North Carolina Press for the Virginia Historical Society, 1956), 88.

56. William Waller Henning, ed., *The Statutes at Large; Being a Collection of All the Laws of Virginia from the First Session of the Legislature in the Year 1619,* 13 vols. (Philadelphia: Thomas Desilver, 1823): 4:208–10, 6:30–31, 475–77; 9:216–17; *Digest of the Laws of the State of Georgia* (1800), 88–89, 98–100, 376–77; Charles McCamic, "Administration of Poor Relief in the Virginias," *West Virginia History* 1 (1940): 175–77; Howard Mackey, "The Operation of the Old Poor Law in Colonial Virginia," *Virginia Magazine of History and Biography* 73 (January 1965): 28–40; Virginia Bernhard, "Poverty and the Social Order in Seventeenth-Century Virginia," *Virginia Magazine of History and Biography* 85 (April 1977): 141–55; David T.

Konig, "'Dale's Laws' and the Non–Common Law Origins of Criminal Justice in Virginia," *American Journal of Legal History* 26 (October 1982): 354–75; Rhys Isaac, *The Transformation of Virginia, 1740–1790* (Chapel Hill: University of North Carolina Press, 1982), 192–98; Barbara Ulmer, "Benevolence in Colonial Charleston," in *South Carolina Historical Association Proceedings 1980*, 5–7; Walter J. Fraser Jr., "Controlling the Poor in Colonial Charles Town," in *South Carolina Historical Association Proceedings 1980*, 14–15; Elizabeth Wisner, *Social Welfare in the South: From Colonial Times to World War I* (Baton Rouge: Louisiana State University Press, 1970), 14.

57. Edmund Ruffin, *The Political Economy of Slavery; or, The Institution Considered in Regard to Its Influence on Public Wealth and the General Welfare* (Washington: Lemuel Towers, 1853), in *Slavery Defended: The Views of the Old South*, ed. Eric L. McKitrick (Englewood Cliffs, N.J.: Prentice-Hall, 1963), 69–80; Edmund Ruffin, *Slave Labor and Free Labor, Described and Compared* (n.p., n.d.), 25–26; Elwood Fisher, *Lecture on the North and South* (Cincinnati: Daily Chronicle, 1849), 32–35; Iveson L. Brookes, *A Defense of the South against the Reproaches of the North* (Hamburg, S.C.: Republican Office, 1850), 17. For comments on free labor and capitalism in the proslavery argument, see Foner, *Free Soil, Free Labor, Free Men*, 66–68; Stanley M. Elkins, *Slavery: A Problem in American Institutional and Intellectual Life*, 2d ed. (Chicago: University of Chicago Press, 1968), 214–16; and Genovese, *Roll, Jordan, Roll*, 85–86.

58. George Fitzhugh, *Slavery Justified, by a Southerner* (Fredricksburg, Va.: Record Printing Office, 1850), in McKitrick, *Slavery Defended*, 41–49; George Fitzhugh, *Cannibals All!, or Slaves without Masters*, ed. C. Vann Woodward (Cambridge: Harvard University Press, Belknap Press, 1960), 108–9, 137, 205, 188, 219.

59. "Extract of a Letter from Robert Greenhow, Esq. President, &c, of the City Overseers of the Poor of Richmond," in Yates, *Report*, 1104–7 (my emphasis); Daniel C. Vogt, "Poor Relief in Frontier Mississippi, 1798–1832," *Journal of Mississippi History* 51 (August 1989): 192; William D. Valentine, Diary, 1837–1855, 15 vols., Southern Historical Collection, Manuscripts Department, University of North Carolina, Chapel Hill, 9:161, April 23, 1849; James Watts to Mrs. Mary Evans, July 5, 1811, McKay-Stiles Family Papers, 1734–1915, Southern Historical Collection, Manuscripts Department, University of North Carolina, Chapel Hill.

60. Valentine, Diary, 9:161, April 23, 1849, 12:28, May 4, 1852; Catherine E. McGolnick to Dr. Grimes, June 4, 1811, McKay-Stiles Family Papers; David Schenck, Diary, 1835–1902, 12 vols., typescript ed., Southern Historical Collection, Manuscripts Department, University of North Carolina, Chapel Hill, 4:113.

61. For overall treatments of the southern poor laws, see James W. Ely Jr., "'There Are Few Subjects in Political Economy of Greater Difficulty': The Poor Laws of the Antebellum South," *American Bar Federation Research Journal* 4 (1985): 849–79;

Wisner, *Social Welfare in the South*, 3–52; and especially Barbara Lawrence Bellows, "Tempering the Wind: The Southern Response to Urban Poverty, 1850–1865" (Ph.D. diss., University of South Carolina, 1983). Although she studies only Richmond, Charleston, and Savannah, Bellows's is the best treatment of social welfare in the Old South. Her subsequent book considers more closely the social welfare history of Charleston. See *Benevolence among Slaveholders: Assisting the Poor in Charleston, 1670–1860* (Baton Rouge: Louisiana State University Press, 1993). See also Vogt, "Poor Relief," 181–99.

62. Bellows, "Tempering the Wind," 4, 29–30, 250–58. See also Ulmer, "Benevolence in Colonial Charleston," 2–3. Ulmer does not really intend to make such an argument, but her analysis points in this direction.

63. On pauper auctions and other older forms of relief, see Vogt, "Poor Relief," 186; Presentments of the Grand Jury of Lancaster District, Fall Term 1821, quoted in Ely, "Few Subjects," 858; Valentine, Diary, 9:161, April 23, 1849; Wisner, *Social Welfare in the South*, 40.

On the authorization of poorhouses, see Henning, *Statutes at Large*, 10:288–90, 12:27–30; *Session Laws of Virginia, 1844*, 77–82; *Session Laws of South Carolina, 1824*, 66–67; Ely, "Few Subjects," 853–55; Vogt, "Poor Relief," 187–88; Valentine, Diary, 9:161, April 23, 1849; *Session Laws of North Carolina, 1831*, 15.

For the continuance of outdoor relief, see *Session Laws of South Carolina, 1824*, 67; "Extract of a letter from the governor of Virginia," in Yates, *Report*, 1102–3; "Extract of a letter from N. Shippard, Esq. Chamberlain of the city of Richmond," Yates, *Report*, 1104; "Extract of a Letter from Robert Greenhow," 1104–7; Vogt, "Poor Relief," 192.

For the figures on Richmond, see Robert Everest, "Pauperism and Crime," *DeBow's Review* 19 (August 1855): 284–85. Everest was an Englishman who was interested in supposed racial and ethnic roots of poverty. Apparently, he undertook the project of collecting statistics on his own, and his figures seem fairly reliable. For other statistics on poverty in Virginia, see "Report of the Second Auditor in Relation to the Number of Poor Children Sent to School . . . ," in *Virginia Convention, 1850–1851, Documents Containing Statistics of Virginia* (Richmond, 1851). The highest incidence occurred among foreign-born inmates, at 1.38 percent of the total foreign population in the city. For whites the corresponding figure was 0.36 percent, and for free blacks, it was 0.63 percent.

For the example from Beckford Parish, see Beckford Parish Poorhouse Account Book, 1799–1838, Shenandoah County, Virginia, Books, 1799–1838, Southern Historical Collection, Manuscripts Department, University of North Carolina, Chapel Hill.

64. *Poindexter v. Wilson and Others*, 3 Munf. 183–84 (Va., 1812); *The Commissioners of the Poor, for Laurens District, v. Lot Dooling*, 1 Bailey 73–75 (S.C., 1827);

Commissioners of the Orphan of the City of Charleston v. William Magill, Cheves 56–59 (S.C., 1840); *Brewer v. Harris & als.*, 5 Gratt 285 (Va., 1848); Ely, "Few Subjects," 863–64; Vogt, "Poor Relief," 187–88.

65. *Poindexter v. Wilson*, 183–84; *Commissioners of the Orphan of the City of Charleston v. Magill*, 56–59; *Bullock v. Sebrell*, 6 Leigh 560–61 (Va., 1835).

66. For the Arkansas and Missouri laws, see *Revised Statutes of Arkansas* (1838), 758–59; *Revised Statutes of Missouri* (1845), 1070–71. In general, this description is based on Henning, *Statutes at Large*, 12:573–80; *Revised Code of Virginia* (1819), 2:264–79; *Code of Virginia* (1849), 258–65; *Code of Virginia* (1860), 291–96; *Session Laws of Virginia, 1856*, 162–63; *Code of Virginia* (1860), 801–2; *Digest of the Statute Laws of Kentucky* (1834), 1521–24; *Revised Statutes of Kentucky* (1852), 531, 690–92; *Laws of Texas, 1822–1897* (Gammel, 1898), 2(1): 39–40; Jeffrey S. Adler, "Vagging the Demons and Scoundrels: Vagrancy and the Growth of St. Louis, 1830–1861," *Journal of Urban History* 13 (November 1986): 3–30. Bellows, "Tempering the Wind," 27, 184–85, 223.

67. *Session Laws of Virginia, 1820*, 22–23; *Session Laws of Georgia, 1859*, 69–70; Ira Berlin, *Slaves without Masters: The Free Negro in the Antebellum South* (New York: Pantheon, 1974), 226; *Code of Mississippi* (1850), 525.

68. Genovese discusses "the hegemonic function of the law" in *Roll, Jordan, Roll*, 25–49. On the relationship between slaves and poor whites, see ibid., 22–23, and Fraser, "Controlling the Poor in Colonial Charles Town," 13–14. While he is primarily interested in local relief in Mississippi, Christopher Johnson also notes the role of southern social welfare law in upholding the social order. See "Poor Relief in Antebellum Mississippi," *Journal of Mississippi History* 49 (1987): 2–3. On the control of poor relief by southern elites, see Bellows, "Tempering the Wind," 9–14, 17–19, 36, 90, and Vogt, "Poor Relief," 193–98.

69. *Revised Statutes of North Carolina* (1837), 1:201; *Compilation of the Laws of Georgia, 1810–1819* (Lamar, 1821), 642. See also *Digest of the Laws of Georgia* (Prince, 1837), 647; *Codification of the Statute Law of Georgia* (1845), 748; *Code of Tennessee* (1858), 359–60; *Revised Code of Mississippi* (1857), 628–29; *Penal Code of the State of Texas* (1857), 74. See also *Digest of the General Statute Laws of the State of Texas* (Oldham and White, 1859); *Texas Laws* (Gammel), 2(1): 40. On the definition of prostitutes as vagrants, see Thomas Clyde Mackey, "Red Lights Out: A Legal History of Prostitution, Disorderly Houses, and Vice Districts, 1870–1917" (Ph.D. diss., Rice University, 1984), 27–67.

70. *Session Laws of North Carolina, 1840–41*, 102; *Session Laws of South Carolina, 1836*, 82; *The State, ex relatione I. H. Coleman v. Hart Maxcy, E. J. Arthur, et al.*, 1 McMul. 341–45 (S.C., 1837). See also Augustin S. Clayton, *The Office and Duty of Justice of the Peace. . . .* (Milledgeville, Ga.: S. Grantland, 1819), 413; *Reports and Resolutions of South Carolina, 1835*, 55; Athens, Alabama, Resolution on Disorderly Persons, January 31, 1852, Southern Historical Collection, Manuscripts Department,

University of North Carolina, Chapel Hill; Jack Kenny Williams, *Vogues in Villainy: Crime and Retribution in Ante-bellum South Carolina* (Columbia: University of South Carolina Press, 1959), 47–50; Bertram Wyatt-Brown, *Honor and Violence in the Old South* (New York: Oxford University Press, 1986), 131–42.

71. *Colson v. Brown*, 2 Brevard 332–33 (S.C., 1809); *Michael P. Walsh ads. The State*, 2 McCord 248–49 (S.C., 1822).

72. Schenck, Diary, 3:8–9, January 10, 1853.

Chapter 3: Northern Principles Go South

1. Carl Schurz, *Report on the Condition of the South* (1865; reprint, New York: Arno Press, 1969), 38; *New York Principia*, repr. in the *Liberator*, March 3, 1863.

2. The best examination of free-labor ideology and the conditions of labor in the postwar South is in the work of the Freedmen and Southern Society Project of the University of Maryland. For a short overview, see Ira Berlin et al., "The Terrain of Freedom: The Struggle over the Meaning of Free Labor in the U.S. South," *History Workshop* 22 (Autumn 1986): 109, and especially Berlin et al., *Wartime Genesis*, 2–8. The FSSP is especially good at noting the influence of northern social welfare concepts on Union policy, though they do not mean vagrancy in particular, Berlin et al., *Wartime Genesis*, 15–16, 29–30. The importance of free-labor ideology is, of course, a main point of Eric Foner. See *Reconstruction*, esp. 54–60. In this work, Foner still adopts much of the previous point of view. Moreover, as noted in the introduction, Foner and others see labor law as anomalous to free-labor ideology.

By making the argument about law and emancipation, I do not mean to suggest that "law" represents a definite point of causation outside the realm of "ideology." Nor do I mean to eliminate the role of northern free-labor ideology in shaping the contours of emancipation. My point is not so much that northerners used labor law directly (though they quite frequently did) but that they structured free labor based on popular versions of the competing legal visions of a capitalist labor market that had originated in courts and legislatures during the antebellum period.

Most historians of emancipation and Reconstruction have not sought to connect legal developments in the postwar South to changes in the antebellum or postbellum North. The most notable exception to this trend is Amy Dru Stanley, who has explored notions of contract and vagrancy in two important articles. See "Conjugal Bonds and Wage Labor: Rights of Contract in the Age of Emancipation," *Journal of American History* 75 (June 1988): 471–500, and "Beggars Can't Be Choosers: Compulsion and Contract in Postbellum America," *Journal of American History* 78 (March 1992): 1265–93.

3. The central works on wartime Reconstruction in Louisiana are Louis S. Gerteis, *From Contraband to Freedmen: Federal Policy toward Blacks, 1861–1865* (Westport, Conn.: Greenwood Press, 1973), esp. 65–115; C. Peter Ripley, *Slaves and Freed-*

men in Civil War Louisiana (Baton Rouge: Louisiana State University Press, 1976), 1–3, 25–90; William F. Messner, *Freedmen and the Ideology of Free Labor: Louisiana, 1862–1865* (Lafayette: Center for Louisiana Studies, University of Southwest Louisiana, 1978), xi–xii, 32–113; Ted Tunnel, *Crucible of Reconstruction: War, Radicalism, and Race in Louisiana, 1862–1877* (Baton Rouge: Louisiana State University Press, 1984), 84–85; Peyton McCrary, *Abraham Lincoln and Reconstruction: The Louisiana Experiment* (Princeton: Princeton University Press, 1978), 66–159; and J. Thomas May, "Continuity and Change in the Labor Program of the Army and the Freedmen's Bureau," *Civil War History* 17 (September 1971): 245–54.

Other wartime experiments included those in low country South Carolina and Georgia and in the Mississippi Valley. The best account is Berlin et al., *Wartime Genesis*, 87–113, 621–50. See also Willie Lee Rose, *Rehearsal for Reconstruction: The Port Royal Experiment* (New York: Oxford University Press, 1964), and Foner, *Reconstruction*, 50–54, 58–60. I have focused on Louisiana because it (along with the Mississippi Valley) is seen by historians as more indicative of what would follow in the postwar period and because Lincoln made it a showcase for wartime Reconstruction. On this point, see Lawanda Cox, *Lincoln and Black Freedom: A Study in Presidential Leadership* (Columbia: University of South Carolina Press, 1981).

While Union policymakers sought to bring capitalist labor relations to the emancipated South via law, other northerners sought to do so through outright enterprise. For this story, see Lawrence N. Powell, *New Masters: Northern Planters during the Civil War and Reconstruction* (New Haven: Yale University Press, 1980). Powell, it should be noted, believes wartime labor regulations grew from "compromises with slavery" and that the labor program in Louisiana laid the basis for Yankee planters' efforts (84–85).

4. Berlin et al., *Wartime Genesis*, 349–54. For other, more complete treatments of Butler's labor policies, see Gerteis, *Contraband to Freedmen*, 65–73; Ripley, *Slaves and Freedmen*, 25–45; Messner, *Freedmen*, 32–43.

5. Fred Harvey Harrington, *Fighting Politician: Major General N. P. Banks* (Philadelphia: University of Pennsylvania Press, 1948), vii–viii, 41–104.

6. *New Orleans Picayune*, December 19, 1862; *War of the Rebellion: A Compilation of the Official Records of the Union and Confederate Armies*, 128 vols. (Washington, D.C.: Government Printing Office, 1880–1901), 1st ser., 15:620 (hereafter cited as *OR*).

7. *New Orleans Picayune*, January 22, 1863; *National Anti-Slavery Standard*, February 21, 1863; *Liberator*, March 6, 1863. Although William Lloyd Garrison later approved of Banks's course, he commented that the arrests showed that "the 'iron hand' of military rule [was] laid almost as tyrannically upon the victimized colored people of New Orleans as was that of the rebel masters. Gen. Banks [was] in fact digging his own political grave."

8. *OR*, 15:667.

9. *New York Tribune*, February 18, 1863. Berlin et al., *Wartime Genesis*, 355–56. The FSSP argues that the vagrancy section "bound [former slaves] to a given plantation for an entire year, [and] violated their conviction that freedom conferred the right to come and go as they pleased." If viewed out of the context of prewar law, this certainly seems to be the intent, but federal officials were more interested in enforcing *work* discipline than in enforcing *plantation* discipline. This distinction was something that none of the parties involved ever grasped fully.

10. *National Anti-Slavery Standard*, April 4, 1863; *Autobiography of Oliver Otis Howard*, 2 vols. (New York: Baker and Taylor, 1907), 2:186; Berlin et al., *Wartime Genesis*, 358. Although pauper auctions had incurred much criticism in the prewar period, they continued even into the late 1860s. See Robert Bremner, *The Public Good: Philanthropy and Welfare in the Civil War Era* (New York: Alfred A. Knopf, 1980), 26, 150–51.

11. *New Orleans Picayune*, January 31, 1863, February 19, 1863; *New York Times*, February 23, 1863.

12. *New Orleans Picayune*, February 19, 1863; *New York Times*, February 23, 1863.

13. *New York Tribune*, March 4, 1863; *New Orleans Picayune*, February 20, 1863; *New York Times*, March 5, 1863.

14. *New York Tribune*, March 11, 1863; Denison to Chase, March 31, 1863, *Diary and Correspondence of Salmon P. Chase*, in *Annual Report of the American Historical Association for 1902* (Washington, D.C.: Government Printing Office, 1903), 378–79.

15. Cecil D. Eby, ed., *A Virginia Yankee in the Civil War: The Diaries of David Hunter Strother* (Chapel Hill: University of North Carolina Press, 1961), 148–49.

16. "The Massachusetts Board of State Charities, and the Westborough Reform School," *Christian Examiner* 83 (July 1867): 117; Bremner, *Public Good*, 30, 172. In the immediate postwar period, this ship became a receptacle for young black men who were arrested for vagrancy after drifting northward.

17. *OR*, 34(2): 228–29.

18. Ibid., 229–30.

19. Even the radical Schurz recognized the importance of seasonality in the Union's labor program. Schurz, *Report*, 16.

20. Thomas W. Conway, *Report on the Condition of the Freedmen* (Washington, D.C.: Government Printing Office, 1864), 4, 8–9.

21. Excerpts from testimony of Thomas W. Conway, January 28, 1865, Testimony Received by the Commission, ser. 736, Smith-Brady Commission, in Berlin et al., *Wartime Genesis*, 576, 578.

22. James B. Yeatman, *Report of the Western Sanitary Commission in Regard to Leasing Abandoned Plantations with Rules and Regulations Governing the Same* (St. Louis: Western Sanitary Commission, 1864), 13–15; Berlin et al., *Wartime Genesis*, 373–74. In the late 1850s, farm wages averaged $140 per year plus board. Bremner, *Public Good*, 12. The contracts I have looked at also suggest that farm wages ranged

between $10 and $16 per month, depending on the duration of the contract and whether the worker got room and board. Under any estimate, they were considerably lower than William P. Mellen's highest levels of $25, $20, and $15 for men and $18, $14, and $10 per month for women. In reality, the army's top rate of $8 was somewhat below the market, while the Treasury Department's was above it. However, wartime inflation makes these figures doubtful. It is unclear what Mellen intended in regard to in-kind remuneration. One section of the orders required lessees to provide room, board, clothing, and one acre of ground, while stipulating that they sell provisions at 15 percent above wholesale.

23. *OR*, 47(1): 1147; *New Orleans Tribune*, March 28, 1865, July 15, 1865, July 16, 1865, August 4, 1865.

24. Circular No. 2, Bureau of Refugees, Freedmen, and Abandoned Lands–Louisiana, in *New Orleans Tribune*, July 16, 1865. On Conway's release of vagrants, see Thomas W. Conway, *The Freedmen of Louisiana: Final Report of the Bureau of Free Labor, Department of the Gulf, to Major General E. R. S. Canby* (New Orleans: Times Book Office, 1865), 4. On Conway's replacement, see Howard A. White, *The Freedmen's Bureau in Louisiana* (Baton Rouge: Louisiana State University Press, 1970), 18–24.

25. *New Orleans Tribune*, October 27, 28, November 3, 1865. Fullerton to Chief of Police of the City of New Orleans, October 25, 1865, United States, Bureau of Refugees, Freedmen, and Abandoned Lands, *Records of the Assistant Commissioner for the State of Louisiana, Bureau of Refugees, Freedmen, and Abandoned Lands, 1865–1870*, 36 rolls, National Archives Microfilm Publication No. 1027, roll 1 (hereafter cited as BRFAL-LA); White, *Freedmen's Bureau in Louisiana*, 25.

26. *Harper's Weekly*, February 21, 1863; *New York Times*, February 23, 1863, March 5, 1863, February 14, 1863. The paper continued to observe Banks with great interest, and by the summer of 1864, the editors feared that Banks's labor system was "Philanthropy Run Mad." Yet they believed he had found the "golden mean" of remunerating the laborer but compelling him to work. *New York Times*, July 23, 1864.

27. *New York Principia*, repr. in the *Liberator*, April 3, 1863; C. K. W. in the *Liberator*, March 11, 1864; *Christian Watchman and Reflector*, repr. in *Liberator*, February 27, 1863; *New York Tribune*, March 4, 1863.

28. Speech before the Massachusetts Anti-Slavery Society, January 26, 1865, printed in the *Liberator*, February 10, 1865; Wendell Phillips, "On a Metropolitan Police," *Liberator*, April 10, 1863.

29. James McKaye, *The Mastership and Its Fruits: The Emancipated Slave Face to Face with His Old Master* (New York: William C. Bryant, 1864), 26–28.

30. Ibid. On problems with provost marshals, see Berlin et al., *Wartime Genesis*, 359–60. Self-reliance was a central theme of the AFIC's preliminary report. See U.S. Congress, Senate, *Preliminary Report Touching the Condition and Management of*

Emancipated Refugees, Made to the Secretary of War by the American Freedmen's Inquiry Commission, 38th Cong., 1st sess., June 30, 1863, S. Exec. Doc. 53, 8, 18–19. Written by labor reformer Robert Dale Owen, this report also connected the issue to images of gender, for it quoted favorably a judge who contrasted the "shiftless" ways of blacks in the towns with the "bold, erect carriage and free bearing" of those in the military. "It makes men of them at once," the judge had said, and the commissioners presumably agreed (7).

31. U.S. Congress, Senate, *Final Report of the American Freedmen's Inquiry Commission to the Secretary of War*, 38th Cong., 1st sess., May 15, 1864, S. Exec. Doc. 53, 110 (hereafter cited as AFIC, Final Report). The commissioners could hold these ideas in part because they had no fear about freedpeople becoming vagrants. They suggested that former slaves were willingly accepting self-restraint and building their own institutions of poor relief. "Scarcely any beggars are found among them," Dale happily noted (100).

Schurz, *Report*, 28–30. Schurz suggested that the cure to vagrancy lay in providing land and a sense of place, not in penal measures.

The influence of the idea of competitiveness on prewar abolitionist thought is best explored in Glickstein, "'Poverty Is Not Slavery,'" 195–209.

32. W. H. Allen, "Free Labor in Louisiana," *Christian Examiner* 78 (May 1865): 385, 387, 395, 398.

33. E. E. Hale, "How to Use Victory," *Atlantic Monthly* 13 (June 1864): 765; Garrison to Francis W. Newman, July 22, 1864, in *The Letters of William Lloyd Garrison*, vol. 5, *Let the Oppressed Go Free, 1861–1867*, ed. Walter E. Merrill (Cambridge: Harvard University Press, Belknap Press, 1979), 231.

The issue of poverty had long troubled the abolitionist movement, and its relationship with the working class had been strained at the best of times. See Glickstein, "'Poverty Is Not Slavery,'" 200–205; Aileen S. Kraditor, *Means and Ends in American Abolitionism: Garrison and His Critics on Strategy and Tactics, 1834–1850* (New York: Pantheon, 1969), 243, 247, 253; Foner, *Politics and Ideology*, 24–25; and Bernard Mandel, *Labor: Free and Slave, Workingmen and the Anti-slavery Movement in the United States* (New York: Associated Authors, 1955), 61–62, 73, 77–78, 89–95.

34. *Liberator*, February 24, 1865, March 3, 1865; *National Anti-Slavery Standard*, April 25, 1863, May 2, 1863; *New York Times*, August 13, 1864. The biblical phrase used by Bowen is from Gen. 3:19. Abolitionists and poor-law reformers were also fond of quoting Paul's injunctions against idleness in 2 Thes. 6:14. Glickstein has also noticed this particular use of Scripture. "'Poverty Is Not Slavery,'" 200.

35. *Congressional Globe*, 38th Cong., 1st sess., 536 (cited hereafter as *CG*, Cong./sess.); P. J. Staudenraus, "The Popular Origins of the Thirteenth Amendment," *Mid-America* 50 (April 1969): 108–15. Where I have applied factional designations below, they are based on Michael Les Benedict, *A Compromise of Principle: Congressional Republicans and Reconstruction, 1863–1869* (New York: W. W. Norton, 1974), 27–33.

36. *CG*, 38/2, 531; Jacobus tenBroek, *The Antislavery Origins of the Fourteenth Amendment* (Los Angeles: University of California Press, 1951), 138–39; Staudenraus, "Popular Origins," 114. The amendment fell twelve votes short of the necessary two-thirds on its first House vote on June 15, 1864. The House managers managed to swing enough votes during the lame duck session in January 1865 by persuading Democrats that the end of slavery was a fait accompli with the end of the war, that 1864 elections had ensured passage in the new session, and that Democrats could save face by voting for the measure. For example, see the speech of Democrat Anson Herrick of New York, who switched his vote. *CG*, 38/2, 526; Herman Belz, *A New Birth of Freedom: The Republican Party and Freedmen's Rights, 1861–1866* (Westport, Conn.: Greenwood Press, 1976), 123.

37. This interpretation differs from the position of some historians in the last thirty years who have seen the Thirteenth Amendment as a truly radical text intended to bring about a revolution in federal-state relations and to broaden civil and political rights. See tenBroek, *Antislavery Origins*, 137–83; G. Sidney Buchanan, *The Quest for Freedom: A Legal History of the Thirteenth Amendment*, repr. from *Houston Law Review* 12 (1976); Harold M. Hyman and William Wiecek, *Equal Justice under Law: Constitutional Development, 1835–1875* (New York: Harper and Row, 1982), chaps. 10–11. Most recently, this view has been urged in Lea S. VanderVelde, "The Labor Vision of the Thirteenth Amendment," *University of Pennsylvania Law Review* 138 (December 1989): 437–504. There are two main problems with these interpretations. First, they privilege Radical Republicans above all others to find the meaning of the amendment, yet Radicals did not hold a preponderance of power in 1864 and 1865. See Michael Les Benedict, *Compromise of Principle*. Second, and more important, they underrate the significant ways in which northern labor law defined what freedom meant for workers, both in the prewar North and in the postwar South.

For an even more limited view on the meaning of the amendment than the one I am suggesting, see Belz, *New Birth*, 113–34. Belz acknowledges that some Republicans saw the amendment as granting rights to both blacks and whites, but he concludes that in 1864 and 1865, most Republicans did not conceive of it as altering federalism significantly or granting much beyond personal liberty. In view of southern resistance, however, Republicans broadened their views based on the amendment's implications.

38. Foner, *Free Soil, Free Labor, Free Men*, 1–39. *CG*, 38/1, 1313 (Trumbull); *CG*, 38/2, 141 (Ashley). See also *CG*, 38/1, 1320, 1369, 1440. For the use of such "catch phrases" as "the dignity of labor" during the debate, see VanderVelde, "Labor Vision," 447, 472–73.

39. *CG*, 38/2, 138 (Ashley). *CG*, 38/1, 1369 (Clark). See also *CG*, 38/1, 1320–24, 2949, 2955. Though I am not exactly referring to the same issue, the following works are helpful on this matter. Foner, *Free Soil, Free Labor, Free Men*, 40–51, 59; Glickstein, "'Poverty Is Not Slavery,'" 212; and Elkins, *Slavery*, 164–93.

40. *CG*, 38/1, 1438, 2980; 38/2, 144, 199, 200. James Harlan cited examples of free blacks supporting themselves in the prewar North, while John Farnsworth pointed to the brave service of black troops and the reliability of African Americans in sheltering soldiers. Radical Josiah B. Grinnell of Iowa maintained that if slaves had supported both themselves and their masters, they could surely support themselves as freedpeople. Hyman and Wiecek also see a hierarchy of rights but do not connect it as directly to ideas about work and family. *Equal Justice*, 396.

41. *CG*, 38/1, 1482, 1439. *CG*, 38/1, 1482; 38/2, 143. By negative and positive, I simply mean negative in the sense of subtracting something and positive in the sense of adding something. This division is partially based on Carl Schurz's observation in 1866: "The general government of the republic has, by proclaiming the emancipation of the slaves commenced a great social revolution in the south, but has, as yet, not completed it. Only the negative part of it is accomplished." Schurz, *Report*, 38. For a similar use of these terms, see VanderVelde, "Labor Vision," 495. For a different interpretation of Sumner's alternative amendment, see VanderVelde, "Labor Vision," 449–50 n. 67.

42. For broader discussion of conflict of laws and antislavery, see William Wiecek, *The Sources of Anti-slavery Constitutionalism in America, 1760–1848* (Ithaca, N.Y.: Cornell University Press, 1977); Paul Finkelman, *An Imperfect Union: Slavery, Freedom, and Comity* (Chapel Hill: University of North Carolina Press, 1981).

43. *CG*, 38/2, 190 (emphasis and brackets in Kasson's original); *CG*, 38/2, 154; 38/1, 2983.

44. *Harmon v. Salmon Falls Manufacturing Company*, 35 Me. 452–55 (1853); Catherine Beecher, *Treatise on Domestic Economy for Young Ladies at Home and at School* (New York: Harper and Brothers, 1847), 25.

45. AFIC, Final Report, 110; *In re Turner*, 24 Fed. Cas. 337 (1867); Schurz, *Report*, 76. On the Turner case, see Hyman, *More Perfect Union*, 484–85, and below, chapter 6. On the antipeonage act, see Hyman, *More Perfect Union*, 391–92, and Steinfeld, *Invention of Free Labor*, chap. 7. Republicans also worried about the fact that indentures continued under the antislavery provisions of the Northwest Ordinance, which were nearly identical in wording to the Thirteenth Amendment. Belz, *New Birth*, 125–26.

For a different view about the "specific prohibitions" the framers had in mind, see VanderVelde, "Labor Vision," 485–95. In part at least, VanderVelde's wider list of prohibitions, which includes such elements as enforcing specific enforcement, wage fixing, enticement laws, and even entirety itself, results from the fact that she looked at debates after the amendment passed. I would agree that *radicals* in Congress and elsewhere (especially in the Freedmen's Bureau) came to oppose a wide range of standard northern labor practices and laws. Yet I would suggest that radicals represented only one part of the discourse about labor law in the immediate postbellum period. Moreover, radicals themselves split over whether labor law should be used to protect workers or to create a radically free market in labor. For an example of this tension within radical thought, see the section on the *New Orleans Tribune* in chap. 5 below.

46. Holman, *CG*, 38/1, 2962; Saulsbury, *CG*, 38/1, 1366; White, *CG*, 38/2, 215. See also 38/1, 2939, 2985, 2987, and 38/2, 151, 178; Belz, *New Birth*, 122. If taken to its ultimate conclusion under an expansive interpretation, the Thirteenth Amendment could produce a genuinely democratic revolution that would dissolve all servile relationships and institute a truly egalitarian society.

47. Henderson, *CG*, 38/1, 1465; Farnsworth, *CG*, 38/2, 202; Kelley, *CG*, 38/1, 2985.

48. The following is taken from Harlan's speech in support of the amendment in *CG*, 1437–38. A lawyer born in Illinois and raised in Indiana, Harlan was a strong supporter of antislavery. Herman Belz, *Reconstructing the Union: Theory and Policy during the Civil War* (Ithaca, N.Y.: Cornell University Press, 1969), 57.

49. For a different view of the concept of reciprocity and vagrancy, see Amy Dru Stanley, "Beggars Can't Be Choosers," 1290–93. Stanley suggests that postbellum reformers invoked the "rule of exchange" from contract language, but she does not make clear how this differed substantially from prewar invocations of reciprocity. It could be argued that Harlan was a forward-looking spokesperson for the kind of discourse Stanley envisions in the postwar period, yet he seems to be calling on older concepts, for his arguments were remarkably similar to those employed by Beecher almost two decades before.

50. VanderVelde, "Labor Vision," 495–504.

Chapter 4: The Mutation of Free-Labor Law

1. *Timmins v. Lacy*, 30 Tex. 120 (1867). On the Black Codes generally, see Theodore B. Wilson, *The Black Codes of the South* (University: University of Alabama Press, 1969). For Howard's comments, see U.S. Congress, Senate, *Reports of the Freedmen's Bureau Assistant Commissioners and Laws in Relation to the Freedmen*, 39th Cong., 2d sess., S. Exec. Doc. 6, 2–3 (hereafter cited as *SED* 6). For an example of claims that southern laws modeled the North, see *Report of the Joint Committee on Reconstruction*, four parts in one volume (Washington, D.C.: Government Printing Office, 1866), 4:56.

2. For general treatments of the bureau, see George R. Bentley, *A History of the Freedmen's Bureau* (Philadelphia: University of Pennsylvania Press, 1955), and Donald G. Nieman, *To Set the Law in Motion: The Freedmen's Bureau and the Legal Rights of Blacks, 1865–1868* (Millwood, N.Y.: KTO Press, 1979). On passage of the legislation, see Belz, *New Birth*, 69–112.

Among the general works critical of the bureau are William S. McFeely, *Yankee Stepfather: General O. O. Howard and the Freedmen* (New York: W. W. Norton, 1968), 7–8, 149–65; Leon F. Litwack, *Been in the Storm So Long: The Aftermath of Slavery*

(New York: Vintage Books, 1979), esp. 364–86; and Gerteis, *Contraband to Freedmen*, 183–92. McFeely, *Yankee Stepfather*, 1–7, is a valuable overview of earlier views.

On the economic outcomes of emancipation, see Ralph Schlomowitz, "The Origins of Southern Sharecropping," *Agricultural History* 53 (July 1979): 557–75; Roger L. Ransom and Richard Sutch, *One Kind of Freedom: The Economic Consequences of Emancipation* (Cambridge: Cambridge University Press, 1977), 94; Peter Kolchin, *First Freedom: The Responses of Alabama Blacks to Emancipation and Reconstruction* (Westport, Conn.: Greenwood Press, 1972), 44–48; Joel Williamson, *After Slavery: The Negro in South Carolina during Reconstruction, 1861–1877* (Chapel Hill: University of North Carolina Press, 1965), 64–95; and R. L. F. Davis, *Good and Faithful Labor: From Slavery to Sharecropping in the Natchez District* (Westport, Conn.: Greenwood Press, 1982), 4–6, 88–115, who sees the freedpeople as the only parties who wanted sharecropping. For contrary views, see Jonathan Wiener, *Social Origins of the New South: Alabama, 1860–1885* (Baton Rouge: Louisiana State University Press, 1978), 35–57, who sees labor arrangements deriving from a process of class conflict in which planters exercised "coercive method[s] of labor control," and Gerald D. Jaynes, *Branches without Roots: Genesis of the Black Working Class in the American South, 1862–1882* (New York: Oxford University Press, 1986), who contends that neither planters nor freedpeople wanted sharecropping; rather, it was forced on both sides by the lack of credit. Harold Woodman has evaluated the older elements of this literature in "Sequel to Slavery: The New History Views the Postbellum South," *Journal of Southern History* 43 (November 1977): 532–54.

Of newer interpretations of the bureau, Foner's *Reconstruction* is the best example. The best work to date on the bureau in a particular state is Paul Cimbala's wonderfully nuanced study of the agency in Georgia. Cimbala does an exemplary job of explaining the influence of northern ideology on bureau policymaking and also sees the central role of the bureau in the failure of Reconstruction. Paul A. Cimbala, *Under the Guardianship of the Nation: The Freedmen's Bureau and Reconstruction in Georgia, 1865–1870* (Athens: University of Georgia Press, 1997). Cimbala expressed some of the points of this work in earlier articles. See, for example, "The 'Talisman Power': Davis Tillson, the Freedmen's Bureau, and Free Labor in Reconstruction Georgia, 1865–1866," *Civil War History* 28 (June 1982): 153–71.

For other examples of generally sympathetic treatments, see Foner, *Politics and Ideology*, 101; Dan T. Carter, *When the War Was Over: The Failure of Self-Reconstruction in the South, 1865–1867* (Baton Rouge: Louisiana State University Press, 1985), 178, 204, 214; Barry A. Crouch, *The Freedmen's Bureau and Black Texans* (Austin: University of Texas Press, 1992), ix–x.

3. For the point about the bureau's structure, see McFeely, *Yankee Stepfather*, 84.

For examples of emancipation as part of the transition to capitalism, see Barbara Jeanne Fields, *Slavery and Freedom on the Middle Ground: Maryland during the*

Nineteenth Century (New Haven: Yale University Press, 1985), esp. chap. 6; Julie Saville, *The Work of Reconstruction: From Slave to Wage Labor in South Carolina, 1860–1870* (New York: Cambridge University Press, 1994); and Joseph P. Reidy, *From Slavery to Agrarian Capitalism in the Cotton Plantation South, Central Georgia, 1800–1880* (Chapel Hill: University of North Carolina Press, 1992), esp. chap. 6. These works, and others like them, have pointed the way toward what I see as a much deeper understanding of emancipation and Reconstruction, yet most of these more recent studies still see law as anomalous to the emergence of capitalist labor relations. Reidy provides a particularly clear example of scholars who see this transition as without "real precedents" (136–37).

For an excellent discussion of the divergent meanings of "freedom" and free labor and their relationship to capitalist development during Reconstruction, see Foner, "Meaning of Freedom," 435–60.

4. For a similar argument about the gap in social conditions, see Fields, *Slavery and Freedom on the Middle Ground*, 163–66.

5. Saxton to Mr. N. C. Dennet, August 15, 1865, United States, Bureau of Refugees, Freedmen, and Abandoned Lands, *Records of the Assistant Commissioner of the Bureau of Refugees, Freedmen, and Abandoned Lands for the State of South Carolina 1865–1870*, 42 rolls, National Archives Microfilm Publication No. M869, roll 1 (hereafter cited as BRFAL-SC and roll number); Saxton to E. A. Wild, no date [probably early July 1865], BRFAL-SC, roll 1; Saxton to E. A. Wild, August 11, 1865, BRFAL-SC, roll 1. Saxton also had control over Georgia and Florida for the first few months of his administration. See also Saxton to Col. James C. Beecher, August 17, 1865, ibid.

On Saxton's background, see *National Cyclopedia of American Biography*, 4:219–20. On Port Royal, see Rose, *Rehearsal for Reconstruction*; Berlin et al., *Wartime Genesis*, 87–113.

6. General Order 11, August 28, 1865; Circular No. 5, October 19, 1865, BRFAL-SC, roll 37; Circular No. 2, U.S. Congress, House, *Orders Issued by the Freedmen's Bureau, 1865–1866*, 39th Cong., 1st sess., H. Exec. D. 70, 92 (hereafter cited as *HED* 70).

7. Saxton to Oliver Otis Howard, December 25, 1865; Saxton to Upham, December 27, 1865; Saxton to Bvt. Maj. Gen. C. Devens, December 13, 1865, BRFAL-SC, roll 1; Upham to Saxton, December 20, 1865, BRFAL-SC, roll 8; Circular No. 4, *HED* 70, 94–95.

8. Saxton to Howard, October 13, 1865, BRFAL-SC, roll 1; O. O. Howard, Special Field Orders No. 1 and No. 2, October 19, 1865, BRFAL-SC, roll 37. Saxton was aware of his precarious position almost from the start. See Saxton to Maj. Gen. James B. Steedman, August 19, 1865, BRFAL-SC, roll 1. Circular No. 1 (1866 series), January 20, 1866, BRFAL-SC, roll 36. Fears about a black insurrection circulated throughout the South in late 1865. For more on these fears, see Dan T. Carter, "The Anatomy of Fear: The Christmas Day Insurrection Scare of 1865," *Journal of Southern History* 42 (August 1976): 345–64.

9. U.S. Congress, Senate, *Reports of Assistant Commissioners of the Freedmen's Bureau, 1865–1866*, 39th Cong., 1st sess., S. Exec. D. 27, 143 (hereafter cited as *SED* 27). For a considerably different interpretation of Kiddoo, see Crouch, *Freedmen's Bureau and Black Texans*, 21–27. Crouch believes Kiddoo did not "favor" planters and overall helped freedpeople to "receive more equitable treatment" (26–27). I think Crouch underestimates the extent to which Kiddoo's rigid stance on contracts and his use of enticement restricted local labor markets in planters' favor. Still, my goal here is not to cast blame or heap praise on one assistant commissioner or another. Rather, I hope to illustrate the diverse positions they maintained regarding the role of the state in labor law. Kiddoo's rigorous use of the law and the power vested in the army, I believe, makes him a viable representative for bureau conservatives.

The most comprehensive treatment of Kiddoo's administration can be found in William L. Richter, *Overreached on All Sides: The Freedmen's Bureau Administrators in Texas, 1865–1868* (College Station: Texas A&M University Press, 1991), 79–145. Richter argues that the bureau represented "a radical program for its day that failed to achieve its idealistic goals because it was administered by white men who acted in an unimaginative, bureaucratic manner, instead of in an inventive, revolutionary fashion" (ix). Richter's rather constricted analytical framework does not allow him to explore the role of northern ideology (as Crouch does) or account for the nature of bureaucratic states.

For a general summary of bureau historiography in the state, see Crouch, *Freedmen's Bureau and Black Texans*, 1–11. For examples of earlier treatments of the bureau in the state, see Richter, "The Army and the Negro in Reconstruction Texas, 1865–1870," *East Texas Historical Journal* 10 (Spring 1972): 8; Claude Elliot, "The Freedmen's Bureau in Texas," *Southwestern Historical Quarterly* 56 (July 1952): 11.

10. *SED* 27, 141. Very few enticement cases reached the appellate level in the prewar North. Based on these few litigations, it seems northern courts had sometimes allowed enticement actions in cases of apprentices or domestic servants but refused to apply the rule to industrial cases. See *James v. Le Roy, Bayard, & McEvers*, 13 Johns. 274 (N.Y., 1810), an apprentice on a ship; *Haight v. Badgeley and Wife*, 15 Barb. 499 (N.Y., 1853), a domestic; *Campbell v. Cooper*, 34 N.H. 49 (1856), another domestic; *Boston Glass Manufactory v. Binney et al.*, 21 Mass. (4 Pick.) 425 (1827). On this last action, see Tomlins, "Ties That Bind," 218–19. Tomlins sees the dicta in this case as another example of judges importing master-servant discourse to empower the industrial employment relation. For the role of enticement in postwar labor law, see chapter 6 below.

11. *SED* 27, 141–42.

12. Ibid., 142–44.

13. Ibid.

14. Ibid., 142, 147; Kiddoo to Richardson, December 19, 1866, United States, Bureau of Refugees, Freedmen, and Abandoned Lands, *Records of the Assistant Com-*

missioner for the State of Texas, Bureau of Refugees, Freedmen, and Abandoned Lands, 1865–1870, 32 rolls, National Archives Microfilm Publication No. M821, roll 1 (hereafter cited as BRFAL-TX; all citations are to roll 1).

15. *SED* 27, 157; Kiddoo to Howard, July 23, 1866, William Sinclair to Phillip Dunn, August 14, 1866, Kiddoo to Dunn, August 21, 1866, BRFAL-TX.

16. *SED* 27, 157; Kiddoo to Howard, August 8, 1866, BRFAL-TX. Kiddoo's racism even extended to everyday matters. In May 1866, he requested from the army "one intelligent and reliable white soldier for duty as [an] orderly and one black soldier for the purpose of taking care of the government's horses." Kiddoo to E. M. Mason, May 26, 1866, BRFAL-TX.

17. *SED* 27, 146; Kiddoo to M. W. Dunn, August 21, 1866, BRFAL-TX; Kiddoo to James W. Throckmorton, September 13, 1866, BRFAL-TX; Barry A. Crouch, "'All the Vile Passions': The Texas Black Code of 1866," *Southwestern Historical Quarterly* 97 (June 1993): 20–22; Wilson, *Black Codes,* 109.

Kiddoo was having other problems with Austin at this time. Legislators had established a joint committee to investigate the charges of violence contained in his monthly reports. See Kiddoo to Throckmorton, September 13, 1866.

18. Crouch, "'Vile Passions,'" 23–30; Wilson, *Black Codes,* 109–11; *Laws of Texas, 1866,* 103–4.

19. James B. Smallwood, *Time of Hope, Time of Despair: Black Texans during Reconstruction* (Port Royal, N.Y.: National University Publications, 1981), 56; Richter, "Army and the Negro," 9.

20. For a general history of the Freedmen's Bureau in Texas, see Elliot, "Freedmen's Bureau in Texas," 1–24.

21. *HED* 70, 147; Smallwood, *Time of Hope,* 40, 53; Richter, "Army and the Negro," 13; Circular letter of October 17, 1865, BRFAL-TX.

22. *HED* 70, 148; *SED* 27, 82. Earlier, Gregory had suggested contracts with heads of households. Circular letter of October 17, 1865, BRFAL-TX.

23. *HED* 70, 148; *SED* 27, 78–79. At this time, wage rates ranged from eight dollars to fifteen dollars per month plus provisions; share contracts stipulated a one-fourth to one-half share plus provisions.

24. *SED* 27, 83–84. If 90 percent of the freedmen were under contract, 10 percent were not. In a state with almost no free black population prior to emancipation, where slavery meant nearly 100 percent plantation employment, this must have been shocking to the planters. On the free black population, see Ira C. Colby, "The Freedmen's Bureau in Texas and Its Impact on the Emerging Social Welfare System and Black-White Social Relations, 1865–1885" (Ph.D. diss., University of Pennsylvania, 1984), 171–73.

25. Gregory to Harris, January 20, 1866; Gregory to Howard, April 18, 1866, BRFAL-TX.

26. *HED* 70, 150; Gregory to Howard, October 31, 1865, BRFAL-TX; Gregory to Harris, January 20, 1866.

27. Gregory to Harris, January 20, 1866; Gregory to Howard, March 17, 1866, BRFAL-TX.

28. Elliot, "Freedmen's Bureau in Texas," 10, 25; Richter, "Army and the Negro," 7.

29. Michael W. Fitzgerald, "Wager Swayne, the Freedmen's Bureau, and the Politics of Reconstruction in Alabama," *Alabama Review* 48 (July 1995): 188–89. Fitzgerald correctly notes that Swayne has often been used by previous scholars as a prototypical bureau conservative. He argues that Swayne's initial labor policies were harsh but that the assistant commissioner liberalized them and other parts of his administration by 1866. Kenneth B. White, "Wager Swayne: Racist or Realist?" *Alabama Review* 31 (April 1978): 93–95. White contends that Swayne's legal education affected him little but that his military training gave him a reverence for regulations.

30. General Order 12, August 31, 1865; General Order 14, September 15, 1865, United States, Bureau of Refugees, Freedmen, and Abandoned Lands, *Records of the Assistant Commissioner for the State of Alabama, Bureau of Refugees, Freedmen, and Abandoned Lands, 1865–1870*, National Archives Microfilm Publication No. 809, roll 17 (hereafter cited as BRFAL-AL and roll number).

31. General Order 4, August 4, 1865, BRFAL-AL, roll 17. See also Elizabeth Bethel, "The Freedmen's Bureau in Alabama," *Journal of Southern History* 14 (February 1948): 51–53, 76, 87. By the fall of 1865, Swayne became aware of the deficiencies of using civil authority and later attributed its failure to "class feeling." See Swayne to Howard, November 28, 1865, BRFAL-AL, roll 2. Report of Major General Wager Wayne, Assistant Commissioner for Alabama, for the Year Ending October 31, 1866, printed copy in BRFAL-AL, roll 2, 4 (cited hereafter as *Annual Report*). These "agents" should not be confused with the subassistant commissioners, whom I mention below. The SACs were drawn mostly from the Union army as in other states.

32. Assistant Adjutant General to Mayor of Selma, September 11, 1865; AAG to Capt. Andrew Geddes, September 8, 1865; AAG to L. T. Pasona, September 21, 1865; AAG to G. A. Washburn, May 10, 1866, BRFAL-AL, roll 1. I have cited letters from the assistant adjutant general without names, assuming they are transmitting orders from the assistant commissioner.

33. For Swayne's involvement with the Alabama legislature and governor concerning the Black Codes, see *Annual Report*, 5, 11–12; *HED* 70, 293–94; Wiener, *Social Origins*, 52. On other policy decisions, see AAG to G. L. Mason, Mayor of Wetumpka, November 20, 1865; AAG to Henry Brown, December 5, 1865; Swayne to Hon. M. L. Williams, December 9, 1865; Swayne to Judge J. M. Henderson, January 27, 1866; Swayne to County Judge, Lowndes Co., January 29, 1866; Swayne to Mrs. Thomas Harrell, April 18, 1866, BRFAL-AL, roll 1.

34. *HED* 70, 287; Swayne to Howard, July 24, 1865, August 21, 1865, BRFAL-AL, roll 2; *Annual Report*, 5; Swayne to Howard, September 4, 1865, BRFAL-AL, roll 2.

35. *Annual Report*, 9; *HED* 70, 298, 287–88 (emphasis in original). Both before and during the war, abolitionists had promoted the salutary influence of poverty in inducing labor. See Glickstein, "'Poverty Is Not Slavery,'" 199.

36. AAG to S. S. Gardner, April 24, 1866; Swayne to Howard, September 1, 1866; AAG to C. W. Pierce, October 18, 1866; AAG to Pierce, January 11, 1867; AAG to Henry Livingston, January 4, 1867, BRFAL-AL, roll 1.

For more examples of interference with vagrancy cases, see Swayne to Sheriff of Elmore County, April 27, 1867; Swayne to Probate Judge of Elmore County, April 27, 1867; Swayne to H. W. Clark, May 4, 1867; AAG to Peck, May 8, 1867, BRFAL-AL, roll 2. Swayne did allow Clark to escape punishment if he forwarded an affidavit stating his ignorance of repeal of the law. Swayne to Clark, May 14, 1867, ibid. In another case, Swayne refused to interfere because the committal occurred before repeal and because the freedman had won release on appeal to the county court. AAG to Shorkley, July 10, 1867, ibid.

For more examples of interference with apprenticeships, see Swayne to Probate Judge, Meacon Co., April 11, 1867; Swayne to C. W. Pierce, April 13, 1867; O. D. Kinsman to Samuel S. Gardner, December 27, 1867, ibid.

37. AAG to Pierce, December 18, 1866; AAG to W. M. A. Mitchell, January 7, 1867; AAG to J. B. Healy, August 9, 1867; AAG to Connelly, September 7, 1867; AAG to Connelly, October 10, 1867; AAG to Mitchell, January 16, 1867; Swayne to Hon. Waller Coleman, January 22, 1867, BRFAL-AL, roll 1; Swayne to Howard, February 14, 1867, BRFAL-AL, roll 1; General Order 3, April 16, 1867, BRFAL-AL, roll 17; Bethel, "Freedmen's Bureau in Alabama," 66–67.

38. Swayne to Howard, January 30, 1867, BRFAL-AL, roll 1. In another letter to Howard on the same date, Swayne referred to the apprenticeship law as "apparently belonging rather to a statute which is greatly needed prescribing a punishment for the continuation of slavery and limiting to a *strict* and well defined construction of the term '*crime*' for which involuntary servitude may be permitted."

39. On the limiting effects of federalism, see Michael Les Benedict, "Preserving the Constitution: The Conservative Basis for Radical Reconstruction," *Journal of American History* 61 (1974): 65–90; and Hyman, *More Perfect Union*.

40. Williamson, *After Slavery*, 77–78.

41. General Order 75, Department of South Carolina, December 15, 1865, BRFAL-SC, roll 36; repr. in the *Free American* (San Francisco), March 27, 1866. My thanks to Harold Hyman for the *Free American*.

42. General Order 5 (1866 series), February 6, 1866, BRFAL-SC, roll 36. On Scott's background, see *National Cyclopedia of American Biography*, 12 : 175–76. On Scott's aversion to politics, see his letter to the editor of the *Great Republic*, May 20, 1867, BRFAL-SC, roll 1.

43. Scott to Mr. J. Cordossa, February 11, 1867; Scott to J. L. Riggs, May 4, 1867, BRFAL-SC, roll 1; Scott to Oliver Otis Howard (Annual Report for 1866), November 1, 1867, BRFAL-SC, roll 1. In 1867, Scott requested copies of state constitutions from Pennsylvania, Massachusetts, and Iowa. See Scott to Gov. John Geary of Pennsylvania, April 21, 1867, and accompanying note that similar letters were sent to the governors of the other two states, BRFAL-SC, roll 1.

44. Circular No. 5 (1866 series), February 5, 1866, BRFAL-SC, roll 36.

45. General Order 14 (1866 series), April 14, 1866; Circular letter of Scott, June 22, 1866, BRFAL-SC, roll 36.

46. Circular letter of Scott, December 26, 1866, BRFAL-SC, roll 36.

47. Circular No. 1 (1867 series), January 1, 1867; Circular No. 2 (1867 series), January 9, 1867; General Order 5 (1867 series), March 4, 1867; Circular letter, June 19, 1867; Circular letter, September 13, 1867, all BRFAL-SC, roll 36.

48. Oliver D. Kinsman to D. T. Corbin, February 1, 1865; Henry W. Smith to Commanding Officer, U.S. forces, Clarendon District, February 28, 1866; Smith to Corbin, March 5, 1866; Smith to all whom it may concern, May 22, 1866; Smith to J. L. Heyward, July 31, 1866; Smith to A. P. Cavaher, August 11, 1866; Edward L. Deane to F. W. Liedtke, March 31, 1867, BRFAL-SC, roll 1. Kinsman, Smith, and Deane were acting adjutant generals in Scott's office. They usually signed correspondence carrying out his orders unless the addressee was a prominent figure. Kinsman, a native of Maine who enlisted in Iowa, later served as assistant adjutant general in Alabama under Wager Swayne and played a key role in the operation of the labor program there. Henry Warren Smith was born in New York and enlisted in Michigan. See Francis Bernard Heitman, *Historical Register and Dictionary of the United States Army, from Its Organization, September 29, 1789, to March 2, 1903* (Washington, D.C.: Government Printing Office, 1903), 602, 899. I have no biographical information for any of the other South Carolina assistant adjutant generals.

49. Edward L. Deane to Corbin, January 27, 1867, BRFAL-SC, roll 1. For similar actions by local agents, see below.

50. Scott to Howard, November 1, 1866, Annual Report for 1866, BRFAL-SC, roll 1; Scott to Orr, December 13, 1866, BRFAL-SC, roll 1 (emphasis in original). The influence of equitable concepts on the bureau's program has been noted by Hoffer, *Law's Conscience*, 128–29.

51. Benedict has divided politicians during Reconstruction into three similar groups though not on this basis. See *Compromise of Principle*, 27–33.

52. As noted above, I have focused on South Carolina in part because of the completeness of the records. I have also investigated local agents in Alabama and found similar divisions. See James D. Schmidt, "'Neither Slavery nor Involuntary Servitude': Free Labor and American Law, ca. 1815–1880" (Ph.D. diss., Rice University, 1992), chap. 5.

53. Report of E. R. Chase, July 17, 1866, BRFAL-SC, roll 34; Report of Chase, July 27, 1866, ibid; Davy v. Wm. Davis, July 6, 1866, Register of Complaints, Barnwell Subdistrict, National Archives Record Group 105 (cited hereafter as BRFAL-SC, RG 105), 33, 73, 29, 47. Chase's use of racial language appears repeatedly in Register of Complaints, Barnwell Subdistrict, BRFAL-SC, RG 105.

54. Report of E. R. Chase, July 17, 1866, BRFAL-SC, roll 34.

55. Register of Complaints, Barnwell Subdistrict, BRFAL-SC, RG 105, 3, 7, 8–12, 17, 23, 71. Many similar actions are recorded in the register.

56. Circular No. 1, November 10, 1865, 4th Subdistrict, Georgetown, BRFAL-SC, roll 37; Report of A. J. Willard, November 13, 1865, BRFAL-SC, roll 34; Report of A. J. Willard, December 6, 1865, BRFAL-SC, roll 34.

57. Register of Complaints, Moncks Corner Subdistrict, BRFAL-SC, RG 105, 1:46; Report of O'Brien, September 5, 1866, BRFAL-SC, roll 34; Report of O'Brien, October 24, 1866, BRFAL-SC, roll 34. O'Brien was also an agent in Maryland. On his time there, see Fields, *Slavery and Freedom on the Middle Ground*, 149–50.

58. Register of Complaints, Moncks Corner Subdistrict, BRFAL-SC, 1:85, 87.

59. Circular No. 1, November 10, 1865, 4th Subdistrict, Georgetown, BRFAL-SC, roll 37.

60. Frank A. Rollin, *Life and Public Services of Martin R. Delany* (1868; reprint, New York: Krause Reprint Co., 1969), 242–43, 229, 239, 244.

61. Acting Adjutant General to C. H. Howard, July 22, 1865, BRFAL-SC, roll 1; Scott to Delany, October 16, 1866, BRFAL-SC, roll 1; Rollin, *Life and Labor*, 273–74; Martin Abbott, *The Freedmen's Bureau in South Carolina, 1865–1872* (Chapel Hill: University of North Carolina Press, 1967), 23, 34; Williamson, *After Slavery*, 28, 113, 354.

62. Repr. in Scott to Howard, November 1, 1866, BRFAL-SC, roll 1; John William De Forest, *A Union Officer in the Reconstruction* (New Haven: Yale University Press, 1948), 29; Abbott, *Freedmen's Bureau*, 24, 115, 127.

63. Repr. in Scott to Howard, May 23, 1867, BRFAL-SC, roll 1; Letters Sent, Greenville Subdistrict, BRFAL-SC, RG 105. Williamson, *After Slavery*, 37, 66, notes that De Forest continued to hold blacks above poor whites in his postwar writings, although his novels helped create and perpetuate the stereotype of the faithful house servant.

64. Report of Runkle in Scott to Howard, October 22, 1866, BRFAL-SC, roll 34.

65. Runkle to H. M. Smith, September 13, 1866, Letters Sent, Aiken Subdistrict, BRFAL-SC, RG 105; Runkle to William Kemble, September 10, 1866, ibid.

66. Annual Report of J. E. Cornelius, October 23, 1866, BRFAL-SC, roll 34; Report of November 30, 1866, ibid.

Agents B. F. Smith, J. M. Johnston, and the German-born Eugene A. Kozlay might also fall into this category. On Smith, see Report of April 25, 1866, BRFAL-SC, roll 34; Report of July 31, 1866, ibid.; excerpt in Scott to Howard (Monthly Report for June 1866), July 29, 1866, BRFAL-SC, roll 1. On Kozlay, see Report of January 29, 1866, BRFAL-SC, roll 34, in which Kozlay noted that he had ordered subordinates to employ unemployed freedmen on public roads as vagrants in order to enforce Sickle's General Order 1. Yet he put their idleness down to their sudden freedom and the tendency to dwell on it. See also his report of February 28, 1866, BRFAL-SC, roll 34, in which he voiced his optimism in freedmen supporting themselves. Biographical information on Kozlay comes from Heitman, *Register*, 608.

67. Annual Report of Garret Nagle, November 1, 1866, BRFAL-SC, roll 34; Report of Garret Nagle, November 30, 1866, ibid.; Nagle to William Davis, October 5, 1866,

Complaint Summons Sent, Marion Subdistrict, BRFAL-SC, RG 105, 1:42; Nagle to Joel M. Witsell, September 7, 1867, BRFAL-SC, RG 105, 168–169. Another agent who fell into this category was A. E. Niles. See Report of A. E. Niles, July 13, 1866, BRFAL-SC, roll 34; Report of A. E. Niles, August 3, 1866, BRFAL-SC, roll 34.

68. Annual Report of Garret Nagle, November 1, 1866, BRFAL-SC, roll 34; Report of Garret Nagle, November 30, 1866, ibid.; Register of Complaints, Summerville Subdistrict, BRFAL-SC, RG 105, 5, 30, 31, 40, 14, 39; Nagle to J. M. Connely, September 27, 1866, Complaint Summons Sent, Marion Subdistrict, BRFAL-SC, RG 105, 1: 36; Nagle to John D. Edwards, September 14, 1867, Complaint Summons Sent, Marion Subdistrict, BRFAL-SC, RG 105, 1:170.

69. Annual Report of George A. Williams, October 24, 1866, BRFAL-SC, roll 34.

70. Williams's Annual Report; Report of George A. Williams, December 31, 1866, BRFAL-SC, roll 34; Scott to Williams, June 11, 1867, BRFAL-SC, roll 1; excerpt in Scott to Howard (Monthly Report for June 1867), July 20, 1867, BRFAL-SC, roll 1. Biographical information from Heitman, *Register*, 1040.

71. Excerpt in Scott to Howard, January 23, 1867, BRFAL-SC, roll 1; excerpt in Scott to Stone, February 23, 1867, ibid.; excerpt in Scott to Howard, March 20, 1867, ibid.

72. Report of F. W. Liedtke, July 31, 1866, BRFAL-SC, roll 34; Report of F. W. Liedtke, August 31, 1866, ibid.; Annual Report of F. W. Liedtke, November 1, 1866, ibid.; excerpt in Scott to Howard, June 20, 1866, BRFAL-SC, roll 1; Register of Complaints, Moncks Corner Subdistrict, BRFAL-SC, RG 105, 1:2–10; Heitman, *Register*, 632.

73. Register of Complaints, Moncks Corner Subdistrict, BRFAL-SC, RG 105, 1: 164–65, 176–77, 2:2–5, 72; Report of Liedtke, August 31, 1866, BRFAL-SC, roll 24; excerpt in Scott to Howard (Monthly Report for December 1866), January 23, 1867, BRFAL-SC, roll 1; Edward L. Deane to Liedtke, March 31, 1867, BRFAL-SC, roll 1.

74. Annual Report of Liedtke, November 1, 1866, BRFAL-SC, roll 34.

75. Report of D. T. Corbin, April 30, 1866, BRFAL-SC, roll 34; Report of Corbin, May 31, 1866, ibid.; excerpt in Scott to Howard (Monthly Report for March 1867), April 20, 1867, BRFAL-SC, roll 1; Williamson, *After Slavery*, 364, 375, 394, 413.

76. Annual Report of J. D. Greene, October 1866, BRFAL-SC, roll 34.

77. Pingree to Ford Parker, May 1, 1867, Letters Sent, Darlington Subdistrict, BRFAL-SC, RG 105, 2:72; excerpt in Scott to Howard, May 23, 1867, BRFAL-SC, roll 1.

78. Pingree to E. L. Deane, October 31, 1867, Letters Sent, Darlington Subdistrict, BRFAL-SC, RG 105, 2:192; Journal of Complaints, Darlington Subdistrict, BRFAL-SC, RG 105, 42, 44, 45, 73–74, 79; Register of Complaints, Darlington Subdistrict, BRFAL-SC, RG 105, 1–15.

79. Excerpt in Scott to Howard (Monthly Report for March 1867), April 20, 1867, BRFAL-SC, roll 1; excerpt in Scott to Howard (Monthly Report for April 1867),

May 23, 1867, ibid.; excerpt in Scott to Howard (Monthly Report for June 1867), July 20, 1867, ibid.

80. Excerpt in Scott to Howard (Monthly Report for April 1867), May 23, 1867, BRFAL-SC, roll 1; excerpt in Scott to Howard (Monthly Report for July 1867), August 24, 1867, ibid.

81. Journal of Complaints, Darlington Subdistrict, BRFAL-SC, RG 105, 93–98.

82. Pingree to E. L. Deane, October 29, 1867, Letters Sent, Darlington Subdistrict, BRFAL-SC, RG 105, 2:190.

83. Excerpt in Scott to Howard, May 23, 1867, BRFAL-SC, roll 1.

84. I have not investigated the actions of Redeemer legislatures. For more on labor law in the post-Reconstruction South, see William Cohen, "Negro Involuntary Servitude in the South, 1865–1940: A Preliminary Analysis," *Journal of Southern History* 42 (February 1976): 31–60; Jonathan M. Wiener, "Class Structure and Economic Development in the American South, 1865–1955," *American Historical Review* 84 (October 1979): 973–83; and Harold Woodman, *New South–New Law: The Legal Foundations of Credit and Labor Relations in the Postbellum Agricultural South* (Baton Rouge: Louisiana State University Press, 1995). For the most comprehensive treatment of the southern labor markets after Reconstruction, see Gavin Wright, *Old South, New South: Revolutions in the Southern Economy since the Civil War* (New York: Basic Books, 1986), esp. chaps. 1–4.

Chapter 5: Southern Reactions and Reformulations

1. *OR*, 49(2), 954, 728–29; Conway, *Freedmen of Louisiana*, 23, 27, 34.

2. For planter desires for labor control in Alabama, see Kolchin, *First Freedom*, 35, and Wiener, *Social Origins*, 35. See also Sylvia H. Krebs, "Will the Freedmen Work? White Alabamians Adjust to Free Black Labor," *Alabama Historical Quarterly* 36 (Summer 1974): 151–63; John B. Myers, "The Alabama Freedmen and the Economic Adjustments during Presidential Reconstruction, 1865–1867," *Alabama Review* 26 (October 1973): 254; and Kenneth B. White, "Black Lives, Red Tape: The Alabama Freedmen's Bureau," *Alabama Historical Quarterly* 34 (Winter 1981): 242, 257. For a more comprehensive treatment of planters during emancipation, see James L. Roark, *Masters without Slaves: Southern Planters in the Civil War and Reconstruction* (New York: W. W. Norton, 1977).

3. Report of Capt. Andrew Geddes, September 7, 1865; Report of Lt. Spence Smith, December 2, 1865, BRFAL-AL, roll 18; *HED* 70, 292; C. W. Buckley, Report of Tour of Eastern Alabama, BRFAL-AL, roll 19; *Report of the Joint Committee on Reconstruction*, 3:9.

4. *SED* 6, 170–74.

5. On Patton's vetoes, see *Annual Report*, 11–12. For examples of convict labor, see *HED* 70, 292, and Special Inspection Report of W. A. Arthur, October 13, 1866, BRFAL-AL, roll 19.

6. Report of William Connelly, August 1, 1867; Report of John B. Callis, January 31, 1867; Report of C. W. Pierce, May 31, 1865, BRFAL-AL, roll 18.

7. On driving away for general reasons or after summer work, see Report of George Tracy, October 31, 1866; Report of George Shorkley, January 4, 1867; Report of James Curtis, June 6, 1868; Report of Pierce, June 30, 1868, BRFAL-AL, roll 18. For discharges for political reasons, see Report of A. C. Taylor, March 1, 1868; Report of Robert T. Smith, March 2, 1868, ibid.; and Julius Hayden to Oliver Otis Howard, March 9, 1868, BRFAL-AL, roll 2. For hiring women and children at harvest, see Report of William H. H. Peck, October 10, 1866, BRFAL-AL, roll 18. For failing to appear for settlement, see Report of Peck, October 20, 1866, BRFAL-AL, roll 18.

8. For ways in which African American initiative was decisive in shaping policy, see Berlin et al., *Wartime Genesis;* Nancy Cohen-Lack, "A Struggle for Sovereignty: National Consolidation, Emancipation, and Free Labor in Texas, 1865," *Journal of Southern History* 58 (February 1992): 58–98. For a summary of the role of labor law in the Reconstruction South, see Harold D. Woodman, "Post–Civil War Southern Agriculture and the Law," *Agricultural History* 53 (January 1979): 319–37.

9. *New Orleans Tribune*, April 9, 1865. For more about the *Tribune*, see William P. Conner, "Reconstruction Rebels: The *New Orleans Tribune* in Post-war Louisiana," *Louisiana History* 21 (Spring 1980): 160–64. The *Tribune* was preceded by a French-language paper, *L'Union*, which published from September 1862 through July 1864. Roudanez also owned *L'Union*, and Trévigne edited it.

10. *New Orleans Tribune*, December 4, 1864, February 18, March 14, 18, 1865. The resolutions passed at the Economy Hall meeting and the exchange with Hurlbut are reprinted in Berlin et al., *Wartime Genesis*, 594–98.

11. *New Orleans Tribune*, April 9, March 29, 1865. In part, the *Tribune*'s ambivalence came from the shifting role of the prewar free black elite. As federal orders began to lump all African Americans together, the elite tried to change from being a separate community and became the leaders of freedpeople. See Berlin et al., *Wartime Genesis*, 373–74. For additional comments on guardianship, see *New Orleans Tribune*, November 23, 1864, March 14, April 9, 1865.

12. *New Orleans Tribune*, February 7, July 22, 1865. For arbitrary arrests, see August 18, 1864. For additional comments on equal application of vagrancy laws, see March 30, July 20, 1865.

13. Ibid., March 14, December 12, 1865; December 31, 1867. See also March 18, December 17, 1865.

14. Ibid., October 13, 1865. See also September 24, October 22, November 30, 1864, December 31, 1867.

15. Ibid., November 26, 1864, March 18, 1865. See also February 7, March 28, 30, 1865, October 31, 1867.

16. Ibid., October 31, 1867.

17. *Proceedings of the Black National and State Conventions, 1865–1900*, vol. 1, ed. Philip S. Foner and George E. Walker (Philadelphia: Temple University Press,

1986), 58, 66, 87, 180, 228, 232, 234. For similar comments about freedpeople returning to work made by the *Colored Tennessean*, see Jaynes, *Branches without Roots*,
64–65.

18. *Proceedings of the Black National and State Conventions*, Walker, 85, 114, 194,
361–62. On the last point, see ibid. and Foner, *Reconstruction*, 112–18, esp. 114.

19. Swayne to Howard, July 24, September 11, 1865, BRFAL-AL, roll 2; Report of
Samuel S. Gardner, October 10, 1865, BRFAL-AL, roll 18. See also Report of George
Tracy, August 18, 1867; Report of James Gillette, May 21, 1868, BRFAL-AL, roll 18.
Donald Nieman finds African Americans of all classes used the law to maintain
community order well into the 1870s. Donald G. Nieman, "Black Political Power
and Criminal Justice: Washington County, Texas, 1868–1884," *Journal of Southern
History* 55 (August 1989): 416–17. For the *Tribune*, see *New Orleans Tribune*, Feb-
ruary 2, January 29, February 24, 1865; Conner, "Reconstruction Rebels," 173–76.
Conner notes that the "associations" were based on the ideas of French socialist
Charles Fourier as well as German radical Franz Hermann Shulze-Delitzsch. The
associations' level of success remains unclear.

20. Report of T. M. Goodfellow, October 18, 1865, BRFAL-AL, roll 18. Swayne to
C. C. Sibley, August 24, 1867, BRFAL-AL, roll 2.

Of course, the eventual outcome for many African Americans' search for land was
their acquiescence in sharecropping arrangements, as many historians have demonstrated. For an example of the freedmen's desire for share arrangements in Alabama,
see Report of Bennett, February 2, 1868, BRFAL-AL, roll 18. Report of Shorkley,
January 4, 1867; Report of Bennett, March 31, 1868; Report of McGogy, August 5,
1867, BRFAL-AL, roll 18.

21. *HED* 70, 297; Report of Connelly, January 31, 1867; Report of Charles Bartlett,
February 6, 1868; Report of Bennett, January 31, 1868, BRFAL-AL, roll 18. Kolchin,
First Freedom, 39, refers to these actions as a "mass general strike."

22. Specific evidence for this point comes from research in the local records of
the Alabama Freedmen's Bureau. See Report of Robert T. Smith, May 2, 1868. *HED*
70, 297. AAG to Hon. A. A. McMillan, June 10, 1867, BRFAL-AL, roll 2. Report of
Tracy, January 31, 1866; Reports of Connelly, January 31, 1868, March 2, 1868; Reports of Blair, December 27, 1867, February 2, 1868, March 1, 1868; Report of Buckley, October 20, 1865; Report of Thomas L. Bevilt [?], April 27, 1868; Report of
Gillette, June 26, 1868, BRFAL-AL, roll 18. Kolchin, *First Freedom*, 8–11; Wiener,
Social Origins, 42–46. On the freedmen's withdrawal from labor generally, see Ransom and Sutch, *One Kind of Freedom*, 44–46.

23. Excerpt in Scott to Howard (Monthly Report for May 1867), June 22, 1867,
BRFAL-SC, roll 1; Report of A. J. Willard, November 13, 1865, BRFAL-SC, roll 34.
On the issue of controlling conditions of labor generally, see Berlin et al., *Wartime
Genesis*, 45–51. For a more detailed discussion of later African American labor
actions in Reconstruction South Carolina, see Eric Foner, *Nothing but Freedom:*

Emancipation and Its Legacy (Baton Rouge: Louisiana State University Press, 1983), 74–110.

24. Charles Buckley, Report of a Tour of Eastern Alabama, January 27, 1866, BRFAL-AL, roll 19; Docket of Cases Tried in Freedmen's Court, Franklin, N.C., January 1 to February 28, 1866, United States, Bureau of Refugees, Freedmen, and Abandoned Lands, *Records of the Assistant Commissioner for the State of North Carolina, Bureau of Refugees, Freedmen, and Abandoned Lands, 1865–1870*, National Archives Microfilm Publication No. 843, roll 31 (hereafter cited as BRFAL-NC). BRFAL-NC, Warren County and Granville County. For unjust discharge cases, see reports of Montgomery agents, October 25, 1867, through September 30, 1868, and esp. Report of John C. Hendrix, January 6, 1868, BRFAL-AL, roll 18. See also excerpt in Robert Scott to O. O. Howard (Monthly Report for March 1867), April 20, 1867, BRFAL-SC, roll 1; excerpt in Scott to Howard, May 23, 1867, BRFAL-SC, roll 1; excerpt in Scott to Howard, July 20, 1867, BRFAL-SC, roll 1.

25. For Alabama, see AAG to G. L. Mason, Mayor of Wetumpka, November 20, 1865; AAG to Henry Brown, December 5, 1865; Swayne to Hon. M. L. Williams, December 9, 1865; Swayne to Judge J. M. Henderson, January 27, 1866; Swayne to County Judge, Lowndes Co., January 29, 1866; Swayne to Mrs. Thomas Harrell, April 18, 1866, BRFAL-AL, roll 1. For a similar case in South Carolina, see H. Smith to Mr. M. A. Moore Jr., April 22, 1866, BRFAL-SC, roll 1.

26. *Freedmen's Bureau v. Richardson*, March 28, 1866, BRFAL-NC, roll 31.

27. *Brown v. State*, 23 Md. 504 (1865). On the Maryland constitution and the situation in the state generally, see Fields, *Slavery and Freedom*, 131–32.

28. *Brown v. State*, 23 Md. 503.

29. Ibid., 509, 511.

30. Swayne to Howard, January 30, 1867, BRFAL-AL, roll 1.

31. Fields, *Slavery and Freedom*, 140–42, 156; Richard Paul Fuke, "Planters, Apprenticeship, and Forced Labor: The Black Family under Pressure in Postemancipation Maryland," *Agricultural History* 62 (Fall 1988): 57–74. I have located twelve of such suits in southern courts, including those in Union slave states, plus one in federal court. This litigation is cited and discussed below. Fields also argues that some apprenticeships were motivated by the revenge of former owners, but such intentions might not appear in a suit, of course. I have not found this dynamic true elsewhere in the South.

32. *Cox v. Jones*, 40 Ala. 299 (1866); *Jack, a Freedman v. Thompson*, 41 Miss. 49 (1866). In the Alabama case, Waddell's actions received an implied sanction from Swayne's office. When the local bureau agent tried to interfere with Waddell's actions, the judge complained. Swayne responded that although he had heard of abuse, the lieutenant involved had no power to intervene directly. Swayne's office then ordered the officer to channel all future action through the assistant commissioner's office. Swayne to J. F. Waddell, Judge of Probate, Crawford, Russell Co., Ala., January 11,

1866; AAG to Lt. Spencer Smith, January 12, 1866, BRFAL-AL, roll 1. For a similar reading of apprenticeship, see Fuke, "Planters, Apprenticeship, and Forced Labor," 62–67. For a more general treatment of the structure of black families during Reconstruction, see Jacqueline Jones, *Labor of Love, Labor of Sorrow: Black Women, Work, and the Family, from Slavery to the Present* (1985; New York: Vintage Books, 1986), 58–68.

33. *Cox v. Jones,* 40 Ala. 298; *Jack v. Thompson,* 41 Miss. 49–50; *Hatcher v. Cutts,* 42 Ga. 616–18 (1871). After Milly Cutts's arrest, a Mr. Ansley paid her bond and arranged for her to pay back the six hundred dollars by working for Mr. Cutts. In September 1870, Milly Cutts obtained a writ of habeas corpus against Hatcher for the release of her children from the Clarke County Superior Court. When Hatcher appealed this action to the Georgia state supreme court, he lost, and Cutts retained control of her children.

34. *Comas v. Reddish,* 35 Ga. 236 (1866).

35. *Adams v. Adams,* 36 Ga. 236–39 (1867).

36. *Adams v. Adams,* 239, 237–40. The price of the contract with Dykes might have been $150 rather than $120. The report of facts gives the first figure, the opinion the latter. Ibid., 241.

37. For more on apprenticeship and its role in postbellum domestic law, see Peter Bardaglio, *Reconstructing the Household: Families, Sex, and the Law in the Nineteenth-Century South* (Chapel Hill: University of North Carolina Press, 1995), 162–63.

38. *Timmins v. Lacy,* 30 Tex. 115; An Act Establishing a General Apprentice Law, and Defining the Obligations of Master or Mistress and Apprentice, reprinted in *Timmins v. Lacy,* 30 Tex. 120, 121, 119–23. The law was repealed in 1871, but the 1876 state constitution reinstated apprenticeship through the county courts. *Vernon's Annotated Revised Civil Statutes of the State of Texas* (1973), 1A: 2. For the Texas Black Codes, see also Foner, *Reconstruction,* 201; Richter, "Army and the Negro," 12; Richter, *The Army in Texas during Reconstruction, 1865–1870* (College Station: Texas A&M University Press, 1987), 61; and Robert A. Calvert, "The Freedmen and Agricultural Prosperity," *Southwestern Historical Quarterly* 76 (April 1973): 465.

39. *Timmins v. Lacy,* 30 Tex. 125–26. The only surname recorded in the case for Sarah is "Lacy." "Lacy" is used throughout, even though it would not have been her proper surname at the time she married Harry Pope.

40. Ibid., 126–29.

41. Ibid., 127–28. In the record of the case, the Lacys' property is referred to as "provisions," but I do not believe this indicates in-kind payment. Rather, it was probably meant to denote personal property such as furniture or tools.

42. Ibid., 127–29.

43. For the efforts of freedpeople to establish family life and economy in Texas, see Smallwood, *Time of Hope.* For family economy and the urban-ethnic working class, see John Bodnar, *The Transplanted: A History of Immigrants in Urban America* (Bloomington: Indiana University Press, 1985), 71–83. For other direct evidence of

freedpeople using apprenticeships to secure land or to augment the family economy, see Rebecca Scott, "The Battle over the Child: Child Apprenticeship and the Freedmen's Bureau in North Carolina," *Prologue* 10 (Summer 1978): 105, 107, 112.

44. *Timmins v. Lacy*, 124, 125. In the supreme court argument, Murray is named an attorney for the Lacys (130). For the record of the case in the lower court, see 123–29. For biographical information on Reeves, see Charles Ramsdell, *Reconstruction in Texas* (New York: Columbia University Press, 1910), 89; Randolph Campbell, "The District Judges of Texas in 1866–1867: An Episode in the Failure of Presidential Reconstruction," *Southwest Historical Quarterly* 93 (January 1990): 361.

45. *In re Turner*, 24 Fed. Cas. 337 (1867); Hyman, *More Perfect Union*, 484–85. For the *Turner* case and the situation in Maryland, see also Richard Paul Fuke, "A Reform Mentality: Federal Policy toward Black Marylanders, 1864–1868," *Civil War History* 21 (September 1976): 214–33, esp. 225; W. A. Lowe, "The Freedmen's Bureau and Civil Rights in Maryland," *Journal of Negro History* 37 (July 1952): 221–47; and Fields, *Slavery and Freedom*, chap. 6. On North Carolina, see *In re Ambrose*, 61 N.C. 91 (1867); List of Indentures Cancelled, April 30, 1868, BRFAL-NC, roll 31. For the *Ambrose* case, see also Scott, "Battle over the Child," 101–13, esp. 111–12. Scott indicates that some agents refused to cancel indentures.

In the thirteen appeals cases I located (see above), African American litigants won in nine and lost in three; one was remanded to the lower court for further proceedings.

46. Fields, *Slavery and Freedom*, 153–55. Fields notes that apprenticeship died slowly in Maryland, partly as a result of declining interest on the part of the bureau and the complex family relationships apprenticeship raised. On the continued use of apprenticeship after 1868, see *Cockran v. State*, 46 Ala. 714 (1871); *Mitchell v. McElvin*, 45 Ga. 588 (1873); *Ballenger v. McLain*, 54 Ga. 159 (1875); *Hatcher v. Cutts*, 42 Ga. 616 (1871); and *Mitchell v. Mitchell*, 67 N.C. 307 (1872).

For some examples of apprenticeship in the postwar North, see *People v. Weissenbach*, 60 N.Y. 386 (1875); *Ex parte McDonald*, 4 Luz. Leg. Reg. 255 (Pennsylvania, 1874); *Hunsucker v. Elmore*, 54 Ind. 209 (1876); and *Fisher v. Lunger*, 33 N.J.L. 100 (1868).

47. *Jack v. Thompson*, 41 Miss. 51; *Comas v. Reddish*, 35 Ga. 237, 238; *In re Turner*, 339–40.

48. *Cannon v. Stuart*, 8 Del. (3 Houst.) 225 (1866); *Cox v. Jones*, 40 Ala. 299. For other decisions relying in part on formalism, see *Timmins v. Lacy*, 30 Tex. 130–35; *Jack v. Thompson*, 41 Miss. 50–51.

49. *Beard v. Hudson*, 61 N.C. 183 (1867). For Reade's comments on prudent actions, see *In re Ambrose*, 61 N.C. 95.

50. The analysis below generally supports Bardaglio's overall conclusions about the rise of maternal rights and the "triumph of state paternalism" in postbellum southern law. See *Reconstructing the Household*, 137–75.

51. *Lamb v. Lamb*, 67 Ky. 214 (1868); *Beard v. Hudson*, 61 N.C. 182.

52. *Thomas v. Newcom*, 64 Ky. 83–85 (1866); *Small v. Small*, 65 Ky. 45–49 (1867); *Adams v. Adams*, 36 Ga. 241–42. See also *Chaudet v. Stone*, 67 Ky. 210–12 (1868) for another example of Hardin breaking an indenture.

53. *In re Ambrose*, 61 N.C. 95, 96, 97.

54. *Timmins v. Lacy*, 30 Tex. 130–31. For background on the Bonners, see James D. Lynch, *The Bench and Bar of Texas* (St. Louis: Nixon-Jones, 1885), 116–18.

55. *Timmins v. Lacy*, 135, 137, 137–38. For an example of a court coming to the opposite and unusual conclusion that slave marriages themselves were legitimate, see *Mitchell v. McElvin*, 45 Ga. 560 (1873). For vagrancy laws that contained clauses proscribing desertion, see *Revised Statutes of Maine* (1847), 218; *Compiled Statutes of New Hampshire* (1853), 268; and *Statutes of Connecticut* (1854), 740. For the general context of marriage laws regarding freedpeople in Texas, see Barry A. Crouch, "The 'Chords of Love': Legalizing Black Marital and Family Rights in Postwar Texas," *Journal of Negro History* 79 (Fall 1994): 334–50.

56. See Woodman, *New South, New Law*.

Chapter 6: The Northern Reconstruction of Free-Labor Law

1. *New York Times*, June 6, 1879.

2. This "discovery of the tramp" in the 1870s has drawn considerable attention by historians. The most complete accounts are Paul Ringenbach, *Tramps and Reformers, 1873–1916: The Discovery of Unemployment in New York* (Westport, Conn.: Greenwood Press, 1973), 3–35, and Michael B. Katz, *Poverty and Policy in American History* (New York: Academic Press, 1983), 157–81, and especially the essays in Monkkonen, *Walking to Work*.

3. *Weaver v. Halsey*, 1 Ill. App. 558 (1878); *Duncan v. Baker*, 21 Kan. 99 (1878); *Thrift v. Payne*, 71 Ill. 408 (1874). As it turned out Halsey was not a model worker. After he had worked for Weaver two weeks, Weaver's other two servants were ready to leave. In that short span, Halsey had complained about the food, tried to get the other hand to do his work, and made sexual advances to the maidservant.

4. *Garfield v. Huls*, 54 Ill. 427 (1870); *Thrift v. Payne*, 71 Ill. 408 (1874); *Parcell v. McComber*, 11 Neb. 209, 212 (1881). This last case is another example in which I cannot be certain the worker was a farmhand. I have assumed he was because of the term and time of making the contract (in October for a year), the place (a rural county in Nebraska's Platte River valley), and the low level of wages. On the point that farm mechanization took hold only after the Civil War, see Schob, *Hired Hands and Plowboys*, 69, 108–9. On hired boys generally, see 173–90, 261. My point about hired boys is based on the fact that cases in which entirety was applied to minors appeared mostly after the war. Before the war, courts had ruled that minors were not bound by contract doctrines. See chap. 1. In contrast, Schob implies that proletarianization of farmworkers was taking place in the Civil War period. See 210, 267–72.

5. *McClay v. Harvey*, 90 Ill. 525 (1878).

6. *Leopold et al. v. Salkey*, 89 Ill. 423 (1878). The court denied recovery in the case.

On skill decline in industrialization, see Laurie, *Artisans into Workers*, chaps. 1–2; Thompson, *Making of the English Working Class;* and Sewell, *Work and Revolution in France*, esp. chaps. 9–10.

7. *Bixby v. Dunlap*, 56 N.H. 458–59 (1876). See also *Noice, Adm'x v. Brown*, 39 N.J. Law 569 (1877); Wood, *Master and Servant*, 450–77. Outside the South, Wood listed only a handful of enticement litigations that reached the appellate level.

8. *Walker v. Cronin*, 107 Mass. 556–57, 563–65 (1871).

9. *Walker v. Cronin*, 557.

10. For descriptions of these practices, see *Collins v. New England Iron Company*, 115 Mass. 23–24 (1874); *Naylor v. Fall River Iron Works Co.*, 118 Mass. 317–18 (1875); *Preston v. American Linen Co.*, 119 Mass. 400–401 (1876); and *Pottsville Iron and Steel Co. v. Good*, 116 Pa. 386–87 (1887).

11. *Harrington v. Fall River Iron Works Co.*, 119 Mass. 82–83 (1875); *Hughes v. Wamsutta Mills*, 93 Mass. 201–2 (1865); *Heber v. United States Flax Manufacturing Co.*, 13 R.I. 304–5 (1881).

12. *Collins v. New England Iron Co.*, 115 Mass. 23 (1874); *Preston v. American Linen Co.*, 119 Mass. 402–3 (1876).

13. *Preston v. American Linen Co.*, 119 Mass. 404. For another decision that knowledge equaled assent, see *Wright v. Trainer*, 32 Legal Intelligencer 62 (Pa.), quoted in *Pottsville Iron and Steel v. Good*, 116 Pa. 386–87 (1887).

14. *Naylor v. Fall River Iron Works*, 317–19. For a similar argument by an employer's attorney, see *Pottsville Iron and Steel v. Good*, 116 Pa. 388–89.

15. *Preston v. American Linen Co.*, 119 Mass. 400; *Pottsville Iron and Steel v. Good*, 116 Pa. 390.

16. Horace Gray Wood, *A Treatise on the Law of Master and Servant* (1877; reprint, Buffalo: William Hein and Co., 1981), 2–4, 278–81.

17. *Beach v. Mullin*, 34 N.J. Law (5 Vroom) 344–46 (1870); *Jennings v. Lyons*, 39 Wis. 553–58 (1876); *Diefenback v. Stark*, 14 N.W. 621–25 (1883).

18. Field on *Damages* quoted in *Duncan v. Baker*, 106; *McClay v. Hedge*, 18 Iowa 68 (1864); *Parcell v. McComber*, 210.

19. *Trobridge et al. v. Barnett*, 30 Wisconsin 661 (1872); *Duncan v. Baker*, 108; Field quoted in *Duncan v. Baker*, 106.

20. *Duncan v. Baker*, 105; *McClay v. Hedge*, 68; *Parcell v. McComber*, 212.

21. For a tabulation of these decisions, see Karsten, "'Bottomed on Justice,'" 241–43.

22. Feinman, "Development of the Employment of the at Will Rule," 125–28, 132–34; Peter Linzer, "The Decline of Assent: At-Will Employment as a Case Study of the Breakdown of Private Law Theory," *Georgia Law Review* 20 (Winter 1986):

335–36; Karsten, "'Bottomed on Justice,'" 250–51. Karsten argues that the at-will rule actually helped workers because it gave them a greater claim to pro rata compensation.

23. Wood, *Master and Servant*, 272–74; *Kansas Pacific Ry. Co. v. Roberson*, 3 Colo. 144 (1876); *Coffin v. Landis*, 5 Phila. 177 (1863); *King & Graham v. Steiren*, 44 Pa. 99, 101, 105 (1862).

24. *DuQuoin Star Coal Mining Co. v. Thorwell*, 3 Ill. App. 394 (1879). The state created this court after the Civil War as an intermediate step between the circuit courts and the state supreme court.

On the coal boom generally, see Chandler, *Visible Hand*, 76–77. For Illinois, see Theodore Calvin Pease, *The Story of Illinois* (Chicago: University of Chicago Press, 1949), 188.

25. *Wilmington Coal Mining and Manufacturing Co. v. Barr*, 2 Ill App. 86–87 (1878). "Yellow-dog contracts" forced workers to renounce participation in unions or union activities as a condition of employment. They originated in England in the early nineteenth century. American companies began to adopt them in the 1870s. Joel I. Seidman, *The Yellow Dog Contract* (Baltimore: Johns Hopkins Press, 1932), 11–38.

26. *Wilmington Coal Mining and Manufacturing Co. v. Barr*, 88–89.

27. *Wilmington Coal Mining and Manufacturing Co. v. Lamb*, 90 Ill. 465 (1878). On the point about hegemony, see Holt, "Recovery by the Worker Who Quits," 728. Holt sees *Britton* and the cases following it in this light, claiming these decisions "operated to lull workers into a false sense of equality and security," although he acknowledges that *Britton* can be seen as a victory of class struggle "from the standpoint of the worker" (706). One point that should be noted is that workers in these cases received compensation for their toil, and that probably made a significant difference in their daily lives.

28. Karsten, "'Bottomed on Justice,'" 251 n. 133. On workplace control, see David Montgomery, *The Fall of the House of Labor: The Workplace, the State, and American Labor Activism, 1865–1925* (New York: Cambridge University Press, 1987).

29. As noted in chapter 3, my analysis here differs considerably from that of Amy Dru Stanley, who sees postwar reformers as having learned the language of contractual reciprocity with regard to beggars in the emancipation South. While it is certainly true that such important postwar reformers as Samuel Gridley Howe played central roles in southern Reconstruction, the central elements of their language of poverty had existed since the antebellum period. See Stanley, "Beggars Can't Be Choosers," 1290–93.

30. Of course, it might be argued that tramp laws had no effect, for their operation depended on local officials. Indeed, Alexander Keyssar, in his study of unemployment in Massachusetts, has pointed out that local officials rarely enforced tramp laws regularly. See Keyssar, *Out of Work: The First Century of Unemployment in Massa-*

chusetts (New York: Cambridge University Press, 1986), 137–38. Even though such laws may not have been enforced regularly (neither are modern traffic laws), I would suggest that, even if most tramps did not face arrest, tramp laws played an important role in the legal and cultural creation of a capitalist labor market by setting the terms of what was acceptable. If viewed as a bourgeois assertion of power, tramp laws strengthened a capitalist conception of the labor market by endowing it with the power of the state.

31. Allan Pinkerton, *Strikers, Communists, Tramps, and Detectives* (New York: G. W. Carelton, 1878), 31. For another acknowledgment of the novelty of these laws, see Francis Wayland and F. B. Sanborn, "Report on Tramp Laws and Indeterminate Sentences," *Seventh Annual Conference of Charities and Corrections* (Boston: A. Williams, 1880), 278. I have used Pinkerton's ambivalent account liberally below. Pinkerton was a complicated figure. The symbol of managerial oppression of the working class, he nevertheless had experienced both working-class life and poverty. Born in Scotland, he supported his family as a cooper's apprentice and became active in the Chartist movement. After the family immigrated to the United States, Pinkerton settled in Illinois, building a successful business in his trade and becoming active in the underground railroad. When he helped uncover a counterfeiting ring, Pinkerton moved into detective work, first in rural Illinois, then in Chicago. By 1855, he had founded a detective agency that would become the tool of the country's rising managerial class. Both his background in the working class and this connection to the new middle-class managers were crucial for the tensions that pervaded his views on tramping. Pinkerton was charged with policing people of his own heritage, while trying to maintain the same middle-class respectability that his employers sought. Frank Morn, *"The Eye That Never Sleeps": A History of the Pinkerton National Detective Agency* (Bloomington: Indiana University Press, 1982), ix–x, 19–25.

32. Laura E. Richards, ed., *Letters and Journals of Samuel Gridley Howe*, 2 vols. (Boston: Dana Estes and Co., 1909), 2:508–36, quotes on 531, 511, 528; Harold Schwartz, *Samuel Gridley Howe: Social Reformer, 1801–1876* (Cambridge: Harvard University Press, 1956), 267–71, 275–76; Bremner, *Public Good*, 169–72.

33. *Session Laws of Massachusetts, 1866*, 229–230; Stanley, "Beggars Can't Be Choosers," 1273.

34. *Session Laws of Pennsylvania, 1866*, 259–60; *Session Laws of Pennsylvania, 1868*, 1031–32.

35. Bremner, *Public Good*, 147, 174–75.

36. *Session Laws of New York, 1860*, 401–2; *Session Laws of New York, 1862*, 393, 980–81; *Session Laws of New York, 1878*, 483–84; Bremner, *Public Good*, 148–49, 158–63.

37. *New York Times*, January 12, 1865, November 21, 1869, September 30, 1873.

38. Ibid., June 3, 1874, July 24, 1874, October 7, 1874.

39. *Session Laws of Pennsylvania, 1876*, 149–54.

40. Ibid., 154–56.

41. The New Jersey law is generally given credit as being the first "tramp" act because it used the term for the first time. However, the New Hampshire law was recognized as a response to the tramp problem. See *Central Law Journal* (St. Louis) 2 (September 3, 1875): 365.

The growth of the legal definition of "tramp" can be seen in David S. Garland and Charles Porterfield, eds., *American and English Encyclopedia of Law*, 2d ed. (Northport, N.Y.: Edward Thompson Co., 1904), 28:445, 451, and 29:571: "Usually . . . a tramp is defined as a person who, outside of his own city or county, or not being a resident of the state, commits an act of vagrancy, and his punishment is usually more severe. *It follows that while all tramps are vagrants, not all vagrants are tramps*" (my emphasis). See also William C. Anderson, *A Dictionary of Law. . . .* (Chicago: T. H. Flood, 1893), 1047, and Francis Rawle, ed., *Bouvier's Law Dictionary* (Kansas City: Vernon Law Book Co., 1914), 3:3307–8.

In the following section on the statutes, I have given specific citations only when quoting. My generalizations are drawn from *Session Laws of Pennsylvania, 1879*, 33–34; *Revised Statutes of Maine* (1884), 925; *Revised Statutes of Delaware* (1915), 1629–32; *Annotated Code of Iowa* (1897), 1981–82; *Revised Statutes of Wisconsin, Supplement* (1883), 332–36; *Revised Statutes of Ohio* (1879), 1654; *Revised Statutes of Illinois* (1885), 425; *Laws of Indiana, Special Session, 1877*, 80–84; *Laws of Maryland, 1880*, 43–45; *Laws of Massachusetts, 1880*, 231–33; *Revised Laws of Vermont* (1881), 766–67; *General Statutes of Connecticut* (1887), 346–47; *Revised Statutes of New Jersey* (1877), 1208–19; *Session Laws of New York, 1880*, 296–97; *Laws of New Hampshire, 1875*, 610–11 for the 1875 law; "The New Hampshire Tramp Law," *New York Times*, September 2, 1878. For the general state of tramp laws through the late 1890s, see Harry A. Millis, "The Law Affecting Tramps and Immigrants," *Charities Review* 7 (September 1897): 587–94. Helpful secondary sources are Sidney Harring, "Class Conflict and the Suppression of Tramps in Buffalo, 1892–1894," *Law and Society Review* 11 (Summer 1977): 873–81, and Michael Davis, "Forced to Tramp: The Perspective of the Labor Press, 1870–1900," in Monkkonen, *Walking to Work*, 161–65.

42. *Session Laws of Pennsylvania, 1879*, 33–34.

43. *New York Times*, September 2, 1878; *Revised Statutes of Wisconsin*, 333.

44. For a useful discussion about the relationship between tramps and local charity officials, see Keyssar, *Out of Work*, 138–42.

45. *Code of Tennessee* (1884), 396–97; *Code of Alabama* (1907), 3:954–57; *Code of North Carolina* (1883), 586–87; *Revised Code of Mississippi* (1880), 772–73. Missouri also passed a law in 1879, which was revised in 1889 and astonishingly declared unconstitutional under the Thirteenth and Fourteenth Amendments in 1893. The state reenacted a vagrancy statute in 1899. See *In re Thompson*, 117 Mo. 83–92 (1893).

46. *New Orleans Picayune* repr. in *New York Times*, December 30, 1877; Wright, *Old South, New South*, 94–96. On southern variations in tramping, see Eric Monkkonen, "Regional Dimensions of Tramping, North and South, 1880–1910," in Monkkonen, *Walking to Work*, 191–209. On black out-migration, see Nell Irvin Painter, *Exodusters: Black Migration to Kansas after Reconstruction* (New York: Alfred A. Knopf, 1977), and Roger G. Athearn, *In Search of Canaan: Black Migration to Kansas, 1879–1880* (Lawrence: Regents Press of Kansas, 1978). Painter discusses reaction to the Exodusters but does not mention tramp laws (203–11).

47. *Compiled Laws of Nevada* (1900), 945–47; *Penal Code of California* (1909), 358–60; *Revised Statutes of Colorado* (1908), 551–52. For more on attempts to bring urban order to the frontier, see Duane A. Smith, *Rocky Mountain Mining Camps: The Urban Frontier* (Bloomington: Indiana University Press, 1967).

48. For a general discussion of this point, see James B. Gilbert, *Work without Salvation: America's Intellectuals and Industrial Alienation, 1880–1910* (Baltimore: Johns Hopkins University Press, 1977), 23–30.

49. "The Disease of Mendicancy," *Scribner's Monthly* 13 (January 1877): 416–17. See also Pinkerton, *Strikers*, 47.

50. *New York Times*, April 27, 1879, January 11, 1876, June 18, 1878, June 19, 1878, October 24, 1879, January 31, 1880; *Baltimore Gazette*, July 22, 1878, repr. in *New York Times*, July 28, 1878. This so-called train stealing in Wisconsin may have been the reason the state's legislature denied tramps the right to assemble. For another example of "train stealing," see *New York Tribune*, July 14, 1876.

51. *New York Times*, December 10, 1875, April 19, 1876, October 13, 1876; Lee O. Harris, *The Man Who Tramps: A Story of Today* (Indianapolis: Douglas and Carlon, 1878), 269. On the identification of tramps with labor radicalism and the 1877 strikes, see "Disease of Mendicancy," 416–17; "What Shall We Do With Our Tramps?" *New Englander and Yale Review* 37 (July 1878): 521–32; *Nation*, January 24, 1878, 50; *New York Tribune*, August 14, 1876, November 28, 1877; Davis, "Forced to Tramp," 141–70; Robert W. Bruce, *1877: Year of Violence* (Indianapolis: Bobbs Merrill, 1959), 20–23, 68–69, 99, 117, 151, 173, 187; Philip S. Foner, *The Great Labor Uprising of 1877* (New York: Monad Press, 1977), 212.

52. Pruyn quoted in Katz, *Poverty and Policy*, 163–64; Ringenbach, *Tramps and Reformers*, 19; C. S. Watkins, "Pauperism and Its Prevention," *Ninth Annual Conference of Charities and Corrections* (Madison, Wis.: Midland, 1883), 95–96; Josephine Shaw Lowell, "One Means of Preventing Pauperism," *Sixth Annual Conference of Charities and Corrections* (Boston: A. Williams, 1879), 195; A. Reynolds, "The Prevention of Pauperism," *Sixth Annual Conference of Charities and Corrections* (Boston: A. Williams, 1879), 214–15.

Katz reanalyzed Pruyn's data and found that, in fact, tramping was primarily the temporary movements of casual laborers (*Poverty and Public Policy*, 157–81). John Schneider reaches similar conclusions: "Tramps were mostly unmarried white men in the prime of life who worked at manual labor and were either natives of the United States or immigrants from the British Isles or Canada," John C. Schneider, "Tramping Workers, 1890–1920: A Subcultural View," in Monkkonen, *Walking to Work*, 226. On casual labor in late-nineteenth-century America, see Montgomery, *Fall of the House of Labor*, chap. 2.

53. "What Shall We Do with Our Tramps?," 521–32 (emphasis in original).

54. *New York Times*, June 17, 1875; Hale quoted in Katz, *Poverty and Policy*, 158; Blair quoted in *New York Times*, December 22, 1877; Pinkerton, *Strikers*, 47–48, 66 (quote). The labor press increasingly adopted this position as the century wore on. See Davis, "Forced to Tramp."

55. The most direct statement of this view is Harring, "Class Conflict," 873–81. Ringenbach, *Tramps and Reformers*, chap. 1, takes a much softer position, but he still sees charitable societies as central. My conclusions on the influence on charitable societies are drawn from F. B. Sanborn, "The Year's Work in Administration and Legislation," *Sixth Annual Conference of Charities and Corrections* (Boston: A. Williams, 1879), 26; State of New York, *Ninth Annual Report of the State Board of Charities, State of New York* (Albany: Jerome B. Parmenter, 1876), 30; *New York Times*, January 19, 1878.

56. Horatio Seymour, "Crime and Tramps," *Harper's New Monthly Magazine* 58 (December 1878): 106–7; *New York Tribune*, December 28, 1877; *American Farmer*, 8th ser., 7 (January 1878): 32–33; "The Tramp Nuisance," *Central Law Journal* (St. Louis) 2 (September 3, 1875): 365; *National Cyclopedia of American Biography*, 19: 28. Unlike many others, Thompson recognized that "whatever [would] remove hard times and give work to thousands of laboring men" was also needed.

57. *New York Times*, February 6, 1875, February 12, 1877, January 9, 1876; *New York Tribune*, April 26, 1879; *American Farmer*, 8th ser., 7 (January 1878): 32–33.

58. Stephenson quoted in *Nation* 26 (January 24, 1878): 50. Stephenson's report also appeared in the *New York Times*, January 21, 1878. On local vigilance actions, see *New York Times*, July 18, 1877, January 24, 1877, December 9, 1876. On local charity activities, see Henry Hill, "Report of the Standing Committee on Organization of Charities in Cities," *Eighth Annual Conference of Charities and Corrections* (Boston: A. Williams, 1881), 114–15.

59. Hill, "Report," 115; *Philadelphia Record*, July 16, 1877, repr. in *New York Times*, July 18, 1877. On popular suppression, see Samuel Walker, *Popular Justice: A History of American Criminal Justice* (New York: Oxford University Press, 1980); Richard Maxwell Brown, "Violence and the American Revolution," in *Essays on the American Revolution*, ed. Stephen G. Kurtz and James H. Hutson (Chapel Hill: University of North Carolina Press, 1973), 81–116.

60. Pinkerton, *Strikers*, 66; Sanborn, "Year's Work," 25; Wayland and Sanborn, "Tramp Laws," 280–81.

61. *Shanley v. Wells*, 71 Ill. 78–83 (1873); "The Illinois Vagabond Law of 1877,"

Monthly Jurist (Bloomington, Ill.) 1, no. 7 (November 1877): 532–33; *Albany Law Journal* 16, no. 24 (December 15, 1877): 423; *Chicago Tribune*, December 6, 1877; *The Luzerne Legal Register*, 12 (1883), 220.

62. *City of Portland v. City of Bangor*, 65 Me. 120–21 (1876). This case is the only direct instance I have found of a judge linking northern and southern Reconstruction.

63. *Prescott v. State*, 19 Ohio St. 184,–89 (1869).

64. Seymour, "Crime and Tramps," 108.

65. *New York Times*, June 3, 1875, June 13, 1875; Peabody quoted in *New York Times*, March 14, 1878; Rodgers, *Work Ethic*, 226–28; "Once More the Tramp," *Scribner's Monthly*, April 15, 1878, 882. For another assertion about tramps' rejection of wage work, see *New York Tribune*, August 10, 1876; Martin B. Anderson, "Labor in Institutions for the Dependent Classes," in State of New York, *Twelfth Annual Report of the State Board of Charities* (Albany: Charles Van Benthuysen and Sons, 1879), 261. See also Pinkerton, *Strikers*, 45.

Gilbert, *Work without Salvation*, 23–30, also discusses tramping as a crisis in the work ethic. Katz, *Poverty and Policy*, 174–81, stresses the point that contemporary observers explained tramping as a personal failure. Keyssar, *Out of Work*, 132, notes how officials in Massachusetts described tramping as willful.

66. Levi L. Barbour, "Vagrancy," in *Eighth Annual Conference of Charities and Corrections* (Boston: A. Williams, 1881), 132 (quote, emphasis mine), 134; C. W. Chancellor, *Report on the Public Charities, Reformatories, Prisons, and Almshouses of the State of Maryland* (New York: Arno Press, 1976, facs. repr. of 1877 ed.), 29; William H. Davenport, "The Work-House–Blackwell's Island," *Harper's New Monthly Magazine* 38 (October 1866): 699–700. John C. Schneider has suggested that while most tramping was caused by the volatile labor market of the late nineteenth century, some tramps may have taken to the road to escape industrial regimentation. Schneider, "Subcultural View," 221.

67. *Nation*, January 24, 1878, 50; Diller Luther, "Causes and Prevention of Pauperism," in *Seventh Annual Conference of Charities and Corrections* (Boston: A. Williams, 1880), 248; Barbour, "Vagrancy," 136; *New York Times*, September 5, 1875, 9; *New York Times*, December 26, 1875, 9; Seth Lowe, "The Problem of Pauperism in the Cities of Brooklyn and New York," in *Sixth Annual Conference of Charities and Corrections* (Boston: A. Williams, 1879), 209; *Nation*, January 24, 1878, 50; "Disease of Mendicancy," 417.

68. State of New York, *Ninth Annual Report*, 30; Lowe, "Problem of Pauperism," 209; Wayland and Sanborn, "Report," 280–81; Wayland quoted in *New York Times*, September 7, 1877, 2. See also Anderson, "Labor in Institutions," 261.

For the point about direct enforcement, see Stanley, "Beggars Can't Be Choosers," 1283–93. Stanley argues that postwar reformers faced the task of explaining compulsory labor in the growing language of contract. To do so, they invoked "the rule of exchange" and defined vagrancy by "the idiom of the marketplace" (1290). Stanley also believes that, in part, reformers such as Edward Pierce, Josephine Shaw Lowell, and Samuel Gridley Howe learned the "coercive aspects" of free labor through their experiences in the postwar South and carried this knowledge back north. Although it is true that some reformers used reciprocity and contract language, it was not as novel in the postwar period as Stanley implies. As noted in the previous chapters, mutual obligation as the basis for work had been a common element of antebellum and early wartime thinking on vagrancy. For more on this issue, see Shklar, *American Citizenship*, esp. 2–4, 72, 92–94.

69. Henry E. Pellew, "Pauperism in the State of New York: The Value of Industrial Training and Enforced Labor," in *Sixth Annual Conference of Charities and Corrections* (Boston: A. Williams, 1879), 217; Barbour, "Vagrancy," 131; Anderson, "Labor in Institutions," 261.

70. Seymour, "Crime and Tramps," 107. Although they do not explore masculinity and tramping in depth and deal with a somewhat later period, the following works are suggestive of this point: Monkkonen, "Regional Dimensions," 207; Schneider, "Subcultural View," 223; Lynn Wiener, "Sisters of the Road: Women Transients and Tramps, 1880–1910," in Monkkonen, *Walking to Work*, 178–79.

71. Anderson, "Labor in Institutions," 262; "The Vilest of the Vile," *New York Times*, January 7, 1877, 5; Watkins, "Prevention," 94. See also Pinkerton, *Strikers*, 26; Chancellor, *Report*, 29. For a discussion of the importance of work in nineteenth-century constructions of masculinity, see Rotundo, *American Manhood*, 167–93.

72. Quoted in Wayland and Sanborn, "Tramp Laws," 279; *New York Tribune*, April 26, 1879, September 26, 1880; Wayland as quoted in *New York Times*, September 7, 1877. Harris also employed this imagery in *Man Who Tramps*, 269.

73. Davenport, "Work-House," 689, 700; Lowell, "One Means," 190–93, 197–98; Dr. Elisha Harris to Josephine Shaw Lowell, in Lowell, "One Means," 198; Anderson, "Labor in Institutions," 265. On the domestic roles of female tramps, see Wiener, "Sisters," 178; Pinkerton, *Strikers*, 52–67. For more on Lowell and the charity work of other bourgeois women, see Lori D. Ginzberg, *Women and the Work of Benevolence: Morality, Politics, and Class in the Nineteenth-Century United States* (New Haven: Yale University Press, 1990).

74. Joseph A. Dacus, *Annals of the Great Strikes* (1877; reprint, New York: Arno Press, 1969), 18, 24; Luther, "Causes," 246. In general, see Russell Lynes, *The Domesticated Americans* (New York: Harper and Row, 1957), and Christopher Lasch, *Haven in a Heartless World: The Family Besieged* (New York: Basic Books, 1977). Although Lasch is talking about a later time period, the argument seems to fit here. See also Schneider, "Subcultural View," 223.

75. Chancellor, *Report*, 27; *The Lancaster Bar*, December 27, 1879, 120.

76. Pinkerton, *Strikers*, 39; *New York Times*, August 24, 1877.

77. Lowell, "One Means," 198; Wayland and Sanborn, "Tramp Laws," 278.

78. "Vilest of the Vile," *New York Times*, January 7, 1877, 5; Snivig C. Trebor [Robert C. Givins], *The Millionaire Tramp* (Chicago: Cook County Review, 1886), 55; Barbour, "Vagrancy," 131. For other examples, see Trebor, *Millionaire Tramp*, 44; "The Prevention of Pauperism," in *Sixth Annual Conference of Charities and Corrections* (Boston: A. Williams, 1879), 41; Pinkerton, *Strikers*, 41.

79. Barbour, "Vagrancy," 133, 134; Pinkerton, *Strikers*, 50. See also Comments of Dr. Charles Hoyt during debate in Reynolds, "Prevention," 41; Trebor, *Millionaire Tramp*, 44; Pinkerton, *Strikers*, 36.

80. Harris, *Man Who Tramps*, 5–14. Harris's work was part of a broader group of novels that responded to the 1877 strikes. Bruce, *1877*, 319.

81. Harris, *Man Who Tramps*, 35, 38.

82. Ibid., 40–45, 267.

83. *New York Tribune*, July 28, 1876, December 28, 1877.

84. Reynolds, "Prevention," 210; Anderson, "Labor in Institutions," 261.

85. Barbour, "Vagrancy," 131, 137; Anderson, "Labor in Institutions," 260; Dacus, *Annals*, 307, iv, 57; Wayland as quoted in *New York Times*, September 7, 1877; "Once More the Tramp," 883. See also State of New York, *Tenth Annual Report of the State Board of Charities* (Albany: Jerome B. Parmenter, 1877), 32.

86. Luther, "Causes," 242, 247–48; Wayland and Sanborn, "Tramp Laws," 218; Harris, *Man Who Tramps*, 269; Pinkerton, *Strikers*, 42.

87. Mrs. W. P. Lynde, "The Treatment of Erring and Criminal Women," in *Seventh Annual Conference of Charities and Corrections* (Boston: A. Williams, 1880), 251; Barbour, "Vagrancy," 136. For other examples of both the preceding points, see State of New York, *Tenth Annual Report*, 30–31; State of New York, *Ninth Annual Report*, 26–27; Sanborn, "Year's Work," 25; Lowe, "Problem of Pauperism," 201.

88. Trebor, *Millionaire Tramp*, 41, 45–46 (quote), 51 (emphasis in original).

89. Chancellor, *Report*, 25–26, 29; Pinkerton, *Strikers*, 48. See also Dacus, *Annals*, 19; Pinkerton, *Strikers*, 39.

90. See T. J. Jackson Lears, *No Place of Grace: Anti-modernism and the Transformation of American Culture, 1880–1920* (New York: Pantheon, 1981), 29 on tramps. Rotundo's discussion of failure and male neurasthenia also sheds light on the anti-modern elements of tramping. Rotundo sees men's nervous breakdowns as a rejection of the work rhythms of an urban-industrial work. See *American Manhood*, 185–93.

91. Lowe, "Problem of Pauperism," 206; Barbour, "Vagrancy," 132; Trebor, *Millionaire Tramp*, 46; State of New York, *Tenth Annual Report*, 32.

92. *New York Tribune*, September 26, 1880.

93. Pinkerton, *Strikers*, 26–28, 30, 33–36, 49.

94. Warner as quoted in Wayland and Sanborn, "Tramp Laws," 279.

Conclusion: Law and Social Change

1. For an example of legal history that treats law (mostly) as a reflection of social change, see Hall, *Magic Mirror.*

2. This point does not mean that the Civil War and Reconstruction would fade as major watersheds, as Peter Bardaglio's work shows. See Bardaglio, *Reconstructing the Household.*

3. For Skowronek's discussion of the intellectual dimension of state building, see *Building the New American State,* 31–34.

Bibliography

PRIMARY SOURCES

Manuscripts

Athens, Alabama. Resolution on Disorderly Persons, January 31, 1852. In the Southern Historical Collection of the Manuscripts Department, University of North Carolina, Chapel Hill.

Robert A. Jones Account Book, 1817–28. In the Southern Historical Collection of the Manuscripts Department, University of North Carolina, Chapel Hill.

McKay-Stiles Family Papers, 1734–1915. In the Southern Historical Collection of the Manuscripts Department, University of North Carolina, Chapel Hill.

Schenck, David. Diary, 1835–1902. 12 vols. Typescript edition. In the Southern Historical Collection of the Manuscripts Department, University of North Carolina, Chapel Hill.

Shenandoah County, Virginia, Books, 1799–1838. In the Southern Historical Collection of the Manuscripts Department, University of North Carolina, Chapel Hill.

United States. Bureau of Refugees, Freedmen, and Abandoned Lands. *Records of the Assistant Commissioner for the State of Alabama, Bureau of Refugees, Freedmen, and Abandoned Lands, 1865–1870.* National Archives Microfilm Publication No. 809.

———. *Records of the Assistant Commissioner for the State of Louisiana, Bureau of Refugees, Freedmen, and Abandoned Lands, 1865–1870.* 36 rolls. National Archives Microfilm Publication No. 1027.

———. *Records of the Assistant Commissioner for the State of North Carolina, Bureau of Refugees, Freedmen, and Abandoned Lands, 1865–1870,* National Archives Microfilm Publication No. 843.

———. *Records of the Assistant Commissioner for the State of South Carolina, Bureau of Refugees, Freedmen, and Abandoned Lands, 1865–1870.* 42 rolls. National Archives Microfilm Publication No. M869.

———. *Records of the Assistant Commissioner for the State of Texas, Bureau of*

Refugees, Freedmen, and Abandoned Lands, 1865–1870. 32 rolls. National Archives Microfilm Publication No. 821.

Valentine, William D. Diary, 1837–1855. 15 vols. In the Southern Historical Collection of the Manuscripts Department, University of North Carolina, Chapel Hill.

Newspapers

Congressional Globe
Free American (San Francisco)
Galveston Daily News
Liberator
National Anti-Slavery Standard
New Orleans Picayune
New Orleans Tribune
New York Times
New York Tribune
Niles Weekly Register

Legal Sources

Clayton, Augustin S. *The Office and Duty of Justice of the Peace.* . . . Milledgeville, Ga.: S. Grantland, 1819.

Dane, Nathan. *General Abridgement and Digest of American Law.* 8 vols. Boston: Cummings, Hilliard & Co., 1823.

Dunlap, John A. *The New-York Justice, or, A Digest of the Law Relative to Justices of the Peace in the State of New-York.* . . . New York: Isaac Riley, 1815.

Freeman, Samuel. *The Massachusetts Justice.* . . . 3d ed. Boston: Thomas and Andrews, 1810.

Parson, Theophilus. *The Law of Contracts.* 2d ed. Boston: Little, Brown, 1855.

Perkins, J. C., ed. *A Practical Treatise on the Law of Contracts not under Seal . . . by Joseph Chitty.* Springfield, Mass.: Merriam, 1851.

Read, Collinson. *Precedents in the Office of a Justice of the Peace.* . . . 3d ed. Philadelphia, 1810.

Reeve, Tapping. *The Law of Baron and Femme.* . . . 3d ed. Albany: William Gould Law Publisher, 1862.

Sedgwick, Theodore. *A Treatise on the Measure of Damages.* 4th ed. New York, 1868.

Wood, Horace Gray. *A Treatise on the Law of Master and Servant.* 1877. Buffalo: William Hein and Co., 1981.

Other Printed Primary Sources

Albany Law Journal 16, no. 24 (December 15, 1877): 423.

Allen, W. H. "Free Labor in Louisiana." *Christian Examiner* 78 (May 1865): 383–99.

American Farmer, 8th ser., 7 (January 1878): 32–33.

Anderson, Martin B. "Labor in Institutions for the Dependent Classes." In State of New York, *Twelfth Annual Report of the State Board of Charities*, 259–67. Albany: Charles Van Benthuysen and Sons, 1879.

Annual Reports of the New York Association for Improving the Condition of the Poor: Nos. 1–10, 1845–1853. Edited by David J. Rothman. New York: Arno Press, 1971.

Autobiography of Oliver Otis Howard. 2 vols. New York: Baker and Taylor, 1907.

Barbour, Levi L. "Vagrancy." In *Eighth Annual Conference of Charities and Corrections*, 131–38. Boston: A. Williams, 1881.

Beecher, Catherine. *Treatise on Domestic Economy for Young Ladies at Home and at School*. New York: Harper and Brothers, 1847.

Berlin, Ira, et al., eds. *The Wartime Genesis of Free Labor: The Lower South*. Ser. 1, vol. 3 of *Freedom: A Documentary History of Emancipation, 1861–1867*. New York: Cambridge University Press, 1990.

Breeden, James O., ed. *Advice among Masters: The Ideal in Slave Management in the Old South*. Westport, Conn.: Greenwood Press, 1980.

Brookes, Iveson L. *A Defense of the South against the Reproaches of the North*. Hamburg, S.C.: Republican Office, 1850.

Carey, Matthew. *Appeal to the Wealthy of the Land, Ladies as well as Gentlemen, on the Character, Conduct, Situation, and Prospects, of Those Whose Sole Dependence for Subsistence Is on the Labour of Their Hands*. 1833. Reprint, New York: Arno Press, 1969.

Chancellor, C. W. *Report on the Public Charities, Reformatories, Prisons, and Almshouses of the State of Maryland*. 1877. Reprint, New York: Arno Press, 1976.

Conway, Thomas W. *The Freedmen of Louisiana: Final Report of the Bureau of Free Labor, Department of the Gulf, to Major General E. R. S. Canby*. New Orleans: Times Book Office, 1865.

———. *Report on the Condition of the Freedmen*. Washington, D.C.: Government Printing Office, 1864.

Dacus, Joseph A. *Annals of the Great Strikes*. 1877. Reprint, New York: Arno Press, 1969.

Davenport, William H. "The Work-House—Blackwell's Island." *Harper's New Monthly Magazine* 38 (October 1866): 683–702.

De Forest, John William. *A Union Officer in the Reconstruction*. New Haven: Yale University Press, 1948.

Diary and Correspondence of Salmon P. Chase. In *Annual Report of the American Historical Association for 1902*. Washington, D.C.: Government Printing Office, 1903.

"The Disease of Mendicancy." *Scribner's Monthly* 13 (January 1877): 416–17.

Eby, Cecil D., ed. *A Virginia Yankee in the Civil War: The Diaries of David Hunter Strother*. Chapel Hill: University of North Carolina Press, 1961.

Everest, Robert. "Pauperism and Crime." *DeBow's Review* 19 (August 1855): 268–85.

Everett, Edward. *A Lecture on the Working Men's Party*. 1831. Reprint, New York: Arno Press, 1969.

Fisher, Elwood. *Lecture on the North and South*. Cincinnati: Daily Chronicle, 1849.

Fitzhugh, George. *Cannibals All!, or Slaves without Masters*. Edited by C. Vann Woodward. Cambridge: Harvard University Press, Belknap Press, 1960.

————. *Slavery Justified, by a Southerner*. Fredricksburg, Va.: Record Printing Office, 1850. In *Slavery Defended: The Views of the Old South*, edited by Eric L. McKitrick. Englewood Cliffs, N.J.: Prentice-Hall, 1963.

Goodloe, A. T. "Overseers." *Southern Cultivator* 18 (September 1861): 287.

Griffith, Lucille, ed. "The Plantation Record Book of Brookdale Farm, Amite County, 1856–1857." *Journal of Mississippi History* 7 (January 1945): 23–31.

Hale, E. E. "How to Use Victory." *Atlantic Monthly* 13 (June 1864): 763–68.

Harris, Lee O. *The Man Who Tramps: A Story of Today*. Indianapolis: Douglas and Carlon, 1878.

Hill, Henry. "Report of the Standing Committee on Organization of Charities in Cities." In *Eighth Annual Conference of Charities and Corrections*, 113–16. Boston: A. Williams, 1881.

"The Illinois Vagabond Law of 1877." *Monthly Jurist* (Bloomington, Ill.) 1, no. 7 (November 1877): 532–33.

Jones, Hugh. *The Present State of Virginia, From When Is Inferred a Short View of Maryland and North Carolina* [1724]. Edited by Richard L. Morton. Chapel Hill: University of North Carolina Press for the Virginia Historical Society, 1956.

Lancaster Bar, December 27, 1879.

Lemon, Sarah McCulloh, ed. *The Pettigew Papers*. Vol. 2, *1819–1843*. Raleigh: North Carolina Department of Cultural Resources, 1988.

Lowe, Seth. "The Problem of Pauperism in the Cities of Brooklyn and New York." In *Sixth Annual Conference of Charities and Corrections*, 200–210. Boston: A. Williams, 1879.

Lowell, Josephine Shaw. "One Means of Preventing Pauperism." *Sixth Annual Conference of Charities and Corrections*, 189–200. Boston: A. Williams, 1879.

Luther, Diller. "Causes and Prevention of Pauperism." *Seventh Annual Conference of Charities and Corrections*, 242–49. Boston: A. Williams, 1880.

Luther, Seth. *An Address to the Working-Men of New-England*. 1832. Reprint, New York: Arno Press, 1969.

Luzerne Legal Register 12 (1883): 220.

Lynde, Mrs. W. P. "The Treatment of Erring and Criminal Women." *Seventh Annual Conference of Charities and Corrections*, 249–51. Boston: A. Williams, 1880.

"The Massachusetts Board of State Charities, and the Westborough Reform School." *Christian Examiner* 83 (July 1867): 117.

McKaye, James. *The Mastership and Its Fruits: The Emancipated Slave Face to Face with His Old Master*. New York: William C. Bryant, 1864.

Merrill, Walter E., ed. *The Letters of William Lloyd Garrison*. Vol. 5, *Let the Oppressed Go Free, 1861–1867*. Cambridge: Harvard University Press, Belknap Press, 1979.

Millis, Harry A. "The Law Affecting Tramps and Immigrants." *Charities Review* 7 (September 1897): 587–94.

Moore, John Hebron, ed. "Two Documents Relating to Plantation Overseers of the Vicksburg Region, 1831–1832." *Journal of Mississippi History* 16 (January 1954): 31–37.

Nation, January 24, 1878, 50.

"Once More the Tramp." *Scribner's Monthly*, April 15, 1878, 882–83.

"Overseers." *Southern Planter* 4 (August 1844): 184.

"Overseers." *Southern Planter* 5 (July 1845): 166.

"Overseers." *Southern Planter* 5 (August 1845): 172.

"Overseers." *Southern Planter* 5 (September 1845): 209–11.

"Overseers." *Southern Planter* 16 (February 1856): 48–49.

"Overseers: Their Duties." *Southern Cultivator* 12 (July 1854): 270.

"Overseers' Rules." *Southern Planter* 18 (July 1858): 410–11.

Pellew, Henry E. "Pauperism in the State of New York: The Value of Industrial Training and Enforced Labor." In *Sixth Annual Conference of Charities and Corrections*, 216–20. Boston: A. Williams, 1879.

Phillips, M. W. "Domestic Economy–Overseers: A Few Thoughts on the Subject." *Southern Cultivator* 14 (November 1856): 338.

Phillips, Ulrich B. *Plantation and Frontier Documents, 1649–1863*. 2 vols. Cleveland: Arthur C. Clark Co., 1909.

Pinkerton, Allan. *Strikers, Communists, Tramps, and Detectives*. New York: G. W. Carelton, 1878.

"Poor Laws." *American Quarterly Review* 14 (September 1833): 66–101.

"The Prevention of Pauperism." In *Sixth Annual Conference of Charities and Corrections*, 36–42. Boston: A. Williams, 1879.

Proceedings of the Black National and State Conventions, 1865–1900, vol. 1, edited by Philip S. Foner and George E. Walker. Philadelphia: Temple University Press, 1986.

Report of Select Committee Appointed to Visit Charitable Institutions Supported by the State and All City and County Poor and Work Houses and Jails: New York Sen. Doc. 8, 1856. New York: Arno Press, 1976.

Report of the Committee Appointed by the Guardians of the Poor. . . . Philadelphia: Samuel Parker, 1827.

Report of the Joint Committee on Reconstruction. Four parts in one volume. Washington, D.C.: Government Printing Office, 1866.

"Report of the Second Auditor in Relation to the Number of Poor Children Sent to School. . . ." In *Virginia Convention, 1850–1851, Documents Containing Statistics of Virginia*. Richmond, 1851.

Reynolds, A. "The Prevention of Pauperism." In *Sixth Annual Conference of Charities and Corrections*, 210–16. Boston: A. Williams, 1879.

Richards, Laura E., ed. *Letters and Journals of Samuel Gridley Howe*. 2 vols. Boston: Dana Estes and Co., 1909.

Rollin, Frank A. *Life and Public Services of Martin R. Delaney*. 1868. Reprint, New York: Krause Reprint Co., 1969.

Ruffin, Edmund. *The Political Economy of Slavery; or, The Institution Considered in Regard to Its Influence on Public Wealth and the General Welfare*. Washington: Lemuel Towers, 1853. In *Slavery Defended: The Views of the Old South*, edited by Eric L. McKitrick. Englewood Cliffs, N.J.: Prentice-Hall, 1963.

———. *Slave Labor and Free Labor, Described and Compared*. N.p., n.d.

Sanborn, F. B. "The Year's Work in Administration and Legislation." In *Sixth Annual Conference of Charities and Corrections*, 24–33. Boston: A. Williams, 1879.

Schurz, Carl. *Report on the Condition of the South*. 1865. Reprint, New York: Arno Press, 1969.

Seymour, Horatio. "Crime and Tramps." *Harper's New Monthly Magazine* 58 (December 1878): 106–8.

"Slaves in Louisiana." *Harper's Weekly*, February 21, 1863.

Southern Planter 1 (April 1841): 58.

Southern Planter 3 (October 1843): 234.

State of New York. *Ninth Annual Report of the State Board of Charities, State of New York*. Albany: Jerome B. Parmenter, 1876.

State of New York. *Tenth Annual Report of the State Board of Charities, State of New York*. Albany: Jerome B. Parmenter, 1877.

T. S. "Overseers." *Southern Planter* 3 (December 1843): 271.

"The Tramp Nuisance." *Central Law Journal* (St. Louis) 2 (September 3, 1875): 365.

Trebor, Snivig C. [Robert C. Givins]. *The Millionaire Tramp*. Chicago: Cook County Review, 1886.

Tuckerman, Joseph. *An Essay on the Wages Paid to Females for Their Labour*. 1830. Reprint, New York: Arno Press, 1969.

———. *On the Elevation of the Poor: A Selection of His Reports as Minister at Large in Boston*. 1874. Reprint, New York: Arno Press, 1971.

———. *Report of the Commissioners . . . on the Subject of the Pauper System of the Commonwealth of Massachusetts*. 1833. Reprint, New York: Arno Press, 1971.

U.S. Congress. House. *Orders Issued by the Freedmen's Bureau, 1865–1866*, 39th Cong., 1st sess., H. Exec. Doc. 70.

U.S. Congress. Senate. *Final Report of the American Freedmen's Inquiry Commission to the Secretary of War*, 38th Cong., 1st sess., May 15, 1864. S. Exec. Doc. 53.

———. *Orders Issued by the Freedmen's Bureau, 1865–1866*, 39th Cong., 1st sess., S. Exec. Doc. 6.

———. *Preliminary Report Touching the Condition and Management of Emanci-*

pated Refugees, Made to the Secretary of War by the American Freedmen's Inquiry Commission, 38th Cong., 1st sess., June 30, 1863. S. Exec. Doc. 53.

―――. *Reports of Assistant Commissioners of the Freedmen's Bureau, 1865–1866*, 39th Cong., 1st sess., S. Exec. Doc. 27.

―――. *Reports of the Freedmen's Bureau Assistant Commissioners and Laws in Relation to the Freedmen*, 39th Cong., 2d sess., S. Exec. Doc. 6.

"Vagrancy in Cincinnati." *Western Law Journal* 2 (December 1849): 589–90.

"Virginia Overseers." *Southern Planter* 5 (June 1845): 136–37.

War of the Rebellion: A Compilation of the Official Records of the Union and Confederate Armies. 128 vols. Washington, D.C.: Government Printing Office, 1880–1901.

Watkins, C. S. "Pauperism and Its Prevention." In *Ninth Annual Conference of Charities and Corrections*, 94–97. Madison, Wis.: Midland, 1883.

Wayland, Francis, and F. B. Sanborn. "Report on Tramp Laws and Indeterminate Sentences." In *Seventh Annual Conference of Charities and Corrections*, 277–81. Boston: A. Williams, 1880.

"What Shall We Do with Our Tramps?" *New Englander and Yale Review* 37 (July 1878): 521–32.

Wright, Francis. *An Address to the Industrious Classes*. 1830. Reprint, New York: Arno Press, 1969.

Yates, John V. N. *Report of the Secretary of State in 1824 on the Relief and Settlement of the Poor*. In *The Almshouse Experience: Collected Reports*, edited by David J. Rothman. New York: Arno Press, 1971.

Yeatman, James B. *Report of the Western Sanitary Commission in Regard to Leasing Abandoned Plantations with Rules and Regulations Governing the Same*. St. Louis: Western Sanitary Commission, 1864.

SECONDARY SOURCES

Books

Abbott, Martin. *The Freedmen's Bureau in South Carolina, 1865–1872*. Chapel Hill: University of North Carolina Press, 1967.

Alexander, John K. *Render Them Submissive: Responses to Poverty in Philadelphia, 1760–1800*. Amherst: University of Massachusetts Press, 1980.

Ashworth, John. *Slavery, Capitalism, and Politics in the Antebellum Republic*. Vol. 1, *Commerce and Compromise, 1820–1850*. New York: Cambridge University Press, 1995.

Atack, Jeremy, and Fred Bateman. *To Their Own Soil: Agriculture in the Antebellum North*. Ames: Iowa State University Press, 1987.

Athearn, Roger G. *In Search of Canaan: Black Migration to Kansas, 1879–1880*. Lawrence: Regents Press of Kansas, 1978.

Bardaglio, Peter. *Reconstructing the Household: Families, Sex, and the Law in Nine-teenth-Century America.* Chapel Hill: University of North Carolina Press, 1995.

Bassett, John Spencer. *The Southern Plantation Overseer As Revealed in His Letters.* Northampton, Mass.: Smith College, 1925.

Bellows. Barbara. *Benevolence among Slaveholders: Assisting the Poor in Charleston, 1670–1860.* Baton Rouge: Louisiana State University Press, 1993.

Belz, Herman. *A New Birth of Freedom: The Republican Party and Freedmen's Rights, 1861–1866.* Westport, Conn.: Greenwood Press, 1976.

———. *Reconstructing the Union: Theory and Policy during the Civil War.* Ithaca, N.Y.: Cornell University Press, 1969.

Benedict, Michael Les. *A Compromise of Principle: Congressional Republicans and Reconstruction, 1863–1869.* New York: W. W. Norton, 1974.

Bentley, George R. *A History of the Freedmen's Bureau.* Philadelphia: University of Pennsylvania Press, 1955.

Berlin, Ira. *Slaves without Masters: The Free Negro in the Antebellum South.* New York: Pantheon, 1974.

Blassingame, John. *Black New Orleans, 1860–1880.* Chicago: University of Chicago Press, 1965.

———. *The Slave Community: Plantation Life in the Antebellum South.* New York: Oxford University Press, 1979.

Blumin, Stuart M. *The Emergence of a Middle Class: Social Experience in the American City, 1760–1900.* New York: Cambridge University Press, 1989.

Bodnar, John. *The Transplanted: A History of Immigrants in Urban America.* Bloomington: Indiana University Press, 1985.

Bremner, Robert. *From the Depths: The Discovery of Poverty in the United States.* New York: New York University Press, 1956.

———. *The Public Good: Philanthropy and Welfare in the Civil War Era.* New York: Alfred A. Knopf, 1980.

Brown, Kathleen. *Good Wives, Nasty Wenches, and Anxious Patriarchs: Gender, Race, and Power in Colonial Virginia.* Chapel Hill: University of North Carolina Press, 1996.

Bruce, Robert W. *1877: Year of Violence.* Indianapolis: Bobbs Merrill, 1959.

Brundage, Anthony. *The Making of the New Poor Law: The Politics of Inquiry, Enactment, and Implementation, 1832–1839.* New Brunswick, N.J.: Rutgers University Press, 1978.

Buchanan, G. Sidney. *The Quest for Freedom: A Legal History of the Thirteenth Amendment.* Reprinted from *Houston Law Review* 12 (1976).

Calavita, Kitty. *U.S. Immigration Law and the Control of Labor, 1820–1924.* New York: Academic Press, 1984.

Carter, Dan. *When the War Was Over: The Failure of Self-Reconstruction in the South, 1865–1867.* Baton Rouge: Louisiana State University Press, 1985.

Chandler, Alfred D., Jr. *The Visible Hand: The Managerial Revolution in American Business*. Cambridge: Harvard University Press, Belknap Press, 1977.

Cimbala, Paul A. *Under the Guardianship of the Nation: The Freedmen's Bureau and Reconstruction in Georgia, 1865–1870*. Athens: University of Georgia Press, 1997.

Clark, Christopher. *The Roots of Rural Capitalism: Western Massachusetts, 1780–1860*. Ithaca, N.Y.: Cornell University Press, 1990.

Clement, Priscilla Ferguson. *Welfare and the Poor in the Nineteenth Century City: Philadelphia, 1800–1854*. Rutherford, N.J.: Fairleigh-Dickinson University Press, 1985.

Cox, Lawanda. *Lincoln and Black Freedom: A Study in Presidential Leadership*. Columbia: University of South Carolina Press, 1981.

Crouch, Barry A. *The Freedmen's Bureau and Black Texans*. Austin: University of Texas Press, 1992.

Davis, David Brion. *The Problem of Slavery in an Age of Revolution, 1770–1823*. Ithaca, N.Y.: Cornell University Press, 1975.

Davis, R. L. F. *Good and Faithful Labor: From Slavery to Sharecropping in the Natchez District*. Westport, Conn.: Greenwood Press, 1982.

Dawley, Alan. *Class and Community: The Industrial Revolution in Lynn*. Cambridge: Harvard University Press, 1976.

Demos, John. *A Little Commonwealth: Family Life in Plymouth Colony*. New York: Oxford University Press, 1970.

Dublin, Thomas. *Women at Work: The Transformation of Work and Community in Lowell, Massachusetts, 1826–1860*. New York: Columbia University Press, 1979.

Dudden, Faye E. *Serving Women: Household Service in Nineteenth-Century America*. Middletown, Conn.: Wesleyan University Press, 1983.

Dunkley, Peter. *The Crisis of the Old Poor Law in England, 1795–1834: An Interpretive Essay*. New York: Garland, 1982.

Elkins, Stanley M. *Slavery: A Problem in American Institutional and Intellectual Life*. 2d ed. Chicago: University of Chicago Press, 1968.

Ellis, David M. *New York: City and State*. Ithaca, N.Y.: Cornell University Press, 1981.

Fields, Barbara Jeanne. *Slavery and Freedom on the Middle Ground: Maryland during the Nineteenth Century*. New Haven: Yale University Press, 1985.

Finkelman, Paul. *An Imperfect Union: Slavery, Freedom, and Comity*. Chapel Hill: University of North Carolina Press, 1981.

Foner, Eric. *Free Soil, Free Labor, Free Men: The Ideology of the Republican Party before the Civil War*. New York: Oxford University Press, 1970.

———. *Nothing but Freedom: Emancipation and Its Legacy*. Baton Rouge: Louisiana State University Press, 1983.

———. *Politics and Ideology in the Age of Civil War*. New York: Oxford University Press, 1980.

————. *Reconstruction: America's Unfinished Revolution, 1863–1877.* New York: Harper and Row, 1989.

Foner, Philip S. *The Great Labor Uprising of 1877.* New York: Monad Press, 1977.

Freyer, Tony A. *Producers versus Capitalists: Constitutional Conflict in Antebellum America.* Charlottesville: University Press of Virginia, 1994.

Friedman, Lawrence. *Contract Law in America: A Social and Economic Case Study.* Madison: University of Wisconsin Press, 1965.

————. *Crime and Punishment in American History.* New York: Basic Books, 1993.

Galenson, David W. *White Servitude in Colonial America.* New York: Cambridge University Press, 1981.

Gates, Paul W. *The Farmer's Age: Agriculture, 1815–1860.* New York: Holt, Rinehart, and Wilson, 1960.

Genovese, Eugene D. *Roll, Jordan, Roll: The World the Slaves Made.* 1974. New York: Vintage Books, 1976.

Gerteis, Louis S. *From Contraband to Freedmen: Federal Policy toward Blacks, 1861–1865.* Westport, Conn.: Greenwood Press, 1973.

Gilbert, James B. *Work without Salvation: America's Intellectuals and Industrial Alienation, 1880–1910.* Baltimore: Johns Hopkins University Press, 1977.

Ginzberg, Lori D. *Women and the Work of Benevolence in the Nineteenth-Century United States.* New Haven: Yale University Press, 1990.

Glenn, Myra C. *Campaigns against Corporal Punishment: Prisoners, Sailors, Women, and Children in Antebellum America.* Albany: State University of New York Press, 1984.

Glickstein, Jonathan A. *Antebellum Concepts of Free Labor.* New Haven: Yale University Press, 1991.

Hall, Kermit. *The Magic Mirror: Law in American History.* New York: Oxford University Press, 1989.

Harrington, Fred Harvey. *Fighting Politician: Major General N. P. Banks.* Philadelphia: University of Pennsylvania Press, 1948.

Hill, Christopher. *Society and Puritanism in Pre-Revolutionary England.* London: Secher and Warbung, 1964.

Himmelfarb, Gertrude. *The Idea of Poverty: England in the Industrial Age.* New York: Alfred A. Knopf, 1984.

Hoffer, Peter Charles. *The Law's Conscience: Equitable Constitutionalism in America.* Chapel Hill: University of North Carolina Press, 1990.

Horwitz, Morton J. *The Transformation of American Law, 1780–1860.* Cambridge: Harvard University Press, 1977.

Hyman, Harold M. *A More Perfect Union: The Impact of the Civil War and Reconstruction on the Constitution.* New York: Alfred A. Knopf, 1973.

Hyman, Harold M., and William Wiecek. *Equal Justice under Law: Constitutional Development, 1835–1875.* New York: Harper and Row, 1982.

Ignatieff, Michael. *A Just Measure of Pain: The Penitentiary in the Industrial Revolution, 1750–1850*. New York: Pantheon, 1978.

Isaac, Rhys. *The Transformation of Virginia, 1740–1790*. Chapel Hill: University of North Carolina Press, 1982.

Jaynes, Gerald D. *Branches without Roots: Genesis of the Black Working Class in the American South, 1862–1882*. New York: Oxford University Press, 1986.

Johnson, Paul E. *A Shopkeeper's Millennium: Society and Revivals in Rochester, New York, 1815–1837*. New York: Hill and Wang, 1978.

Jones, Jacqueline. *Labor of Love, Labor of Sorrow: Black Women, Work, and the Family, from Slavery to the Present*. New York: Vintage Books, 1986.

Karsten, Peter. *Heart versus Head: Judge-Made Law in Nineteenth-Century America*. Chapel Hill: University of North Carolina Press, 1997.

Katz, Michael B. *In the Shadow of the Poorhouse: A Social History of Welfare in America*. New York: Basic Books, 1986.

———. *Poverty and Policy in American History*. New York: Academic Press, 1983.

Keyssar, Alexander. *Out of Work: The First Century of Unemployment in Massachusetts*. New York: Cambridge University Press, 1986.

Kolchin, Peter. *First Freedom: The Responses of Alabama Blacks to Emancipation and Reconstruction*. Westport, Conn.: Greenwood Press, 1972.

Kraditor, Aileen S. *Means and Ends in American Abolitionism: Garrison and His Critics on Strategy and Tactics, 1834–1850*. New York: Pantheon, 1969.

Kulikoff, Allan. *The Agrarian Origins of American Capitalism*. Charlottesville: University Press of Virginia, 1992.

Lasch, Christopher. *Haven in a Heartless World: The Family Besieged*. New York: Basic Books, 1977.

Laurie, Bruce. *Artisans into Workers: Labor in Nineteenth-Century America*. New York: Hill and Wang, 1989.

Lears, T. J. Jackson. *No Place of Grace: Anti-modernism and the Transformation of American Culture, 1880–1920*. New York: Pantheon, 1981.

Litwack, Leon F. *Been in the Storm So Long: The Aftermath of Slavery*. New York: Vintage Books, 1979.

Lynch, James D. *The Bench and Bar of Texas*. St. Louis: Nixon-Jones, 1885.

Lynes, Russell. *The Domesticated Americans*. New York: Harper and Row, 1957.

Mandel, Bernard. *Labor: Free and Slave, Workingmen and the Anti-slavery Movement in the United States*. New York: Associated Authors, 1955.

Marx, Karl. *Wage Labour and Capital*. In *Karl Marx: Selected Writings*, edited by David McClellan. New York: Oxford University Press, 1977.

Marx, Karl, and Friedrich Engels. *The Communist Manifesto*. In *Karl Marx: Selected Writings*, edited by David McClellan. New York: Oxford University Press, 1977.

McCoy, Drew R. *The Elusive Republic: Political Economy in Jeffersonian America*. Chapel Hill: University of North Carolina Press, 1980.

McCrary, Peyton. *Abraham Lincoln and Reconstruction: The Louisiana Experiment.* Princeton: Princeton University Press, 1978.

McFeely, William S. *Yankee Stepfather: General O. O. Howard and the Freedmen.* New York: W. W. Norton, 1968.

Messner, William F. *Freedmen and the Ideology of Free Labor: Louisiana, 1862–1865.* Lafayette: Center for Louisiana Studies, University of Southwest Louisiana, 1978.

Mohl, Raymond. *Poverty in New York, 1783–1825.* New York: Oxford University Press, 1971.

Monkkonen, Eric, ed. *Walking to Work: Tramps in America, 1790–1935.* Lincoln: University of Nebraska Press, 1984.

Montgomery, David. *Beyond Equality: Labor and the Radical Republicans, 1862–1872.* New York: Alfred A. Knopf, 1967.

———. *Citizen Worker: The Experience of Workers in the United States with Democracy and the Free Market during the Nineteenth Century.* New York: Cambridge University Press, 1993.

———. *The Fall of the House of Labor: The Workplace, the State, and American Labor Activism, 1865–1925.* New York: Cambridge University Press, 1987.

Morn, Frank. *"The Eye That Never Sleeps": A History of the Pinkerton National Detective Agency.* Bloomington: Indiana University Press, 1982.

Morris, Richard B. *Government and Labor in Early America.* 1946. New York: Harper, 1965.

Nelson, William E. *The Roots of American Bureaucracy, 1830–1900.* Cambridge: Harvard University Press, 1982.

Nieman, Donald G. *To Set the Law in Motion: The Freedmen's Bureau and the Legal Rights of Blacks, 1865–1868.* Millwood, N.Y.: KTO Press, 1979.

Novak, Daniel A. *The Wheel of Servitude: Black Forced Labor after Slavery.* Lexington: University of Kentucky Press, 1978.

Oakes, James. *The Ruling Race: A History of American Slaveholders.* New York: Alfred A. Knopf, 1982.

Orren, Karen. *Labor, the Law, and Liberal Development in the United States.* New York: Cambridge University Press, 1991.

Painter, Nell Irvin. *Exodusters: Black Migration to Kansas after Reconstruction.* New York: Alfred A. Knopf, 1977.

Paladun, Phillip S. *A Covenant with Death: The Constitution, Law, and Equality in the Civil War Era.* Urbana: University of Illinois Press, 1975.

Pease, Theodore Calvin. *The Story of Illinois.* Chicago: University of Chicago Press, 1949.

Pessen, Edward. *Most Uncommon Jacksonians: The Radical Leaders of the Early Labor Movement.* Albany: State University of New York Press, 1967.

Powell, Lawrence N. *New Masters: Northern Planters during the Civil War and Reconstruction.* New Haven: Yale University Press, 1980.

Ramsdell, Charles. *Reconstruction in Texas.* New York: Columbia University Press, 1910.

Ransom, Roger L., and Richard Sutch. *One Kind of Freedom: The Economic Consequences of Emancipation.* Cambridge: Cambridge University Press, 1977.

Reidy, Joseph P. *From Slavery to Agrarian Capitalism in the Cotton Plantation South.* Chapel Hill: University of North Carolina Press, 1992.

Richter, William L. *The Army in Texas during Reconstruction, 1865–1870.* College Station: Texas A&M University Press, 1987.

———. *Overreached on All Sides: The Freedmen's Bureau Administrators in Texas, 1865–1868.* College Station: Texas A&M University Press, 1991.

Ringenbach, Paul. *Tramps and Reformers, 1873–1916: The Discovery of Unemployment in New York.* Westport, Conn.: Greenwood Press, 1973.

Ripley, C. Peter. *Slaves and Freedmen in Civil War Louisiana.* Baton Rouge: Louisiana State University Press, 1976.

Roark, James L. *Masters without Slaves: Southern Planters in the Civil War and Reconstruction.* New York: W. W. Norton, 1977.

Rodgers, Daniel T. *The Work Ethic in Industrial America, 1850–1920.* Chicago: University of Chicago Press, 1974.

Roediger, David R. *The Wages of Whiteness: Race and the Making of the American Working Class.* London: Verso, 1991.

Rose, Willie Lee. *Rehearsal for Reconstruction: The Port Royal Experiment.* New York: Oxford University Press, 1964.

Ross, Stephen J. *Workers on the Edge: Work, Leisure, and Politics in Industrializing Cincinnati, 1788–1899.* New York: Columbia University Press, 1985.

Rothman, David J. *The Discovery of the Asylum: Social Order and Disorder in the New Republic.* Boston: Little, Brown, 1971.

Rotundo, E. Anthony. *American Manhood: Transformations in Masculinity from the Revolution to the Modern Era.* New York: Basic Books, 1993.

Ryan, Mary P. *Cradle of the Middle Class: The Family in Oneida County, New York, 1790–1865.* New York: Cambridge University Press, 1981.

Salinger, Sharon V. *"To Serve Well and Faithfully": Labor and Indentured Servants in Pennsylvania, 1682–1800.* New York: Cambridge University Press, 1987.

Saville, Julie. *The Work of Reconstruction: From Slave to Wage Labor in South Carolina, 1860–1870.* New York: Cambridge University Press, 1994.

Scarborough, William Kauffman. *The Overseer: Plantation Management in the Old South.* Baton Rouge: Louisiana State University Press, 1966.

Schneider, David M. *The History of Public Welfare in New York State, 1609–1866.* 2 vols. Chicago: University of Chicago Press, 1938.

Schob, David E. *Hired Hands and Plowboys: Farm Labor in the Midwest, 1815–1860.* Urbana: University of Illinois Press, 1975.

Schwartz, Harold. *Samuel Gridley Howe: Social Reformer, 1801–1876.* Cambridge: Harvard University Press, 1956.

Scott, William B. *In Pursuit of Happiness: American Conceptions of Property from the Seventeenth to the Twentieth Century.* Bloomington: Indiana University Press, 1977.

Seidman, Joel I. *The Yellow Dog Contract.* Baltimore: Johns Hopkins Press, 1932.

Sewell, William. *Work and Revolution in France: The Language of Labor from the Old Regime to 1848.* Cambridge: Cambridge University Press, 1980.

Shklar, Judith N. *American Citizenship: The Quest for Inclusion.* Cambridge: Harvard University Press, 1991.

Skocpol, Theda. *Protecting Soldiers and Mothers: The Political Origins of Social Policy in the United States.* Cambridge: Harvard University Press, Belknap Press, 1992.

Skowronek, Stephen. *Building the New American State: The Expansion of National Administrative Capacities, 1877–1920.* New York: Cambridge University Press, 1982.

Smallwood, James B. *Time of Hope, Time of Despair: Black Texans during Reconstruction.* Port Royal, N.Y.: National University Publications, 1981.

Smith, Duane A. *Rocky Mountain Mining Camps: The Urban Frontier.* Bloomington: Indiana University Press, 1967.

Stampp, Kenneth. *The Peculiar Institution: Slavery in the Antebellum South.* New York: Alfred A. Knopf, 1956.

Stansell, Christine. *City of Women: Sex and Class in New York, 1789–1860.* Urbana: University of Illinois Press, 1982.

Steinfeld, Robert J. *The Invention of Free Labor: The Employment Relation in English and American Law and Culture, 1350–1870.* Chapel Hill: University of North Carolina Press, 1991.

Taylor, Albion Guilford. *Labor Law and Labor Problems.* New York: Prentice-Hall, 1944.

TenBroek, Jacobus. *The Antislavery Origins of the Fourteenth Amendment.* Los Angeles: University of California Press, 1951.

Thompson, E. P. *The Making of the English Working Class.* New York: Penguin, 1968.

Tomlins, Christopher L. *Law, Labor, and Ideology in the Early Republic.* New York: Cambridge University Press, 1993.

———. *The State and the Unions: Labor Relations, Law, and the Organized Labor Movement in America, 1880–1960.* New York: Cambridge University Press, 1985.

Trattner, Walter I. *From Poor Law to Welfare State: A History of Social Welfare in the United States.* 3d rev. ed. New York: Free Press, 1984.

Tunnel, Ted. *Crucible of Reconstruction: War, Radicalism, and Race in Louisiana, 1862–1877.* Baton Rouge: Louisiana State University Press, 1984.

Walker, Samuel. *Popular Justice: A History of American Criminal Justice.* New York: Oxford University Press, 1980.

Way, Peter. *Common Labour: Workers and the Digging of North American Canals, 1780–1860.* New York: Cambridge University Press, 1993.

Weber, Max. *The Protestant Ethic and the Spirit of Capitalism.* Translated by Talcott Parsons. New York: Charles Scribner's Sons, 1958.

White, Howard A. *The Freedmen's Bureau in Louisiana.* Baton Rouge: Louisiana State University Press, 1970.

Wiecek, William. *The Sources of Anti-slavery Constitutionalism in America, 1760–1848.* Ithaca, N.Y.: Cornell University Press, 1977.

Wiener, Jonathan. *Social Origins of the New South: Alabama, 1860–1885.* Baton Rouge: Louisiana State University Press, 1978.

Wilentz, Sean. *Chants Democratic: New York and the Rise of the American Working Class, 1788–1850.* New York: Oxford University Press, 1984.

Williams, Jack Kenny. *Vogues in Villainy: Crime and Retribution in Ante-bellum South Carolina.* Columbia: University of South Carolina Press, 1959.

Williamson, Joel. *After Slavery: The Negro in South Carolina during Reconstruction, 1861–1877.* Chapel Hill: University of North Carolina Press, 1965.

Wilson, Theodore B. *The Black Codes of the South.* University: University of Alabama Press, 1969.

Wisner, Elizabeth. *Social Welfare in the South: From Colonial Times to World War I.* Baton Rouge: Louisiana State University Press, 1970.

Woodman, Harold. *New South–New Law: The Legal Foundations of Credit and Labor Relations in the Postbellum Agricultural South.* Baton Rouge: Louisiana State University Press, 1995.

Wright, Gavin. *Old South, New South: Revolutions in the Southern Economy since the Civil War.* New York: Basic Books, 1986.

Wyatt-Brown, Bertram. *Honor and Violence in the Old South.* New York: Oxford University Press, 1986.

———. *Southern Honor: Ethics and Behavior in the Old South.* New York: Oxford University Press, 1982.

Articles and Essays

Adler, Jeffrey S. "Vagging the Demons and Scoundrels: Vagrancy and the Growth of St. Louis, 1830–1861." *Journal of Urban History* 13 (November 1986): 3–30.

Benedict, Michael Les. "Preserving the Constitution: The Conservative Basis for Radical Reconstruction." *Journal of American History* 61 (1974): 65–90.

Berlin, Ira, et al. "The Terrain of Freedom: The Struggle over the Meaning of Free Labor in the U.S. South." *History Workshop* 22 (Autumn 1986): 108–30.

Bernhard, Virginia. "Poverty and the Social Order in Seventeenth-Century Virginia." *Virginia Magazine of History and Biography* 85 (April 1977): 141–55.

Bertoff, Rowland. "Independence and Attachment, Virtue and Interest: From Republican Citizen to Free Enterpriser, 1787–1837." In *Uprooted Americans: Essays in Honor of Oscar Handlin,* edited by Richard L. Bushman et al., 97–124. Boston: Little, Brown, 1979.

Bethel, Elizabeth. "The Freedmen's Bureau in Alabama." *Journal of Southern History* 14 (February 1948): 49–92.

Bonner, James C. "The Plantation Overseer and Southern Nationalism as Revealed in the Career of Garland D. Harmon." *Agricultural History* 19 (January 1945): 1–11.

Brown, Richard Maxwell. "Violence and the American Revolution." In *Essays on the American Revolution,* edited by Stephen G. Kurtz and James H. Hutson, 81–116. Chapel Hill: University of North Carolina Press, 1973.

Bushman, Richard L. "'This New Man': Dependence and Independence, 1776." In *Uprooted Americans: Essays in Honor of Oscar Handlin,* edited by Richard L. Bushman et al., 77–96. Boston: Little, Brown, 1979.

Calvert, Robert A. "The Freedmen and Agricultural Prosperity." *Southwestern Historical Quarterly* 76 (April 1973).

Campbell, Randolph. "The District Judges of Texas in 1866–1867: An Episode in the Failure of Presidential Reconstruction." *Southwestern Historical Quarterly* 93 (January 1990): 357–77.

Carter, Dan T. "The Anatomy of Fear: The Christmas Day Insurrection Scare of 1865." *Journal of Southern History* 42 (August 1976): 343–64.

Chambliss, William J. "A Sociological Analysis of the Law of Vagrancy." *Social Problems* 12 (Summer 1964): 67–77.

Cimbala, Paul A. "The 'Talisman Power': Davis Tillson, the Freedmen's Bureau, and Free Labor in Reconstruction Georgia, 1865–1866." *Civil War History* 28 (June 1982): 153–71.

Clement, Priscilla Ferguson. "The Transformation of the Wandering Poor in Nineteenth-Century Philadelphia." In *Walking to Work: Tramps in America, 1790–1935,* edited by Eric Monkkonen, 56–79. Lincoln: University of Nebraska Press, 1984.

Cohen, William. "Black Immobility and Free Labor: The Freedmen's Bureau and the Relocation of Black Labor, 1865–1866." *Civil War History* 30 (September 1984): 221–34.

———. "Negro Involuntary Servitude in the South, 1865–1940: A Preliminary Analysis." *Journal of Southern History* 42 (February 1976): 31–60.

Cohen-Lack, Nancy. "A Struggle for Sovereignty: National Consolidation, Emancipation, and Free Labor in Texas, 1865." *Journal of Southern History* 58 (February 1992): 58–98.

Conner, William P. "Reconstruction Rebels: The *New Orleans Tribune* in Post-war Louisiana." *Louisiana History* 21 (Spring 1980): 159–81.

Crouch, Barry A. "'All the Vile Passions': The Texas Black Code of 1866." *Southwestern Historical Quarterly* 97 (June 1993): 13–31.

———. "The 'Chords of Love': Legalizing Black Marriage and Family Rights in Postwar Texas." *Journal of Negro History* 79 (Fall 1994): 334–50.

Crouch, Barry A., and L. J. Schultz. "Crisis in Color: Racial Separation in Texas during Reconstruction." *Civil War History* 16 (March 1969): 37–49.

Cummings, John. "The Poor Laws of Massachusetts and New York." *Publications of the American Economic Association* 10 (July 1895): 546–63.

Daniel, Michael J. "Samuel Spring Gardner: A Maine Parson in Alabama." *Maine Historical Society Quarterly* 23 (1984): 151–76.

Davis, Michael. "Forced to Tramp: The Perspective of the Labor Press, 1870–1900." In *Walking to Work: Tramps in America, 1790–1935*, edited by Eric Monkkonen, 141–70. Lincoln: University of Nebraska Press, 1984.

Dubin, Gary V., and Richard H. Robinson. "The Vagrancy Concept Reconsidered: Problems and Abuses of Status Criminality." *New York University Law Review* 37 (January 1962): 102–36.

Earle, Carville, and Ronald Hoffman. "The Foundation of the Modern Economy: Agriculture and the Costs of Labor in the United States and England, 1800–1860." *American Historical Review* 85 (December 1980): 1059–94.

Elliot, Claude. "The Freedmen's Bureau in Texas." *Southwestern Historical Quarterly* 56 (July 1952): 1–24.

Ely, James W., Jr. "'There Are Few Subjects in Political Economy of Greater Difficulty': The Poor Laws of the Antebellum South." *American Bar Federation Research Journal* 4 (1985): 849–79.

Ely, James, Jr., and David Bodenhamer. "Regionalism and the Legal History of the South." In *Ambivalent Legacy: A Legal History of the South*, edited by James Ely and David Bodenhamer, 3–29. Jackson: University of Mississippi Press, 1984.

Feinman, Jay M. "The Development of the Employment of the at Will Rule." *American Journal of Legal History* 20 (April 1976): 118–35.

Fitzgerald, Michael W. "Wager Swayne, the Freedmen's Bureau, and the Politics of Reconstruction in Alabama." *Alabama Review* 48 (July 1995): 188–218.

Foner, Eric. "The Meaning of Freedom in the Age of Emancipation." *Journal of American History* 81 (September 1994): 435–60.

Foote, Caleb. "Vagrancy-Type Law and Its Administration." *University of Pennsylvania Law Review* 104 (1956): 603–50.

Fraser, Walter J., Jr. "Controlling the Poor in Colonial Charles Town." *South Carolina Historical Association Proceedings 1980*, 13–35.

Friedman, Lawrence. "The Law between the States: Some Thoughts on Southern Legal History." In *Ambivalent Legacy: A Legal History of the South*, edited by

James Ely and David Bodenhamer, 30–46. Jackson: University of Mississippi Press, 1984.

Fuke, Richard Paul. "Planters, Apprenticeship, and Forced Labor: The Black Family under Pressure in Post-emancipation Maryland." *Agricultural History* 62 (Fall 1988): 58–74.

———. "A Reform Mentality: Federal Policy toward Black Marylanders, 1864–1868." *Civil War History* 21 (September 1976): 214–33.

Glickstein, Jonathan A. "'Poverty Is Not Slavery': American Abolitionists and the Competitive Labor Market." In *Antislavery Reconsidered: New Perspectives on the Abolitionists*, edited by Lewis Perry and Michael Fellman, 195–218. Baton Rouge: Louisiana State University Press, 1979.

Hall, Kermit L., and James W. Ely Jr. "The South and the American Constitution." In *Uncertain Tradition: Constitutionalism and the History of the South*, edited by Kermit L. Hall and James W. Ely Jr., 3–16. Athens: University of Georgia Press, 1989.

Harring, Sidney. "Class Conflict and the Suppression of Tramps in Buffalo, 1892–1894." *Law and Society Review* 11 (Summer 1977): 873–911.

Haskell, Thomas. "Capitalism and the Origins of Humanitarian Sensibilities." *American Historical Review* 90 (April 1985): 339–61 (June 1985): 547–66.

Holt, Wythe. "Recovery by the Worker Who Quits: A Comparison of the Mainstream, Legal Realist, and Critical Legal Studies Approaches to a Problem of Nineteenth Century Contract Law." *Wisconsin Law Review*, no. 4 (1986): 677–732.

Johnson, Christopher. "Poor Relief in Antebellum Mississippi." *Journal of Mississippi History* 49 (1987): 1–21.

Jones, Douglas Lamar. "The Strolling Poor: Transiency in Eighteenth-Century Massachusetts." *Journal of Social History* 8 (1975): 28–54.

———. "The Transformation of the Law of Poverty in Eighteenth-Century Massachusetts." In *Law in Colonial Massachusetts, 1630–1800*, 153–190. Boston: Colonial Society of Massachusetts, 1984.

Karsten, Peter. "'Bottomed on Justice': A Reappraisal of Critical Legal Studies Scholarship Concerning Breaches of Labor Contracts by Quitting or Firing in Britain and the U.S., 1630–1880." *American Journal of Legal History* 34 (July 1990): 211–61.

Kealy, Linda. "Patterns of Punishment: Massachusetts in the Eighteenth Century." *American Journal of Legal History* 30 (April 1986): 163–86.

Klebaner, Benjamin J. "Poverty and Its Relief in American Thought, 1815–1861." *Social Service Review* 38 (December 1964): 382–99.

Konig, David T. "'Dale's Laws' and the Non–Common Law Origins of Criminal Justice in Virginia." *American Journal of Legal History* 26 (October 1982): 354–75.

Krebs, Sylvia H. "Will the Freedmen Work? White Alabamians Adjust to Free Black Labor." *Alabama Historical Quarterly* 36 (Summer 1974): 151–63.

Lacey, Forrest W. "Vagrancy and Other Crimes of Personal Condition." *Harvard Law Review* 66 (May 1953): 1203–26.

Lahan, P. Michael. "Trends in the Law of Vagrancy." *Connecticut Law Review* 1 (Spring 1968): 350–68.

Ledbetter, Billy D. "White Texans' Attitudes toward the Political Equality of Negroes, 1865–1870." *Phylon* 40 (September 1979): 253–63.

Linzer, Peter. "The Decline of Assent: At-Will Employment as a Case Study of the Breakdown of Private Law Theory." *Georgia Law Review* 20 (Winter 1986): 323–427.

Lowe, W. A. "The Freedmen's Bureau and Civil Rights in Maryland." *Journal of Negro History* 37 (July 1952): 221–47.

Lubove, Roy. "The New York Association for Improving the Conditions of the Poor: The Formative Years." *New York Historical Society Quarterly* 43 (1959): 307–26.

Mackey, Howard. "The Operation of the Old Poor Law in Colonial Virginia." *Virginia Magazine of History and Biography* 73 (January 1965): 28–40.

May, J. Thomas. "Continuity and Change in the Labor Program of the Army and the Freedmen's Bureau." *Civil War History* 17 (September 1971): 245–54.

McCamic, Charles. "Administration of Poor Relief in the Virginias." *West Virginia History* 1 (1940): 171–91.

Monkkonen, Eric. "Regional Dimensions of Tramping, North and South, 1880–1910." In *Walking to Work: Tramps in America, 1790–1935*, edited by Eric Monkkonen, 190–211. Lincoln: University of Nebraska Press, 1984.

Myers, John B. "The Alabama Freedmen and the Economic Adjustments during Presidential Reconstruction, 1865–1867." *Alabama Review* 26 (October 1973): 252–66.

Nieman, Donald G. "Black Political Power and Criminal Justice: Washington County, Texas, 1868–1884." *Journal of Southern History* 55 (August 1989): 391–420.

Prude, Jonathan. "The Social System of Early New England Textile Mills: A Case Study, 1812–1840." In *Working-Class America: Essays on Labor, Community, and American Society*, edited by Michael H. Frisch and Daniel J. Walkowitz, 1–35. Urbana: University of Illinois Press, 1983.

Richter, William L. "The Army and the Negro in Reconstruction Texas, 1865–1870." *East Texas Historical Journal* 10 (Spring 1972): 7–19.

Rothenberg, Winifred B. "The Emergence of Farm Labor Markets and the Transformation of the Rural Economy: Massachusetts, 1750–1855." *Journal of Economic History* 58 (September 1988): 537–66.

Schaffner, Margaret A. "The Labor Contract from Individual to Collective Bargaining." *Bulletin of the University of Wisconsin*, no. 182 (December 1907): 1–135.

Schlomowitz, Ralph. "The Origins of Southern Sharecropping." *Agricultural History* 53 (July 1979): 557–75.

Schneider, John C. "Tramping Workers, 1890–1920: A Subcultural View." In *Walk-*

ing to Work: Tramps in America, 1790–1935, edited by Eric Monkkonen, 212–34. Lincoln: University of Nebraska Press, 1984.

Scott, Rebecca. "The Battle over the Child: Child Apprenticeship and the Freedmen's Bureau in North Carolina." *Prologue* 10 (Summer 1978): 101–13.

Shepherd, Rebecca A. "Restless Americans: The Geographic Mobility of Farm Laborers in the Old Midwest, 1850–1870." *Ohio History* 89 (Winter 1980): 25–45.

Stanley, Amy Dru. "Beggars Can't Be Choosers: Compulsion and Contract in Postbellum America." *Journal of American History* 78 (March 1992): 1265–93.

———. "Conjugal Bonds and Wage Labor: Rights of Contract in the Age of Emancipation." *Journal of American History* 75 (June 1988): 471–500.

Staudenraus, P. J. "The Popular Origins of the Thirteenth Amendment." *Mid-America* 50 (April 1969): 108–15.

Steinfeld, Robert J. "Property and Suffrage in the Early American Republic." *Stanford Law Review* 41 (January 1989): 335–76.

Stott, Richard. "British Immigrants and the American 'Work Ethic' in the Mid-Nineteenth Century." *Labor History* 25 (Winter 1984): 86–102.

Sydnor, Charles S. "A Slave Owner and His Overseers." *North Carolina Historical Review* 14 (January 1937): 21–38.

Thompson, E. P. "Time, Work-Discipline, and Industrial Capitalism." *Past and Present* 38 (December 1967): 56–97.

Tomlins, Christopher. "The Ties That Bind: Master and Servant in Massachusetts, 1800–1850." *Labor History* 30 (Spring 1989): 193–227.

Ulmer, Barbara. "Benevolence in Colonial Charleston." *South Carolina Historical Association Proceedings 1980*, 1–12.

VanderVelde, Lea S. "The Labor Vision of the Thirteenth Amendment." *University of Pennsylvania Law Review* 138 (December 1989): 437–504.

Vogt, Daniel C. "Poor Relief in Frontier Mississippi, 1798–1832." *Journal of Mississippi History* 51 (August 1989): 181–99.

Walsh, John T., Jr. "Vagrancy: A Crime of Status." *Suffolk University Law Review* 2 (Spring 1968): 156–78.

White, Kenneth B. "Black Lives, Red Tape: The Alabama Freedmen's Bureau." *Alabama Historical Quarterly* 34 (Winter 1981): 241–58.

———. "Wager Swayne: Racist or Realist?" *Alabama Review* 31 (April 1978): 92–109.

Wiener, Jonathan M. "Class Structure and Economic Development in the American South, 1865–1955." *American Historical Review* 84 (October 1979): 970–92.

Wiener, Lynn. "Sisters of the Road: Women Transients and Tramps, 1880–1910." In *Walking to Work: Tramps in America, 1790–1935*, edited by Eric Monkkonen, 141–70. Lincoln: University of Nebraska Press, 1984.

Wilentz, Sean. "Artisan Republican Festivals and the Rise of Class Conflict in New York City, 1788–1837." In *Working-Class America: Essays on Labor, Community, and American Society,* edited by Michael H. Frisch and Daniel J. Walkowitz, 37–65. Urbana: University of Illinois Press, 1983.

Wood, Gordon. "Interests and Disinterestedness in the Making of the Constitution." In *Beyond Confederation: Origins of the Constitution and American National Character,* edited by Richard Beeman, Stephen Botein, and Edward C. Carter II, 69–109. Chapel Hill: University of North Carolina Press, 1987.

Woodman, Harold. "Post–Civil War Southern Agriculture and the Law." *Agricultural History* 53 (January 1979): 319–37.

———. "Sequel to Slavery: The New History Views the Postbellum South." *Journal of Southern History* 43 (November 1977): 532–54.

Unpublished Secondary Sources

Bellows, Barbara Lawrence. "Tempering the Wind: The Southern Response to Urban Poverty, 1850–1865." Ph.D. diss., University of South Carolina, 1983.

Colby, Ira C. "The Freedmen's Bureau in Texas and Its Impact on the Emerging Social Welfare System and Black-White Social Relations, 1865–1885." Ph.D. diss., University of Pennsylvania, 1984.

Mackey, Thomas Clyde. "Red Lights Out: A Legal History of Prostitution, Disorderly Houses, and Vice Districts, 1870–1917." Ph.D. diss., Rice University, 1984.

Scarborough, Jane L. "George W. Paschal: Texas Unionist and Scalawag Jurisprudent." Ph.D. diss., Rice University, 1972.

Schmidt, James D. "'Neither Slavery nor Involuntary Servitude': Free Labor and American Law, ca. 1815–1880." Ph.D. diss., Rice University, 1992.

Stanley, Amy Dru. "Contract Rights in the Age of Emancipation: Wage Work and Marriage in Post Civil War America." Ph.D. diss., Yale University, 1990.

Index

DATE DUE

MAY 14 99 FA			
AUG 0 2 REC'D			
OCT 0 4 2000			
NOV 7 NYC			
DEC 2 2 2001			
FEB 0 5 2002			
AUG 1 9 2002			
DEC 2 8 2002			
DEC 21 REC'D			
OhioLINK JUN 0 4 REC'D			
GAYLORD			PRINTED IN U.S.A.